THE PERILOUS TRADE

BOOKS BY ROY MacSKIMMING

Shoot Low Sheriff, They're Riding Shetland Ponies
(with William Hawkins)

Formentera, a novel

Out of Love, a novel

On Your Own Again
(with Keith Anderson)

Gordie: A Hockey Legend

Cold War: The Amazing Canada–Soviet
Hockey Series of 1972

THE PERILOUS TRADE
Publishing Canada's Writers

ROY MacSKIMMING

M&S

National Library of Canada Cataloguing in Publication

MacSkimming, Roy, 1944-
The perilous trade : publishing Canada's writers / Roy MacSkimming.

Includes index.
ISBN 1-55199-073-3

1. Publishers and publishing–Canada–History–20th century. I. Title.

Z481.M323 2003   338.4'70705'0971   C2003-903649-9

We acknowledge the financial support of the Government of Canada through the Book Publishing Industry Development Program and that of the Government of Ontario through the Ontario Media Development Corporation's Ontario Book Initiative. We further acknowledge the support of the Canada Council for the Arts and the Ontario Arts Council for our publishing program.

Acknowledgments on pages 425 and 426
represent a continuation of this copyright page.

Text design by Terri Nimmo

Typeset in Minion by M&S, Toronto
Printed and bound in Canada

This book is printed on acid-free paper that is 100% recycled, ancient-forest friendly (100% post-consumer recycled).

McClelland & Stewart Ltd.
The Canadian Publishers
481 University Avenue
Toronto, Ontario
M5G 2E9
www.mcclelland.com

1   2   3   4   5   07   06   05   04   03

CONTENTS

PREFACE

This book tells the story of Canadian English-language book publishing from the Second World War to the present. It is not an exhaustive or scholarly history but an impressionistic, opinionated journey through the landscape. Since my professional life has taken place in and around the publishing industry, it could scarcely be otherwise. After working in publishing for a decade, first for an established firm and later as a co-founder of a small press, I've been successively a literary journalist, a publishing officer at the Canada Council for the Arts, and an industry analyst. My books have appeared from six Canadian firms, including two French-language houses, and one in the United States. Inevitably *The Perilous Trade* is coloured by those experiences.

But it would have been impossible to draw a true portrait from personal experience alone. In my research, I was generously assisted by many publishers, writers, and book industry professionals willing to share their memories and insights. The core of that research is more than a hundred interviews, most of them audiotaped and conducted from 1998 to 2002; together they represent an oral history of English-Canadian publishing. They are listed and cited in the sources at the end of the book.

I've focused on English-language trade publishers and publishing, since that is what I know best. The richly accomplished French-language industry centred in Quebec operates in a very different cultural and economic milieu and demands a book unto itself. I've focused also on publishers I consider builders of the industry: the pioneers, mavericks, and idealists who risked greatly and took personal leaps of faith, often against conventional wisdom and their own financial interests. I discuss many highly skilled and dedicated professionals, especially in the foreign-owned sector, only briefly if at all; this is essentially the story of the indigenous industry.

For all their remarkable diversity, Canadian publishers are a small clan. Just as Margaret Laurence likened Canadian writers to a tribe, our publishers inhabit a village. Visitors remark how everyone in the village refers to everyone else by first names. Their houses are widely scattered geographically yet owned by people who know one another well, having worked side by side in professional organizations or in one of the established firms before starting their own companies. This is one native's guide to the village.

R.M.
Perth, Ontario
May 2003

INTRODUCTION

A CANADIAN EXPERIMENT

Publishing Canadian books has always been an experiment. Like the great experiments of building a transcontinental railway and a national broadcasting system, it constitutes one of the nation's defining acts. Publishing, after all, is a people's way of telling its story to itself.

Economically speaking, publishing Canadian books doesn't make a lot of sense. It's a high-risk, low-margin business conducted on the fringes of empire. Only in recent times have some of the country's authors become international stars, commanding large followings and spectacular royalty advances.

Publishing Canadian books isn't the same thing as publishing books in Canada. Publishers have existed in this country since the early nineteenth century, yet they weren't usually publishing Canadian authors; most were capitalizing on the fact that the colonists wanted to read the latest works of Sir Walter Scott, Charles Dickens, or James Fenimore Cooper. Few of those "publishers" – really importers or distributors – cared to invest in Canadian writers who had no audience in Great Britain or the United States. Although it was possible to make money distributing books from the two imperial centres, the costs of editing, designing, typesetting, printing, and marketing titles for Canada alone were prohibitive. Textbooks, with a captive market in the school system, were another matter. But "trade" books – titles published for the general public – were long regarded as a recipe for disaster. There simply weren't enough Canadians to buy them.

As a result, comparatively few Canadian books appeared for nearly a century after Confederation. The publishers who issued them were daring adventurers, but no publisher who wanted to survive published indigenous books exclusively, at least not for long. That truism prevailed until the late 1960s, when publishing, like so much else in Western society, changed radically, and a new generation of publishers arrived who were willing to stake everything on Canadian writing.

That generation would not have come forward without the groundbreaking work of their predecessors. The modern era in English-Canadian publishing really began *circa* 1950, with the careers of four men who founded the industry we know today: John Gray of Macmillan of Canada, Jack McClelland of McClelland & Stewart, Marsh Jeanneret of the University of Toronto Press, and William Toye of Oxford University Press. The half-century from their time to the present was transformed by concurrent revolutions in culture, politics, technology, and mores. For Canada, the cultural transformation was even more sweeping than for other Western democracies. Being "dead-set in adolescence," as Earle Birney wrote, the country had farther to grow as it matured; Canadian literature mirrored, encouraged, and accelerated that maturing. Because English-speaking Canadians hadn't developed a mythology to explain our existence, writing and publishing became vital to our process of self-definition.

Consequently literature is English Canada's greatest cultural achievement. Canadians have written some of the memorable books of our time. In the fiction of Robertson Davies, Mavis Gallant, Alice Munro, Margaret Atwood, or Rohinton Mistry, in the poetry of Irving Layton, P.K. Page, Leonard Cohen, or Anne Carson, in the creative thought of Northrop Frye, Marshall McLuhan, George Grant, or the philosopher Charles Taylor, our literature has taken a clear-eyed and distinctive measure of the era. These and many other Canadians have produced a currency whose acceptance abroad came with startling swiftness.

That acceptance dates roughly from 1992 and Michael Ondaatje's Booker Prize for *The English Patient*. Critics in London and New York later discovered, as the literary editor of the *Sunday Times* declared, that much of the English-speaking world's most exciting new fiction was coming from Canada. Suddenly Canadians were winning the big international literary awards: the Orange and IMPAC and Commonwealth Prizes, Bookers for Atwood and Yann Martel, a National Book Critics Circle Award in the United States for Carol Shields, even a Pulitzer, thanks to

Shields's dual citizenship. Suddenly German publishers were calling on Toronto literary agents in search of the next hot writer. Suddenly Mordecai Richler was a national anti-hero in Italy.

But of course, the making of those accomplishments wasn't sudden at all. As Ondaatje acknowledged in accepting his Governor General's Literary Award for *The English Patient*, "Writers don't just spring up out of the landscape, fully formed, ready to get honours. Canadian writing today evolves from a dedicated nurturing." By the time our writers began receiving international acclaim, the country's literature had been evolving for decades, nurtured by men and women who gambled talent, energy, and professional capital on the proposition that Canada deserves books of its own. They are Canadian publishers.

A singular, stubbornly idiosyncratic clan, Canada's publishers have seldom told their own story. "For an industry devoted to the dissemination of information, book publishing has appeared remarkably reticent . . . about discussing in print its own activities," wrote the Ontario Royal Commission on Book Publishing in 1973. Thirty years on, that observation remains largely true. The literature on Canadian publishing is still sparse, heavier on policy analysis than on narrative or anecdote. With the occasional exception, publishers have been too preoccupied with producing other people's books to write their own.

It's unlikely they were too busy having a good time – although publishers' chronic anxieties are mixed with irrational optimism and fitful exuberance. Publishing for an English-language population less than one-tenth the size of the American market is an exacting and unforgiving business. Comparing publishing in Canada with that in the United States, the royal commission observed, "The same percentage of publishing misjudgments is more costly in Canada and the same percentage of publishing successes provides less income with which to underwrite the mistakes."

Canadian publishers must get all the fundamentals right: from the choice of manuscripts and cover designs and marketing strategies to that crucial decision, how many copies to print. When things beyond their control go wrong – routine problems like non-delivering authors or computer breakdowns, or outright disasters like a distributor's bankruptcy or a bookstore chain's implosion – the margin of error is narrow. On the other hand, as a headline in the American trade magazine *Publishers Weekly* once said, if you can make it in Canadian publishing, you'll make it anywhere. A harsh environment breeds resourcefulness and cunning.

That environment is conditioned by two factors. First, there is no such language as Canadian. English Canadians share the mother tongue of the world's two largest book-exporting nations, which between them produce about 140,000 new titles each year compared with our 10,000. Second, our liberal humanist tradition demands that we keep our borders open to books and ideas from abroad. Canadians enjoy direct physical access to probably the widest international selection of books in the world.

In the exceptionally crowded market that results, foreign competition extends beyond sheer numbers to price. Since Canadians are accustomed to paying for American and British books that are much cheaper to produce, thanks to economies of scale (the bigger the printing, the lower the cost per copy), Canadian publishers face an interesting dilemma: in addition to the constraints of a small population, they must underprice their books to compete. Little wonder that Morley Callaghan, writing in the *University of Toronto Quarterly*, once called Canada "a country that is no publisher's paradise."

Against those odds, Canadian publishers in the second half of the twentieth century built an industry of extraordinary diversity and breadth. Those who put their top priority on publishing Canadian books paid the financial price: a price that first became apparent from the struggles of Canada's greatest publisher, Jack McClelland. But by the time the extent of McClelland's troubles had become common knowledge in the 1970s, the next generation had already set off in his footsteps.

The post-war period has seen prodigious growth: in number of firms, number of titles, total sales, and literary stature. In January 1950, the trade journal *Quill & Quire* listed forty book publishers in English-speaking Canada, all but two based in Toronto. Now Statistics Canada identifies 450, located all through the country. The first reliable government survey of the industry, taken by Ernst & Ernst in 1970, found Canadian publishers in both official languages had earned revenues of $222 million in the previous year. Thirty years later, Statistics Canada put the figure at $2.2 billion, a 1,000 percent increase – $1.8 billion of it in English-language books. Exports of Canadian books tripled during a five-year period in the mid-1990s.

Amid that explosive growth, and despite the proliferation of internationally admired Canadian authors, the industry has remained financially precarious. The media have given major play to the succession of perils afflicting the trade: the American takeovers of 1970; the recurring calamities at McClelland & Stewart; assorted bankruptcies and bailouts; and most recently, the trauma inflicted on publishers, authors, and independent booksellers alike by the former management of the retail giant Chapters Inc. and the related collapse of the Stoddart Publishing empire. But somehow Canadian publishers have struggled on, staggering with élan from one near-catastrophe to another, all the while generating a literature of astonishing richness.

By the turn of the millennium, a significant part of that publishing was being conducted not only by the Canadian-owned firms that have long been its primary producers but by subsidiaries of foreign-owned conglomerates. Well capitalized by their wealthy multinational parents and endowed with lucrative imported titles, the subsidiaries were harvesting much of the crop of outstanding fiction writers that smaller Canadian presses had sown. They have bought up rights to works by both promising newcomers and established veterans, especially novels. Canadian-owned publishers still originate by far the lion's share of new trade titles, but few can afford the high-stakes game of bidding for the priciest authors.

That situation converged with the Chapters debacle in 2000 and the Stoddart crash in 2002 to leave the indigenous industry in an economically battered, even attenuated state. As this book was being written, Canadian-owned publishing had reached a crossroads. Whether it will regain the vigour of its experimental, innovative, risk-taking youth, infused with fresh human and financial capital, or subside into working as a seed farm for writers destined for the multinationals is a question yet to be settled. Neither outcome is inevitable. Much depends, as we'll see in chapters to come, on the actions of individuals and governments. Given publishing's importance to Canadian identity and the near-heroic attempts to build an industry under domestic control, the outcome has profound cultural, political, and psychological consequences for the nation.

CLARKE, IRWIN

1

THE PUBLISHING LIFE

My impression is that authors discover themselves and that
publishers sometimes recognize these discoveries.

Jack McClelland, *Quill & Quire* (April 1985)

Like others of my generation, I fell sideways into book publishing. Unlike dentistry or engineering or organized crime, publishing in the 1960s was an accidental profession, requiring no specialized training. Now there are college programs and even master's degrees in publishing; pragmatic, worldly people plan to become editors or marketing specialists or production managers, even publishers with their own firms. But in spring 1964, my ambition was more elementary: I was looking to scrape together some cash so I could drop out of the University of Toronto and go to Europe for a while. After all three Toronto newspapers turned me down, on the sensible grounds that I lacked any useful journalistic or life experience, I landed a summer job in the editorial department of a major Canadian publisher.

The company was Clarke, Irwin, then managed by a rosy-cheeked, formidable Scot named R.W.W. Robertson, "Robbie" to his friends. Clarke, Irwin wasn't the biggest Canadian book publisher of the time, nor the oldest. But after thirty-four years, it was profitably ensconced in the top tier of English-Canadian firms, then numbering about a dozen, all based in Toronto. Like its competitors – W.J. Gage, the Ryerson Press, Copp Clark, Macmillan of Canada, Oxford University Press, J.M. Dent & Sons

(Canada), Thomas Nelson & Sons (Canada), McGraw-Hill Co. of Canada, and Holt, Rinehart & Winston of Canada – Clarke, Irwin was primarily a textbook publisher. Unlike some of them, it also originated trade books. Trade publishing made far less money than school publishing, but it was more fun.

In addition, Clarke, Irwin acted as Canadian distributor – "exclusive agent," in trade parlance – for a select group of British and American publishers. It employed nearly a hundred people. In some respects, it was an archetypal Canadian publisher, more so than the flamboyantly extroverted McClelland & Stewart, then just beginning its glory days under Jack McClelland. But Clarke, Irwin too harboured its eccentricities and internal contradictions.

All I knew as I entered Clarwin House, the firm's two-storey brick headquarters on St. Clair Avenue West, was that I wanted Mr. Robertson to employ me long enough so I could take it on the lam to London, Paris, and points south, for the sake of my higher education as a writer. He'd granted me an interview largely, I realized, because he knew my father, William MacSkimming, the public school superintendent in Ottawa: a fellow Scot, and even more significantly a fellow graduate of the University of Edinburgh.

Mr. Robertson was not a large man, but he exuded authority. Below his beetling eyebrows, his eyes were alert for signals of sincerity and right thinking, his lips compressed yet straining towards kindliness. It wasn't merely his brogue that reminded me of my dad.

He opened the interview with a challenge. "So! You've settled on a life in publishing!"

"I'm sure it's a wonderful profession," I replied lamely.

"Now, I understand you write *poetry*."

"I've had some poems published," I conceded.

Mr. Robertson nodded, indicating he was dimly aware of the existence of the obscure literary mags where my work had appeared. I didn't mention that I'd also co-authored a chapbook with William Hawkins, *Shoot Low Sheriff, They're Riding Shetland Ponies*, after attending the now legendary University of British Columbia poetry conference in 1963, where everyone had smoked grass on the lawn with Allen Ginsberg.

"We don't *do* poetry at Clarke, Irwin," Mr. Robertson said, "but if you *were* to work in our editorial department, a command of the Queen's English is a prerequisite. We would train you in the rigours of editorial style and usage. But we also have manuscripts that need evaluating, and that requires another sort of talent. You're taking English and history at Varsity?"

"Yes, sir."

"Very good. Now, I've selected a manuscript from the pile. I will ask you to read it, consider its merits or lack thereof, and write a two-page report describing plot, characters, and so on. Conclude by clearly stating whether it deserves to be published and if so, why. Clarke, Irwin seldom takes on *novels*, but never mind. I would like the report and manuscript back on Monday. Any questions?" At this, Mr. Robertson's lips parted in a tentative smile.

Rattling home on the streetcar, I felt an electric curiosity about the contents of the thick brown envelope on my lap. Some struggling writer had sweated blood to write an entire novel, something I planned to do myself one day, and now it was up to me to pass judgment on it. I was intimidated but thrilled.

I sat down immediately in my rented room and began reading the neatly typed manuscript. What I discovered astonished me: it was competently written, with what seemed a plausible Irish setting and dialogue, but its author had lifted his entire plot and most of his characters from Sean O'Casey's *Juno and the Paycock*, a play I'd seen performed at the Crest Theatre not long before. It had never occurred to me that a fellow writer would stoop so low. I sat down and typed my report, summarizing as instructed, and delivered my verdict that here was not an impressive new talent but a talented new plagiarizer.

The following Monday, I waited silently in Mr. Robertson's office while he scanned my report. Grinning and turning slightly pinker, he hired me on the spot. But his expression turned severe again: "You wish to start immediately after your exams, but the editorial department can't accommodate you until June. In the meantime, are you willing to lug books around until you pray you'll never see another?"

I was.

At the beginning of May 1964, I reported to the warehouse in the high-ceilinged basement of Clarwin House. On my first day, I learned how to punch a time clock, how to handle books without smearing their dust jackets, how implacably heavy book cartons become after you've carried a few dozen from the delivery truck to the loading dock to the wooden pallet in the rear storage area. Forklift trucks were not in use at Clarke, Irwin.

As Bill, the warehouse manager, had explained, warehouse functions were divided between shipping and receiving. My job was to assist the receiver, John, a lanky Australian with a crumpled face and roguish sense of humour, who called cartons "cartoons" and the young secretaries who came downstairs for complimentary copies "darlin'." John worked like a Trojan whenever the trucks arrived bearing whole printings of books, shipments from agency publishers, or returns from the bookstores. At such times, my challenge was just to keep up with him. But I was also learning an eternal truth about publishing. There are always too many books: books to be stacked by the carton, books to be unpacked and shelved, books shipped to their destinations only to be returned a few months later, still unsold, and to be reshelved or, tragically, consigned to the shredder.

When things quieted down, John armed me with a feather duster and sent me to patrol the rows of high metal racks while he went for a smoke on the loading dock. This became my favourite part of the job. It gave me a chance to browse at will among thousands of titles, dipping into the interesting ones.

The titles that excited me certainly weren't Clarke, Irwin's textbooks, their utilitarian covers all too familiar from my school days: *Living Latin*, *Cours moyen de français*, *Pirates and Pathfinders*. These were the firm's bread and butter, core texts approved for classroom use years earlier, still selling in the tens of thousands and returning tidy profits. Clarke, Irwin had also published significant trade books from time to time: *The Firebrand*, William Kilbourn's stirring and elegant biography of the rebel leader William Lyon Mackenzie; *The Ancestral Roof*, a handsome study of Upper Canadian domestic architecture; the writings of the West Coast painter Emily Carr; the plays of Gratien Gélinas; and the early works of Robertson Davies, edited by Mr. Robertson himself. But the books I was drawn to were the ones from elsewhere.

Clarke, Irwin distributed major British publishers such as Harrap, Jonathan Cape, and Chatto & Windus; this was before those houses, like so many others, lost their independence to multinational conglomerates. Harrap was best known for its popular English-French dictionary, Chatto for its literary authors such as Iris Murdoch and V.S. Pritchett; and Cape published not only Ian Fleming but the new espionage sensation Len Deighton and the inspired nonsense verse of John Lennon. Since Chatto had absorbed the Hogarth Press, the imprint founded by Leonard and Virginia Woolf, hardcover editions of some of Virginia's novels also reposed on the shelves I dusted, alongside biographical studies of twentieth-century authors published by Oliver and Boyd in Edinburgh and books published by E.P. Dutton in New York. On the Dutton backlist were Dostoevsky's *Notes from Underground*, Lawrence Durrell's *The Black Book*, and a compilation of letters between Durrell and Henry Miller, two of my favourite writers.

As I learned, the agency business could be problematic. If your agencies published too many titles of marginal appeal to Canadians, you lost money. If you were too successful, the foreign publisher would reward you by establishing its own branch in Canada and taking the business away. And yet import distribution was considered an essential part of Canadian publishing: if you aspired to originate trade books, you had to offset the inevitable losses by profitably distributing American and British lines.

One day at noon, John disappeared instead of eating his bag lunch on the loading dock with the rest of us. After lunch, he was still nowhere to be seen. Bill's face darkened.

By 3:30, when a truck pulled in, I was still working alone. A tense silence prevailed among the usually gossipy shippers as they picked books off the racks and packed them at the long plywood table. Just before 5 o'clock, a shipper came over to clue me in. John, it seemed, had gone off on one of his toots. Bill had told Mr. Robertson of John's defection, and the two men had driven over to confront him at his favourite watering hole, where they'd found him dead drunk.

Alarmed, I asked what would happen to John now. Nothing much, was the answer, apart from being docked a day's pay; John pulled this stunt every six months or so, but he'd be back in the morning. Clarke, Irwin enforced a strictly teetotal policy at all company functions, from author lunches to book launches, but as a traditional family firm it always took care of its own.

One day I was schlepping books around in jeans and a T-shirt, the next I was working upstairs in a suit and tie, learning the rudiments of editing. Clarke, Irwin turned out to be the perfect place to apprentice. There were seven of us in the editorial department: a senior educational editor, a senior trade editor, four junior editors, and now, temporarily, me. We were confined to a single room, sitting at two rows of desks crammed end to end, like medieval clerks; in fact, the Clarke, Irwin logo was a twelfth-century monk poring over a manuscript. Since half the editors were Brits, my arrival tipped the balance in the Canadians' favour, and the male contingent rose to two.

Clarke, Irwin adhered religiously to the traditional method of proof-reading. One editor read aloud from the typed and edited manuscript, using verbal equivalents for every punctuation mark: "stop" for period, "shriek" for exclamation mark, "para" for paragraph break. The proof-reader followed along on the galleys (sheets of type not yet divided into pages) or the page proofs, marking printer's errors, as typesetting mistakes were called, in red pencil, and author's changes or our own editorial second-guessing in blue. In a vacant office, I communed over the long, floppy galleys of Dominion Archivist Gustave Lanctot's history of New France with Eileen, a bespectacled former teacher from the Prairies. Eileen demonstrated for me the stylized hieroglyphics by which editors conveyed instructions to typesetters, then still composing in hot metal. Every hour or so, we switched roles. By the end of the first day, my eyeballs felt as if they'd been yanked out of their sockets, but at least there was no heavy lifting.

At the front of the building was a reception area opening into a library of first editions of every title Clarke, Irwin had published since 1930, where teachers and librarians occasionally visited to browse and order books. One sweltering July afternoon, I was sitting in the library doing research on titles the company was considering reprinting. Sweat was trickling down my sides, so I removed my suit jacket and draped it carefully over the back of my chair. It wasn't long before the blue-haired grandmotherly receptionist rose from her switchboard and strode across the broadloom to press a note firmly into my palm; written in fountain pen in a familiar-looking hand, it read, "Roy, please restore your jacket. R.W.W.R." How Mr. Robertson had seen my breach of protocol from his closed office down the hall remained a mystery.

Since the real editors were busy editing books, I was soon assigned to the slush pile of unsolicited manuscripts. At first I pictured myself as a prospector panning for gold, but soon I came to see I was shovelling dross. The pile contained an inordinate number of frontier memoirs, reminiscences by grizzled men and women who'd endured trials with nature in the Yukon or northern Alberta and lived to tell the tale in endless, shapeless detail. Clarke, Irwin had published a popular northern memoir with sled dogs on the cover called *Land of the Long Day*, by Doug Wilkinson, and offerings by Wilkinson's less talented imitators poured over the transom. On my office Olympic I typed, with one carbon copy, the prescribed two-page report on each failed attempt, following the example of my jaded colleagues. Since manuscript reports were circulated within the editorial department, reading them became one of our chief amusements; each editor competed to be more urbane and witty than the rest, as if we were writing for *The New Yorker* and not one another.

Unexpectedly I was assigned a book to edit myself. *Canada's Fighting Pilots* had been placed on the 1965 spring list and required only routine copy-editing, I was told. But on reading the manuscript, I decided it needed more elaborate attention to tell the story dramatically and economically. It would be the latest title in the Canadian Portraits series, which featured patriotic, wholesome mini-biographies aimed straight at the public library and school library markets. I got out my pencil, rolled up my sleeves, and went happily to work.

The author of *Canada's Fighting Pilots*, Edmund Cosgrove, seemed more of a PR man than what I snobbishly considered a "writer," but clearly he felt a boy's own passion for the heroic exploits and hair-raising escapades of Canadian aces in the two world wars. I found myself sharing his passion as I worked. I moved sentences and paragraphs around, cut redundant passages, and tried to snap the narrative into sharper focus.

Worried I might be overstepping my authority, I suggested to Cosgrove that we meet to discuss my proposed changes. He turned out to be an affable guy, so pleased to be getting published that he was glad to let me mess with his prose. When the heavily marked-up manuscript was ready for his approval, I decided there ought to be a small ceremony to mark the occasion. Cosgrove was a former journalist: that must mean he liked to drink. I invited him to meet me downtown after work. I'd be subverting Clarke, Irwin's prohibition on alcohol, but what the hell, I'd be doing it on my own time and money.

I suggested the Twenty-Two, a piano bar in the elegant old Windsor Arms Hotel. I'd never been inside the place, but as a student I had often walked past and thought it looked surpassingly worldly, as indeed it was: dim, smoky, and crowded with animated drinkers whose conversation drowned out the pianist in the white jacket. Arriving first, I ordered what I thought you were supposed to drink in such a place, a dry martini with three olives. Cosgrove groped like a myopic halfback through the bodies and gloom and asked for a beer. The lights were too low for him to see how much I'd changed his manuscript, but he didn't seem particularly concerned.

When we left the Twenty-Two, the pianist was playing "Moonlight in Vermont," but the sky above Toronto was piled with rain clouds. The lights on Bloor Street had come on early, and fashionable women hurried past under umbrellas. As I strolled westward towards my room in the Annex, the warm summer rain on my face, I felt I'd entered at last into possession of the world.

My work in publishing paid miserably, but I was still able to save enough for a few months in Europe. Everything in London from pub food to accommodation was dirt cheap, and in Franco's Spain, cheaper yet again. Buses and hitchhiking were reasonable ways to get around; in the Balearics, entire farmhouses rented for $20 a month without running water or electricity, and the *vino del pais* was 15 cents a bottle.

On my return home, flushed with adventures and dead broke, I faced a choice: finish my degree or work to support myself. It was no contest. I petitioned R.W.W.R. for my old job back, full-time. He was doubtful at first, not so much about my ability as about my leaving university without a degree. In the end, he confirmed there was a permanent spot for me in the editorial department but cautioned, "Now, we expect you, Roy, to make a long-term commitment to Clarke, Irwin." My starting salary as a junior trade editor would be $4,500 a year. At twenty-one, that would do.

The company president, to whom Mr. Robertson himself reported, was both a Clarke and an Irwin. Mrs. Irene Clarke was a plump, silver-haired widow who had been a partner in the firm's founding with her late husband, W.H. (William) Clarke, and her brother, John C.W. Irwin, both formerly with Macmillan of Canada. Irwin had left the company in 1944 over some forgotten difference of opinion to form another publishing house, the Book Society of Canada. Clarke had died unexpectedly in 1955 at the age of fifty-two; his black and white portrait photograph still glowered from a wall overlooking the reception area, keeping a steadfast eye on the house he and his wife had built. Mrs. Clarke herself had a large office over-looking an open-air courtyard, but her health was poor and she preferred to oversee business from her apartment on Spadina Road. At one time, the office had been destined for the Clarkes' brilliant older son, Gary, who had attended Oxford. But after trying out publishing under his parents for several years, Gary Clarke had enrolled in theological studies, becoming a lay minister in the United Church and later a university teacher.

I was immediately given two manuscripts to edit, both by pets of Mrs. Clarke's. Roy Greenaway was a retired reporter who'd spent his life at the *Toronto Star* covering fires, murders, elections, and other disasters, using every trick in the book to scoop the arch-rival *Telegram*. *The News Game* would be his account of fifty years as a hard-digging newshound. Christilot Hanson, nineteen years old, had written *Canadian Entry*, a sincere and only moderately gushy memoir of riding as a member of the national dressage team in the 1964 Tokyo Olympics. Christilot and her mother, the dance teacher Willy Blok Hanson, were part of Toronto's social elite. Neither of these books seemed to me to have a compelling reason to exist. But since Clarke, Irwin's trade list was subject to Mrs. Clarke's personal control, so was I; and yet I rarely saw her except at Christmas, when employees were summoned to receive from her gloved hand a sealed envelope containing a holiday bonus.

Soon a more interesting project came my way. With the passion for all things Canadian that accompanied the approaching Centennial, the National Press Club in Ottawa was compiling *A Century of Reporting/Un siècle de reportage*, a bilingual anthology of the best print and photo journalism since 1867. The chief compilers were the journalists Christopher Young and Jean-Louis Gagnon, who along with the historian Frank Underhill would write introductions to each item. It was some indication of Clarke, Irwin's prestige that the Press Club had brought the project to us. I was assigned as in-house editor, responsible for overseeing text, photo research, captions, and translation and for expediting the project as it travelled between Chris Young at the *Ottawa Citizen* and Miss Isobel Walker, our fearsome production manager. I'd spend almost two years on *A Century of Reporting*; it would stretch my knowledge of Canadian history, Quebec culture, Toronto's archival resources, and Clarke, Irwin's internal nervous system.

Simultaneously I edited a curious work of religious history by another of Mrs. Clarke's friends (deceased), with the teasingly misleading title *Calvin and the Libertines of Geneva*. I ghost-wrote a chapter to update a new edition of A.Y. Jackson's memoir, *A Painter's Country*; working with the elderly member of the Group of Seven, I discovered a small talent for literary mimicry. Although I didn't get to handle Clarke, Irwin's most celebrated title of that period, the political journalist Richard Gwyn's *The Shape of Scandal*, I did edit a fascinating memoir of the First World War, Will R. Bird's *Ghosts Have Warm Hands*. But for all my absorption in what I was doing, I detected a stirring within, a restless craving to move beyond editorial housekeeping and create my own literary list – the stigmata of the aspiring publisher.

On the face of it, this was a hopeless dream. It had been ages since Clarke, Irwin had published the likes of Robertson Davies. And the company's genteel sensibility was light-years removed from the contemporary writing that excited me; I might have had better luck persuading the firm to operate an off-track betting pool or an all-night booze can than championing some raunchy experimental novel. But by various twists of fate, I received support for my ambition.

William H. Clarke Jr. arrived in 1966 to inhabit the large office off the courtyard. At twenty-six, Bill Clarke wore dark Tory-blue suits and a sober expression, and he had the brisk self-assurance of someone groomed for power at the best schools. His features were a younger, gentler version of his father's portrait in the corridor. Bill was eleven years younger than his brother Gary. It was obvious that Bill too possessed a formidable intelligence, which had already taken him far in a demanding field; he'd studied mathematics, physics, and astronomy at the University of Toronto and had recently earned a Ph.D. in astrophysics at UCLA, where he'd had access to one of the most advanced computing facilities in the world. He might have stayed in the States, except that, deemed to have the blood of publishers in his veins, he'd been plucked from his orbit, brought back to Toronto, and made part-time assistant to the president. With his pipeline to the boss, his presence soon created conflicts for Mr. Robertson, who, with little fuss or fanfare, stepped out of the company he'd served for twenty years and joined a smaller rival, Burns & MacEachern. Since Mrs. Clarke's heart problems persisted, Bill was compelled to move into the courtyard office full-time as vice-president.

The editorial department threw a farewell party for Mr. R. off the premises, complete with fine French wines. It was sad to see him leave. Still, his departure opened the door for much-needed modernization. Bill Clarke soon raised the salaries of us editorial peons to a less shameful level and, happily, seemed prepared to expand the trade program and extend me some autonomy as an editor.

My other ally was Lionel Trippet, a thirty-something Englishman who'd joined the editorial department shortly after me. Lionel was an autodidact with a droll wit, a chain-smoker who stood outside in all weathers to indulge his habit, since Clarke, Irwin prohibited smoking inside the building. Lionel's prior experience at Chatto & Windus lent him a certain prestige within the firm. Through our shared enthusiasms for travel and literature, we became friends. I urged him to read Canadian writers: Irving Layton, Leonard Cohen, John Newlove, and Gwendolyn

MacEwen, whom I'd visited at the cottage she shared with her fellow poet Milton Acorn, on Ward's Island in Toronto Harbour. Lionel would soon return to England, where he would become a senior editor at Arrow Books, Granada Publishing, and elsewhere. But before leaving, he gave Bill Clarke an earful: Clarke, Irwin was creatively moribund, Lionel informed him, and ought to be publishing brilliant young Canadian writers like Leonard Cohen – as unlikely a prospect as I could imagine, given the scatology of *Beautiful Losers*.

Naturally Clarke found Lionel's arguments impertinent, the arrogance of a condescending Englishman. But when I arranged a meeting to ask Bill if I could solicit fiction and poetry in the firm's name, he gave me the go-ahead, as if to refute Lionel's charges on the spot.

I started by approaching three writers whose work I'd read in the little mags: Margaret Atwood, Alden Nowlan, and Dave Godfrey. Atwood, whose first professionally published book of poetry, *The Circle Game*, had recently appeared from Contact Press, wrote a friendly reply to my inquiry; she had a novel in manuscript, but it was with McClelland & Stewart for the moment. Nowlan, a wonderful New Brunswick poet, was a different story. At seventeen, I'd introduced myself to him on a trip through Hartland, New Brunswick, where he was editor of the local paper, and later we'd corresponded. To my delight, Nowlan now replied by sending me a thick sheaf of unpublished poems. Although only thirty-three, he was recovering from surgery for cancer in his throat and neck.

Nowlan's new poems were earthy and dark, crafted in a colloquial, highly personal voice: an advance over his previous work published by Ryerson, Contact, and the poet Jay Macpherson's private press, Emblem Books. In my editorial report, I strongly recommended that Clarke, Irwin publish a scaled-down version of the collection; then I sent the manuscript down the hall for Bill Clarke's response. I knew he'd have to get it past his mother; I doubted she'd care for Nowlan's street language and rough candour, but the big unknown was Bill's own attitude.

A couple of months after submitting my report, I was none the wiser. I pictured the Clarkes, *mère et fils*, engaged in some ferocious battle of wills: whether over Nowlan's poetry or over the question of taking their trade list in this weird new direction, I couldn't know. I wrote Nowlan a letter from home, apologizing for "the endless messing around over your ms." and holding out the hope, however slim, that the Clarkes might still accept it.

Astonishingly, two months later, they did. Nowlan had meanwhile published several strong new poems in *The Tamarack Review* and *The Canadian Forum*, so I added those to the manuscript while jettisoning about a third of the original batch. We now had a tight collection, and after *Bread, Wine and Salt* was published in an attractive hardcover format in fall 1967, it shared the Governor General's Award for poetry with Eli Mandel's *An Idiot Joy*.

Whatever her earlier misgivings, Mrs. Clarke was now chuffed, as Lionel would have said, and she and Bill set off for Ottawa to squire their prize author to the presentation ceremony at Rideau Hall. They forgot to invite me along; but as a consolation prize, I got to accompany them to the Granite Club for lunch with Leslie Frost, the former Conservative premier of Ontario, whose memoirs we were chasing. In the next couple of years, Clarke, Irwin published poetry by George Woodcock, Raymond Souster, and Francis Sparshott, and Nowlan would remain with the firm for the rest of his foreshortened career, through several more books of poetry and fiction. Although it was never an entirely comfortable fit, what with Alden's backwoods origins and penchant for the bottle, the Clarkes were proud to have a literary lion on their list, and he seemed gratified to have landed a home in a Toronto publishing house, however uptight. And yet, even when I brought forward Nowlan's next manuscript, a story collection called *Miracle at Indian River*, I had to defend it strenuously against the Clarkes' niggling doubts.

They had a similar response to another writer I brought into the house. I was assembling the first in a series of anthologies I'd proposed, to be called *New Canadian Writing*, a paperback annual that would showcase several short stories by each of three young writers. I'd acquired some superb stories from Clark Blaise, including one called "How I Became a Jew." While visiting Toronto from Montreal, where he taught, Blaise came to the office to meet Bill. The two men were remarkably similar in some ways, both brash and outspoken, with a patrician manner beyond their years, yet culturally they were miles apart. "What would you say," Clarke asked Blaise, "to changing the title to 'How I Became a Jewish Person'?" But for all the awkwardness of his struggles to emerge from his mother's control, Bill Clarke was perceptive enough to see the widening gap between a rapidly changing world and Clarke, Irwin. In time, he'd try hero- ically to do something about it.

I couldn't take credit for discovering Blaise; I'd come across his work through Dave Godfrey. Twenty-nine when I met him in 1967, Godfrey would come to exercise a deep influence on Canadian publishing. Already a brilliant writer of short fiction, he was a vocal anti-imperialist and neo- phyte publisher, all the while teaching English at his alma mater, Trinity College in the University of Toronto, which had expelled him nine years earlier. Wiry, tightly wound, with a long, bony face split by sudden laugh- ter or frozen by anger, Godfrey had a stare that burned through walls. His constant state of readiness to act on his convictions would galvanize my own resolve.

I'd been reading Godfrey's stories in literary magazines and, struck by their austere intelligence, particularly in a series of hunting tales that were appearing in *Saturday Night*, I asked him for a manuscript. As with Atwood, I was a little late. Too impatient to wait to be discovered, Godfrey decided to push his work into print through a small press he'd just started with the poet Dennis Lee. His book came out in fall 1967 as *Death Goes Better with Coca-Cola*, one of the first titles from House of Anansi Press. These were the hunting tales, but luckily, Godfrey had other stories that hadn't yet appeared in book form, and I took some of those for *New Canadian Writing 1968*. Characteristically, Godfrey liked to think the series had been his idea all along. In a letter, he told me Anansi had been plan- ning the same sort of thing, but that was okay: "We're fertile; we can be stolen from."

Alongside work by Blaise and Godfrey, the first *New Canadian Writing* anthology featured stories by David Lewis Stein, a fine and underrated writer. The second, *New Canadian Writing 1969*, would include pieces by John Metcalf, C.J. Newman, and Douglas Spettigue. But by that time, I'd be gone from Clarke, Irwin. The series wouldn't survive my leaving, although Metcalf would stick around long enough to publish his first collection of short fiction, *The Lady Who Sold Furniture*, with the company.

Nothing particularly dramatic precipitated my departure after four years; I'd simply bumped up against my psychic limits at Clarke, Irwin. Continuing to persuade the firm to publish my kinds of books would be an endless, exhausting struggle. Besides, my wife, Suzette, and I wanted to return to Europe. But the other catalyst for change was what I saw Godfrey and Lee creating at Anansi. It would be fantastic to publish books out of your basement as they did, to crank out whatever you believed in, whatever the country and the world needed to read and know. That was what I wanted to do someday, and the sooner the better.

GEORGE J. McLEOD

COPP CLARK | W. J. GAGE

MUSSON BOOK COMPANY

J. M. DENT & SONS | THOMAS ALLEN

RYERSON PRESS

2

AT MID-CENTURY

Is it true, then, that we are a people without a literature?

Report of the Royal Commission on National
Development in the Arts, Letters and Sciences (1951)

T he plaintive query above was posed a mere half-century ago. The
questioners were five royal commissioners appointed by Prime
Minister Louis St. Laurent's government to study Canada's cultural and
intellectual life and decide what, if anything, the state ought to do about it.
Known at the time as the Massey commission after its chairman, Vincent
Massey, and more recently as the Massey-Lévesque commission in recognition of the sole francophone member, Père Georges-Henri Lévesque, the
commission faced a formidable task: to survey, assess, and make recommendations on "national development in the arts, letters and sciences,"
consulting widely with Canadians in the process. The commission's report
would lead, among other things, to creation of the Canada Council and the
National Library of Canada.

Following their appointment in 1949, the commissioners issued a call
for written briefs, then travelled across "this young nation, struggling to be
itself" to hold hearings in sixteen cities. Their final report's air of anxious
hand-wringing reflected what they'd heard from members of the public
concerned about broadcasting, the arts, and scholarly and scientific
research. About the state of the writing profession, the commissioners
were gloomy. "Not only the critics but the briefs," they intoned, "agree that

Canadian literature has not yet achieved the status of a 'national litera-ture.'" And: "In Canada, it seems, the cultural environment is hostile or at least indifferent to the writer."

When it came to book publishing, the commissioners found even more cause for gloom. In 1948 English-language publishers had issued a mere fourteen books of fiction and thirty-five works of poetry and drama. That output was far lower than at the turn of the century or during the 1920s. It reflected a prolongation of the lean times, economically and cre-atively, that had begun with the Depression and continued throughout the Second World War.

Massey-Lévesque identified systemic causes of Canada's cultural malaise. At all levels of the educational system, dependence on American textbooks and learning materials was "excessive." Even in higher educa-tion, "the comparative smallness of the Canadian university population, and the accessibility of American publishing houses with their huge markets has resulted in an almost universal dependence on the American product." Consequently it was difficult for Canadian universities to offer courses that weren't taught in American universities, to function as centres of indigenous research, or to foster intellectual exchange between the country's English- and French-language cultures. Very few books were translated from the other language. There was a lack of Canadian books, period, which resulted in a lack of Canadian studies, and a grievous lack of knowledge about the country.

The report advocated no limits on access to the books, magazines, movies, or other cultural products spilling constantly over the border. Instead it put the onus squarely on Canadians to remedy the problem. They had been poor patrons of their own artists to date, and even poorer custodians of their own culture and heritage. Out-of-print Canadian books were treated better in the United States than in their home country, the commissioners scolded, pointing to "the countless invaluable Canadian books now available only in the U.S.," and the fact that the three best collections of print Canadiana were at the Library of Congress, the New York Public Library, and Harvard University.

Such distressing facts highlighted the desperate need for a national library. The commission agreed with intervenors who had called this lack "a national disgrace," and one of its major recommendations was that such an institution be established "without delay." Yet even though Parliament brought a national bibliographic centre into being in 1950, with the task of preparing a union catalogue of all books in Canadian libraries, and would establish the National Library itself in 1953 to begin the comprehensive collection of Canadiana, a dedicated building for the institution wouldn't open until Centennial Year.

New life was stirring in Canadian literature nonetheless. A remarkable three-day gathering took place at Queen's University in Kingston, Ontario, in July 1955. The Canadian Writers' Conference assembled for the first time a large group of literary professionals, many of whom scarcely knew one another, including several who worked on what the conference's prime mover, F.R. (Frank) Scott, termed "the literary assembly line": magazine editors, broadcasters, and book publishers.

Eighty-one invitees attended the Kingston conference, including poets, novelists, and non-fiction writers, mostly from Toronto, Montreal, and Vancouver. The roll call was impressive. Present were Earle Birney, Morley Callaghan, Irving Layton, James Reaney, Malcolm Ross, A.J.M. Smith, and a twenty-one-year-old poet listed as "L.N. Cohen." Delegates who didn't attend but sent moral support included Pierre Berton, Robertson Davies, Northrop Frye, Hugh MacLennan, and Marshall McLuhan. The conference offered writers a rare chance to converse with one another, and an even rarer opportunity to meet people who could help their careers: Ralph Allen of *Maclean's*, Hugh Garner of *Liberty*, John Gray of Macmillan, S.P. Kite of Penguin Books Canada, young Jack McClelland, young Robert Weaver of the CBC. The irony lay in the fact that the event was funded, like much Canadian scholarship at the time, by the Rockefeller Foundation.

Participants spent the evenings arguing about papers they'd heard during the day, and for relaxation they lounged on the grass during afternoon poetry readings organized by the energetic Layton. Debate grew heated as delegates from different worlds clashed. The committed socialist Frank Scott, poet and legal scholar, and the lapsed socialist Hugh Garner, novelist and journalist, disagreed vehemently over the idea of (then non-existent) grants to creative writers. Garner alleged that they'd go to "the wrong people," i.e., the safe and the sober; Scott called Garner's attitude "defeatist." The poet Miriam Waddington reported a tentative consensus after the dust had settled: "Everyone agreed that there is no inherent evil in subsidies." The novelist Henry Kreisel's discussion group felt the development of Canadian literature was hindered by the problem of keeping books in print, and therefore subsidizing standard editions of important works would be appropriate, "if the Canada Council were ever set up."

From today's perspective, the conference appears remarkably self-doubting. Here was a gathering of the country's finest writers, a generation now seen as the progenitors of contemporary Canadian literature, debating what John Gray called "the conditions under which Canadian literature might come into existence." The conference discourse seemed to echo Frye's famous question, "Where is here?"

Facts cited in Frank Scott's introduction to the conference proceedings, published by Macmillan the following year, resolve the paradox. Only two literary magazines then existed in English-speaking Canada. Very few universities offered courses in Canadian literature, and those that did were "hard pressed to find copies of the books students should read." The Governor General's Awards were "a hollow gesture" because they carried no monetary value; the winners even had to pay their own way to Rideau Hall to receive their awards. Scott decried the paucity of bookstores across the country (the Massey-Lévesque commission had counted no more than twenty-five stores devoted solely to books) and deplored the "dismal situation" of the nation's libraries, which lacked adequate funds to buy books. Although he found hope in CBC Radio's growing role in creating an audience, and advocated other steps to encourage young writers, Scott described the landscape for Canadian writing and publishing as "inexcusably black."

Things could only improve.

The outlook for Canadian books hadn't always been so discouraging. Several Canadian authors had become internationally prominent around the turn of the twentieth century: Robert Service, Sir Charles G.D. Roberts, Ernest Thompson Seton, Bliss Carman. Even more successful were the Reverend Charles Gordon and Lucy Maud Montgomery. Writing under the pen name Ralph Connor, Gordon published his first international best-seller, *Black Rock*, in instalments in *The Westminster*, the periodical of the Presbyterian Church of Canada. When Westminster Press issued the novel in book form in 1898, it sold out a first Canadian printing of 5,000 copies, still a very respectable sale more than a century later. American rights went to Revell in Chicago, which sold hundreds of thousands more. Connor, a prolific writer as well as an influential public figure, produced *The Sky Pilot* a year later and *The Man from Glengarry* two years after that; those three titles alone would sell 5 million copies throughout the English-speaking world. Like other writers of his day, Connor appealed to the public's appetite, both inside and outside Canada, for fiction about the frontier.

Between 1905 and 1914, an average of twenty-one new Canadian novels appeared each year. Lucy Maud Montgomery's first book, *Anne of Green Gables*, was published in 1908 by an American company. Like Connor's, her success was atypical; unlike him, she remains popular today. But even though Canadian authors could break into the international market under foreign imprints, they scarcely made their domestic publishers rich.

The size of the home market had been a problem from the very beginning. In 1836 Joseph Howe, the newspaper proprietor and future premier of Nova Scotia, issued *The Clockmaker*, Thomas Chandler Haliburton's satirical sketches about the sharp Yankee trader Sam Slick. Although the book sold well enough to justify a reprint and earned the author healthy royalties, Howe complained that he netted only £35 on his investment. For the rest of his long writing career, Canadian-born Haliburton published instead in Britain and the United States, to reach the largest readership.

Nineteenth-century Canadian publishers, many of them also printers or booksellers, issued cheap reprints of British and American authors for domestic consumption. Some, such as John Lovell of Montreal and Hunter-Rose of Toronto, paid royalties to the authors. But Toronto's Belford Brothers took advantage of an 1875 Canadian law extending copy-right only to authors domiciled in Canada and mercilessly ripped off popular American writers and their publishers, selling their books not only in Canada but barefacedly in the United States by mail order. Mark Twain litigated against the Canadian pirates, who ate up a good portion of his American market. In support of Twain, the New York press condemned the "Canadian invasion." What may have been Canadian trade publishers' most lucrative hour, if not their finest ethically, was brought to an end by a U.S.-Canada copyright agreement in 1891. From then on, the agency business took hold, and distributing imported titles overshadowed original publishing, when not pre-empting it altogether.

Among the early Canadian booksellers and printers who eventually mutated into publishers were two educational firms whose names have survived into the present. Copp Clark (part of British-owned Pearson Education Canada) traces its origins to a Toronto retailing and printing operation begun in 1841, which became Copp Clark in 1869. And Gage Learning Corporation, still Canadian-owned, extends all the way back to the Toronto booksellers and publishers A. and R. Miller; it became W.J. Gage in 1880.

More than a dozen publishing houses sprang up in Toronto during the two decades before the First World War. They included the Musson Book Company (1896), G.N. Morang (1897), George J. McLeod (1898), University of Toronto Press (1901), Oxford University Press (1904), John C. Winston (1904), Macmillan of Canada (1905), McClelland & Goodchild (1906, later McClelland & Stewart), J.M. Dent & Sons (1913), Thomas Nelson & Sons (1913), and Thomas Allen (1916). Oxford, Macmillan, Dent, and Nelson were all branches of British firms.

Four of the new houses were headed by men who'd begun their careers with the oldest Canadian publisher of all. Established in 1829, the Methodist Book Room and Publishing House, renamed the Ryerson Press in 1919, was a church-owned operation producing the weekly *Christian Guardian*, forerunner of the *United Church Observer*, and supplying religious materials to circuit riders, the itinerant preachers who travelled the Canadian colonies. Egerton Ryerson, future father of public education in Ontario, became the house's first "book steward" at twenty-three, acting as both editor and business manager. Ryerson arranged for one of the earliest printing presses in Upper Canada to be shipped from New York up the old industrial canals, across Lake Ontario by boat, and then by ox cart to Muddy York. Although his primary obligation was to print religious titles, Ryerson soon caught the publishing bug and by 1833 was issuing some secular books.

The most influential of Ryerson's successors was the Reverend William Briggs, appointed book steward in 1878. A man of the cloth with a taste for business, Briggs became an ambitious publisher of both trade and educational books; in 1897 he published thirty-seven Canadian titles, an output that the Ryerson Press would not exceed until the expansive 1920s. Briggs also trained several leading publishers of the next generation. McClelland & Stewart's founders, John McClelland and Frederick Goodchild, both learned their profession under him, as did George Stewart, who joined them seven years later via Oxford University Press. Three others left the Methodist Book Room to head up new houses: Samuel B. Gundy to open the Canadian outpost of Oxford, George J. McLeod and Thomas Allen to start their own companies.

Although a time of severe shortages and tragedy on a vast scale, the First World War gave a tremendous boost to publishing as a surge of patriotism lifted book sales to new heights. The war replaced the frontier as the subject everyone wanted to read about. In 1914 publishers started to enjoy record-breaking Christmas seasons; titles by Ralph Connor and the fighter ace Billy Bishop led the field. After the war ended, Hugh Eayrs, who would soon become president of Macmillan of Canada, reported that some books achieved sales of 25,000 to 40,000 copies during the conflict.

Eayrs and gentlemanly John McClelland were two of three key figures to emerge between the wars. The third was Lorne Pierce, a Methodist scholar with six university degrees who joined the Ryerson Press in 1920 and quickly became editor-in-chief. Pierce's ambition was to restore Ryerson to its former eminence as English Canada's leading trade publisher. He never quite fulfilled his aim, but his fervour and idealism had a formative impact on Canadian writing and on public perceptions of it. Convinced that the nation had come of age in the war and was ready to express a new spiritual identity through literature, Pierce ransacked the country for writers on his cross-country tours. Too often he unearthed quantity rather than quality – he published a record eighty-four titles in 1930 – but his labours generated a fertilization process that would produce better writing in years to come.

Pierce nurtured a notion called Canadian literature. He published copious amounts of it, commissioned critical studies of it, edited school readers bursting with it, and wrote, lectured, and pamphleteered endlessly about it. There was an evangelical industry about the man. His successor a generation later in promotional zeal, Jack McClelland, remembered Pierce as "a sort of wild, strange fellow" who "always seemed to be in a hurry" but was "a very good publisher." Above all, Pierce wanted to publish nothing but Canadian authors. Six years before his retirement in 1960, he allowed himself to describe his utopian dream in *The House of Ryerson*, published to mark the press's 125th anniversary. "As the years pass," Pierce wrote, "we shall become a completely independent publishing house, developing our own line, in our own time, and in our own way. More and more we shall be free of the halter of the agencies."

Pierce identified closely with Hugh Eayrs and John McClelland. Looking back at the three of them in the 1920s, he wrote, "We were at the beginning of things as a nation and we felt under obligation to assist as many spokesmen of our time as we could . . . It was simply that a birth, and then possibly a rebirth, of Canadian letters had to begin somewhere, and it might as well begin with us."

The Depression and the Second World War cast Canadian publishing into a state of suspended animation. The strong survived by hunkering down until the storm had passed, but two promising firms founded during the 1920s were too fragile to last. Louis Carrier of Montreal and Graphic Press of Ottawa both tried to publish Canadian trade authors without benefit of either agency or educational lines. Graphic, the more productive of the two, declared bankruptcy in 1932 after seven years and eighty-three titles, including works by Frederick Philip Grove, who served briefly as the press's editor, and the first Canadian political *roman à clef*, *The Land of Afternoon*, by Madge Macbeth writing as Gilbert Knox. Publishers with firmer foundations stayed in business by cutting back on Canadian titles and releasing staff. McClelland & Stewart, after issuing twenty-nine Canadian titles in 1929, reduced its output to an average of seven a year during the Depression.

The impact of the Second World War was very different from that of the First. Although publishing didn't come to a halt in English Canada, it remained quiescent as many key personnel left home to fight. In French Canada, the war was unpopular, but it produced an unexpected bonanza for publishers. With publishing in Paris shackled by the Nazi occupation, Montreal firms filled the gap by supplying the book needs of the rest of the francophone world, issuing reprints of standard French authors while developing their own writers, such as Gabrielle Roy and Roger Lemelin. Montreal in the early 1940s was a great place to be a book publisher: "a time of real luxury," according to Pierre Tisseyre, a Frenchman who had emigrated to Montreal and begun a book club and publishing house called the Cercle du livre de France. But the bubble burst with the war's end and the resumption of France's normal export trade. The Quebec industry returned to the status quo ante, remaining dominated by clerical publishing houses and their conservative editorial policies until the Quiet Revolution of the 1960s.

In publishing, as in Canadian culture generally, a kind of mini-depression followed the Second World War. John Gray told the Kingston writers' conference that a decision to publish a Canadian trade book equalled a decision to lose money. Canadian publishers enjoyed neither American-style income from the sale of paperback, book club, broadcast, or movie rights, nor latter-day grant funding from government programs. During the 1950s, the traditional Canadian publishing model became more deeply entrenched than ever, based on the twin revenue streams of agency business and schoolbooks, to use the term then in style.

American educational publishers were at first content to be represented by Canadian firms, obtaining access to Canadian schools and libraries through the agency system. Several major British subsidiaries had been established early in the century, partly out of imperial habit, partly because the parent company wanted a closer eye on things. In January 1950, the trade journal *Quill & Quire* listed a dozen foreign publishers operating Canadian branches, only four of them American: Doubleday,

Ginn, McGraw-Hill, and Random House. Many more American firms would arrive during the next two decades, but for now, Canadian-owned houses benefited from representing about 700 American and British publishers. The school-age population exploded as the post-war baby boom started moving through the educational system. For publishers with texts approved for classroom use, the schoolbook business could be very lucrative indeed.

Robin Farr worked at the heart of Canadian educational publishing in that expansive period. Farr, who would distinguish himself as the first director of McGill (later McGill-Queen's) University Press and a key cultural bureaucrat in the Canada Council and the Ontario government, started out as a teacher in British Columbia. He began his publishing career at the century's midpoint, joining Copp Clark on January 1, 1950.

Like the Ryerson Press, Copp Clark still operated its own printing presses. When Farr joined the company, it drew much of its editorial and managerial strength from Marsh Jeanneret, who would leave three years later for the University of Toronto Press. But ownership lay in the hands of two brothers, Alan and Dudley Thomas, who had inherited the firm. Having reached the rank of brigadier general in the Canadian army, Alan Thomas liked to be called "the Brig" and insisted on being transported to and from the old Copp Clark building on Wellington Street in a chauffeur-driven limousine that flew the company flag. A dedicated inventor, Thomas would suffer the most bizarre death of any Canadian publisher. He had invented an early version of the snowmobile, powered by a propeller mounted on the rear of the vehicle, and one day, as he was demonstrating the device to army brass at Camp Borden, the propeller came loose and decapitated him.

In 1950 Copp Clark was one of the main Toronto publishers supplying textbooks to the "el-hi" (elementary and high school) market. Robin Farr went on the road as a sales rep, or traveller, presenting the company's titles to educators across the western provinces. From Winnipeg he'd take the Canadian Pacific line through Regina and Calgary to the west coast; the return trip was on the Canadian National through Edmonton and

Saskatoon. At each stop he'd set up book displays in hotel rooms. The textbooks Farr sold hadn't necessarily been originated by Copp Clark; rather than risk large sums to create a series of readers or math or science texts, which might or might not be adopted by provincial governments to teach the approved curriculum, publishers often simply obtained the rights to American titles and Canadianized them. Farr remembered sitting in his hotel room in Regina, cutting pictures of American coins out of the display copy of a textbook and replacing them with pictures of Canadian coins.

According to C.J. Eustace, a prominent publisher with Dent during the period, the great influx of American textbooks into Canada had begun during the 1940s. By the 1950s, Eustace estimated, about 60 percent of textbooks used in schools were either direct American imports or American in origin, adapted for Canadian students. Leading the field was the famous Dick and Jane reading series, distributed in Canada by Gage.

It wasn't only Dick and Jane's pedagogical qualities that made it so successful; Gage was also widely known to throw the best parties and dinners, an indispensable feature of successful schoolbook publishing. Gage's top traveller was a genial gent named Frank Strowbridge, who seemed to his competitors to enjoy an unusually large expense account for wooing educators and curriculum officials. And yet those same competitors appreciated Strowbridge's generosity with rookies. Both Robin Farr and Gladys Neale of Macmillan remembered benefiting from his advice. Young Farr visited Strowbridge's hotel room during a trip across the west: "Frank must have taken pity on this kid. He up and poured me a drink, then poured himself one. He put half a glass of milk in his drink and said to me, 'Now, the drink is for me, and the milk is for my ulcer.'"

The average print run for a Canadian novel was then about 2,000 copies, but school readers and spellers were routinely printed in runs of 50,000. Back in the 1920s, C.J. Eustace noted, Macmillan had produced 100,000 copies of titles in its Ontario-authorized Canadian Readers series. Robin Farr might return from his western sales trips with orders totalling 175,000 copies for a single book, provided it had received education ministry authorization in several provinces. Copp Clark's *The Story of Canada*, a social studies text, could easily sell 50,000 copies in each province. "It was just staggering," Farr recalled at the turn of the millennium, "especially when you consider the fight to sell 5,000 or 6,000 copies now." Moreover, there were no returns to worry about.

According to Campbell Hughes, who spent thirty-one years in educational publishing at Ryerson and Van Nostrand Reinhold of Canada as well as in the United States, it wasn't unusual to ship three or four freight cars of books to a western ordering depot. "Old-time publishers still remember with glee," he once wrote, "the time the Saskatchewan Book Bureau burned down at the peak of the shipping season and all of the books had to be replaced, sending some publishers back for an extra press run. It was, as one publisher remembers, like having two harvests in one year."

With Canadian educational publishers reaping big profits, major American companies such as John Wiley & Sons, Prentice-Hall, D.C. Heath, Addison-Wesley, and Holt, Rinehart soon superseded their agents by moving into Canada themselves. Meanwhile most Canadian publishers avoided the higher risks of trade publishing, particularly in fiction and serious non-fiction. Copp Clark was typical in that regard, issuing only a few trade books a year on such popular topics as curling or hockey. There was no trade editorial department as such at Copp Clark, Farr remembered: "It was a question of which manuscripts came floating in over the transom. Somebody would decide, 'We've had an awfully good year in educational sales, so we can do this or that trade book.'"

Trade publishing retained vestiges of colonialism, with all the self-doubt that condition entails. An editorial in the January 1950 issue of *Quill & Quire* admiringly cited a recent novel by David Walker, a Scottish author of adventure and spy fiction who had come to Canada in the 1930s as aide-de-camp to Governor General Lord Tweedsmuir (a.k.a. the novelist John Buchan and creator of the Governor General's Literary Awards). One of the characters in Walker's *The Storm and the Silence* was a publisher turned commando officer, who described his former profession as being "creative because you help other people to create." The anonymous *Quill & Quire* editorialist opined that this character stood for good old-fashioned chivalry and asked rhetorically: "Is publishing, then – is the book business generally – one which attracts the chivalrous? Certainly it has little to attract anyone interested primarily in making money."

The prevailing notion was that publishing was a profession for gentlemen, preferably gentlemen with English or Scots accents. Snobbery was equally evident in *Quill & Quire*'s lead story covering the writers' delegations that had appeared recently before Vincent Massey's royal commission: "A felicitous blend of dignity and informality characterized the Toronto hearings of the Royal Commission on National Development in the Arts, Letters and Sciences, held during the second week in November in the University Senate Chamber in Simcoe Hall. The dignity was inherent in the setting – the high square chamber, furnished in the rich simplicity of polished walnut, its tall windows hung with royal blue velour – with a stab of colour from the coat of the Mountie who stood at ease in polished boots before the ponderous doors. There was dignity too in the group who sat in high-backed chairs before the broad head table: the finedrawn domed countenance of the Honourable Vincent Massey."

Amid all that dignified high-mindedness, the writers begged for crumbs. They requested that the Governor General's Awards be endowed with money (but not too much), and that eight grants ("scholarships") be awarded annually to "serious writers": "$1,500 for single persons [read 'women'], $2,500 for heads of families."

Throughout the 1950s, the book trade journal featured tips about selling greeting cards, gift wrapping, and stationery, then important staples for booksellers. Consumers patronized the thriving book sections in department stores such as Eaton's, Simpsons, and Woodward's, and publishers often decried the paucity of dedicated bookstores. S.P. Kite, who managed Penguin Books Canada, told the 1955 Kingston conference: "The one great shortage in Canada is bookshops upon which, of course, so much depends for the promotion of reading." When the Canadian Retail Booksellers Association (later the Canadian Booksellers Association) started up in 1952, it had only thirty-five stores in its membership.

The shortage of bookstores was linked to a shortage of readers. The situation would improve as Canada's population grew and the reading public expanded with the spread of higher education. Mel Hurtig opened his first bookstore in Edmonton in 1956; Bill Duthie started his first Vancouver store in 1957. These and other independents, such as Munro's in Victoria, Evelyn de Mille Books in Calgary, Mary Scorer Books in Winnipeg, Britnell's, Lichtman's, and the Book Cellar in Toronto, Shirley Leishman Books in Ottawa, and the Book Room in Halifax (originally owned by the Ryerson Press), would play crucial roles in their communities for decades. The Coles and Classics bookstore chains existed only in embryonic form, confined in the early 1950s to Toronto and Montreal respectively. Both would eventually extend from coast to coast in direct and finally fatal competition with each other and with the third chain, British-owned W.H. Smith, which drew a big crowd to the opening of its first Canadian store on Yonge Street in Toronto in 1950.

Quill & Quire did its bit to boost book sales by publishing an annual Christmas catalogue, *Books for Everybody*. Then as now, publishers bought advertising space in the catalogue, which booksellers offered free to customers. The 1950 edition led with the fiction bestsellers *Joy Street*, by Frances Parkinson Keyes, and *Across the River and into the Trees*, by Ernest Hemingway. The popular novelists A.J. Cronin, Frank Yerby, Nevil Shute, Agatha Christie, W. Somerset Maugham, C.S. Forester, and Georgette Heyer were showcased. Canadian authors were ghettoized in a "Canadian Themes" section, which highlighted two novels by writers popular in the States: Thomas B. Costain's *Son of a Hundred Kings*, "a period novel of an Ontario town in The Gay Nineties," and Thomas Raddall's *The Nymph and the Lamp*. That was also the year of Roger Lemelin's *The Plouffe Family*, Edward McCourt's *Home Is the Stranger*, and the all but forgotten *Blaze of Noon* by Jeann Beattie, winner of the Ryerson Press's All-Canada Fiction Contest. In non-fiction, the catalogue featured regional books, published in Toronto, by Bruce Hutchison and Roderick Haig-Brown of British Columbia and Will R. Bird of Nova Scotia, as well as the travel book *We Fell in Love with Quebec*. All were destined to be outsold by *Skate with Me*, the story of the 1948 Olympic gold medallist Barbara Ann Scott.

Substantive issues also engaged the trade. One of these achieved the rare feat of uniting all parts of the book industry in both official languages: the struggle to abolish a federal sales tax on books. Despite appeals to the government from the forerunner of the Canadian Book Publishers'

Council, the St. Laurent government had kept the tax in place and in 1952 had actually raised it, from 8 to 10 percent. But in his 1953 budget speech, Finance Minister Douglas Abbott announced that the tax would be eliminated, declaring, "I have been impressed with the breadth and sincerity of the representations for this action, and I have been convinced that it would be in the public interest to forego the modest amount of revenue now received from this source."

Earlier that year, Abbott had met in Ottawa with a delegation of English- and French-language publishers and booksellers. A key factor in their success was the support of the Canadian Library Association/ Association canadienne des bibliothèques. The librarians brought supporting letters from Canadian universities, labour groups, writers', teachers', and school trustees' associations, even medical associations. Canada "should encourage . . . the intellectual and spiritual development of her citizens," they argued. "A revenue tax on books is not worthy of a great nation."

The book industry had been trying to roll back the tax for thirty years before the victory, ever since the first W.L. Mackenzie King administration had levied it in the early 1920s. The arguments then were largely identical to more recent ones against the goods and services tax on books. The main difference lay in *Quill & Quire*'s remark that the 1953 federal budget had reduced the cost not only of a book but of a pack of cigarettes to enjoy while reading it.

A dearth of media coverage plagued Canadian books from the 1950s until well into the '70s. *Quill & Quire* ran a blunt assessment of the situation in its August and September 1954 issues. "We sometimes feel as inferior about our book reviewing as we do about our publishing," an unsigned editorial confessed. "Britain has 'The [*Times*] Literary Supplement,' the United States has 'The Saturday Review of Literature'; but Canada has nothing of the kind and there's no reason why she should have. There are not yet by any means enough Canadian books published to warrant a special magazine devoted to essays and reviews on contemporary literature."

That salvo was followed by patronizing praise for the ability of the few newspaper reviewers of the time (William Arthur Deacon of the *Globe and*

Mail, Jean Swanson of the *Saskatoon Star-Phoenix*) to tailor their reviews to a generally unsophisticated audience: "This is made up for the most part of people with a high school education, who depend on knowledgeable people 'on the inside' to direct their thinking." The editorial proceeded to the nub of its argument: "The one criticism we might make is that there is sometimes a disproportionate emphasis on Canadian books . . . Thus to encourage reading and buying simply on the basis of Canadianism is unwise; only a satisfied public will turn out eventually to be a well-read and discriminating one."

Quill & Quire's position was similar to that of Nathan Cohen of the *Toronto Star* towards Canadian theatre: demand higher standards from homegrown artists and producers, Cohen argued ceaselessly, and the result will be a better product and a more enlightened audience. The trade journal claimed that Canadian literature would develop "a healthy backbone" only if criticism in the newspapers and on CBC Radio were more fearless and rigorous. As an illustration, it cited the overly kind reception given Gabrielle Roy's second book, *Where Nests the Water Hen*. The novel had been found wanting by only one critic, who "happens to belong to the academic group which takes its burden of intellectual honesty seriously, and [who] made his criticism over a radio program that deserves every praise for the freedom, responsibility, and quality of its reviews."

That program was almost certainly *Critically Speaking*, heard each week on the CBC. Its producer, Robert Weaver, was one of a tiny band who expected better things of Canadian writing than most authors and publishers were delivering. Weaver, who had joined the CBC in 1948, had an international outlook that would later fall out of step with a resurgent cultural nationalism, but his outlook was needed in the 1950s, a period of blandness and insularity. At the 1955 Kingston conference, Weaver took issue with the truism that Canadians pay no attention to their artists until their work is praised abroad, arguing that he detected the opposite trend: Canadians were in fact suspicious of writers who had been successful internationally. Books by Ethel Wilson, Mordecai Richler, and Ernest Buckler had been recognized abroad but slighted by Canadian reviewers. Other writers (unidentified), whose talents Weaver considered inferior, had fared better with domestic critics and the public, in part because "their books are so obviously Canadian." Morley Callaghan, Buckler, and Richler had all secured American paperback publication, Weaver said, "which would never have happened if these novelists had been content with a Canadian public alone."

Weaver set about using the CBC as a vehicle for promoting Canadian short fiction, poetry, drama, and criticism that satisfied his modernist literary values. He brought fresh contemporary voices to a national audience. Programs such as *Canadian Short Stories, CBC Wednesday Night, Critically Speaking,* and later *Anthology* acquainted listeners with the work of Callaghan, Richler, Sinclair Ross, Hugh Garner, Mavis Gallant, Alice Munro, and others who became household names. Compensating for the shortage of both publishers and booksellers, CBC Radio enacted an early form of audio publishing: a medium particularly appropriate to Canada, with its small public widely dispersed across a huge land mass.

Weaver was highly cognizant of how electronic media were shaping mass audiences, homogenizing taste and experience regardless of national borders. He saw how recent developments in the book world were following that trend and told the Kingston conference that Penguin Books was "consciously exploiting a public spread over several countries." The inexpensive mass-market paperback was creating a new commercial and cultural phenomenon, multinational publishing. The paperback's growing ascendancy, along with the success of book clubs such as Book of the Month Club and the Literary Guild (both popular in Canada), was creating simultaneous bestsellers in more than one country. Canada could not and should not be immune to such internationalism, Weaver believed, but he envisioned the flow going both ways; Canadians should also be contributors to the process, exporting our best writers.

Paradoxically, just as media were creating mass audiences, they could also target programming to small, special-interest publics. That was exactly what Weaver was doing with his commercial-free CBC literary programs, which he estimated (in the absence of today's audience measurement tools) were reaching 25,000 to 50,000 listeners across the country. If Weaver was, in a sense, a publisher, he truly paralleled a magazine publisher. The content of his radio programs was diverse and created by many hands. Because the medium's time constraints demanded fiction that was brief yet vivid, it was no accident that many Canadian writers came to excel at the short story sooner than the novel. Some of the writers Weaver nurtured, such as Gallant and Munro, began appearing in *The New Yorker*. In 1956, Weaver would co-found, with several others, *The Tamarack Review*, which remained Canada's leading literary quarterly until its final issue in 1982.

And yet even someone as crucially positioned as Weaver could find it hard to get his hands on Canadian books. Both Weaver and Robert Fulford, who in 1959 began writing the country's only daily book column in the *Toronto Star*, recalled the infuriating difficulty of obtaining review copies from some Toronto firms. This was particularly true of agency houses that published little, if anything, themselves and sometimes weren't even aware that they had Canadian authors in their warehouse. In 1958, while an editor at *Chatelaine*, Fulford had complained, "The eccentricity of Canadian publishers in the matter of publicity continues to astonish me . . . The appalling fact is that the only people in this country who ever write about books are those who care enough to break down the curtain of secrecy that publishers erect around themselves under the title 'Publicity Department.' "

At that time, according to Fulford in an interview, "You could be pretty well-read in Canadian literature without spending a lot of time reading." In his *Star* column, he reviewed literally all the Canadian fiction published in English and much of the non-fiction as well. In the late 1950s and early '60s, there might be only half a dozen first novels and no more than twenty novels in total published during a whole year. Fulford found the quality of some of them deplorable, particularly those produced by Ryerson during Lorne Pierce's twilight years. But when he was eager to review the latest book by Mavis Gallant, a Canadian living in Paris and published in the United States, Fulford found review copies so hard to come by that "to get them from the, quote, 'publishers,' unquote, you practically had to go down there with automatic weapons and hold them up. You certainly couldn't get one in the stores, because there wouldn't be any." The distributor of Gallant's book had ordered only fifty or a hundred copies to supply the whole country, having no inkling of her growing reputation.

If Canadians were a people without a literature in the 1950s, it was in part because publishers hadn't taken trade publishing seriously; it was a sideline indulged in for reasons of pride or prestige, not profit. That antiquated attitude persisted well into the 1960s, even in productive houses such as Macmillan, Oxford, and Clarke, Irwin. It would take the energy, brashness, and unfettered imagination of Jack McClelland to explode the mystique of publishing as a gentleman's calling with his commitment, aggressive advertising, and theatrical promotion stunts. By breaking the mould, McClelland would rebel against not only his own father but the founding father of Canadian publishing's modern era: John Gray.

Macmillan

MACMILLAN OF CANADA

3

GRAY'S LUCK

I never wonder why I am in publishing; for all its responsibilities it is a rare privilege.

John Gray to Hugh MacLennan (1958)

I n one of the stories he relished telling on himself, John Gray arrived at the old Macmillan building on Bond Street in Toronto for his first day at work. It was August 1930, and the twenty-three-year-old had obtained the job by a circuitous route. After failing two years at the University of Toronto while enjoying himself immensely, he'd barnstormed around Europe with a pickup hockey team, toyed with being a writer in London, and spent a year as a junior master at his alma mater, the boys' prep school at Lakefield, Ontario. Presented with a casual offer from Hugh Eayrs of Macmillan based on his prowess at bridge, Gray had passed it up, opting to work his way around the world on a freighter. But he soon thought better of that and wrote explaining his change of heart to Eayrs, who had assured him the door to Macmillans (as everyone called it) would remain open. Gray waited days, then weeks for a reply. His other options had closed by the time he was told Eayrs had departed on a voyage to England. Gray fired off a cable to Macmillan's London headquarters, politely insisting on a decision. A reply arrived from Eayrs within twenty-four hours: "Awfully sorry completely forgot letter join us August 18th."

"And so by chance encounters, by blind luck, and perhaps guided by some instinct," Gray wrote in his memoirs, "I stumbled into what was to be

43

my career." This remarkable man wouldn't be the country's most innovative publisher nor its most flamboyant, but without him – as exemplar, mentor, setter of standards – the profession would not have developed as it did.

Curiosity and optimism help make a book publisher, especially if combined with a modicum of luck. On all counts, young John Morgan Gray was superbly qualified. Unsure where his destiny lay, he renewed nightly his pledge of "fun tomorrow," a bright and adventurous day ahead. His luck resulted partly from being born into an affectionate and privileged family. As a boy, Gray lived in London with his mother and older brother so that the family could be together while his father served in the First World War. Schoolmates taunted the boys for their Canadian accents until they learned to ape English diction. Later the brothers boarded at Lakefield and attended Upper Canada College, where John became "something of a connoisseur of caning" and played first-team hockey.

Gray's luck was often reinforced by sound intuition: as in his decision to marry Antoinette Lalonde, for example, who had "more lovely, bubbling vitality and enjoyment of life than I had ever encountered," or his later refusal to be lured away from Macmillan by job offers elsewhere. Even so, as a young publisher he got into scrapes. After a liquid lunch in 1936 to celebrate the record-breaking Canadian sales of *Gone with the Wind*, he committed a minor hit-and-run on Spadina Road involving the company car and a brand new Cadillac, fortunately parked. The Cadillac's owner didn't press charges, however, since Gray "seemed to be a nice young man." The idea of John Gray as an amiably blundering buffoon and young rakehell belies the Ashley and Crippen portrait on the jacket of his memoirs: the very image of a judicious publisher of the old school, with all the English tics of the genre intact down to the thoughtfully flourished pipe and white handkerchief tucked up the grey gabardine sleeve.

Gray's patina of Britishness suited him well for rising through the ranks. Long a bastion of empire, the publisher of Kipling and Tennyson, Macmillan had opened a Canadian office in 1905. The branch's fortunes were entrusted to Frank Wise, an Englishman with ten years' experience in the New York office. Wise built up the Canadian market for Macmillan's

British and American books and published a few Canadian authors, as long as their views were consistent with his own imperial convictions.

Under Wise's direction, the Bond Street building was erected in 1910. Two years later, Wise made a valuable acquisition for the firm by taking over G.N. Morang, a leading Toronto textbook publisher. But as the historian A.B. McKillop entertainingly recounts in *The Spinster and the Prophet*, Wise also proceeded to enrich himself at his employer's expense, running various personal enterprises out of the Macmillan building and siphoning off company resources. When the previously sound Canadian branch began to falter, investigations revealed Wise's misdemeanours, and he resigned in disgrace in 1921.

His successor was Hugh Eayrs, another Englishman, only twenty-five on being elevated to president. Eayrs was also a budding author; he'd written a biography of General Isaac Brock for Macmillan's Canadian Men of Action series and collaborated on a novel with Thomas B. Costain, when the future bestselling author was still editor of *Maclean's*. Eayrs combined ability and energy with a skill for self-promotion. On a business trip to London, the "bumptious boy from Yorkshire," as Gray described him, disarmed the three elderly Macmillan brothers so completely with "his charm and wit, his cockiness and real capacity," that he overcame their doubts about his youth and limited experience.

One of the first books Eayrs published, an English translation of Louis Hémon's historical novel of Quebec, *Maria Chapdelaine*, became an overnight success in Britain and the United States. Subsequently London gave him a more or less free hand in running the Canadian show. During the 1920s and '30s, he drove a Stutz Bearcat touring car and entertained at the Toronto Club, black tie only. One of his guests was the rising young novelist Morley Callaghan, who fifty years later was still reminiscing about Eayrs's "magnificent champagne parties and dinners."

John Gray wrote this assessment of his first boss, whom he greatly liked and admired: "At the core of his confidence was a belief in his luck; a belief all gamblers – and publishers – must have, but none should have too much; at once a great and dangerous gift. I was to see it make him by turns unbeatable and intolerable, and to see it contribute to his destruction long before his time."

During the 1920s, Eayrs had been fortunate in hiring an ambitious young man, W.H. Clarke, who quickly learned the educational side of the business. Clarke took charge of all Macmillan's school publishing, plus its college and medical books, and was soon guiding projects to profitable conclusions. But he and Eayrs were temperamentally too alike, according to Gray, and at the same time too different in their natures to coexist comfortably. "Both were forceful, fiercely competitive, and stubborn," but whereas Eayrs played and drank hard, the teetotalling Clarke "seemed never to play." Clarke believed his successes entitled him to a greater share of authority and rewards within the firm, and when he didn't get them, he and his brother-in-law John C.W. Irwin left Macmillan "in great bitterness" to start Clarke, Irwin. In the wake of their departure, the untested Gray arrived.

Eayrs sent his recruit on the road as a sales rep to Ontario schools, and Gray took to the work immediately. When the firing of a colleague required him to travel to the Maritime provinces, Gray was exuberant. Although he'd make the trip many times in the future, "I was never to lose that sense of privilege and pleasure. It had been there all through the twenty-four-hour train trip aboard the Ocean Limited from Montreal, but it swept over me with a peculiar joy as I stepped off the train at last in Halifax, and walked along the still-panting train at the edge of the harbour, sniffing the sea and hearing a distant fog-horn. This was the life!"

Much of that life was spent on trains, accompanied by giant sample trunks full of books, and in hotel rooms, entertaining visiting educators and sharing a drink with rival travellers. Like any enterprising sales rep, Gray soon found himself metamorphosing into a field editor. His first big find came when a tip from an educator in Truro, Nova Scotia, led to a meeting with a superintendent of schools in Amherst, which provided an introduction to a professor of chemistry at Mount Allison University, who ultimately co-authored one of Macmillan's most successful textbooks, *Dominion High School Chemistry*. On another occasion, Gray and his colleague Frank Upjohn asked one of Macmillan's authors, the distinguished poet and professor E.J. Pratt, to co-edit an anthology of narrative poems for high schools. *A Pedlar's Pack* filled the niche so well that it remained in print for over forty years.

After only two years with the firm, Gray became manager of the educational department, with Upjohn, a year younger at twenty-four, as assistant manager. Their swift ascent was paved by the dismissal of two older colleagues, victims of what Gray acknowledged as publishing's "occupational disease," alcoholism. He soon learned to recognize the potential for corruption in educational publishing; subtler than money changing hands, it could be as simple as offering a textbook contract to an educator who had influence on the provincial selection committee. But as Gray worked more closely with Eayrs, he became implicated in some seriously compromised situations. Eayrs's health was deteriorating and his judgment dimming as he himself became alcoholic. Still only in his late thirties, he tended to make snap decisions, committing the company to costly projects without a business rationale.

The most ambitious publishing project Macmillan had yet attempted was a set of readers for all four western provinces, from elementary grades through high school. The investment necessary to compete for such a major contract was beyond Macmillan's means, so the company joined forces with Ryerson, while W.J. Gage collaborated on a competing bid with Thomas Nelson.

To win an advantage, Eayrs resorted to the high-handed tactic of denying competitors the right to use any selections to which Macmillan or its agencies held copyright, including works by Kipling, Hardy, Yeats, and many other authors. When the competitors objected that this would deprive the authors or their estates of permission fees, Gray had to agree. He took up the issue with Eayrs, but the boss stuck to his legalistic justification. The Macmillan-Ryerson volumes for grades seven, eight, and nine were edited by Lorne Pierce of Ryerson and Dora Whitefield (in private life Mrs. Hugh Eayrs, who had little experience to qualify her for the task).

The comeuppance came after the Macmillan-Ryerson reader for grade seven won the contract for Alberta and seemed likely to sweep the other provinces. Ten thousand copies had already been printed and shipped when Gage and Nelson alleged that the winning book contained teachers' notes plagiarized word for word from American readers. If their complaints weren't satisfied, the two companies would seek a court injunction.

With Eayrs and Pierce away on holiday, the young manager of Macmillan's school department had to face the flak alone. During a three-day train journey to Edmonton, Gray racked his brains for a solution to salvage Macmillan's investment, coming up with a compromise at the eleventh hour: if Alberta used Macmillan's grade seven book without changes for a year, he proposed, the company would cede the grade eight contract to Gage and Nelson, clearing all copyrights for their book, and eliminating all plagiarism in its own future editions. Gray was gambling that the fall term was about to begin and Alberta needed its books quickly. His calculations proved correct: the province's deputy minister of education told the rival publishers to accept Gray's proposal. The offending book went on to be revised and live a happy and profitable life for another twenty-five years.

The young publisher's life wasn't all schoolbooks. Rubbing shoulders with prominent Macmillan authors at the Eayrses' parties, Gray chauffeured Grey Owl, before the English imposter's unmasking, to sign books at Eaton's and lecture at the King Edward Hotel; he squired stately Mazo de la Roche, winner of the Atlantic Monthly prize for *Jalna*, to lunch at the York Club. Mixing with celebrity writers inspired Gray to continue his own writing in his off-hours. His most substantial accomplishment of the period was a boys' thriller modelled on his experiences at Lakefield; after many rejections by publishers, it appeared as *The One-Eyed Trapper* from the British firm Blackie, which offered him "an iniquitous type of old-fashioned contract" and a flat royalty of £40 in return for world rights. That experience gave Gray a lifelong empathy with the precariousness of the writing life. "Every publisher should write at least one book and try to find a publisher for it," he wrote.

John Gray was thirty-two when the Second World War began. He and his new recruit in the educational department, Barney Sandwell, were in the elevator of a Belleville, Ontario, hotel when the operator told them the Germans had marched into Poland. Several months later, Gray received an equally profound shock in another hotel, the Palliser in Calgary: he opened a telegram to read that Hugh Eayrs had dropped dead at forty-six. For all his bluster and self-importance, Eayrs had been Gray's mentor, initiating him into the world of books and authors, and his death was a desolating blow.

The firm too had been unprepared for losing Eayrs. Distracted by the war, London simply promoted the financial officer, Robert Huckvale, to assume command. In his memoir, Gray portrayed "Bob Harvey," Huckvale thinly disguised, as devoid of publishing instincts.

Called up for active service, Gray took a military intelligence course at Royal Military College, Kingston, and made captain. With his five-year-old son, John, riding on his shoulders on the way to the railway station, Gray left for Halifax and shipped out for England; he wouldn't see his family again for three and a half years. He was posted to the newly formed II Canadian Corps as the officer responsible for counter-intelligence. In Normandy, he survived an errant bullet fired by a Canadian soldier, which singed the skin above his left ear. In Antwerp, he had his portrait taken; the surviving photograph reveals a tanned, lean, unsmiling face with pene-tratingly wary eyes, thoroughly stripped of boyish innocence.

The route back to the post-war world seemed to fork in two directions, writing and publishing. Gray wasn't sure which to follow; he entertained the idea of working part-time for Macmillan and writing the rest of the time. Passing through London on his way home, he dropped in at company headquarters and broached that possibility with Rache Lovat Dickson, a Canadian who had run his own publishing house in London and was now responsible for liaison with Macmillan's Toronto branch. Dickson dis-couraged the notion. He cautioned that the firm, then headed by Harold Macmillan (the future prime minister) and his brother Daniel, would think Gray wasn't serious about the business.

Gray's wartime experience had bred in him a skeptical mind, "an ability to check my normally intuitive or emotional response to problems." He followed Dickson's advice and, back home at the beginning of 1946, did indeed become serious about the business. When Huckvale offered him his old position at exactly the salary he'd been earning five years earlier, Gray objected vigorously. Huckvale reluctantly upped the offer from $4,000 a year to $4,800. Frank Upjohn, back for two months since leaving the air force, was finding the company's lack of direction intolerable and thinking of moving on, but he and Gray pledged to stay together and work for change from within.

The firm's lack of publishing vision was typified by its treatment of Robertson Davies. For several years, Davies had been entertaining readers of the *Peterborough Examiner* and the *Kingston Whig-Standard* with extravagantly satirical columns written under the pen name Samuel Marchbanks. Davies offered Macmillan a book-length collection of his columns, but the trade editor, Ellen Elliott, declined. Davies took the proposal to Clarke, Irwin, which agreed to publish it as *The Diary of Samuel Marchbanks*. Macmillan wouldn't get another chance to publish Davies until twelve years and many successful books later.

Gray's resolve to stay was tested on his next train journey west. Macmillan and Ryerson were revising their pre-war reading series, and Gray was travelling with Lorne Pierce to visit provincial education officials when Pierce asked, "How would you like my job?" Shouting his regrets above the rattling of the train, and flourishing a Scotch in one hand and a cigarette in the other, Gray pointed out that smoking and drinking were discouraged by Ryerson's owner, the United Church. Privately Gray also harboured doubts about the quality of the Ryerson list.

Before 1946 was out, Rache Lovat Dickson arrived from London on a tour of inspection. Over after-dinner drinks at the King Edward, Gray and Upjohn spilled out their grievances about Huckvale, insisting they just wanted a genuine publisher to work with, someone who understood the profession of books. They waited weeks while their fate was decided across the Atlantic, but the decision went in their favour: Huckvale, the Macmillans decreed, was to retire on pension, and John Gray was to replace him. With one stroke of a British pen, the modern era in Canadian publishing could begin.

It was an ideal time to take command of a publishing house in Canada. The economy, kick-started by the war, would expand in a few years in a full-scale boom. A steady rise in school enrolments would lift the educational publishing business for years to come, and the 1960s would bring expansion in both college and trade publishing.

Gray's first concern was building up the two most profitable areas, the agency list and educational publishing. His management team was the envy of his competitors: Frank Upjohn ran the trade department, and Barney Sandwell would take over the college and medical departments. One of Upjohn's key salespeople was another returned serviceman and future publisher, Jack Stoddart Sr., who would later move up to become trade sales manager. As for the schoolbook department, Gray had to decide who should succeed him.

Shortly before the war, he'd plucked a young woman from the clerical ranks and added her to his department. Gladys Neale had trained to be a teacher at what was then called normal school, but she accepted a pay cut to work at Macmillan for $12.50 a week – the minimum wage for women – simply because, like so many before and since, she wanted to work with books. During the war years, Huckvale had appointed Miss Neale acting manager of the schoolbook department. Without the benefit of a mentor on staff, she wrote Huckvale a memo explaining that she needed to travel across the country to learn about curriculum in the various provinces. To her astonishment, he agreed.

Respectable women didn't travel alone in the early 1940s, and on her first trip, Neale was accompanied by Ellen Elliott. Ever after, Neale went by herself, the lone woman among the publishers' travellers criss-crossing the country. Although the provinces were making few curriculum changes during the war, she managed to persuade Huckvale to publish several new textbooks.

Gray's return bumped Neale back down the ladder, the usual fate of women who had done men's jobs in wartime. When he moved upstairs, Gray again appointed her acting manager of the schoolbook department and hired a new traveller, with the intention of promoting him over Neale's head once he'd learned the ropes. It turned out, however, that the man was more inclined to academic life than to publishing, and he left the firm. When Neale later asked Gray if he thought she'd have put up with being demoted again, he replied, "Well, why not, if you respected him and admired his work?"

The reply left her speechless. "I'm quite sure, looking back," she said years later in an interview, "that I would not have stayed."

But by 1950, Gray had confirmed Gladys Neale as manager on a permanent basis: the first woman, after Ellen Elliott, to hold such a senior position in Canadian publishing without owing it to a husband's influence. Neale would become one of the most successful and respected educational publishers of her generation. "I always said," she recalled nine months before her death in 1999, "that I made my contribution to Canadian culture, because it was the revenues of the schoolbook department which enabled John Gray to do his trade publishing. So I took a little credit."

Gray once confessed he'd thought Neale wouldn't be up to the job because of the impropriety of her sitting up late, drinking and talking shop with male educators. She told him tartly, "That's not the way we do business these days. I accomplish just as much talking to people in their offices." But drinking was considered such an integral part of the profession that, after her promotion, Neale adopted the rule that, at a business lunch or dinner, she'd never take more than one drink: "I felt I had a reputation to uphold." Colleagues and competitors alike knew her as a formidable woman who grew more so with age. Within the company, male employees learned to keep their distance. Jim Douglas, who sold Macmillan books across the west from 1958 to 1971 before founding his own publishing house, described her as "a powerful lady in every way."

Gray's long-term support was vital to Gladys Neale's success, but if he counted on her to operate the schoolbook department, he also exacted a personal price. One of Neale's most profitable projects was a series of Canadian spelling books, developed to replace a series from Macmillan in New York, which had become a separate company in 1950. Her series sold so well that its authors earned a lot of money; one bought a new car and a mink coat with her share of the royalties. Neale had contributed materially to the books' contents, and the educator who served as the general editor of the series recommended that she too receive a royalty. But John Gray forbade it. If Neale had a personal stake in these books' success, he declared, it might lead her to neglect the rest of her list. She conceded in an interview that his point may have been valid in principle, yet he'd allowed a male staff member to accept royalties on a Macmillan book.

Gray practised a similar double standard in the matter of employees furthering their education. After putting in two summers at Columbia Teachers' College in New York, Neale requested a year's sabbatical to complete her degree in education. Gray raised objections: she'd be seduced by life in New York, she'd be hired by an American publisher, a year was too long to leave her position unfilled. Although the company had assisted men in her own department to improve their education, she stayed home.

Gladys Neale was a pioneer at a time when women customarily remained in the lower echelons of the industry. By promoting her to head a division, and later appointing her to sit on the Macmillan board, John Gray joined, however reluctantly, the vanguard of social change. "It took him some time and hard thinking," Neale recalled, "but he finally did right as far as I was concerned."

With Macmillan's various departments in capable hands, Gray could turn to rebuilding the trade list. Two world wars and the Depression had involved him in great events and reinforced his love of reading history. Seeking historians who could write for a general audience, he found a source close by in the University of Toronto, whose history department had been supplying Macmillan with authors since the 1920s.

Gray set the bar high by contracting with Donald Creighton – already the author of a work of mythic scope, *Dominion of the North* – to publish his magisterial, two-volume biography of Sir John A. Macdonald. In 1952 Creighton's *John A. Macdonald: The Young Politician* outsold all other Macmillan trade titles and received the Governor General's Award for non-fiction; Frank Upjohn told *Quill & Quire* the book had even outsold John Steinbeck's *East of Eden* "by a nose." The sequel, *John A. Macdonald: The Old Chieftain*, won the award for 1955. Creighton, Carl Berger has stated in *The Writing of Canadian History*, inspired his fellow scholars to make political biography the dominant form in Canadian historical studies, and a spate of biographies soon followed: J.M.S. Careless on George Brown (Macmillan), William Kilbourn on William Lyon Mackenzie (Clarke, Irwin), Kenneth McNaught on J.S. Woodsworth (University of Toronto Press), George Stanley on Louis Riel (Ryerson).

Gray's love affair with Canadian history and politics continued to enrich the Macmillan trade list right through to the 1980s: from Frank Underhill's *In Search of Canadian Liberalism* and Pierre Elliott Trudeau's *Federalism and the French Canadians* to Ramsay Cook's studies of Canadian and Quebec nationalism, former prime minister John Diefenbaker's memoirs, and Christina McCall's *Grits*. By chronicling the national drama in an authoritative yet accessible manner, these and other Macmillan titles made a major impact on Canadians' knowledge of their country. Macmillan published Gray's own historical work, *Lord Selkirk of Red River*, in 1963; meticulously researched and elegantly written, the book earned Gray the University of British Columbia Medal for best Canadian biography of the year.

And yet John Gray's best-known authors were neither historians nor politicians but novelists. Some he inherited from his predecessors, others he pursued and won, so that most of Canada's leading fiction writers of the 1950s published with Macmillan. A few were already known internationally: Mazo de la Roche, Morley Callaghan, Hugh MacLennan, Ethel Wilson, Robertson Davies. Working with novelists let Gray live closer to his feelings and produced some of his warmest friendships.

In 1951 Callaghan completed *The Loved and the Lost* after the long hiatus since *More Joy in Heaven* in 1937. The new novel was set in the Montreal underworld, which Callaghan had come to know by mixing with boxers and gangsters in a bar and grill on Dorchester Street. Gray and Upjohn decided to launch *The Loved and the Lost* at Montreal's tony Ritz-Carlton Hotel, inviting guests such as Frank Scott from McGill and the city's mayor, Camillien Houde. At Callaghan's request, they also invited the proprietors of his Dorchester Street hangout, who had everyone back to their establishment afterwards for dinner and more drinks. As Callaghan's son Barry told it in *Barrelhouse Kings*, everyone had such a wonderful time that the jovial mayor, famed for his underworld contacts, insisted the great writer sign his "golden book" of distinguished visitors at city hall. Gray and Upjohn piled into Houde's limousine with Callaghan and his wife, Loretto, some newspaper cronies, and the oversized mayor, and were chauffeured to City Hall at 2 in the morning. Having forgotten his keys, Houde ordered his driver to break in through a window, and the signing was enacted in the mayor's chambers, sanctified by the ceremonial passing of a silver flask.

Gray and Callaghan lunched regularly in Toronto for years afterwards, and in 1959 Macmillan published a handsome hardcover edition of Callaghan's masterly short fiction. *Morley Callaghan's Stories* contained the author's own selection of work previously published in *The New Yorker* and in two earlier collections. It was the most important book of short stories published in Canada to that point and for years afterwards. But Gray sometimes confided to colleagues that, as much as he admired Callaghan, he felt more comfortable with other Macmillan authors who were less prickly and combative and, frankly, more British: Ethel Wilson, the Vancouver-based novelist who had grown up in England, or Robertson Davies.

Gray had long coveted the prolific Davies as an author, but he was reluctant to poach him from Clarke, Irwin, which had published all of Davies's fiction, non-fiction, and drama. In 1958, however, Davies and Clarke, Irwin had a falling-out over the rights to his next novel, *A Mixture of Frailties*, the third in what is now known as the Salterton Trilogy. Davies had acquired a New York agent, Willis Kingsley Wing, who proceeded to sell Canadian, American, and British rights separately, to maximize the return to Davies and to himself. Previously Clarke, Irwin had held world rights to Davies's books, controlling sales of foreign editions; now the company insisted that the option clause in Davies's contract for his previous novel gave it the right to do so again. Legally it was a groundless position, but rather than sensibly cut a deal with Wing for Canada only, Clarke, Irwin declined the manuscript.

When Gray caught wind of the dispute, he promptly negotiated Canadian rights to *A Mixture of Frailties* for publication later in 1958. It also appeared from Scribner's in New York and Weidenfeld and Nicholson in London. Davies wouldn't produce another novel until *Fifth Business* twelve years later, when the great outpouring of his later period began, but Macmillan would continue publishing him until Gray's retirement and beyond. Meanwhile Gray and Davies enjoyed a friendship based on their shared anglophilia and a common taste for history and literary gossip.

Becoming Hugh MacLennan's publisher involved Gray in a more complex relationship, professionally and personally. Gray sought out MacLennan in 1946 at a Canadian Authors Association meeting, where they agreed on the iniquity of publishing contracts from the author's point of view: a rare stance for a publisher. Their formal association began after MacLennan, disappointed by sales of his third novel, *The Precipice*, sought publishers for his next book. In the United States, he left Duell, Sloan and Pearce and found Little, Brown. In Canada, he left William Collins Sons and found John Gray.

Along with Callaghan, MacLennan was the most admired Canadian novelist of the day, yet he was barely scraping by financially. Facing mounting debts from his wife's illness, he was desperate to make *Each Man's Son* both a critical success and a bestseller. MacLennan's American editor, Angus Cameron of Little, Brown, conferred with Gray on reshaping the manuscript, and MacLennan relied heavily on their responses as he revised. During the editing, MacLennan became close to Gray, sharing his ambitions for his work and his ideas about literature, history, and society. In fact, MacLennan depended on his publisher's judgment so much that Gray urged him not to lose touch with his own instincts: "I think a publisher's vantage point should permit him, and his job occasionally require him, to tell an author what course the publisher thinks he is making in relation to his public – never (or almost never) in relation to his art."

Gray functioned as both MacLennan's publisher and his editor, also working with Frank Upjohn on the marketing of *Each Man's Son*, released in 1951. In addition to print ads, the campaign featured an excerpt in *Saturday Night*, a profile in *Liberty*, radio ads, an appearance as Morley Callaghan's guest on the CBC Radio quiz show *Now I Ask You*, point-of-sale posters and postcards, specially bound reviewer's copies, and launch parties in Toronto and Montreal.

MacLennan received $1,500 as an advance against Canadian royalties, a respectable sum at the time; the American advance was $3,000. Gray was unsuccessful in interesting his parent company in taking British rights, but he placed the novel with Heinemann. In its first year, *Each Man's Son* had Canadian hardcover sales of 10,000 copies: a major success, but not as big as MacLennan had hoped. Despite favourable American reviews and a Literary Guild selection, American sales also disappointed him. Gray explained to his author that the advent of television was combining with movies and paperbacks to erode the market for serious fiction. To his friend William Arthur Deacon, MacLennan wrote: "At least *Each Man's Son* settled one question – nobody can live by writing novels in Canada at the present time." He requested early payment of his royalties in order to pay for his wife's recent hospitalization, and Gray responded immediately with a cheque. MacLennan, who had produced six highly praised books including *Barometer Rising* and *Two Solitudes*, still had to resort to teaching at McGill and writing for magazines and the National Film Board.

Gray provided practical, moral, and editorial support when MacLennan threw himself into perhaps his finest novel, *The Watch That Ends the Night*, amid the emotional turmoil before and after his wife's death. Published in 1959, *The Watch That Ends the Night* sold resoundingly well: 18,000 copies in Canada by the end of the first year. In the United States, it was published by Scribner's, stayed on the *New York Times* bestseller list for several months (where it kept company with *Doctor Zhivago*, *Lolita*, *From the Terrace*, and *Mountolive*), and was bought by the Doubleday Book Club and Hollywood. In the United Kingdom, it was issued by Heinemann. The overall response to the novel was, in fact, far better than Gray's own cautious predictions: anxious to cushion MacLennan from further blows, he'd warned him not to set his hopes too high.

Gray had similarly warned the assembled writers at the 1955 Canadian Writers' Conference in Kingston not to expect too much of domestic publishers: "I doubt that any Canadian publisher is strong enough for any great adventures in original publishing even if the market conditions held the possibility of reward for such adventures, which they don't. The picture is much less feverish, much less dangerous, much less promising than elsewhere." Even in the United States, Gray pointed out, trade publishers did little better than break even on book sales and relied on selling subsidiary rights to push their companies into the black. In Canada, lacking paperback and feature-film industries as well as large magazines or book clubs, subsidiary rights income was negligible. Canadian trade publishers and authors hadn't developed strong relationships, Gray conceded frankly, because they didn't need each other financially: "I doubt that any Canadian publisher derives any important part of his revenue (or *any* net profit) from Canadian general publishing; his commercial welfare is therefore not identified with that of Canadian writers." And if trade authors earned any decent money, it was usually from sales abroad. Trade publishing in Canada was, therefore, "an act of faith," since it lacked a rational commercial basis "and must for years to come."

Under those conditions, it was no surprise that most writers were discouraged from producing more than a book or two. "But," Gray asked, "will a national literature achieve solidity or stature when built out of a succession of first and second books?" His proposed solution: grants for professional authors. Buying writers time to write, he argued propheti-cally, would help them produce their best work.

Despite those constraints, Gray continued to pursue authors he admired, such as W.O. Mitchell, who hadn't yet followed up on his 1947 debut novel, *Who Has Seen the Wind*. At the Kingston conference, one of Gray's editors, Kildare Dobbs, met a young woman from Winnipeg named Adele Wiseman, who gave him the manuscript of her novel about Jewish immigrants on the Prairies. Gray agreed with Dobbs's enthusiastic assess-ment of the book, and Macmillan published Wiseman's *The Sacrifice* the following year, with an American edition appearing from Viking. It won the twenty-eight-year-old author a Governor General's Award.

Gray wasn't always so prescient. Fatefully, he turned down a proposal from Malcolm Ross, the distinguished critic and head of the Queen's University English department. Publishers were partly responsible for the absence of Canadian literature in schools and universities, Ross told Gray, because they put Canadian fiction beyond students' reach, issuing it only in hardcover editions, then letting it go out of print. The solution was both simple and daringly ambitious: an inexpensive paperback reprint series that would include all the Canadian fiction worth preserving.

Ross's proposal was visionary in a way scarcely comprehensible today. The paperback revolution still hadn't arrived in Canada. Even in the United States, quality paperbacks, led by Doubleday's Anchor Books, had only recently begun to emulate the success of Penguin Books by making serious literature available at affordable prices.

Gray's answer to Ross was sympathetic but hard-headed. He approved the motive, but he was adamant about declining the risk. "We'd lose our shirt!" Ross remembered him saying. Gray couldn't see paperbacks, with their narrow profit margins depending on long print runs and high sales, ever succeeding in Canada, especially when the target market of Canadian literature courses didn't even exist. But in Ross's view, it was a chicken-and-egg situation. He took his proposal to Jack McClelland, who possessed the riverboat gambler's instinct that Gray had admired yet feared in Hugh Eayrs. In 1958 McClelland & Stewart launched the New Canadian Library, the heart of the CanLit courses that burgeoned in the decades to come.

According to Kildare Dobbs, John Gray was uncertain of his own literary judgment and sought a favourable consensus among his editors before committing to a book. When Sheila Watson submitted *The Double Hook*, Dobbs admired it, but other in-house readers found the novel too difficult or obscure. After Macmillan declined, M&S published it in 1959, and today it is considered a classic. Other novels that slipped from Macmillan's grasp included Jack Ludwig's *Confusions* and Jock Carroll's *The Shy Photographer*, which offended house sensibilities. Carroll, like another Canadian, John Glassco, wrote fiction too steamy for Canada *circa* 1960; both writers published in Paris with censorship-defying Olympia Press, publisher of Beckett, Genet, Henry Miller, and *The Story of O*.

Dobbs was an accomplished writer himself, one of several who worked under Gray. Educated in Ireland and England, he began trade editing and production under Frank Upjohn in 1953. Gray wanted him to work on schoolbooks, but Dobbs with his Cambridge degree and Gladys Neale with her normal school training didn't hit it off, and Dobbs remained in trade. After several years, Gray applied to Dobbs the dictum from which there was no appeal: all Macmillan editors must have some commercial savvy instilled in them by hitting the road to sell books.

Dobbs considered Gray's maxim "nonsense, a salesman's idea of publishing": salespeople always want a book to repeat last year's success, whereas an editor looks for the next big thing. Following several disastrous weeks of slogging across the west with the Macmillan trade list, Dobbs returned gratefully to editing. He was ably assisted by Richard B. Wright, a refugee from the advertising world and a would-be novelist, whose sub-stantial body of fiction would begin with *The Weekend Man* in 1970 and continue through *Clara Callan*, winner of multiple awards thirty-one years later. The two were joined by Leo Simpson, an Irish-born literary satirist who worked variously in sales, publicity, and editorial at Macmillan before publishing five works of fiction between 1971 and 1996. When Dobbs moved on to journalism in the early 1960s, he was succeeded by another novelist, James Bacque.

Even while employing young writers, Gray preserved customs from Macmillan's imperial past. Tea time was observed in the office every afternoon. "We drank thin tea from thick cups," Bacque remembered. For many years, an aging telephone receptionist sat in her cubicle responding to each caller in an English accent; promptly at the close of each business day, she'd yank the connections out of the old-fashioned switchboard, heedless of cutting off conversations in progress. There was a proofreading unit headed by Hugh Eayrs's sister, a small Englishwoman with a fondness for gin, who occasionally consulted Dobbs on fine points of editorial usage. He recalled a conversation that began, "Can this author be allowed to have an unfinished sentence, Mr. Dobbs?"

"Oh yes, Miss Eayrs, it's okay."

"Do you know, Mr. Dobbs, since my brother died, you're the only man in this building with any brains."

"Thank you, Miss Eayrs."

"And you can call me Winifred."

"Oh, Miss Eayrs, I wouldn't dare!"

One of Dobbs's duties was to attend Mazo de la Roche's Christmas Eve soiree at the Forest Hill home she shared with her companion, Caroline Clement. "Mazo would say things like, 'A writer needs a public, Mr. Dobbs,' very stiffly. I could see her wondering, 'How can I entertain this young man?' And she'd get out her photo album and say, 'Now that's Harold and that's Lady Dorothy and this is Mr. Daniel' – the Macmillans, you know. They were all great pets of hers."

Macmillan's trade sales manager, Donald Sutherland, had arrived from Oxford University Press in 1957 to replace Jack Stoddart Sr. when Stoddart left to run General Publishing. A fervent believer in American-style marketing, Stoddart had tried to modernize what he considered Macmillan's prissy, old-fashioned approach to selling books. Sutherland was a more traditional sort, an anglophile not enamoured of sharp sales techniques. He was also a bona fide scholar, having worked as a curator of Chinese art and archaeology at the Royal Ontario Museum. Beneath his urbane, courteous demeanour, Sutherland could be eccentric; while presiding over a sales conference, he'd take notes in Mandarin so that others couldn't read them.

Both Dobbs and Sutherland felt affection and respect for John Gray, but they were well aware that he could be paternalistic, testy, unjust at times. As the years passed, Gray showed an increasing distaste for any sort of conflict; he was reluctant to dismiss staff, and even when reconciled to the necessity of firing someone, he often delegated the odious task to others. Dobbs remembered offering to do the deed on one occasion, but Gray insisted on doing it himself, then procrastinated so long that the unfortunate employee wasn't informed until Christmas Eve. Gray also began avoiding the company of authors he found difficult. Sutherland assumed responsibility for the care and feeding of high-strung thoroughbreds in the Macmillan stable such as Creighton, Callaghan, and even MacLennan. Gray's employees observed wryly that the undercover work he'd done during the war was the opposite of publishing.

The most enduring John Gray story is of an incident towards the end of his career, on one of the rare visits to Canada by Sir Harold Macmillan. Gray organized a dinner in Macmillan's honour at the King Edward Hotel and invited the media to cover the former prime minister's speech. Still the colonial boy, Gray introduced Macmillan at such interminable, fawning length that a reporter, frantic to make his deadline, bawled out, "Oh, for Christ's sake, man, *get on with it!*" Eyewitnesses remember Gray being so flustered that it was several minutes before he could compose himself and finish the introduction.

And yet Gray relished his post at Macmillan, with all its perks and prestige. Occasionally he'd invite a junior colleague to play hooky with him, taking an afternoon off to attend an antiquarian book auction; at lunches he favoured the midday whiskies and Martinis then in vogue. It was thought that Rache Lovat Dickson coveted his job, but Gray wasn't about to oblige him by moving aside, and when Dickson finally returned to Canada, it was to retire and write his memoirs of the London publishing world. Both Dickson and Gray were involved in setting up St. Martin's Press, which became a well-known New York publisher. After the American branch of Macmillan broke away in 1950, the parent firm created St. Martin's to be its American subsidiary, and Dickson appointed a man to run it. When his appointee faltered, Dickson asked Gray to find a replacement; Gray chose his long-time right hand, Frank Upjohn.

Gray didn't like "big timber" standing too close, in Kildare Dobbs's phrase. He always seemed to be grooming some young up-and-comer to be his successor, only to dash the expectations he'd created. Dobbs remembered a line of Gray's: "We're standing in your light." It might have meant "The company is holding you back," but to Dobbs it signified "I wish you'd leave." Dobbs did leave, to serve as managing editor of *Saturday Night* and later books editor of the *Toronto Star*, but he didn't hold a grudge: "I loved the man. I thought he was wonderful company."

After Dobbs, Jim Bacque was pegged as a potential successor. Bacque appreciated Gray's mentoring, but over time he began to feel like "the parakeet on the admiral's shoulder." Towards the end of his seven years at Macmillan, Bacque concluded that the firm was too rigid in its ways to risk the creative publishing he was itching to try, and he began talking up ideas for a fresh new publishing venture, which would eventually take the form of New Press. When Gray caught wind of this, he sniffed treason and called Bacque on the carpet. The result was Bacque's departure in 1968, a bruising experience mitigated only years later when the men met by chance and Gray praised the New Press publishing program.

Jim Douglas was also shaped by his years with Gray. After creating a Vancouver-based sales agency in 1957, Douglas handled trade sales for Macmillan and McClelland & Stewart, working closely with both Gray and Jack McClelland, but it was Gray he regarded as his mentor. "At M&S," Douglas recalled, "it was jackets off, very informal. And it was 'Jack' and 'Hugh' [Kane, M&S vice-president] to the whole staff. At Macmillan, almost no one called John Gray 'John.' He and Frank Upjohn both kept their handkerchiefs up their sleeves." On the editorial and production side, Macmillan had its controls firmly in place, ensuring that its books were thoroughly copy-edited and proofread. M&S titles, on the other hand, were notorious for sloppy editing and proofing, having been rushed through the system by a harassed and overworked staff. By the early 1970s,

M&S was churning out a hundred new titles a year, some of which Douglas found "embarrassing," while Macmillan was producing half as many, twice as carefully.

In 1967 John Gray distilled nearly forty years' experience in an essay for a special "Publishing in Canada" issue of George Woodcock's quarterly, *Canadian Literature*. The essay was marked by a concern for the writer as much as the publisher; Gray understood in his bones how thoroughly their difficulties intersected. With qualified optimism, he revised his statement of twelve years earlier, when he'd detected no mutual economic benefit in the relationship: "The publisher's 'no net profit' has at least become 'a possible profit'." And he pointedly distinguished between companies that were merely jobbers of foreign-authored books and those that published original work. Developing Canadian literature, he wrote, "could not have been done quickly or well by those interested only or chiefly in the selling of other publishers' books."

Arguably the most important title Gray published towards the end of his career was *Fifth Business*, first in the succession of brilliant late novels that secured Robertson Davies's international reputation. (Millions of copies of his works are now in print.) And yet, surprisingly, although Gray had been Davies's publisher for over a decade, he waffled before committing to the book. When Davies delivered the manuscript at the end of 1969, Ken McVey, one of the editors, was not impressed. McVey wrote in his report that only Davies's name on the manuscript might save it from rejection. Another editor, Ramsay Derry, had exactly the opposite response: he "just knew this was a wonderful book." When Gray himself read the manuscript, he was satisfied Macmillan should indeed publish it, with some changes, but he remained strangely unmoved by the novel's power. He was not alone. Scribner's, which had published Davies previously in the United States, had rejected the novel, and both Viking in New York and Macmillan in London were dragging their feet.

Over drinks at the York Club, Gray and Alan Maclean, managing director of Macmillan in London, met with Davies to explain their hesitation. "What are all these changes you want me to make?" Davies asked them in exasperation. "Should I change my men to women? Do you want me to put the beginning at the end?" But at bottom, the publishers' concerns were nothing he couldn't manage, and the meeting ended with an agreement to publish in fall 1970. *Fifth Business* appeared to enormous critical acclaim and commercial success, particularly in the United States, where early reviews in the *New York Times*, the *Washington Post*, and the *Chicago Tribune* were ecstatic. The book made bestseller status in both the *Times* (briefly) and the *Toronto Star*, the country's only bestseller list at the time, where it remained for forty-two weeks. Davies's writing career was resoundingly relaunched.

Men of letters such as Davies – like branches of British publishers such as Macmillan – were out of style in the cultural politics of 1970; *Fifth Business* didn't win the Governor General's Award, which went to a more experimental work, Dave Godfrey's *The New Ancestors*. The *Zeitgeist* celebrated the new and the radical, and nothing was newer at that point than Godfrey's edgy, iconoclastic style. But Davies's sequel to *Fifth Business*, *The Manticore*, won the award for 1972 over Margaret Atwood's *Surfacing*. The honour came just in time to be a fitting conclusion to Gray's career.

During Gray's final year at Macmillan, the company changed into something very different from the firm he'd known. Having failed to identify a younger successor in whom he felt confidence, Gray had chosen in 1969 a veteran publisher of his own generation as second-in-command, Hugh Kane. For the better part of two decades, Kane had occupied a similar position under Jack McClelland, but moving from M&S to Macmillan was like sailing out of constant, life-threatening storms into calm seas. Seasoned, respected in the trade, Kane must have seemed to Gray an obvious choice to succeed him.

Kane was a trade publisher and hard-driving marketer in the M&S tradition, and his natural inclination was to reinforce the Macmillan trade program, injecting greater panache into the company's promotional efforts. Shortly after his arrival, *Fifth Business* was launched at a party aboard a floating restaurant at the foot of Yonge Street, the spot where Boy Staunton, one of the novel's characters, had driven off the pier and drowned. Some of Kane's new colleagues, however, were less than thrilled by his arrival. Donald Sutherland's life was made difficult by Kane's usurping his authority as head of the trade department. Gladys Neale found Kane dismissive of her schoolbook program, with, she felt, insufficient appreciation of educational publishing and its importance to the bottom line. But those internal stresses were supplanted in 1972 by a common enemy.

In London, the knowledge that Gray would soon be retiring set the Macmillan directors to wondering if they wanted a Canadian branch at all. It was a question they'd sometimes put to Gray personally, and for twenty-six years he'd been answering them in the affirmative, shoring up their confidence in their distant outpost. Gray's son, John, by then a journalist, later recalled that visiting head office was a mixed blessing for his father: "He loved being there, and was probably more respectful than he should have been. But he was constantly having to prove it was worthwhile having a Canadian operation. In the end they left him alone to run his own show, but he always had to check in." With their trusted lieutenant leaving, the owners finally decided it was time to cut Canada loose. In Neale's understanding, they needed the cash.

There were two leading suitors: McClelland & Stewart and the Toronto communications conglomerate Maclean-Hunter. Jack McClelland saw in Macmillan a desperately needed source of profit from educational publishing, where he was weak, in addition to a wonderful trade backlist. But it was only a year since an emergency loan from the Ontario government had saved McClelland from having to sell M&S, and it was difficult for him to arrange the necessary financing. In his formal offer to purchase Macmillan, he proposed to finance the deal by making a public offering of shares in the merged company – a prospect that paled, for the Macmillans in London, alongside Maclean-Hunter's solid cash offer.

One can only speculate how different the future of Canadian publishing would have been if McClelland's bid had trumped Maclean-Hunter's. The merged company might have become the well-capitalized, diversified Canadian-owned publisher that the country had always lacked. Hugh Kane had tried his damnedest behind the scenes to deliver Macmillan into McClelland's hands, and the two old cronies would have had a shot at running a publishing house with sufficient economies of scale, for once, to succeed. Instead, as John Gray prepared to step out, Kane had to reconcile himself to working for Macmillan's new masters.

It has never been entirely clear why Maclean-Hunter wanted to own Macmillan. The corporation published magazines, which might have been a source of book content; it also operated an illustrated book division and a very small schoolbook division, and since 1970 it had held a minority interest in New Press. But aside from folding its schoolbook division into Macmillan, Maclean-Hunter didn't take advantage of potential synergies. On the one occasion it attempted rationalization between Macmillan and New Press, imposing a computerized order fulfillment system, the result was a fiasco for both houses. According to Neale and Sutherland, Macmillan was virtually shut down, unable to ship orders for four to five months, and lost not only a disastrous quantity of business but a previously sterling reputation for service. "And then, of course," observed Neale, "Maclean-Hunter blamed us because we didn't make a profit."

Maclean-Hunter could never reconcile its expectations of profit with the realities of book publishing. Even in the States, book publishing profits are chronically below corporate targets, as conglomerates from RCA Victor to Viacom to Time Warner have discovered. And it was inevitable that Hugh Kane wouldn't last under the new regime; he was an old-fashioned "bookman," not up to Maclean-Hunter's notion of an efficient modern executive, and he had actively campaigned against its takeover offer. Before Kane returned to M&S in 1976, Maclean-Hunter installed a succession of younger CEOs above him to turn the company around. None could perform the trick as quickly as the corporation demanded.

At Maclean-Hunter's request, John Gray remained on the Macmillan board after his retirement in 1973, and the firm continued to publish many of his authors. Gladys Neale continued to preside over the schoolbook department, with Douglas Gibson, recruited from Doubleday Canada, installed as editorial director of the trade division. Fine new fiction writers such as Alice Munro and Jack Hodgins were coming on board; the former publisher at House of Anansi Press, Dennis Lee, who had acted as an editorial adviser to Hugh Kane, emerged in 1974 in a new incarnation as a wildly inventive and popular poet for children with *Alligator Pie*. But Gray was uncomfortable watching his old firm struggle under Maclean-Hunter's stewardship. The media empire was too philistine to care deeply about books, too beholden to the profit motive to conceive of publishing as he saw it: a lifelong commitment to investing in books of quality.

Fortunately Gray had set to work on his autobiography. *Fun Tomorrow* is a high-spirited portrayal of publishing in a vanished era, with a small gem of a war memoir embedded at its core; it remains out of print at the time of writing, waiting to be reissued in paperback by some enterprising publisher. Unfortunately *Fun Tomorrow* stopped at the point when Gray took up the reins at Macmillan after the war; although he intended a sequel, he never seriously began it. He had contracted cancer, and his oncologist told him in late 1977 (accurately, as it turned out) that he had just eight months to live. His son offered to tape his father's recollections as the basis for a second volume of the memoirs, but Gray demurred, reluctant to breach the privacy of living colleagues and perhaps also to reveal too much about himself.

In the meantime, *Fun Tomorrow* was going through production. Its editor, Doug Gibson, knowing how gravely ill Gray was, thought to spare his author the usual tasks of checking proofs and worrying about publication details. But when Gray sent him "a hurt letter," Gibson realized that this author, more than any, needed to be fully involved in the publishing process. He began including Gray every step of the way, down to the wording of the jacket blurb and the advertising copy.

When the book went on press, Gray was dying. The printer was Hunter-Rose, headed by Guy Upjohn, Frank's son. Upjohn pulled out all the stops, and Gibson was able to put a finished copy of *Fun Tomorrow* into Gray's hands as he lay in his hospital bed. Deeply appreciative, Gray shared the precious moment with his family. Two days later, he died, "the most respected and best-loved figure," as his colleague Marsh Jeanneret called him, "in English-Canadian book publishing."

OXFORD
UNIVERSITY PRESS

OXFORD UNIVERSITY PRESS

4

TOYE AND HIS ILK

*The editor's first job is that of a midwife, helping the author
to set free his book, as it has been conceived – to realize his
full potential.*

John Gray, *Canadian Literature* (Summer 1967)

I f his career in Canadian publishing had begun twenty years later, Bill
Toye would almost certainly have received his own imprint. Given his
accomplishments as editor, designer, and author, it would have been a
mark of distinction for any book to have "A William Toye Book" on the
title page. By the close of his forty-three years in the trade – in reality more
than fifty, since he continued to work after his "retirement" in 1991 – Toye
was the most influential publisher, after Macmillan's Gray and the
University of Toronto Press's Marsh Jeanneret, whose name didn't appear
in a company logo.

But in Toye's prime, it wasn't fashionable to adopt the style "A
Douglas Gibson Book," as later at McClelland & Stewart, or "A Phyllis
Bruce Book," as at HarperCollins. Toye also did his publishing at a house
whose bestseller was the Bible and whose imprint dates from the seven-
teenth century. Oxford is a long way, geographically and culturally, from
Toronto. Partly it was Oxford University Press's distance from its
Canadian branch that allowed Toye and his colleagues to undertake
the discerning publishing that exercised such a formative influence on
Canadian poetry, children's literature, book design, and especially the

evolutionary process of canon-building. And partly it was Toye's talent, hard work, high standards, and stubborn high-handedness.

When young William Toye joined Oxford in 1948, the press had already been in Canada for forty-four years. It had opened its first Toronto office in 1904 on Richmond Street, just west of Yonge, in a block known as Booksellers' Row; in 1929 the office moved to University Avenue. OUP was chiefly interested in selling its British titles. Unlike many of its competitors, it had the advantages of a guaranteed list and a grand publishing tradition, and it generated cash by concentrating on those old Oxford reliables: dictionaries, prayer books, and the King James Version.

The parent firm had a hybrid structure that was as much academic as corporate. Governed from the university by a body of senior dons from various disciplines, known as the Delegates, it maintained a publishing and sales staff in London and operated its own printing presses. It undertook a great deal of exclusively scholarly, non-profit publishing under the Clarendon Press imprint but expected the London operation, which published trade books and schoolbooks, to stick to business and turn a profit. The Canadian manager reported to the publisher in London. If the Toronto branch hadn't published a single Canadian title, it's doubtful the parent company would have minded a great deal, as long as it earned a respectable return from Oxford's voluminous list in Canada.

A strain of nepotism was not unknown in OUP culture. The first manager, as the head of the Canadian branch was known, was Samuel B. Gundy, who played a leading role in the delegation that met with the finance minister in the 1920s to protest against the new federal tax on books. Gundy's teenaged son Fred, brought into the business to sell Bibles, became a minor industry legend for his decidedly un-biblical lifestyle. Donald Sutherland, who worked under him for four years before going to Macmillan, remembered Fred Gundy as "a wild character, who'd wine, women, and song his way across Canada selling Bibles and prayer books." Gundy often travelled in company with his drinking and bookselling buddy Bill McLeod, another scion of a publishing family. But Gundy's wares had a big market in mid-century Canada, and he was well liked by peers of both sexes.

Ironically, when the older Gundy died in 1936, his son acquired for a boss the teetotalling W.H. Clarke. Struggling to survive the Depression, Clarke contracted with the Delegates to manage OUP's business in Canada while continuing to operate Clarke, Irwin. He published trade titles under the Oxford imprint, schoolbooks under his own, and the two firms were housed together at Amen House, an imposing replica of a Jacobean London townhouse on University Avenue; later demolished, the building was located across the street from present-day McClelland & Stewart. The arrangement was eminently favourable for Clarke, Irwin, since it reduced the company's overheads and greatly increased its revenues. A similar arrangement existed between M&S and J.M. Dent & Sons: John McClelland served as chairman of Dent's board in Canada, with Dent producing the textbooks, M&S the trade books. Such cooperative alliances allowed Canadian-owned firms to profit from the presence of foreign-owned publishers without losing their identity or independence.

The alliance between Oxford and Clarke, Irwin lasted thirteen years. One of its historic claims was publication of the first Bible completely printed and bound in Canada; Clarke obtained the plates from England during the war, when seaborne book shipments were unsafe, and issued a Canadian-manufactured edition in 1943. Shortly before leaving OUP in 1949 and taking his ambitions uptown to St. Clair Avenue, Clarke hired two young men who would set Oxford's publishing direction in Canada.

A University of Toronto graduate named Ivon Owen, son of a professor of Greek and nephew of a primate of the Anglican Church, arrived in 1947. Owen was joined a year later by twenty-two-year-old Bill Toye, a music lover (he'd once met Rachmaninoff backstage at Eaton Auditorium) and polymath fresh from Northrop Frye's domain at Victoria College, University of Toronto. Both started off in the order department in the basement of Amen House, the site of occasional flooding during heavy rains.

It was "eccentric," Toye admitted years later, to want to enter book publishing, since the industry was small and undeveloped, but he'd entertained the idea since his student days at North Toronto Collegiate Institute. He remembered being fascinated by Oxford's antique-looking headquarters and telling his parents he wanted to work there. At first he was content to perform his duties in the basement, recording every order by customer name on cards for each title and reducing stock levels accordingly. In the process, Toye learned the extensive Oxford list and began his lifelong habit of working evenings. Whenever a new shipment of an Oxford dictionary arrived, the order clerks had to stay late filling back orders.

W.H. Clarke and his wife, Irene, who had her own office in Amen House, enforced a strict ban on smoking and drinking. The staff's Christmas bonus came in the form of a dinner at the King Edward Hotel – dry, of course, and highlighted by an OUP author as guest speaker, skits by the staff, and the gift of a silver spoon to each employee. At the 1948 dinner, Bill Toye had a singing part in a pastiche of Gilbert and Sullivan tunes spoofing the planned parting of Clarke, Irwin from Oxford. In some mysterious way, Toye's spirited performance won over his imperious boss, who previously had ignored him.

Toye then pushed his luck by asking Clarke for the raise he'd been promised after six months on the job but still hadn't received after twelve: "In an act of courage that surprises me today, I asked for an appointment with Mr. Clarke. It was granted, and I entered his impressive oak-panelled office with fireplace across from the library, and reminded him of my promised raise." Clarke heard Toye out and later notified him on engraved OUP stationery that he would be receiving "a substantial increase but one which in my view has been well earned," to $40 a week.

When Toye made his first forays into editing, he characteristically assumed a larger role than the one he'd been assigned. Clarke handed him the galleys for three forthcoming books and told him to get them produced. Undaunted, Toye sought out the company's suppliers to learn the mysteries of typesetting, printing, and binding. He found the suppliers' reps eager and willing to help; the Oxford name and publishing program opened doors.

By a fortunate coincidence, one of the three authors was a former English professor of Toye's at Victoria, Kathleen Coburn, an internationally known Coleridge scholar. Professor Coburn had built up Toye's confidence in his own undergraduate writing; now he found himself proofreading her novel, *The Grandmothers*, coming across not only typos but passages he felt were unclear or awkward, not up to her standards at all. "What to do?" Toye recalled. "How could I make changes in the work of my former professor? But an appointment was arranged, we went over my changes, and she accepted everything! That was the beginning of my career as an editor." Other authors, as Toye would discover, wouldn't take to his busy blue pencil so kindly. But his belief in his ability to prune, reshape, and burnish other people's prose became established early on.

If Toye had a mentor in those early years, it was Ivon Owen. Although Owen didn't have a great deal more experience, a single year's seniority made a big difference so early in their careers. With the departure of Clarke, Irwin, Oxford reassumed responsibility for educational publishing, and Owen, who had begun editing books before Toye, found he *was* the educational department. He went out on the road selling books, with Toye his man on the ground back home. Eventually Owen evolved into the college manager, developing textbooks as well as selling them, and Toye became production manager, a position he would fill for some thirty years while continuing to edit.

The choice of successor to W.H. Clarke was another instance of Oxford nepotism. The Delegates despatched to Toronto one Charles Johnson, an Englishman who, at twenty-nine, was barely older than Owen and Toye but happened to be the son of John Johnson, Printer to the University. Charles was an unhappy young man who had wanted to be an engineer but had been made to study classics by his domineering father, then was packed off to India to work for OUP. He was reassigned to Canada in 1949, as if, in Owen's phrase, running the Canadian outpost was "like managing a bank branch on the corner."

There were problems with the appointment. Charles Johnson knew little about publishing and less about Canada; worse, he was terrified of spending money. He had a drinking problem (he kept a supply of beer hidden in a closet in his office) and a tendency to throw tantrums. On the other hand, Owen found him conscientious, anxious to do a good job. He and Toye tried to educate Johnson about his new country, but persuading him to invest in any particular title was like pulling teeth; Johnson not only was parsimonious and insecure, but he didn't believe, according to Owen, that any Canadian book could be much good. Although Johnson became more pro-Canadian with time, the list grew slowly, and Oxford's output during the 1950s was sometimes fewer than ten titles a year.

One of those titles, however, was the kind a publisher could live on for a long time. OUP had established a cartographic department in England. Since Canada had a lot of geography, head office proposed to the Toronto branch that it publish a Canadian atlas. Owen found Ontario's school curriculum director, Colonel Stanley Watson (father of the broadcaster and author Patrick Watson), receptive to the idea, and work began on the *Canadian Oxford School Atlas*. Tailored to the requirements of the Ontario Ministry of Education, with maps expertly drawn in Oxford, the first edition appeared in 1957. It filled a major need in Canadian schools and was soon selling in six figures every year; several later editions were issued. In Owen's estimation, the atlas became "probably the bestselling Canadian textbook ever," although reliable statistics on these matters are impossible to come by.

As Owen and Toye slowly built up a Canadian program of educational and trade books, Johnson's health deteriorated. In 1962 he suffered an alcoholic breakdown and was admitted to a Toronto treatment facility. After a further period of recovery in Oxford, he resumed working at head office, expecting to be restored eventually to his position in Toronto. But in 1963, while still in England, he either fell or jumped from a moving train, still carrying his briefcase, and was killed. The coroner's jury returned an open verdict on the possibility of suicide.

The Delegates had appointed Owen acting manager in Johnson's absence, and now they confirmed him in the position. Owen began playing a prominent role in publishing industry affairs. In 1964 his peers elected him fourth president of the Canadian Book Publishers' Council, the name adopted three years earlier by the council's forerunner, the Book Publishers Association of Canada, which had begun in 1910 as a branch of the Toronto Board of Trade. Owen's three predecessors at the CBPC were all pillars of the educational publishing establishment: Wilfred Wees of Gage, Victor Seary of Ryerson, and C.J. Eustace of Dent.

In his first address as president, Owen delivered a surprisingly scathing (for such a mild-mannered man) commentary on the practice of "buying around," the time-honoured professional custom of circumventing authorized Canadian distributors of British or American books by obtaining them at source. "Any librarian or professor," he said, "will gladly address any luncheon we care to organize on the subject of our cultural indispensability – if he is not already engaged that day in addressing his colleagues on 'How to Buy Books More Cheaply and Quickly Abroad.'"

Toye, meanwhile, was multi-tasking. He edited schoolbooks, including a French grammar text for Alberta classrooms accompanied by a sound recording, for which he did the casting and directing at the RCA Victor studios. He edited all the trade books. He was production manager, responsible for seeing the entire list through the press. And for some time he was printing stationery, flyers, and forms too, occasionally leaving his other duties to ink up a Multilith press and turn out whatever documents were required.

Even more remarkably, Toye also became the press's chief designer. He studied typography and design on his own time, teaching himself from books. When Oxford was planning its handsome new building on Wynford Drive in the Toronto suburb of Don Mills, where it moved in 1963, Toye seconded himself to advise the architect, Robert Fairfield, who had designed the theatre at Ontario's Stratford Festival, on changes to the office plans.

Blessed with curiosity, energy, and single-minded dedication, Toye was impatient with mediocrity. "Canadian publishing was very feeble back then," he recalled. "There was a kind of amateurishness everywhere." In the 1950s, the standard of Canadian book design was generally stodgy and drab: "shockingly poor," Toye called it. Happily, gifted immigrants such as Frank Newfeld and Leslie Smart joined like-minded Canadians Carl Dair, Allan Fleming, and other designers in raising standards and founding the Society of Typographic Designers (later Graphic Designers of Canada) in 1956 to promote greater sophistication in print design. Toye, who had employed Fleming's services, joined the group to learn all he could. At first he wasn't allowed to become a full member: his design work wasn't deemed skilled enough. But in 1960 he was accepted into full membership and later he became president of the society.

Toye attributed that acceptance to his design work on a 1959 OUP title, *The St. Lawrence*: a history of the river which, it so happened, he'd also written. Now he was not only editing, designing, and producing Oxford's books but writing them too. The book was a natural outgrowth of his fascination with Canadian history; planned to mark the opening of the St. Lawrence Seaway, it was intended for high school readers but also appealed to an adult trade market and went into several printings. An American edition appeared, attracting a glowing review in *The New Yorker*. The book's success led to an invitation from Collins in the United Kingdom for Toye to compile and edit an anthology of Canadian writings; *A Book of Canada* was published in 1962 as part of Collins's National Anthology series. With the royalties from these titles, Toye was able to purchase and renovate the charming midtown row house that has been his Toronto home for many years.

Publishing anthologies was a way of showing the world that Canadian literature existed, by presenting a cross-section of the country's best writing. However arbitrary and exclusionary that taste-making process was, it stimulated wider recognition of a nascent national literature. As it had done in other English-speaking countries, Oxford became associated with the process through anthologies bearing its name: *The Oxford Book of Canadian Verse*, *The Oxford Book of Canadian Short Stories in English*, *The Oxford Anthology of Canadian Literature*. It also became closely linked, through professional and personal ties, with *The Tamarack Review*.

In the mid-1950s, English-Canadian literary magazines were few and far between. The most enduring vehicle for poetry, short stories, and criticism was the left-wing *Canadian Forum*, published monthly since 1920, whose chief thrust had always been political. *The Fiddlehead* appeared from Fredericton and included mostly poetry. Alan Crawley's *Contemporary Verse*, originating on the West Coast, had ceased publication in 1952. Mimeographed poetry magazines with tiny circulations came and went like butterflies, devoted to a particular poetics of the moment.

An important outlet for literary modernism after the war had been *Northern Review*. But by the 1950s, *Northern Review* was running out of creative steam, and in 1956, a year after it relocated from Montreal to Toronto, its disappearance coincided with the death from tuberculosis of its editor, John Sutherland. It was no coincidence that *The Tamarack*

Review emerged later that same year. According to its prime mover, Robert Weaver, he and the other *Tamarack* editors held off because they'd been waiting for *Northern Review* to vacate the field; it had seemed ungracious to push it aside while Sutherland was dying. A more pragmatic consideration, since the Canada Council didn't exist yet, was that literary mags subsisted on subscriptions and private donations, and the supply of both was too limited to support two competing titles in Toronto.

From the start, *Tamarack* radiated elegance. It was stylishly designed and typeset, and professionally printed on top-quality paper by the University of Toronto Press. The editing reflected a consistent level of contemporary sophistication in poetry, fiction, essays, and reviews. It was less nationalistic than the *Forum*, projecting a literary cosmopolitanism that was both its strength and its limitation.

Weaver had taken up the idea for *Tamarack* with Ivon Owen, who had taken it up with Bill Toye, and the three of them threw in $100 each to get it going, becoming the core of its editorial board. Weaver had already begun collaborating with the pair in 1952. Oxford had published *Canadian Short Stories*, an anthology of pieces originally broadcast on his CBC program of the same name. To *Tamarack*'s first editorial board they added Kildare Dobbs, the poet Anne Wilkinson (whose family memoir, *Lions in the Way*, Dobbs had edited for Macmillan), and the critic and University of Toronto professor Millar MacLure. Wilkinson, descended from the wealthy Osler family, was not only gifted poetically but blessed with an inheritance. As Weaver put it, "*Tamarack* would never have lived if Anne Wilkinson hadn't been our secret admirer and benefactor."

Wilkinson would die in 1961; Dobbs and MacLure would leave the board, and others (Owen's wife, Patricia Owen, John Robert Colombo, Naim Kattan, William Kilbourn, Janis Rapaport) would join. But over the course of twenty-six years and eighty-six issues, Weaver and Toye were the driving forces. Weaver gave the CBC to understand that he was merely a member of *Tamarack*'s editorial collective, but for all practical purposes, he was editor-in-chief. His work for the CBC and for the magazine became so intermingled that "sometimes I wasn't sure which of these organizations I was working for." Weaver's CBC colleagues used to kid him about it; his boss, the author Harry Boyle, would find Weaver at his desk typing rejection letters for the magazine and say, "The CBC is so tight, they won't even hire you a secretary to do the *Tamarack Review* rejections." Finally, when the magazine was in danger of falling apart for lack of organization, Weaver told his fellow board members, "Somebody's got to run this thing," and his name began appearing on the masthead as editor. The CBC didn't object, or perhaps it didn't even notice.

Busy as he was at Oxford, Bill Toye made time to proofread, paste up, and produce every issue. "I loved the *Tamarack*," he said. "I felt very privileged to be part of it." Toye designed some issues and ensured consistently high design quality by commissioning covers from Allan Fleming, Frank Newfeld, Theo Dimson, and Fred Huffman. A handsome, colourful, perfect-bound volume, *Tamarack* stood out brightly on bookstore and library shelves and on the few magazine stands that displayed it. When an issue arrived from the printer, the board would convene at Ivon Owen's home, joined by friends of the magazine such as the writers Marian and Howard Engel, to label and stuff and stamp envelopes. Weaver and Toye would tote the mailbags down to the post office, then drive around Toronto delivering copies to bookstores. Weaver would personally walk the magazine into stores whenever he visited St. John's or Montreal or Winnipeg on CBC business.

At its height, *Tamarack*'s circulation was never more than 2,000, but its impact was larger than circulation figures would suggest. With hindsight, the journal appears solidly mainstream, which simply proves its influence; appearing in its pages helped build readership and prestige for many of the Canadian writers considered important today. A typical issue would contain the latest work of Earle Birney, Jay Macpherson, Hugh Hood, Irving Layton, Mordecai Richler, Alice Munro, or Timothy Findley, writers whose work Weaver was also broadcasting over CBC Radio. In 1962 Oxford published *The First Five Years*, a selection of pieces from *Tamarack*. Symbiotic relationships with both *Tamarack* and the CBC shaped OUP's role in Canada's literary evolution.

That alignment produced a shift in the critical spirit in which Canadian short fiction was presented to the public. Previously readers seeking an overview had to turn to anthologies compiled by the academic critic Desmond Pacey, of the University of New Brunswick. Pacey's *A Book of Canadian Stories*, published by Ryerson in four different editions between 1947 and 1962, had become the standard reference after Raymond Knister had edited the first edition in 1928. Weaver was equally industrious, preparing five distinct "series" or editions of *Canadian Short Stories* for Oxford between 1960 and 1991. But Weaver's selections were more adventurous and bracing than Pacey's, his sensibility more contemporary, his critical standards more exacting.

In addition to Weaver's solo anthologizing, Oxford issued many compilations over the years. The critic A.J.M. Smith oversaw a new *Oxford Book of Canadian Verse* in 1960, followed in 1967 by his *Modern Canadian Verse*, containing a rich selection of mainly contemporary work in English and French and wrapped in a psychedelic jacket by the hip young designer Blair Drawson. *Fifteen Canadian Poets*, edited by Gary Geddes and Phyllis Bruce, became a perennial CanLit text after its publication by Oxford in 1971, succeeded by *Fifteen Canadian Poets Plus 5*.

Oxford anthologies helped to popularize Canadian short fiction. *The Oxford Book of Canadian Short Stories in English*, which Weaver co-edited with Margaret Atwood, was published in 1986, followed by *The New Oxford Book of Canadian Short Stories* in 1995. These volumes were thicker than Weaver's other series and very successful commercially (about 40,000 of the 1986 edition were sold), in part because they carried Atwood's name but also because they tapped into an expanding readership for Canadian short stories in both trade and educational markets. Atwood acknowledged the role played behind the scenes by Bill Toye as "goad, fellow-reader and tie-breaker" in a triumvirate with her and Weaver. The Oxford tradition continues in such anthologies as *The Oxford Book of Stories by Canadian Women in English*, edited by Rosemary Sullivan.

But for magnitude, bulk, and sheer indispensability, nothing could surpass what would become Toye's own magnum opus. In 1967 Oxford had published the landmark *Oxford Companion to Canadian History and Literature*, single-handedly written by the retired archivist Norah Story. Because it spanned both historical and literary territory, Story's massive, wide-ranging work was inevitably uneven and occasionally superficial, especially since her entries on contemporary literature were soon outdated. Yet her 935-page tome broke new ground and was unquestionably a highlight among the 300-odd books about Canada published during Centennial Year. It became, along with a 318-page *Supplement* that Toye assembled in 1973, an essential research tool.

After Story's *Companion* had lived out its natural life, Toye committed himself to a completely new reference work: a volume that would address Canadian literature alone, in an attempt to capture the explosion of creative writing in both official languages since Story's volume had appeared. Unlike her book, Toye's *Oxford Companion to Canadian Literature* would consist of contributions by diverse hands. Whatever consistencies of approach, tone, and quality it achieved would largely be due to the editor's judgment and blue pencil.

In compiling the work, Toye coped with tortuous logistical and policy questions: determining which authors and themes to include, which to exclude; deciding which authors should receive a separate article, which could be subsumed within a genre survey; assessing which books deserved their own entry (*The Apprenticeship of Duddy Kravitz*, *Jalna*, *The Wars*, *Who Has Seen the Wind*, but not *St. Urbain's Horseman*); and, equally critical, which writers should be invited to write on which subjects. Throughout a process more than three years long of commissioning and editing entries, Toye also had to struggle with his own perfectionism, with nagging doubts that he'd found the right contributors, suspicions that "there weren't all that many who were first-class," and worries that he'd simply commissioned too much material.

Toye had a nightmare while on holiday in France: the *Companion*, then in the galley-proof stage, had somehow expanded of its own accord to 1,200 pages. When finally published in 1983, the first edition weighed in at a mere 898 pages, comprising 770 entries written by 193 individuals. For all Toye's doubts, the review in the *Globe and Mail* by Robertson Davies was glowing: "It deserves something far beyond a library circulation," Davies wrote. "Buy it. Read it. Think about it." The *University of Toronto Quarterly* termed it "one of the major works of reference in Canadian studies." The fundamental need for a comprehensive and authoritative reference eventually resulted in sales of close to 14,000 copies. Perhaps Toye slept easier after the work was so well received, perhaps not. He was an inveterate "fusser," in his friend Weaver's description, and an encyclopedist's work is never done.

By the time Toye's *Companion* was published, Ivon Owen had been gone from OUP for a decade. In 1973, while living under painfully difficult personal circumstances (the loss of both a son and his marriage), Owen had been relieved of his duties as manager. OUP's financial performance had been lacklustre during the previous two fiscal years – the result, in the view of one former colleague, of Owen's seriously overestimating the Canadian market for *The New English Bible*, co-published by Oxford and Cambridge University Press. A committee of the Delegates informed Owen of their decision on a visit to Toronto. Ironically, while the Delegates were still in the city, a financial statement arrived for the last fiscal year, showing that the press had returned to the black; but it came too late to change their minds.

After twenty-six years with OUP, Owen reverted to his first love, editing. He continued in his voluntary capacity with *The Tamarack Review*, freelanced for M&S and other firms, and was retained for many years by *Saturday Night* as an editorial court of last resort, saving the magazine from assorted errors before it went to press. Toye, whose title at OUP changed to editorial director in 1969, acted in Owen's place for six months until the manager's position was filled permanently. Oxford's new Canadian manager was Lorne Wilkinson, who moved over from McGraw-Hill Ryerson.

After Wilkinson's arrival, Toye was once again free to concentrate on editorial, design, and production. But Toye insisted that the innumerable books he edited, produced, and in some cases created couldn't be considered a full-fledged publishing program. "I thought up a number of books and saw them through," he said without false modesty, "and some just came to me [as unsolicited manuscripts]. But it was more or less unplanned. Because I was doing so many other things, I wasn't building up the kind of list in each area that would have really made a mark. Overheads were always a problem. It seemed to be a matter of doing everything, because the press couldn't afford to have it done properly. And the books were too expensive, and the gross margin was not high enough, so the only way out of it, I thought, was to do everything myself."

At the same time, Toye avowed, he had complete editorial autonomy. In the one genre where he did consciously plan a program, he was inspired by the parent company's list. Great Britain was a nation where children's literature had long been an art. In Canada, at that point, it was anything but; the majority of Canadian children's books were earnest, didactic, and pedestrian. That depressing picture was thoroughly documented by Sheila Egoff in her 1967 study, *The Republic of Childhood: A Critical Guide to Canadian Children's Literature in English* – published, not coincidentally, by Oxford.

Canadian children's publishing then displayed less originality, high spirits, and joy than the books that have poured forth in such profusion since the mid-1970s. Most titles fell into the categories of animal tales, Indian legends, or Canadian history, as suggested by numerous series titles: Macmillan's Great Stories of Canada, Clarke, Irwin's Canadian Portraits, Gage's Frontier Books. There was nothing wrong with those genres per se, except that so much of the writing and illustration was dull and pedantic. As Egoff wrote, responsibility for the dearth of creativity ultimately lay with publishers, particularly in the visual realm: "In the final analysis, good design and good illustrations bring a children's book to its highest form. And why, in books at least, children should not have the best of all possible worlds is mainly a question for publishers to answer."

In 1947 the Canadian Association of Children's Librarians had begun presenting an annual award to the best children's book in English Canada. During the 1950s, the national output was so meagre that no award was given in four separate years. Of that period, Toye observed, "There was a great lack, and I felt we could make a contribution, as the parent business was doing." Once he got his children's program up and running, Oxford won five of the ten awards presented from 1957 to 1966.

The freshness of Toye's approach to children's publishing lay in his flair for strong design and in the imaginative illustrations he commissioned. Two books he wrote himself, *The St. Lawrence* and *A Picture History of Canada* (co-authored with Owen), both received high marks from the hard-to-please Egoff. The artist Leo Rampen illustrated Toye's St. Lawrence book and also Anne Wilkinson's unusual fantasy, *Swann and Daphne*, published by Oxford in 1960 and cited by Egoff as "an important example in the development of the Canadian illustrated book for children."

The apogee of Toye's children's publishing came with his discovery of Elizabeth Cleaver, an artist known for her vivid, sensuous colour and startling visionary forms. He worked with her on nine books, and their fruitful collaboration smacked a little of *The Phantom of the Opera*. When Cleaver was a young artist in 1967, she was introduced to Toye, who was then working on the first anthology of Canadian poetry for children. He found Cleaver's collages so beautiful that he offered her the chance to illustrate the book. Toye heard nothing further until Cleaver called him many weeks later, her voice hoarse and weak; she was in the hospital, having barely survived an operation for cancer. He urged her to begin work as soon as she could, and her recovery immediately took an upward swing: now, she told her physician, she had something to live for. Three months later, she began her illustrations for *The Wind Has Wings: Poems from Canada*, edited by Mary Alice Downie and Barbara Robertson, which Oxford published in fall 1968 to wide acclaim.

Cleaver's method was to make linocuts of her figures and set them against backgrounds created from torn pieces of brightly coloured monoprints, a technique that gave her collages their distinctive volume, space, and texture. Her work was strikingly suited to the myths of transformation that she illustrated, such as *How Summer Came to Canada* and *The Loon's Necklace*. But Toye was an exacting taskmaster and always believed she could do better: "I felt, Now *there* was a talent that could be developed."

After Cleaver moved to Montreal, Toye travelled to her studio apartment to work with her on every page of every book. Usually he'd written the text himself and would insist she redo her compositions over and over, often pushing her to tears. "I was a very, very demanding and arrogant editor," he acknowledged. "But she knew that I was probably right." Cleaver's books won national and international recognition and were published in the United States. But eventually her cancer returned, and her final book, *The Enchanted Caribou*, appeared after her death, in 1985, at the age of forty-five.

Cleaver wasn't the only one to be subjected to the hyperactive Toye treatment. Norah Story first made contact with Oxford in 1962; about to retire as head of the manuscript division of the Public Archives of Canada, she persuaded Ivon Owen that she had the experience and the time to undertake her *Companion* project. When Toye began receiving her entries in manuscript, however, he found them slight, hardly more developed than bibliographic listings, and he began to suspect Story was a better archivist and historian than literary scholar. He demanded more detailed entries. On receiving them, he festooned the pages with changes, suggestions, and queries squiggled in his small, precise hand and sent them back to her. Only when a reworked version arrived would Toye feel the text was satisfactory.

Story began to chafe under his demands and became, in his recollection, "furious." Finally she wrote to Owen complaining about "that young man" (Toye was nearing forty) whose editing, she claimed, had driven her to see a psychiatrist. Owen politely pointed out that Toye had in fact made her text better, and the battles continued.

Matters improved only after Story sold her Ottawa home and moved to an apartment in Toronto, just two blocks away from Toye's house. Every Sunday, she'd invite him over, serve him a glass of rye and a good dinner, and begin discussing the latest batch of edited entries. On that basis, working face to face instead of at long distance, they got along famously. Five years after the project began, *The Oxford Companion to Canadian History and Literature* was published and captured the Governor General's Award for non-fiction. It went on to make Norah Story's retirement more comfortable by selling some 20,000 copies.

For Toye too, the project brought benefits, since working on Story's *Companion* launched his own career as an encyclopedist. And he made, in the end, a good friend, whose table talk was so entertaining that he often wished he'd recorded it. He particularly relished Story's reminiscences of her ritualized relationship with William Lyon Mackenzie King. The prime minister would send his chauffeur to bring her to Laurier House, where they would dine, then withdraw upstairs to converse in the sitting room, overlooked by King's mother's portrait glowing supernaturally in the lamplight. Toye attempted to get a rise out of Story by asking if the bachelor PM had ever made a pass at her. "Oh no," she replied firmly, "the only personal thing he ever said to me was, 'Your eyes are like Mussolini's.'"

Toye couldn't resist repeating the story to a *Time Canada* correspondent when the *Companion* was launched. Oxford was holding an unusually splashy party for its entire list in the ballroom of the Royal York Hotel, and to Toye's mingled horror and delight, *Time* came out the day before with a feature about the book and a photograph of Story over the caption, "Eyes like Mussolini's." Story phoned him, bubbling over with excitement, and asked, "But how did they *ever* get that story about Mackenzie King?" When Toye confessed, she let him off with a lecture about not making fun of such an important national leader.

Other writers accepted his "transformations," to use Toye's term, of their work. These included the noted curator Dennis Reid, author of *A Concise History of Canadian Painting*. While collaborating with Toye, Reid was on staff at the National Gallery of Canada and travelled to Toye's home on weekends, or Toye travelled to Ottawa, so that the two could pore over the latest section of Reid's manuscript. Reid appreciated Toye's pragmatism and professionalism: "We worked out upfront what purposes the book was meant to serve. So first we fashioned a vessel, then filled it."

Senator Eugene Forsey, the distinguished constitutional expert, was in his mid-eighties when Toye persuaded him to write about his long career in politics and the labour movement. Toye would visit Forsey in Ottawa for lengthy editing sessions, sitting in his Senate office overlooking the Parliament Buildings, but asked him once too often to clarify a sentence. In exasperation, Forsey threw the manuscript to the floor and exclaimed, "This book will be the death of me! I should never have started it!" Then he shuffled morosely to the window, stared outside for a long moment, and dictated the perfect revision. Vastly relieved, Toye said meekly, "Thank you, Eugene. That's just right. Don't *you* think it's better?" On the publication of *A Life on the Fringe* in 1990, Forsey wrote Toye "the most extravagant tribute I've ever had from an author."

With every book he edited, Toye's rationale for his interventions was the same. "The choice was to let books be incomprehensible, illogical, boring, and possibly incomplete in their information, or to try to make their texts clear and readable. I chose the latter course every time." Using an approach like invisible mending, he considered his work was in the best interests of the text, the reader, and hence the writer. "I wanted to make changes that would be strictly faithful to the style of the author and the content of the book and completely faithful to the author's intent. The truth is that, when these books are finished, I don't know what I've done and what the author has done. It all reads seamlessly to me, and my part in it vanishes: in my own mind, and certainly in the author's."

Toye did more minimal editing on Oxford's poetry list, where he usually restricted himself to selection and arrangement of a book's contents. During his career, he published not so much widely in the genre as deeply. Oxford was the house of choice for A.J.M. Smith, Jay Macpherson, John Glassco, Miriam Waddington, George Johnston, and, notably, Margaret Atwood. Toye also published collections by F.R. Scott, P.K. Page, Margaret Avison, Raymond Souster, D.G. Jones, Phyllis Gotlieb, Francis Sparshott, Pat Lowther, and Patrick Lane. He was literary executor of the estates of Scott, Smith, and Glassco (whose classic *Memoirs of Montparnasse* he edited), an indication of the trust those authors placed in him.

With Atwood, Toye developed a long professional friendship that he characterized as "close" and "loyal." A.J.M. Smith had originally recommended her to Toye. Soon after *The Circle Game* appeared from Contact Press in 1966, Toye made a cold call over the phone, inviting her to lunch at the Inn on the Park near his office: "During lunch, she asked me what sign I'd been born under. I told her Gemini, and that satisfied her." (Atwood is a Scorpio.) By then, Contact Press was winding up; the House of Anansi, which had reissued *The Circle Game*, was still very new and small; and McClelland & Stewart hadn't exactly covered itself with glory by misplacing the manuscript of Atwood's first novel, *The Edible Woman*. Oxford must have seemed a model of stability by comparison, and Toye a model of probity and organization.

In 1968 Oxford published *The Animals in That Country*, Atwood's first title to appear also in the United States. She'd promised another book to her friend Dennis Lee at Anansi, where she would soon become involved as an editor, but Toye was so "absolutely enthralled" by her next poetry manuscript, inspired by the nineteenth-century pioneer author Susanna Moodie, that he entreated Atwood to let him publish it. *The Journals of Susanna Moodie* appeared from Oxford in 1970, containing collages created by Atwood herself from period illustrations supplied by Toye. A year later, Anansi published her almost equally well-known *Power Politics*. But Lee would soon be gone from Anansi, and Atwood remained loyal to Toye as a poet while publishing her fiction primarily with M&S. Oxford has released ten more of her collections, including three volumes of selected poems, up to *Morning in the Burned House* in 1995.

By that time, Toye had retired from OUP, but his presence continued to be felt in the press where he'd worked for nearly half a century. He was still editing the occasional book, and OUP kept after him to assemble a new version of his *Oxford Companion to Canadian Literature*. Well aware of the heavy workload involved, Toye declined, saying he didn't have the strength. But when the author and critic Eugene Benson, who had edited a similar reference work for Toye on Canadian theatre, suggested they collaborate on a revision, Toye couldn't resist.

Toye and Benson elected to keep all the entries from the first edition, published fourteen years earlier, and update them. In addition, the editors commissioned 342 articles on new authors and on subjects as diverse as literary awards, gay and lesbian literature, and sports writing: nearly half again as many entries as had appeared in the first edition. It was a mammoth undertaking, and it ran all the way to the 1,200 pages that had once featured in Toye's nightmare.

Published in 1997, when Toye was seventy-one (and eventually followed by a concise version, which he prepared entirely by himself four years later), the *Companion* in its second incarnation remains as indispensable as ever, a claim few books can make. And few publishers can truthfully state, as Toye can, that such an important work grew inevitably out of his entire career. "It was," as he said, "a culmination. I'd been preparing for it all my life."

Since 1901

UNIVERSITY OF MANITOBA PRESS | McGILL-QUEEN'S UNIVERSITY PRESS

UNIVERSITY OF TORONTO PRESS

UNIVERSITY OF ALBERTA PRESS | UNIVERSITY OF BRITISH COLUMBIA PRESS

UNIVERSITY OF CALGARY PRESS

5

THE SCHOLARLY ENTREPRENEUR

Book publishing . . . is the profession of professions, and
blends the most enticing features of many kinds of enterprise:
creative, critical, artistic, scholarly, recreational, technical,
political, informational, and financial. Its scope is infinite.

Marsh Jeanneret, *God and Mammon:*
Universities as Publishers (1989)

Before the 1950s, scholarly publishing scarcely existed in Canada. English-Canadian scholars had to go outside the country to publish their research in book form. Harold Innis broke ground for his exploratory work in economics and communications with *The Fur Trade in Canada* (1930) and *The Cod Fisheries* (1940), both published by Yale University Press. Influenced by Innis, Donald Creighton produced his first book, *The Commercial Empire of the St. Lawrence: 1760–1850*, for a series on Canada–United States relations published by one of the Carnegie foundations. In 1947 Barker Fairley's *Study of Goethe* and Northrop Frye's *Fearful Symmetry* appeared, from Oxford's Clarendon Press and Princeton University Press respectively.

But while Canadian scholars were achieving distinction abroad, no university at home could publish them adequately. The Massey-Lévesque commission summarized the negative consequences in 1951: "In a country where few but professors write learned books, it may be expected that few but professors will buy learned books. Canadian publishing houses cannot as a rule bear the inevitable loss, nor can the professor who has written the book. It may be assumed that much useful material goes unpublished, and it is probable that in the past many potential scholars have been discouraged even from writing."

Equally important, no funding body existed with a national mandate to support research in the humanities and social sciences. During wartime, there had even been public debate about closing down Canada's faculties of arts, law, commerce, and education for the duration of the conflict. Only determined opposition by Innis and other scholars persuaded Prime Minister Mackenzie King's government to ensure that the faculties, supposedly not essential to the war effort, were kept open. Such anti-intellectualism explains why Massey-Lévesque remonstrated, "We are in fact neglecting matters essential to a healthy national life."

The climate for research improved significantly with the founding of the Canada Council in 1957. The council's original mandate included support for the social sciences and humanities as well as the arts (twenty years later, its academic granting programs would be transferred to a newly created sister body, the Social Sciences and Humanities Research Council). A tremendous expansion in Canadian universities and graduate programs was accompanied by the extraordinary post-war growth of a single university press, led by an extraordinary publisher. Marsh Jeanneret didn't invent Canadian scholarly publishing, but no other individual has made a comparable impact on the field.

Although the University of Toronto Press has existed since 1901, its main functions during its first half-century were printing and bookselling. "The Press," as its adherents continue to call it, with a capital P, operated the campus bookstore and a printing plant that turned out everything from scholarly journals to labels and exam papers. The core of its publishing program was four journals: the *Canadian Historical Review*, the *Canadian Journal of Economics and Political Science*, the *University of Toronto Law Journal*, and the *University of Toronto Quarterly*.

A young graduate student named Francess Halpenny arrived to work at the press in 1941. With University of Toronto degrees in English and

American literature, she'd hoped to take her doctorate in the United States, but a fellowship was unavailable. She apprenticed as a copy editor on the *University of Toronto Quarterly* and soon was compiling the bibliography for "Letters in Canada," the annual critical survey initiated by two of her former professors, A.S.P. Woodhouse and E.K. Brown. Her tasks involved listing the literary titles produced in Canada the previous year, plus every last Canadian story or poem published in a periodical, English or French.

Separated from the rest of UTP's operations, the editorial department was tucked into a corner of Baldwin House, a rundown Victorian building occupied by the history department. The two departments had tea together every afternoon at 4 o'clock, and since the ladies always made the tea, and the editorial department consisted of ladies, Halpenny found herself serving tea to male history professors. A year later, enlisting in the Women's Division, Royal Canadian Air Force, she served with an anti-submarine patrol based in Newfoundland.

On her return to UTP, Halpenny became the senior editor overnight, in the absence of more experienced staff. The press was on the verge of a transformation instigated, like much of the university's post-war development, by its ambitious president, Sidney Smith, later a secretary of state for external affairs in the Diefenbaker government. Smith's administration commissioned three professors to recommend future directions for the press: the political economist Vincent Bladen, the historian George W. Brown, and the literary scholar Woodhouse. After conducting a grand tour of six major American university presses, the "BBW" committee delivered a report in 1946, laying down the principles that would continue to inform UTP's publishing program for years.

The BBW report aspired to make the University of Toronto "a national leader in developing scholarship and letters," and therefore a vigorous publishing operation was essential. The report stated that the press should not be "parochial" but should publish for the whole country, remaining open to authors from other universities. No scholarly press in the United States was expected to perform such a national service, but in English Canada, the field was wide open.

The report contained one anomaly, which contrasted oddly with the scope of its ambitions: it assumed that a national scholarly press could be financed on the cheap. The three professors posited the notion that profits from UTP's printing and bookstore divisions could cover the expenses of the publishing program. Once lodged in the minds of university administrators, that untested idea kept pressure on the press to pay its own way, a pressure that would decisively shape its list and operations.

George Brown, previously editor of the *Canadian Historical Review*, became the press's part-time editor-in-chief. He reported to a publications committee consisting of senior academics who made publishing decisions based on assessors' reports. Brown's main experience of publishing had been co-authoring a successful history text for schools, *The Story of Canada*, which had made a great deal of money for Copp Clark. In 1946 Brown recruited one of his co-authors, a Copp Clark editor named Eleanor Harman, to become associate editor and production manager at UTP.

Harman was a reserved but strong-willed woman who had received her professional training at Clarke, Irwin in the 1930s. She had imbibed the editorial values imported from Macmillan by W.H. Clarke and John C.W. Irwin, and she had experienced scholarly publishing through Clarke, Irwin's association with Oxford. Moving on to their rival Copp Clark in 1942, Harman worked with Marsh Jeanneret, a rising young publisher who had collaborated with her and Brown on writing *The Story of Canada*.

Harman had her work cut out for her at UTP. Its manufacturing was done at the press's printing plant, which had only two typefaces and bound its unjacketed books in one of two colours, dull green or dull red. Harman took on the challenge of raising design and production standards. She encouraged the evolution of Francess Halpenny and her colleagues from journal editors into book editors, a task that involved handling more complex texts and approaching specialists in many disciplines to obtain peer evaluations of manuscripts.

Halpenny began travelling to the meetings of learned societies in search of prospective authors and assessors. Over the years she would train many UTP editors, who would become known, with the occasional male exception, as "Francess's girls." Part of their job was the care and feeding of academic egos. One such belonged to Professor R. MacGregor Dawson. Equipped with a stentorian voice that could be heard around the block,

Dawson supervised the Canadian Government Series, the press's most ambitious project to date: an attempt to publish a comprehensive study of Canada's system of governance. With her tact, thoroughness, and sharp editorial eye, Halpenny won Dawson's appreciation and support, especially for her work on his own contribution, *The Government of Canada*, a text that hundreds of thousands of political science undergraduates have studied since its first publication in 1947.

In 1952 a milestone occurred in Canadian scholarship: the millionaire businessman James Nicholson, co-founder of Nicholson and Brock, the firm that produced Brock's Bird Seed, died at the age of ninety-one. Nicholson left a large part of his fortune to the University of Toronto to publish "a work similar in principle and scope to the Dictionary of National Biography published in England" but devoted to biographies of eminent Canadians. George Brown was ecstatic; a dictionary of Canadian biography had long been a dream of his. The only hitch was that the bequest would go first to Nicholson's widow, not reaching the university until her death. Since Mrs. Nicholson was some years younger than her husband, and in alarmingly robust health, there was no telling when UTP might launch the massive project; but in the meantime, there was no harm in planning.

The press's general manager, Alex Rankin, immediately thought of his old classmate Marsh Jeanneret, working downtown at Copp Clark. The huge challenges posed by the biographical dictionary would require a combination of publishing and business expertise; in addition, Rankin would soon be leaving the general manager's position. Along with youth and energy, Jeanneret had the experience to fill all those roles. Just thirty-five, he was a self-described "child of the campus" whose father, the eminent French professor and author F.C.A. Jeanneret, was principal of the University of Toronto's University College. The younger Jeanneret began lunching with Rankin and Brown to discuss the press's exciting prospects. And yet, attracted as he was to the idea of running UTP, he entertained doubts.

"I detoured into book publishing in the first place mostly by accident," Marsh Jeanneret would write. After graduating from the University of

Toronto Law School in 1938, the large, shy, studious young man was more inclined to teach law than to practise it. He planned to take graduate studies at Harvard, but he needed paying work for a year. One of his professors, Norman A.M. MacKenzie, a future member of the Massey-Lévesque commission, scribbled a name on a piece of paper and told Jeanneret, "This chap is my brother-in-law. He and his brother own the Copp Clark company."

Jeanneret obtained interviews with the president of Copp Clark, Major Dudley Thomas, and "his even more military younger brother," Alan Thomas, the vice-president known as "the Brig." They offered Jeanneret a job in the textbook department at $15 a week, which he negotiated upward to $20. The Brig advised him: "The three cardinal principles of business are profit, profit, and profit. If you remember them, we shall get along just fine."

Jeanneret was dismayed to discover that although Copp Clark was an important educational publisher, it placed little value on education. One of the Thomas brothers (Jeanneret was too discreet to say which one) once sent a memo to the textbook department calling off a search for the text of Shakespeare's *Ibid.*, since he'd learned at his club that the play did not exist after all. None of Jeanneret's departmental colleagues had graduated from university or even high school.

Copp Clark's editorial policy was to hand an unedited manuscript to the foreman of the in-house printing shop, with instructions to have the book ready before school opened. Jeanneret filled that vacuum by teaching himself editing. The grateful printing foreman coached him in proofreading and marking up manuscripts, and Jeanneret assumed responsibility for the contents. He found the work fascinating; but since the firm published only half a dozen new titles a year and made its biggest profits from reprinting or Canadianizing existing texts, he found himself spending more time pursuing provincial adoptions.

Jeanneret rose quickly at Copp Clark. A high point was co-authoring *The Story of Canada* with Harman and Brown; the book came to be adopted in every province except Quebec and sold over a million copies. With his share of the royalties, Jeanneret and his wife, Beatrice, bought a summer home on Lake Muskoka. Harman used hers to buy a cottage nearby.

By the time Brown and Rankin approached him about managing UTP, Jeanneret had spent nearly fifteen years with Copp Clark, becoming publisher in all but name. He was a trusted associate of both Thomas brothers, who called on him to arbitrate such weighty matters as which of them had first call on the company chauffeur. He had also become a director, with the possibility of acquiring a controlling interest someday. Clearly he was ambitious, and his biggest doubts about going to UTP concerned "whether headship of the University of Toronto Press would carry with it the publishing freedom I already enjoyed downtown."

John Gray recounted a chance meeting with Jeanneret in Fredericton just before the war, which revealed something of the younger man's aspirations. Jeanneret confided to Gray that his father might be interested in bankrolling the two of them to start their own publishing house. Gray considered the idea but soon entered the army; afterwards, he wondered what might have happened if the times had been different.

Now, however, F.C.A. Jeanneret advised his son to resist UTP's approaches, arguing that he'd fare better financially by staying in the private sector. Jeanneret admitted that the idea of moving onto his father's territory concerned him; one can only speculate that his father felt the same way. But when invited to meet with the chairman of the university's board of governors late in 1952, Jeanneret pressed ahead nonetheless. Lieutenant Colonel W. Eric Phillips was, in Jeanneret's description, "the most powerful, experienced, outspoken, and ruthless businessman anywhere on the horizon." As chairman of the giant holding company Argus Corporation, Phillips ran the university board as if it were one of his many enterprises. When Phillips met Jeanneret to discuss the UTP appointment, his mind was already made up.

Ill at ease, Jeanneret spent the first part of the meeting listening. Phillips stretched one leg across a mahogany desk as he smoothly summarized the reasons why he wanted Jeanneret as general manager. Jeanneret almost felt "it would be ungracious for me not to accept [the position] forthwith. I stifled an impulse to say 'yes'." He explained why he was reluctant to leave Copp Clark, making clear that if he did, he was interested in far more than the general manager's job: he wanted to be publisher at UTP, with clearly defined powers of decision-making.

Jeanneret argued that, although publishing academic research was the press's raison d'être, scholarly books could never be expected to support themselves, even when subsidized by the printing and bookstore operations. Therefore, unless the university was prepared to sink a lot of money into the program (it wasn't), UTP would need to develop a revenue-producing, "parallel semi-commercial" program: that is, a general trade list. That program should be compatible with the university's ethos, yet – and this was a large condition – *not* be subject to approval by the academic publications committee. A commercial publisher, Jeanneret explained, makes judgments based on production costs and a keen sense of the market. Publishing opportunities can be fleeting, requiring decisiveness and authority to negotiate. If the publisher's hands were tied by a committee, he'd lose those opportunities to the competition.

"I had unintentionally aroused the chairman's spirit of adventure," Jeanneret recalled. Phillips approved of Jeanneret's suggestion that the publications committee have authority only over scholarly manuscripts that required subsidy. By the time the two men got around to discussing money, they'd improvised the broad lines of the system by which the press would function. It remained only for Jeanneret to check things out with Sidney Smith and his own father.

F.C.A. Jeanneret's sole positive comment stemmed from his admiration for the skills of Eleanor Harman, with whom he'd worked on textbooks at Clarke, Irwin and Copp Clark: "With Miss Harman around it ought to be possible to turn the place into a Canadian Oxford." But the university president was more encouraging. At first, Sidney Smith was uncomfortable with delegating so much power to a press "director" – a new title, in line with usage at American university presses – but gradually he warmed to the idea. In the end, Jeanneret received the authority to expand the publishing program along more commercial lines; he'd combine the functions of both editor-in-chief and general manager and would report directly to President Smith. The arrangement gave Jeanneret practically everything he wanted, except a big salary.

When Jeanneret started work on March 1, 1953, he strode into his office and found a mountain of unopened mail on his desk: "I was pawing at it when Eleanor Harman walked in to say she had thought it would be informative for me to sort the letters myself for a few days to gain an idea of who did what in the Press." Substituting for the mail clerk was an original idea, he had to agree, and a foreshadowing of the influential role Harman would play in their twenty-four-year collaboration.

As Jeanneret discovered, the press's backlist was eclectic; it ranged from Guido Cavalcanti's *Theory of Love* to *Zoogeographical Study of the Land Snails of Ontario*. Copies of T.F. McIlwraith's two-volume, 1,500-page *The Bella Coola Indians* were stacked like sandbags against the warehouse wall, making it nearly impossible to reach the men's room. Jeanneret soon realized the press was running out of space: "Persons of more generous dimensions (like mine) could barely find usable openings at all in some directions." He seized the first opportunity to demonstrate the problem to the president. Inviting Smith, also a large man, up to his office, Jeanneret steered him down non-existent aisles lined by filing cabinets and into cul-de-sacs from which he had to back out.

If one indicator of a successful administrator is expanding his territory, Jeanneret quickly proved himself. He took over all of Baldwin House, where Francess Halpenny and her small band of editors still worked, renovated the house from top to bottom, and installed his administrative, sales, and accounting staff. But that was only a stopgap measure. Not long afterwards, Jeanneret successfully laid a claim to "the last piece of usable land facing the Front Campus," where a handsome stone structure was built to house the UTP offices and the bookstore. The press moved there in 1959, paying every last cent of the construction cost, plus interest. Seven years later, Jeanneret relocated the printing operations to a new facility in suburban Downsview.

After just one month on the job, Jeanneret travelled to New Orleans to attend his first of many annual meetings of the Association of American University Presses. Even though publishing was still a small fraction of UTP revenues, more than half its publishing sales already came from the United States, mainly from academic libraries. Raising the press's profile south of the border not only made business sense but served the needs of scholarly authors. Jeanneret was pleasantly surprised by the collegial attitudes of his AAUP counterparts: they willingly shared their knowledge and experience instead of hoarding it, as his commercial competitors had.

Jeanneret made an important alliance with one of the association's largest members, the University of Chicago Press. Wilfred Wees of W.J. Gage had told Jeanneret that Gage wouldn't be renewing its agency arrangement with Chicago, so he seized the chance to pitch UCP officials about making UTP their representative in Canada. Chicago agreed, and a year later Jeanneret hired the press's first field representative, thirty-two-year-old Hilary Marshall, a Cambridge graduate and British war veteran, to sell the two presses' books across the country. Marshall began travelling to universities, libraries, and bookstores and further developed the market for both houses through a much-expanded promotion program. Under Marshall's care, Chicago's business in Canada would increase more than forty times, before the agency arrangement came to an end in 1968; UTP's sales would eventually increase by an even bigger multiple, making it one of the largest university presses in North America.

But to make that growth possible, Jeanneret had to generate some commercial projects. At Copp Clark, he had come to know Jack C. Jones, publisher of business reference books such as the *Toronto Legal Directory*. Jeanneret worked out an agreement with Jones to co-publish the directory with UTP and eventually purchased it outright, along with Jones's other annual publications. With their advertising content and more or less captive subscribers, these titles produced profits enabling the press to publish numerous scholarly works. Jones, a self-made man with little formal education, grew so proud of his association with UTP that he willed it nearly half a million dollars.

Far stranger was the case of Atamus Richards, pseudonymous author of *A Light Shining in Dark Places* and *Revelation Revealed*. A mysterious gentleman had drowned accidentally, leaving a will requiring his executors to devote the entire proceeds of his estate to publishing two works by the said Richards. When the executors approached Jeanneret, he offered them a deal: UTP would meet the terms of the will to the letter, producing the two works and offering them to the public free of charge, with any unspent balance from the bequest going into the scholarly publications fund.

Jeanneret's only condition was that under no circumstances must the name of the press or the university be associated with the books.

The executors accepted the condition, and Eleanor Harman and Hilary Marshall went into action. The books were produced at minimal cost. A tiny edition was printed. Mail-order ads were placed, and a post office box rented at a branch remote from the university to receive orders. After the requests for free copies were filled (about 200, mainly from clergymen), the balance of the money was added to the scholarly publications fund. It was three times the amount of the press's normal annual contribution.

That lucrative little scam, which Jeanneret managed to keep more or less secret for thirty-five years, got him into no trouble whatsoever, but a more legitimate publishing idea did. He proposed to the university board of governors that UTP publish school textbooks, seeking co-publishing alliances with commercial firms to ensure the goodwill of the private sector. W.H. Clarke, who sat on the board of governors, was offended by the very notion: a university press, he declared, had no business in the schoolbook trade, and Jeanneret backed off.

But the UTP director wasn't deterred from exercising his entrepreneurial instincts. John R. Seeley, the prominent American sociologist then teaching at the University of Toronto, showed him a seventeen-page sample of an unfinished manuscript called "Crestwood Heights." The book was to be based on an in-depth sociological study documenting, for the first time, the mores of a whole Canadian community – the affluent Toronto neighbourhood of Forest Hill. Although Jeanneret was impressed by Seeley's "perceptive style," he faced a quandary: if he made a commitment to Seeley, he'd be gambling that the unwritten book would need no subsidy from the scholarly publications fund; but if he didn't commit himself right away, he'd have to refer the completed manuscript to the committee, and by then Seeley would have signed with an American press.

Jeanneret elected to seize the opportunity. He gave Seeley a verbal offer to publish, conditional only on the university president's approval. After Smith gave his agreement, Jeanneret handed Seeley over to Francess Halpenny, who "masterfully held the [800-page] manuscript of *Crestwood Heights* on course." Jeanneret also profitably sold U.S. rights to Basic Books in New York. Published in 1956, *Crestwood Heights* received positive reviews in both countries, with sensational coverage in the *Toronto Star* under the headline "Children Spoiled by Rich Forest Hill Parents – Research." Curiously Jeanneret expressed regret years later over the fact that the book had sold so well, reaching about 25,000 copies. "In the end the temptation to commercialize *Crestwood Heights* proved irresistible," he wrote repentantly. "I later decided that our decision to do this was unwise and improper . . . We should have concentrated on bringing it to the attention of its scholarly audience."

Jeanneret didn't hesitate to go after American foundation money. In 1957 the Ford Foundation announced a $2.75-million program of grants to American scholarly presses, and Jeanneret fired off a letter explaining the extent of UTP's publishing commitments and financial needs, his bid strengthened by letters of support from some of his AAUP colleagues. When he and Harman visited the Ford's program director in New York, they presented their case so effectively that the press received a five-year funding commitment for its scholarly list, renewed for another three years in 1962.

At the same time, Jeanneret competed as fiercely as any commercial publisher for rights to the official biography of Mackenzie King. The late prime minister's literary executors had chosen R. MacGregor Dawson for the assignment, providing him with privileged access to King's voluminous private diaries, which would not be released to other researchers for many years. John Gray of Macmillan took the lead in paying court to the four executors in Ottawa, who included King's confidant Jack Pickersgill; indeed, Macmillan seemed a logical choice for the rights, given the strength of its history list. But the executors left the choice of publisher up to Dawson, and UTP had published Dawson's *The Government of Canada*. That didn't prevent him from keeping all suitors, including Jeanneret, in the dark for several years while he worked on the project. Jeanneret had an ace up his sleeve, however, in Francess Halpenny, and when UTP published *William Lyon Mackenzie King: A Political Biography, 1874–1923* in 1958, it became a national bestseller. Dawson had died suddenly before its publication, but his work was continued by the historian Blair Neatby in collaboration with UTP.

Next King's executors appointed Pickersgill to abridge – that is, bowd-lerize – the famous diaries for publication. Four volumes covering the years 1939 to 1948 (the final three co-edited by D.F. Forster) appeared on the UTP list as *The Mackenzie King Record*. The 1970s would see further books by and about eminent Liberals: Pickersgill's political autobiography, *My Years with Louis St. Laurent*, and three volumes of former prime min-ister Lester B. Pearson's memoirs, *Mike*.

Jeanneret had an original cast of mind, but he sometimes found other people's originality offputting. UTP's most renowned author struck him at first as an oddball and a nuisance. As far back as 1953, when Marshall McLuhan and his colleagues had begun issuing *Explorations*, their spo-radic journal on culture and communications, Jeanneret found McLuhan "underfoot at the Press." The unbuttoned professor of English irked the straitlaced publisher by dropping into his office unannounced, trailing cigar smoke and learned puns, and hanging around the print shop during production of *Explorations*, egging on the compositors to try typographic experiments that Jeanneret considered "harebrained."

McLuhan had started working on the book that he first called "Gutenberg and His Galaxy." He'd stop by to tell Jeanneret about the difficulties he was having, but Jeanneret was baffled by McLuhan's cryptic discourse. Yet he kept hearing from others, including the university's new president, Claude Bissell, that McLuhan was a brilliant and original mind. Eleanor Harman was in far less doubt about McLuhan's importance; she warded off an approach to McLuhan by an editor from Longman Canada, declaring fiercely, "Marshall is the *Press's* author!"

In spring 1961, Jeanneret decided to offer McLuhan a contract. The following fall, the author walked in, "flopped a bundle on my desk saying: 'There it is!' and just as abruptly walked out." The manuscript flummoxed yet fascinated Jeanneret. When he placed it in Francess Halpenny's hands, he expressed his ambivalence in a note: "I am certain you will agree with me that it is at once exciting, wild, controversial, unconvincing in places, utterly brilliant in others, etc. I do believe that we have a book here that holds the possibilities of being one of the most talked-about and worth-while works we have published in a long while. But I shudder to think of the copy-editing it requires, containing the proportion it does of typos, quotations and citations, etc. . . . Nevertheless, I think we should give this book everything we have."

The manuscript that became *The Gutenberg Galaxy: The Making of Typographic Man* was indeed challenging, both intellectually and visually: so challenging that most mainstream publishers wouldn't have touched it. But as scholarly publishers, Jeanneret and his staff believed in their responsibility to publish original thought. The work was assigned to a young Scots editor, Rik Davidson, recently arrived via Thomas Nelson & Sons (Canada), and to Harold Kurschenska, a staff designer whose use of typography and layout married well with McLuhan's unorthodox style and enhanced comprehension of the text. In later years, McLuhan told Jeanneret that none of the American publishers who subsequently snapped him up ever gave his books such sensitive treatment.

Published in 1962, *The Gutenberg Galaxy* would eventually sell over 60,000 copies for UTP in both hardcover and quality paperback editions. The press also shared in royalties from the New American Library mass-market paperback edition and from numerous foreign-language editions. Jeanneret relished the moment when McLuhan, a Roman Catholic, accepted the Governor General's Award at Rideau Hall with a feudal gesture of obeisance: "When he was summoned to stand before His Excellency, Marshall characteristically threw protocol to the winds, dropped on his knees, and placed his hands in those of Governor General [Georges] Vanier throughout the reading of the citation, and we loved him for it."

Surprisingly, however, McLuhan's famous work was not the press's best-selling scholarly title. That distinction belongs to a book published three years later, *The Vertical Mosaic: An Analysis of Social Class and Power in Canada*, by the Carleton University sociologist John Porter. Subsidy was set aside to cover the expected publication deficit, but it was never needed; sales as of this writing are well over 100,000 copies.

During the years leading up to the Centennial, UTP published other seminal works: Ramsay Cook's biography of John W. Dafoe of the *Winnipeg Free Press* (1963); *In Defence of Canada*, a three-volume study of defence policy by James Eayrs, son of Hugh Eayrs (1964 and 1965, with the third volume in 1972); the architect Eric Arthur's *Toronto: No Mean City* (1964);

the first edition of *Literary History of Canada*, edited by Carl F. Klinck (1965); Russell Harper's monumental *Painting in Canada: A History* (1966). In their different ways, all were landmark books, scholarly yet accessible. Jeanneret had every reason to be proud of the "general list" he'd built in fourteen years at Toronto. He was also proud of the fact that, on $6 million in revenues for 1967, the press earned a 3 percent profit *after* plowing monies back into the scholarly publications fund. He noted tartly that those profits "were astronomical in relation to the parent body's invest-ment in the enterprise." The university's reluctance to invest in UTP became a bitterly sore point with him, especially when rival publishers complained about unfair competition from "subsidized" presses, the pam-pered playthings of public institutions.

In 1957 the president of Maclean-Hunter, Floyd Chalmers, introduced Jeanneret to "the most sensitive, difficult, charming, and successful author it has been my privilege to publish." Armenian-born Yousuf Karsh was eager to produce a coffee-table book of his portraits of the powerful and famous. Jeanneret felt "utterly petrified" by the probable cost, but when he visited Karsh at the photographer's studio in Ottawa's Château Laurier Hotel, they hit it off and signed a contract then and there. UTP would control world publishing rights to the book, and Karsh would retain an artistic right of approval over the photographs.

At a later session to select the contents of *Portraits of Greatness*, Karsh sat on the floor, "kissing adieu to this screen actress and gently calling that actor a bastard as he flicked one picture after another across the room to land on a heap of other culls." The casualties included Ingrid Bergman, Glenn Gould, Adlai Stevenson, Marshal Tito, Herbert von Karajan, and Henry Ford (although many would appear in later books). The portraits Karsh considered acceptable for his first volume ran the gamut from Winston Churchill and Pope John XXIII to George Bernard Shaw and Carl Jung. The engaging text was ghost-written by UTP's editorial staff, using Karsh's anecdotes about the sittings for each portrait.

Karsh's insistence on the highest possible reproduction quality and his indifference to cost regularly gave his publisher the vapours. In that respect, the two were a perfect mismatch; Jeanneret always fretted about going over budget on any UTP book. When Karsh entertained a rival publishing offer from Jack McClelland, he had to be reminded that he was under contract. But that was the least of Jeanneret's problems. Right up to publication day in late 1959, the project seemed dogged by disaster.

First the Canada Council rejected Jeanneret's request for a grant. The deficit Jeanneret feared, however, was covered when Nelson made a commitment to buying editions for the United States and the United Kingdom from a shared print run. Then the fine Dutch printers, Enschedé, almost missed getting finished books across the Atlantic in time for the Christmas season. When the shipment finally arrived in Toronto just before the November 21 publication date, the final and worst calamity occurred. Jeanneret rushed to Eleanor Harman's office to find her weeping over a heap of gorgeously printed black and white portraits, which had tumbled into her lap out of the first copy she opened: the binding didn't hold.

The stress this placed Jeanneret under can only be imagined, but it produced one of his most ingenious strokes as a publisher. He ordered inserted into every copy of *Portraits of Greatness* a handsome, two-page notice printed on deckle-edged art paper, which read, in part: "The reproductions in this book represent a unique achievement in the history of printing . . . A special thermoplastic binding has been used instead of sewing. The volume opens flat and yet shows no unsightly threads. It is also possible to remove, if desired, individual portraits for mounting and framing, without destroying the other contents. Readers are cautioned, however, not to expose the pages to rough handling that might cause separation at the hinge."

Somehow Jeanneret got away with this stratagem, which "came as close to an intentional deception of the public as any of which I have been guilty." Nelson used the same notice with similar results. No review mentioned the defect *as* a defect. The first printing sold out, and when a second printing followed, somehow it lacked the special feature that had made the first unique. In the end, an admiring public bought over 40,000 copies of *Portraits of Greatness* and gobbled up several Karsh sequels from UTP over the next twenty-five years. Jeanneret and Karsh became fast friends; the photographer even named a lane behind his Ottawa property after his publisher.

Yet photographs, however iconic, were not what the University of Toronto Press was supposed to be about. Jeanneret could expect to be remembered by several major editorial projects, the most gargantuan of which had brought him to UTP in the first place.

The *Dictionary of Canadian Biography* has been the longest-running and most expensive publishing project in Canadian history. It remains, by definition, a work in progress; it will not end as long as there is a Canada. As of this writing, it has reached fourteen volumes, covering the lives of eminent Canadians who died up to 1920. It may not be, as Jeanneret claimed, the most ambitious Canadian book project in *every* respect; *The Canadian Encyclopedia*, first published by Mel Hurtig, has its own claim to make. But the *DCB* is unquestionably ambitious and unique, a bilingual expression of Canada's historic duality. Never before have English-language and French-language publishers collaborated so extensively to generate a publication of value to both cultures.

The *DCB*'s current general editor, its fourth, is the historian Ramsay Cook; his counterpart at the Presses de l'université Laval in Quebec City is Jean Hamelin. For three decades, the two presses have cooperated to create the series, which they publish one volume at a time in separate English and French editions. Laval and UTP maintain parallel editorial offices that conduct research into the period spanned by each volume, jointly deciding which lives to include, according to date of death. The two offices then divide up the biographical articles to be commissioned from leading scholars. Each article is written in the language of the author's choice and rigorously checked by both institutions before being copy-edited and translated. How that arrangement came about is a tale in itself; James Nicholson's birdseed fortune was only the beginning.

Shortly after Jeanneret became director, the UTP editor-in-chief, George Brown, conveniently left for Britain on a year's fellowship. On his return, Jeanneret persuaded Sidney Smith to make Brown "honorary editor" of the press with a small honorarium, an arrangement that "left [Brown] at least a toe in publishing." In other words, Jeanneret shunted Brown aside, but with dignity. Yet Brown's passion was history, not publishing, and the two came together in the *DCB*.

The project was in limbo pending Mrs. Nicholson's demise. The widow, then seventy-eight, invited Jeanneret, Brown, and their wives to tea at her Rosedale home; Jeanneret found her a gracious, delightful person and avidly perused her late husband's set of the British *Dictionary of National Biography*, complete with handwritten marginal notes. Shortly afterwards, Mrs. Nicholson wrote to ask what she could do to speed the launch of the *DCB*. She and her husband's executors accepted Jeanneret's proposal that the estate pay her a guaranteed income for life, with the balance of the estate's annual proceeds devoted to work on the dictionary. In 1959 publication plans were announced by the university president, Claude Bissell. George Brown would be the first general editor, an appointment Jeanneret gladly endorsed.

A troubling question was how to fulfill the university's promise that the dictionary would be truly national. Better than most English Canadians of his generation, Jeanneret understood that a mere translation of an English text would be rejected out of hand in Quebec, and a text with a sprinkling of French articles would be denounced as tokenism. He did something he normally avoided: consulted his father, now the university's chancellor and a man with close ties to Quebec. "I think we had better pay a visit to His Eminence," F.C.A. Jeanneret replied.

The two Jeannerets and Brown travelled to Montreal for a two-hour meeting with Paul-Émile Cardinal Léger, conducted entirely in French, at the archbishop's palace. They emerged with the cardinal's blessing and, more crucially, his advice. A small committee was needed, His Eminence told them, consisting of leading scholars representing French Canada's three principal universities at that time – Laval, Montréal, and Ottawa – to plan and orchestrate the project's implementation. Cardinal Léger even proposed the names of three individuals to serve on the committee. All accepted readily.

A year later, the spadework was complete. Université Laval, which since 1950 had operated Quebec's only French-language university press (the University of Ottawa had begun a bilingual press in 1936), committed itself to becoming an equal partner and assuming the heavy financial burden. In 1961, the project's full title became *Dictionary of Canadian Biography/Dictionnaire biographique du Canada*; the historian Marcel Trudel of Laval became *directeur adjoint*. The machinery was set in motion to prepare the first volume, covering the years 1000 to 1700, and after five years of meticulous preparation, it was vice-regally launched at a ceremony in Ottawa in 1966. Mrs. Nicholson, still going strong at ninety, went on her first airplane journey, accompanied by UTP's business manager, Harald Bohne. "Ecstatically" (Jeanneret's term), she presented the first numbered copies of a deluxe edition of volume I to Governor General Vanier, a Laval alumnus.

George Brown had died of a heart attack three years earlier. His work was continued by David M. Hayne, a French professor at the university, who served as general editor from 1965 to 1969. By that point, volume II (1701–1740) was completed, and volumes III and X were well under way. Hayne's successor was Francess Halpenny, who would continue as general editor of the *DCB* until 1989, when she was succeeded by Cook. Halpenny even maintained an apartment in Quebec City, so that she could work more effectively with her colleagues at Laval. Simultaneously she pursued a new but parallel career in librarianship, becoming dean of the University of Toronto Faculty of Library and Information Science in 1972. There she drew on her professional experience to teach courses in Canadian literature, as well as a long-running course on publishing that helped make CanLit activists out of a generation of librarians.

In his memoir, *Halfway up Parnassus*, Claude Bissell described Marsh Jeanneret as "a man committed to success on a grand scale and, in this respect, body and spirit were exact images of each other." Bissell also acknowledged that an essential element in Jeanneret's success was his talent for attracting skilled and committed colleagues. One of the most versatile in a highly versatile group was Harald Bohne.

Over the course of his career, Bohne was successively a librarian, a bookseller, and a publisher. After the war, he worked in the library of U.S.

Army headquarters in his home town of Heidelberg, Germany, immersing himself in English-language literature. Emigrating to Toronto in 1954, he landed a job at the University of Toronto Book Room and began a steady ascent within UTP: bookstore manager to business manager to assistant director to associate director. Before succeeding to the director's position in 1977, Bohne became, wrote Jeanneret, "the business conscience of the Press, as Francess Halpenny had become its editorial conscience."

Jeanneret's description didn't encompass the many services Bohne has rendered to Canada's book community. He was creator in 1967, and first editor, of the essential reference tool *Canadian Books in Print*, which hugely facilitated the business and bibliographic aspects of publishing and bookselling. For the Canadian Booksellers Association, he designed a correspondence course for apprentice booksellers. For neophyte publishers, he co-authored, with his UTP colleague Harry van Ierssel, *Book Publishing: The Creative Business*, a guide that helped many small presses stay on their feet. And as sometime president of both the CBA and the Association of Canadian Publishers, and later as chair of the Book and Periodical Council and the Canadian Copyright Institute, Bohne was an indefatigable campaigner for the causes of writing and publishing.

Jeanneret's description alluded to the role that Bohne played in raising and managing the pool of public funds required to keep massive projects like the *DCB* afloat. Beginning with a $17,000 grant towards the translation costs of volume I, the Canada Council and, after its creation in 1977, the Social Sciences and Humanities Research Council (SSHRC) cumulatively invested millions of dollars in the dictionary. Without assistance on that scale, it would have been impossible for UTP and Laval to continue the *DCB* on any reasonable timetable, since the resources allocated by both institutions were soon spent.

At the same time, the press was conducting other major editorial projects, each with its own degree of complexity. In 1959, when A.S.P. Woodhouse proposed an annotated collection of the works of John Stuart Mill, Jeanneret's first response was interest mixed with alarm: "I found the enormity of the project, whose preliminary blueprint anticipated more than twenty volumes, disquieting." As usual, he worried about where the money would come from, how much of his editors' time the project would consume, how many commercial titles he'd need to pull out of his hat to finance it. On the other hand, Mill's works crossed several disciplines, a fact that, along with Mill's Olympian stature as a political philosopher, guaranteed the project's importance throughout the scholarly world.

In the end, UTP proceeded with the *Collected Works of John Stuart Mill*, beginning with the letters in 1962. Much of the required legwork and textual editing was accomplished by the Victoria College scholar John M. Robson, who would eventually chair the editorial board overseeing the Mill project and became so versed in the ways of the press that he also chaired its publications committee. The Canada Council and later SSHRC contributed materially to offsetting the heavy costs of the series.

Similarly, large dollops of external funding were needed when the press committed itself to an annotated English translation of the fifteenth-century scholar Erasmus, whose collected works number some sixty volumes in medieval Latin. The initiative for that enormous undertaking came from UTP's senior humanities editor, Ron Schoeffel. After determining the level of support for such a project in the scholarly community, Schoeffel and Francess Halpenny submitted "a memo of considerable scope" to Jeanneret for his consideration. Once persuaded of the need, Jeanneret threw his weight behind the project. Financial support for the first five years, starting in 1969, came from the Killam Foundation; in succeeding years, the granting councils contributed over $2 million, based on a twenty-five-year schedule, to defray research, translation, and publishing costs.

Other major projects were less text-based. The *Economic Atlas of Ontario* entailed a nine-year process to plan and produce a huge volume containing 542 maps and 113 colour plates. The atlas posed many intricate design and production challenges and demanded unusually skilled cartography, supplied by Geoffrey Matthews. Jeanneret proudly called it "a masterpiece of book production," a claim borne out by the 1969 gold medal for design at the Leipzig International Book Fair. Another UTP project marrying history with gorgeous design, the *Historical Atlas of Canada*, was published in three volumes beginning in 1987. To date, that high-priced series has sold over 50,000 copies, making it one of the press's all-time top revenue generators. Not strictly a Jeanneret project, it was nevertheless part of his legacy.

A significant aspect of that legacy was the visual attractiveness of the press's books. Jeanneret claimed that UTP was the first Canadian publisher to employ a full-time staff designer, having hired Antje Lingner in 1954. In 1967 the press published a book on graphic design, Carl Dair's *Design with Type*, winner of a medal at the Nice International Book Fair. Dair, who had studied typography in Holland and brought his ideas home to enrich Canadian design through his work and teaching, also created Cartier, the first typeface designed in this country in over a century.

Jeanneret outdid himself in 1968 by hiring Canada's most illustrious graphic designer, Allan Fleming, as chief designer. Fleming, who had created famous logos for Ontario Hydro and Canadian National, had designed the Centennial Year blockbuster photographic book *Canada: A Year of the Land*. He'd been working at MacLaren Advertising but let it be known he would take a salary cut if he could design books full-time. Fleming would stay at UTP until his death nine years later, heading and inspiring an all-star team including Laurie Lewis, Harold Kurschenska, Peter Dorn, and Will Rueter. Jeanneret himself had ambivalent feelings about beautiful books: the aesthete in him wanted to publish them, but the puritan didn't want to pay for them. He once called Fleming's design ideas "unacceptably extravagant." Jeanneret was better able to reconcile himself to the cost of publishing two periodicals about publishing itself, even though both absorbed staff time and other resources.

The first periodical begat the second. *Press Notes*, reporting on current projects and preoccupations at UTP, was born in 1959 out of Jeanneret's penchant "to explain, explain, explain what you were doing," as Francess Halpenny put it, and to expand awareness and recognition of the press's work. Eleanor Harman edited and wrote much of the eight-to-sixteen-page pamphlet. *Press Notes* appeared, with photographs, every two months or so; it was distributed free to authors, faculty members, publishers at home and abroad, and the media. Early articles from *Press Notes* appeared in *The University as Publisher*, an anthology edited by Harman and published to mark the press's diamond anniversary in 1961.

Press Notes attracted so much admiration that Jeanneret saw a demand for a periodical dealing with scholarly publishing at large, "a voice for the whole university press movement." Inevitably Harman ended up as editor of the new quarterly, *Scholarly Publishing*, which debuted in autumn 1969. It boasted an editorial advisory board, chaired by Jeanneret, consisting of distinguished university press directors from around the world. The quarterly soon found acceptance internationally as the authoritative source on the subject. It enlarged Harman's reputation outside the halls of UTP; when she retired in 1975, after forty-five years in publishing, she continued to edit the journal for four more years before turning it over to Ian Montagnes, Halpenny's successor in the editorial department. On Harman's death in 1988, she left her entire estate to support *Scholarly Publishing*.

Marsh Jeanneret inspired admiration, loyalty, and affection in his closest associates. In those who knew him only from a distance, including a majority of his staff, his austere manner inspired something more akin to intimidation. He was always "the Director" or "Mr. Jeanneret," and he practised the opposite of an open-door policy. He was consumed by every aspect of press operations, becoming famous for communicating with colleagues via his "mustard memos," long, single-spaced, dauntingly detailed missives that he typed at top speed on yellow copy paper. "When he had an idea about something," recalled Harald Bohne, "he would write and write and write and think of all the pitfalls, everything that might happen, and then ask you for your comments. When you tried to write back a response, it was awfully hard to find anything that you could add or correct."

According to colleagues who knew him well, Jeanneret's severity was a cover for shyness and social awkwardness. Robin Farr, who had worked under him at Copp Clark and became his good friend, saw him as an introvert who had struggled to emerge from his powerful father's shadow. Jeanneret had adopted his father's august persona, "but underneath it, he was such a warm man." Bohne concurred: "His image was much more conservative than he actually was."

Jeanneret was uncomfortable in public situations demanding spontaneity. As the acknowledged industry expert on copyright, he wrote the publishers' brief to the 1954 federal Royal Commission on Patents, Copyright and Industrial Designs and presented it before the commission with John Gray and W.H. Clarke. When asked by the chair, J.L. Ilsley, why, as intelligent businessmen, they'd entered such an unprofitable industry, Jeanneret became tongue-tied. He was rescued by Gray, who took the floor to declare: "Mr. Chairman, we are in Canadian book publishing because that is the place we wish to be!"

And yet, paradoxically, Jeanneret excelled at networking. In the early 1960s, he helped establish the Canadian presence at the Frankfurt International Book Fair, and he and his staff became heavily involved in the work of the Association of American University Presses, which Jeanneret served as president in 1970. He travelled with AAUP delegations to French West Africa in 1963 and Australia in 1965 to advise on the development of scholarly publishing there. He participated in a 1964 Canadian business mission to the Soviet Union and in Centennial Year hosted the AAUP's annual meeting in Toronto. More than 300 members came from the United States, "the largest assemblage of publishers ever in Canada for any purpose," Jeanneret noted proudly, to participate in panels chaired by UTP staff and to hear Marshall McLuhan inform them, "Clear prose indicates the absence of thought."

Jeanneret's international involvements increased opportunities to co-publish abroad. Above all, they strengthened UTP's presence in the American academic market. The press had begun shipping to American customers through a Brooklyn distributor in 1959 and opened its own office and warehouse in Buffalo, New York, in 1968, the first Canadian publisher to do so. In 1972 Jeanneret convened the founding meeting of the International Association of Scholarly Publishers in Toronto; in 1976 he become its second president.

As *Press Notes* spread the word of Toronto's publishing activities, Jeanneret was increasingly consulted by other Canadian universities about starting presses of their own. The first was McGill University Press, founded in 1960 under the directorship of Robin Farr. McGill was soon publishing a mixture of trade books and academic titles in the university's areas of strength – medicine, law, and Islamic studies – and distributing Yale University Press books. Farr ensured that McGill's titles had a distinctive appearance by employing the gifted West Coast designer Robert R. Reid. After seven years, Farr returned to Toronto to become editor-in-chief at the Ryerson Press and was succeeded by Robin Strachan, Macmillan's college publisher. Under Strachan, the press became McGill-Queen's in 1969, with editorial offices in both Montreal and Kingston.

Farr found Jeanneret and his colleagues exceptionally generous with their time and advice. It was in UTP's own best interests to share the field, since scholarly presses seldom compete in a commercial sense; on the contrary, at a time of tremendous growth in universities and faculties, when professors all over the country were compelled to "publish or perish," the emergence of new presses relieved the pressure. Jeanneret and Eleanor Harman were consulted when the Université de Montréal started its press in 1962, and again when the Universities of Alberta and British Columbia founded theirs in 1969 and 1971 respectively. The University of Manitoba Press had begun in 1967; Wilfrid Laurier University Press would appear in 1974, and the University of Calgary Press in 1981. In 1972, the same year he was nudging the international association into existence, Jeanneret instigated creation of the Association of Canadian University Presses, to which publishers in both language groups belong, and became its founding president.

Most significantly, Marsh Jeanneret fathered Canada's unique system of public support for private-sector publishing. The Ontario Conservative government created the Royal Commission on Book Publishing in December 1970 in response to the American takeovers of Gage and the Ryerson Press. Media attention fell not on Jeanneret but on the commission's other two members: its chair, Richard Rohmer, a lawyer and Tory bagman (but not yet a bestselling novelist), and the advertising executive and Tory backroom organizer Dalton Camp (not yet a respected political columnist). But at the outset Jeanneret was the only one of the three who knew beans about book publishing. He commissioned a book of highly knowledgeable essays on the profession, issued as the royal commission's *Background Papers* in 1972, and ensured that his colleagues asked informed questions during public hearings. Above all, he held the pen on the commission's final report, *Canadian Publishers and Canadian Publishing* (1973), the single most incisive analysis of the subject yet published. Along with the commission's interim reports, that document laid the foundations for three decades of innovative public policy, both federally and provincially, by making a detailed and cogent case for government support.

Jeanneret knew intimately the perils of original Canadian publishing, having spent much of his career financing titles that couldn't subsist on market revenues alone. He'd revealed the gist of his policy ideas in 1969, in a speech marking his second term as president of the Canadian Book Publishers' Council. Under the title "Publishing: A National Responsibility," he championed government support and outlined measures that would in fact be adopted over the next decade. He proposed that the Canada Council provide funding for translation of books between English and French; he favoured direct subsidies for non-commercial titles of cultural value; and he advocated assistance to underwrite collective industry cataloguing, advertising, and distribution. He envisaged "Canadian book centres" in New York, London, and Paris and urged support for publishing education. He even suggested that "we should generate a responsible literature about book publishing in Canada," without clarifying what would constitute an irresponsible literature on the subject.

Some of the royal commission's recommendations bore a distinct resemblance to Jeanneret's earlier proposals. Harald Bohne remembered Jeanneret testing out ideas, such as a loan guarantee program, on senior UTP colleagues. Alone among publishers of his generation (John Gray, for example, was firmly opposed to subsidizing publishers), Jeanneret recognized government support and domestic ownership as essential to the existence of a broad range of Canadian-authored books. It was a question, he'd told his CBPC colleagues, of rendering "a national service": a far cry from the three principles of profit, profit, and profit.

Steering the royal commission and writing its 371-page report, on top of his continuing duties at UTP, nearly killed Marsh Jeanneret. A few months later, in fall 1973, he suffered cardiac troubles that forced him into what appeared to be early retirement. But he couldn't stay away; when he learned that the university would be conducting a thorough study of all UTP operations, he returned to work the next year to deal personally with the committee conducting the study. The report that emerged a year later gratified him by recommending that the university increase its equity in the press, either by investing $1 million or by absorbing the interest on

$1 million of press debt. To Jeanneret's frustration, however, the university acted on the report's administrative ideas only, not its financial ones. He experienced a recurrence of his heart problems, and on his doctor's advice he retired in early 1977, at the age of sixty, leaving the running of UTP to his successor, Harald Bohne.

Jeanneret served as a consultant to the press part-time until he reached sixty-five and began his memoirs; but getting *God and Mammon: Universities as Publishers* to publication proved draining. The research and writing dragged on for several years, and when Bohne finally received the forbiddingly long manuscript, he and Francess Halpenny found it contained far too much material about the printing and bookselling sides of UTP and not nearly enough about publishing. Feeling Jeanneret had been too modest about his own achievements, the two responded with a three-page critique designed to help their former boss revise his manuscript. Instead he withdrew it from the press. Officially it was deemed inappropriate for UTP to publish a book by its recent director; privately Jeanneret was hurt by his old colleagues' lack of enthusiasm. But he did prune the manuscript considerably and, with the discreet assistance of Robin Farr, submitted it to Macmillan of Canada, where the publisher, Linda McKnight, accepted it for publication in 1989.

Marsh Jeanneret died the year after his memoirs were published. He deserves to be honoured as both the founder of Canadian scholarly publishing and the catalyst whose ideas helped release the publishing energy of another generation. In the latter capacity, he made possible the second half of the career of Canada's most spectacular publisher.

McCLELLAND AND GOODCHILD

McCLELLAND, GOODCHILD & STEWART

McCLELLAND & GOODCHILD

McCLELLAND, GOODCHILD & STEWART

McCLELLAND & STEWART

NEW CANADIAN LIBRARY

6

PRINCE OF PUBLISHERS

I am ideally equipped for publishing because I know a little bit – very little, almost nothing in fact – about almost everything.

Jack McClelland (*circa* 1958)

Like Jay Gatsby, he was found in a swimming pool. In his case, no one had pulled the trigger.

The distinguished-looking seventy-four-year-old, whose hair was once described as not white but pewter, had been walking unsteadily beside the pool of his Florida condominium. He'd had too much to drink, and he pitched forward into the water, then began to sink. Luckily a woman saw the incident from her balcony and dialled 911.

By a second stroke of luck, two young women happened by the pool. Diving in, fully clothed, they brought the man to the surface and pulled him over the side. As they were performing artificial respiration, help arrived. Paramedics later estimated he'd been in the pool nearly four minutes. In another thirty seconds, he would have drowned.

Although the man survived, later returning to the pool to swim just to prove he could do it, a long-term consequence of the incident was that he no longer remembered things so well. A short-term consequence was that he couldn't attend a ceremony in his honour held soon afterwards, in November 1996, in Guadalajara, Mexico. The Guadalajara International

Book Fair, feting Canada as the guest nation that year, was paying tribute to him as the outstanding Canadian publisher of his generation. Once again, he was rescued by two women. Jack McClelland's daughters Suzie and Anne accepted the honour on his behalf. McClelland hid out in Toronto, recuperating, profoundly grateful he'd missed the whole thing.

He received all manner of lavish compliments in Guadalajara, some spoken, some written in the bilingual book of homage prepared for the occasion, *Jack McClelland: El editor de la literatura canadiense*. Farley Mowat wrote of Jack's "magnificent elan even in dire adversity." Pierre Berton declared, "Every writer in Canada, old and young, is in his debt." The novelist Aritha van Herk called him "a trickster" for whom "we would do anything." Leonard Cohen contributed a poem lovingly recalling Jack's "gallantry in the face of overwhelming odds" and extolling him as "the real Prime Minister of Canada." His fellow publisher Anna Porter dubbed him "the Prince of Publishers . . . the most successful, the most colourful, certainly the most persistent and imaginative publisher to have erupted onto the world stage."

The mythic McClelland was on abundant display. But the guest of honour missed it all, and a good party too. It would likely have been too much for him anyway, and all too far in the past. Problems with his hearing and eyesight made it damned difficult to hold a conversation any more, much less address a crowd. For a man who'd always been the centre of the action, Prince Jack would be strangely content with second-hand accounts of those tributes to an unparalleled career.

In the summer of 1947, twenty-five-year-old Jack McClelland lit out from Toronto for the west in search of Canadian literature. The trip was his father's idea: if Jack was to be a publisher, he needed to broaden his professional horizons, introduce himself to the book trade, discover a Canada he barely knew. Accompanying him was his wife, Elizabeth, and they travelled in style, behind the wheel of the first Ford convertible to roll off the Oakville, Ontario, assembly line after the war.

His father, John McClelland, a self-made man who'd married late, was already seventy when Jack drove west, old enough to remember watching the troops leave Toronto's Union Station to fight Louis Riel. John McClelland had gone to work in the Methodist Book Room and Publishing House at fourteen. His own father, an Irish immigrant, had been an alcoholic, and young John had left school to support the family; he'd remain an abstainer all his life.

After sixteen years in the trade, latterly as manager of library sales for the Methodist Book Room, John co-founded McClelland & Goodchild with his colleague Frederick Goodchild in 1906. The firm distributed books from Doubleday and other publishers, mainly to libraries. After welcoming George Stewart as a partner in 1913, it became McClelland, Goodchild & Stewart and added Dent, Cassell, and Dodd, Mead to its catalogue. Stewart brought with him his slogan from Oxford, "The Devil weeps when he sees Bibles sold as cheap as these." In 1918, the company became McClelland & Stewart, after an incident involving Goodchild, liquor, and scantily clad women – on a Sunday.

Enjoying record sales during the First World War, M&S moved from Adelaide Street to Victoria Street and doubled its office space. John McClelland's own slogan was "Late to bed, and late to rise / Hustle all day and advertise." The firm branched into publishing Canadians such as Lucy Maud Montgomery, Ralph Connor, Bliss Carman, and Frederick Philip Grove. But M&S curtailed its domestic program during the Depression as the partners repurchased, with painful slowness, the half interest in their company that had been sold to the British firm Cassell to finance their expansion. In 1935 they arranged to manage the Canadian branch of Dent as a hedge against further hard times.

After Jack's graduation from the private St. Andrew's College, John McClelland steered his only son into science and engineering at the University of Toronto. The elder McClelland knew that publishing was no business for a young man with prospects. In addition, he'd acquired as junior partners two no-nonsense Baptists, Wilfred Ford and George Nelson, who didn't believe in taking unnecessary risks on Canadian books. To discourage nepotism, the four partners had agreed that none of their children should enter the firm. It was planned that Jack would go on to Osgoode Hall Law School and a comfortable life, but before that fate could befall him, war intervened.

Leaving the University of Toronto for the navy, he was posted to St. John's and revelled in the drama of his new existence, especially after receiving a command of his own. At sea he was captain of the ship, ashore a handsome young naval officer with an air of danger about him. He volunteered aboard a Canadian flotilla of motor torpedo boats, small craft that dashed about under cover of darkness and torpedoed enemy ships, unless surprised in the English Channel by their nemesis, the deadlier German E-boats. The MTBs' mortality rate offered worse odds than book publishing: before the war was over, eight of the sixteen Canadian MTBs would be blown up, and many of Jack's young comrades would be dead. But Captain "Jake" McClelland's command wouldn't be among the missing, despite the daring raids it undertook. "I lived every day as if it was the last," he remembered. "I had fun all the bloody time."

After the war, McClelland married Elizabeth Matchett and finished off a B.A. at Toronto. In 1946, as John Gray was about to succeed to the top post at Macmillan, a notice appeared in *Canadian Bookseller* magazine: "John McClelland, Jr. has recently joined the staff of McClelland and Stewart, Toronto . . . and now plans to follow his father's footsteps in book publishing." The situation had changed at M&S. Ford and Nelson had left in 1944 to establish the Canadian branch of the Literary Guild, and John McClelland was eager to have his son alongside him in the firm.

During his swing across the west, Jack hosted small gatherings of booksellers, librarians, and academics, meeting authors such as W.O. Mitchell in Alberta and Roderick Haig-Brown in British Columbia. But in recollection, he always dwelled on one special encounter: his introduction to Gabrielle Roy. Roy's first novel, *Bonheur d'occasion*, had been a critical and commercial sensation on publication in Montreal. Just two months before the McClellands' trip, the English version had appeared to acclaim in Canada and the United States as *The Tin Flute*; by the end of its first year, it would sell nearly 14,000 copies for M&S. A monthly selection of the Literary Guild, it would win the Governor General's Award (in the English translation, since the awards were then unilingual) and the Prix Fémina in France.

Gabrielle Roy's status as an M&S author was reason enough for McClelland to meet her, but when he drove from Winnipeg's Fort Garry

Hotel to her home in St. Boniface, he was swept off his feet. Still unmarried, Roy was thirteen years older than McClelland. They drove together through the Manitoba countryside while she told him about her life, her prairie upbringing, and her extensive European travels. Over forty years later, McClelland wrote, "I would have to say that I fell instantly in love."

The rush of emotion posed no threat to his marriage, he hastened to add, even though he saw in Roy "an ethereal beauty that never showed up in photographs." His would be an idealized devotion, practised from afar. Still, Roy's vivacity and intellectual sophistication captivated him; she had a quality that her biographer, François Ricard, has described as an "aura of freedom about her entire person." McClelland would publish twelve more of Roy's books in translation, almost her entire oeuvre in book form. She was among those writers he saw as gifted and exceptional beings, and over the course of their friendship, which would last until her death in 1983, McClelland believed Roy "taught me more about writing and life than anyone else along the way."

Gabrielle Roy was a harbinger of the social changes stirring in post-war Canada. But staid M&S was still very much Jack's father's creation: a company that cozily styled itself "The Home of Good Books" and earned most of its revenue from agency titles. Officially the firm maintained the teetotal, anti-smoking policy John McClelland had laid down in 1906; he was a man who didn't hesitate to walk up to strange women on the street and tell them to butt out their cigarettes. George Stewart, who used to irritate Jack by calling him "sonny boy," was "the party guy," McClelland remembered. If guests wanted liquor at an M&S function, "Stewart would take them away from Dad into a private office and give them a drink."

Jack began serving liquor openly at company events when his father wasn't present. Around that time, Robert Weaver attended what he believed was the first M&S drinking party. At a hotel in London, Ontario, where a Canadian Authors Association convention was taking place, McClelland corralled Weaver, William Arthur Deacon of the *Globe and Mail*, and some University of Western Ontario professors for "a riotous party" that lasted late into the night.

In later years, Jack McClelland's favourite metaphor for book publishing would be the man in the rose garden. The man wanders through a bewitching garden in the moonlight, drifting through the shadows, breathing in the perfume of roses. Then he steps on the head of a rake, which springs up and cracks him on the head. In 1947 Gabrielle Roy was the rose garden, Doubleday the rake.

Ford and Nelson, whose move to the Literary Guild had been financed by Doubleday, now announced they were setting up Doubleday Canada, removing agency revenues built into the foundations of M&S for decades. More than any other event, that blow made a Canadian publisher out of Jack McClelland. If the company was to have any solidity in the future, he concluded, it couldn't depend on foreign publishers. He determined to do something seldom tried before: putting original Canadian trade books at the heart of the operation.

That meant discovering new authors for a new era. If they were out there, McClelland was sure to find them; energetic, charming, and open-minded, he was eager to take risks and easily bored. His formal education and professional training had been somewhat perfunctory, and he'd often rely on intuition in choosing what to publish. When he read the manuscript of the poet Earle Birney's picaresque novel *Turvey* in 1949, McClelland responded with gleeful recognition to the subject matter – Canadians at war – and to the author's satirical, ribald treatment of it.

Even as McClelland and Birney battled by letter over the permissible degree of raunchiness in the soldiers' dialogue, Jack, who cursed as if he'd never left the navy, was fighting for the novel within the house. He let Birney know he had to slip the final version past "certain parties" to get it into print. Publisher and author sparred over usage: "fug," as in Norman Mailer's recent bestseller, *The Naked and the Dead*, versus "buck"; "crunt" versus "gunt"; "b-lls" versus "b —." Society's will to censor was still strong, and would be for another decade and more, until court rulings in the United States and Canada cleared *Ulysses*, *Tropic of Cancer*, and *Lady Chatterley's Lover* for sale.

McClelland's championing of *Turvey* was vindicated by the market-place. M&S printed 5,000 copies, sold them all in three weeks, and moved another 2,000 in the next six months. In spite of Birney's recurring fits of pique – he often complained about real and imagined deficiencies in his contracts, royalty payments, and the promotion of his books – M&S

continued to publish him over the years. Loyalty to his major authors would become a McClelland trademark, along with his blithe imperiousness and irrepressible sense of humour. He once apologized to Birney for losing his temper in their correspondence but added, "Even though the letter may have been rude and unjustified, I still feel that it was an excellent piece of work, and I am proud of it. It is one of the few letters of its type that I have written for posterity . . . Cheers!"

Jack McClelland took charge of M&S in 1952, the year he turned thirty. The company had scheduled only eleven Canadian titles that year. John McClelland Sr. remained president, and his signature was still mandatory on cheques over a certain amount, but at seventy-six he was leaving day-to-day management and long-term planning to his son. The company – and Canadian publishing – would never be the same again.

Sybil Hutchinson had resigned as editor-in-chief two years earlier, unhappy with the young heir's incursions. And in 1951 the general manager, Robert Nelson, had suffered a stroke, which, McClelland would later acknowledge, "made it much easier for me to take over." He put a hard-headed business plan in front of his father. They should consolidate the company offices (since 1948 M&S had shared space with Dent on Bloor Street, across from Varsity Stadium, in addition to keeping the Victoria Street premises). They should drop unprofitable agency lines, dispose of unsaleable inventory, reduce staff, thin the ranks of management, but – in a characteristic statement of priorities – not touch editorial or promotion budgets.

M&S joined the Toronto middle class in moving to the suburbs. Staff were reunited in a one-storey, flat-roofed headquarters dubbed Hollinger House, in the new industrial part of East York. Under the headline "Eastward Ho for McClelland & Stewart," a reporter in the March 1953 *Quill & Quire* waxed lyrical after a guided tour of the premises: "Surely it would give anyone a lift, a new outlook and an added zest to be working in the beautiful new offices and warehouse . . . at 25 Hollinger Road . . . The whole place has an air of cheerful tranquillity which is conducive to concentration."

The reporter's tour revealed the firm's five directors all at their posts: white-haired, mustachioed Mr. McClelland Sr., beaming in his large corner office; young Mr. McClelland in a windowed office beside the sample room; genial George Stewart looking across his desk at a portrait of His late Majesty, George V; Mark Savage, educational sales manager; and the trade sales manager, Hugh Kane, who was "discovered learning the intricacies of a brand-new piece of equipment," a Dictaphone. Under the new order, Kane was already Jack McClelland's right hand. The comrades-in-arms had ousted the older executives Robert Nelson, George Foster, and John Scott and were busy transforming the forty-seven-year-old firm from "The Home of Good Books" into what would become "The Canadian Publishers."

Kane, born in Belfast, had joined M&S in 1936, leaving to serve in the army in 1941 and returning in 1946. As a salesman he'd covered the country many times and knew all the booksellers and librarians, but he also brought to the firm a pragmatism that counterbalanced McClelland's impulsiveness. Eleven years older than his boss, Kane looked even more senior because his hair had prematurely turned white. Like McClelland, he was a dedicated smoker and drinker, and they shared an outspokenness, a reluctance to suffer fools, and a love of laughter.

McClelland, who already owned a quarter of the company, purchased the balance of his father's shares in 1955 for $30,000, giving him 51 percent. George Stewart died that same year at seventy-nine, and Jack would arrange to buy his 49 percent for $65,000. But it would take him some time to pay for Stewart's shares; he received help from Savage and Kane, who both agreed to forgo part of their salaries in return for a minority interest in the company. Kane received 24 percent of M&S: a bit of financial security for the future, he thought, and an incentive and reward for his hard work.

M&S wasn't yet an author's first choice for publishing a trade book in Canada. An up-and-comer named Pierre Berton didn't consider *any* Toronto publisher worth approaching in 1953 when he sent a 25,000-word outline for his first book to Willis Kingsley Wing, the New York agent who acted for Robertson Davies and Berton's boss, Ralph Allen, editor of *Maclean's*. Wing submitted the proposal for *The Royal Family: The Story of the British Monarchy from Victoria to Elizabeth* to the distinguished

American publisher Alfred A. Knopf, who told Berton, "You write like an angel," and accepted the book for the following year.

Berton would have preferred Macmillan to handle the book at home, since he considered John Gray "certainly the pre-eminent publisher in Canada," but his contract stuck him with Knopf's agent, M&S. "So I went to see these unknown people. I hadn't even met Jack," Berton recalled. He was impressed by the young CEO, who took one look at the Knopf jacket design, declared, "This looks like *The Funeral Directors' Annual*," and tore it off the book. McClelland ordered a more buyer-friendly jacket for the Canadian market, and he and Berton were off to one of the most enduring and lucrative collaborations in Canadian publishing.

McClelland's other big "discovery" of the early 1950s also arrived via one of the company's American agencies. Farley Mowat had published his first book, *People of the Deer*, with Little, Brown, but McClelland issued Mowat's next book, *The Regiment*, under the M&S imprint in 1955. When the publisher met his author for the first time, he found in Mowat "a brashness, even an abrasiveness that might not have appealed to everyone." But it appealed to him. The two war veterans were combative, manic in their high spirits; both loved sailing and drinking, and they became such fast friends that, according to McClelland, Mowat once asked him to break the news to his first wife that he was ending their marriage. "To hell with that," McClelland replied. "There's a limit to what a publisher will do for his author."

Their friendship had few other limits, to judge by *The Boat Who Wouldn't Float*, Mowat's hilarious comic-opera account of their sodden attempts to sail an old South Shore bummer (a type of two-masted schooner) in the waters off Newfoundland. Like the *Happy Adventure*, the friendship sometimes ran aground but never sank. On one occasion, McClelland severed their publishing relationship when wounded by some drunken insult, but Mowat couldn't remember uttering it, so they made up and carried on.

Mowat was McClelland's accomplice in subverting the firm's strait-laced customs. On M&S's fiftieth anniversary in 1956, McClelland feared the worst: the anniversary dinner would be deadly dull, he told Mowat, bone-dry "out of deference to Dad." McClelland egged on Mowat to crash the party, since "it is typical of the cheap, mean, one-horse policy of the firm that we haven't even invited any authors to the dinner." He urged Mowat to rhyme off the chronic complaints of the aggrieved author: "I think you could say that all your early dealings were with me, but that you had always suspected that there must be someone more intelligent behind the scenes – that eventually this led to meeting Mr. Stewart, who was very friendly and reassuring and patted you on the back, but called you Sonny Boy because he obviously couldn't remember your name; and Mr. McClelland, who was dignified and reserved but who revolted you by pulling some dirty-looking seaweed, which he called dulse, out of his coat pocket and insisting that you eat it (I don't know whether he has ever done this to you, but if he hasn't you haven't lived)."

When the historic evening arrived, Mowat was smuggled into the Fantasy Farm dining room in Toronto's Don Valley, armed with a bottle of rum and hidden under the dry bar. With the speeches about to begin, Mowat leaped out and declaimed before the startled diners, "I am here to speak for the rights of injured authors!" In one hand he gripped the bottle, in the other a Mills hand grenade from the Second World War, with the detonator missing. "Mr. McClelland, you've got thirty seconds to make amends!"

The Mowat caper notwithstanding, Jack customarily showed great respect for his father, warmly welcoming him on his visits to the office and tolerating his habit of hiding the ashtrays. The author and editor John Robert Colombo, who freelanced extensively for M&S, remembered, "Jack wouldn't hear a harsh word" about McClelland Sr. Jack's former employee and long-time friend Beverley Slopen, later a literary agent, recalled, "Jack always treated him with great affection." Eventually it was no longer necessary to get his father's signature on large cheques. It had bothered the old gentleman when Jack asked him to sign blank ones.

Once termed "the perfect publisher" by H.L. Mencken, Alfred Knopf had become a legend after founding his New York firm in 1915. His backlist included Thomas Mann, Albert Camus, and Jean-Paul Sartre. "I learned more from Alfred than I ever learned from my father," McClelland would say years later. "I considered him to be the best publisher in the United States, if not in the world. He led a very special life."

An elegant gentleman with a flourishing moustache, Knopf took Jack under his wing. When McClelland visited Knopf at his office at 57th Street and Fifth Avenue, he'd be ushered in ahead of other people. Knopf invited Jack to spend weekends at his country house at Purchase, New York, where they drove together in the back seat of a chauffeured Rolls-Royce, talking books and writers. "Alfred knew everything there was to know about authors. I learned a lot from him about how to read a manuscript, what to look for, how to deal with writers. He was serious, very intelligent. He could laugh. He was just a remarkable guy."

Knopf's wife, Blanche, and son, Alfred Jr., known as Pat, both worked in the firm. But Pat subsequently broke with his father to start a rival firm, Atheneum, which M&S also distributed, and Knopf may have seen in McClelland a surrogate son open to tutelage. For McClelland, Knopf was a paragon of taste and judgment, issuing distinguished authors under his Borzoi Books imprint. Knopf openly disdained the commercial writers on his list who made the real money, calling Irving Wallace and Harold Robbins "hacks." When the Knopfs finally elected to cash out by merging their company with Random House in 1960, McClelland lost yet another agency – the most desirable, in his eyes, if not the most profitable – but he continued to set his sights on becoming a Canadian Knopf.

An element of mentorship also existed in McClelland's relationship with Malcolm Ross, who'd been one of his favourite professors at the University of Toronto. When Jack had asked for advice about what to read, Ross had steered him towards Canadian authors. Now Ross pitched his idea for a paperback series of the best in Canadian literature to his former student. Where John Gray had recoiled, McClelland plunged in. "I seemed to convince him," Ross recalled, "that such a series would *create* a market in the universities and schools of the country."

Ross would act as general editor of the New Canadian Library, as the series came to be known, selecting titles in consultation with McClelland and writing or commissioning critical introductions to each book. McClelland was under no illusion that the series would make either of them rich. In a 1955 letter declaring his intent to proceed, "sink or swim," he told Ross candidly, "The one great difficulty that we see now is that there doesn't seem to be a hell of a lot of money in it for anybody . . . It will mean damn little remuneration for you in relation to the effort involved. In view of this, you may want to chuck the whole thing." As a tenured professor, Ross had no problem with the economics; it was McClelland who would bear the financial risk.

McClelland explained to Ross that NCL titles would have to retail at one dollar. A royalty of 7 percent would be split between author and editor, each of whom would receive the princely advance of $100. Initial orders totalled only 300 copies for each of the first four titles, and McClelland didn't proceed with releasing the books until further sales efforts upped the orders to 1,800. Frederick Philip Grove's *Over Prairie Trails*, Morley Callaghan's *Such Is My Beloved*, Stephen Leacock's *Literary Lapses*, and Sinclair Ross's overlooked 1941 novel, *As for Me and My House*, launched the NCL in 1958, bearing 1957 publication dates. Four more titles followed, by Gabrielle Roy, Thomas Chandler Haliburton, Charles G.D. Roberts, and Hugh MacLennan, and a steady stream thereafter. McClelland tried to include as many popular M&S authors as possible; in the years before CanLit was considered a legitimate subject for study, Leacock's sales helped keep the series afloat. There were also early appearances by books not originally published by M&S, mainly from Macmillan authors such as Callaghan, MacLennan, Ethel Wilson, and Gwethalyn Graham.

Ultimately Ross and McClelland were proved right. For the next generation, the NCL underpinned a host of undergraduate Canadian literature courses, a growth industry in Canadian literary studies at the graduate level, even a presence for Canadian literature in high schools. A title's inclusion in the series came to confer quasi-canonical status; the critical introductions stimulated further study and debate. The critic W.J. Keith asserted, "The founding of the series represented a crucial step – I would say *the* crucial step – in demonstrating the existence of a mature Canadian literature and in making possible its extensive study in schools and universities."

But the fulfillment of that dream took at least twenty years. If the NCL eventually turned out to be, as McClelland said, "one of the more profitable things we did," that was simply an incentive to keep it growing.

In the end the NCL's quirks, omissions, and flawed choices, noted by critics, were less important than its ability to keep many significant works in print. It also prodded other publishers into starting paperback series: the Laurentian Library, published (ironically) by Macmillan; Clarke, Irwin's Canadian Paperbacks; University of Toronto Press's Canadian University Paperbooks; General Publishing's PaperJacks and New Press Canadian Classics; Penguin's Canadian fiction reprints. No longer an esoteric pursuit, Canadian literature parachuted into the academic marketplace on McClelland's leap of faith.

There would be further bold moves during the 1950s and '60s. To liberate money and energy for his Canadian trade list, McClelland amputated whole limbs of the business his father and George Stewart had built.

Jack once conceded that "all the profit in Canadian book publishing was in the educational field." When his father had contracted to manage Dent in 1935, M&S had pledged not to compete with the British firm in the Canadian schoolbook market. But in 1956 McClelland informed Dent he'd decided to enter that market himself. Accordingly, Dent took back all its educational business and its trade representation as well, including the lucrative Everyman's Library series.

M&S launched its own schoolbook program, which would consist mainly of English literature and composition texts for high schools, along with some textbooks in geography and Canadian history. Over the years, McClelland employed highly capable staff to develop el-hi and college programs (Mark Savage, Jim Totton, Paul Audley, Peter Milroy, and James Marsh, among others), but his heart simply wasn't in education; he kept diverting resources to the trade side. As Robin Farr, who worked briefly for McClelland, later observed, "Jack never understood educational publishing and had little interest in it, which was a great pity. He paid so little attention to what was a money-maker for the company. [Otherwise] I'm sure some of his financial problems could have been avoided."

Severing the Dent connection presaged even bigger and more fateful steps towards independence. M&S's growing trade program was still dwarfed by its numerous agency lists. Jim Douglas, who began selling M&S

across the west in 1958, remembered he had to carry "these great stacks of agency catalogues, and the Canadian lists were like little pimples, which you tackled at the end." But with the arrival of the 1960s, the M&S trade list expanded rapidly, and soon Douglas was starting off his sales calls with the Canadian books. In 1960 M&S's output jumped from nineteen original titles to thirty, including first novels by Margaret Laurence and Marie-Claire Blais. The next year, thirty-eight titles appeared, among them Leonard Cohen's *The Spice-Box of Earth*, Irving Layton's poetry and short-fiction collection *The Swinging Flesh*, future Liberal finance minister Walter Gordon's *Troubled Canada*, and Stanley Knowles's *The New Party* (as the NDP was first called).

In 1962 Hugh Kane recruited Douglas to work in Toronto as M&S sales and marketing director. From personal experience, Douglas knew that the burden of selling the Canadian and imported catalogues together had become unmanageable. He remembered telling Kane, "You're overloading your travellers. You're going to need two different sales forces, one for the agencies and one for the Canadian books." It was either that, Douglas argued, or get rid of agencies. He leaned towards the latter solution. Kane agreed. So did McClelland, and in 1963 M&S surprised the trade by dropping twenty-three of its twenty-eight agency lines. Only the strongest and swiftest remained: Little, Brown; Van Nostrand Reinhold; Lippincott; Dodd, Mead; and Atheneum.

The Canadian program more than doubled in the six years leading up to the Centennial, hitting eighty-one titles in 1967. Meanwhile overall company revenues swelled from $1.5 million to over $5 million. To some extent, the growth resulted from Centennial fever, but Canada was also producing a whole new generation of writers, a great many of whom published with M&S, and the program's momentum would roll on steadily beyond Centennial Year. Its significance lay not in quantity alone but in the radical shift in publishing priorities.

There is no more renowned motto in the trade than McClelland's "We publish authors, not books." He had first expressed a conscious sense of national purpose to the historian W.L. Morton as far back as 1956, when proposing the multi-volume national history that became known as the Canadian Centenary Series. "I think this history is needed," he told

Morton, "for the same reason that we needed railways in this country; that we needed a Canadian Broadcasting Corporation and a National Film Board. None of the foregoing are any more commercially feasible than the history, but they are not any the less important because of it." M&S adopted the epithet "The Canadian Publishers" around 1962 to accompany its logo of Apollo in his chariot.

There were casualties of McClelland's nationalism. M&S held agency rights to *Canada Made Me*, Norman Levine's 1958 account of a rough journey he'd made across the country, which portrayed Canadians as complacent and parochial. But McClelland didn't publish a separate edition of *Canada Made Me* under the M&S imprint, as he had six years earlier with Levine's war novel, *The Angled Road*. In fact, he made little effort to promote it at all, despite the book's potential for controversy. He told Levine, "I don't think the book is honest from the standpoint of Canada; that is to say, I don't think it presents a fair or valid picture of this country."

McClelland had a dramatically different response to three writers he published shortly afterwards: Sheila Watson, Irving Layton, and Patricia Blondal.

Watson's novel *The Double Hook* had already been rejected by Macmillan. McClelland asked Earle Birney to read her manuscript, which was experimental for its time, and Birney responded with an ambivalent letter in which he called it "a remarkable piece of writing" and "a stylistic *tour de force*," yet also "monotonous, self-conscious, artificial and lacking in real fictional interest." McClelland decided to publish anyway in 1959. In time Watson's novel acquired such iconic status that it became one of the few books in any country to have a bookstore named after it. As the critic Frank Davey noted, *The Double Hook* is considered by many to be "the first truly modern Canadian novel."

Although he always disclaimed any expertise in poetry, McClelland did some adventurous and important publishing in the genre. The Indian File series ran from 1948 to 1958, featuring hardcover volumes by nine poets, among them James Reaney, P.K. Page, Phyllis Webb, and John Glassco. In 1959 McClelland published a far more substantial collection, Layton's richly sensual *A Red Carpet for the Sun*. With its powerful emotional range, accessible technique, and flaunting of sexuality rare for its time, the book broke Layton out of the confines of literary small-press circles. McClelland spent heavily on promotion, launching the book at parties in Montreal and Toronto and creating a new Canadian phenomenon, the poet as public figure. June Callwood assisted the process with her profile of Layton, "The Lusty Laureate from the Slums," in the *Star Weekly*. *Red Carpet* achieved astonishing popularity for a poetry title, selling 8,000 copies and carrying off a Governor General's Award.

McClelland's reaction to Patricia's Blondal's novel *A Candle to Light the Sun* typified his instinctual response to writers. A complete stranger to McClelland, Blondal called to say she was arriving the next day from Montreal to reclaim her manuscript, which had been sitting in the slush pile unread. She seemed particularly impatient to get published. His curiosity aroused, McClelland dug out the manuscript for a quick look, and three hours after closing time, he was still in his office reading. He became so absorbed that he didn't arrive home until 3 in the morning, elated, convinced he'd made a major discovery: "It was the first truly gutsy, tough Canadian novel that I had ever seen."

Meeting Blondal for lunch at the Royal York clinched the matter. The thirty-two-year-old writer struck McClelland as "articulate, intelligent, and, as a plus, extremely beautiful . . . I was absolutely enchanted and decided to publish her novel at the earliest possible date. I offered to marry her, too, if that was a requirement, but I pointed out that I would have to get permission from my wife."

His spontaneous promise to publish Blondal earned a reprimand from Hugh Kane, who chided him about reneging on an agreement to make no commitments without prior consultation with Kane and the senior trade editor, Claire Pratt. But McClelland held to his high opinion of the manuscript: "My view is that she is easily the best novelist that has come to my attention in Canada in years. She has the vigour, the power and the flow, and the eye for significant detail that has been one of the prime lacks in Canadian writing to date." The exchange shows that McClelland knew what he was looking for in fiction. But he soon learned the reason Blondal was pressing so hard to be published: she had been diagnosed with advanced breast cancer. She would die later that year, before M&S could bring out *A Candle to Light the Sun*. The novel was edited by Joyce Marshall, herself a gifted fiction writer, before being released in 1960.

When McClelland first met Leonard Cohen, the twenty-five-year-old exerted a similarly electric influence. "Such was the charm of the very young Leonard Cohen," McClelland recalled in an outline of his un-published memoir, "My Rose Garden," that after skim-reading a few pages of manuscript, he decided, "OK, we're going to publish this guy. I don't give a shit whether the poetry's any good." For insurance, he had Layton's opinion that his young friend was a marvellous poet.

The designer Frank Newfeld's treatment for the 1961 edition of *The Spice-Box of Earth* featured French flaps, a lush black paper cover with flowing gold script, and an image of the author peering darkly through a die-cut rectangle. As in his design for Layton's *Red Carpet*, Newfeld created a powerful visual aura around the author. The poems were printed on heavy creamy stock, embellished with drawings by Newfeld that reflected Cohen's amalgam of sacrament and voluptuous hedonism. There was something a touch decadent about the production, something distinctly *de trop*. It was brilliant packaging, serving to establish Cohen as the next big Canadian writer long before he'd recorded his first album of songs.

With *Spice-Box* still in production, Cohen mailed McClelland a draft of his first novel. McClelland sent it back with suggestions for revision. He didn't want to rush Cohen's fiction into print prematurely, he said, and it wouldn't be doing the author any favour to publish *The Favourite Game* as it stood. ("A protracted love-affair with himself," one M&S reader had called it.) When he wrote Cohen later to inquire about the manuscript, the author replied from London that it was already sold: "I will always consider you my publisher and I will never forget the wonderful treatment you gave my book of poems and as far as possible I will always come to you first. But I just signed away Commonwealth rights to Secker and Warburg."

When Cohen's next collection of poems, *Flowers for Hitler*, was ready, he sent it to McClelland first. He also gave M&S first crack at Canadian rights to his novel *Beautiful Losers* while it was under consideration by Viking. The novel was so unusual that eight reports were needed before the New York firm decided to publish; one of Viking's readers dubbed it

"Canada with the Maple Leaf snatched off . . . rich and raunchy, terrifying and funny." McClelland worried about being hauled up in court on obscenity charges but told Cohen that *Beautiful Losers* was "marvellously well written, and at the same time appalling, shocking, revolting, disgusting, sick and just maybe it's a great novel." McClelland anxiously consulted no fewer than four critics, Claude Bissell, Northrop Frye, Kildare Dobbs, and Robert Weaver, about the advisability of publication, just as he would consult Robertson Davies a decade later about the wisdom of publishing Marian Engel's *Bear*. Both times, he forged ahead. "All I have to decide now," he wrote Cohen, "is whether I love you enough to want to spend the rest of my days in jail because of you."

Beautiful Losers was published in 1966, this time with jacket art by Harold Town. Canadian sales were disappointing; the original hardcover edition sold only about a thousand copies in its first season. But in other respects, McClelland was prophetic: the book is recognized today as a brilliantly representative novel of the 1960s. McClelland continued to defend the novel to all comers, including Malcolm Ross, who refused his publisher's entreaties to include it in the New Canadian Library. *Beautiful Losers* didn't enter the NCL until 1991, after the critic David Staines had succeeded Ross as general editor of the series.

McClelland fought hard for his writers, even as he fought with them, but at times his loyalty was severely tested. Although he held Irving Layton in high esteem, he acknowledged that "it was difficult for anybody to get close to Irving because he would start reciting poetry at you, crazy bugger." In 1977, having published nineteen of Layton's books, McClelland hosted a surprise party for the poet's sixty-fifth birthday at Casa Loma in Toronto, attended by the city's literary and media elite. In gratitude, Layton called McClelland "a beautiful soul." But three years later, Layton infuriated him by jumping ship to bring out a new collection, *For My Neighbours in Hell*, with little Mosaic Press in Oakville. Finally McClelland wrote the matter off to the poet's unbridled ego and continued publishing him.

McClelland's raw language and barroom candour were legendary. Sometimes he had his tongue in his cheek, sometimes he meant every word. Either way, it was a sailor's code for intimacy, and a code he used almost exclusively with men. With women authors, he was more likely to be courtly, solicitous, and protective.

McClelland had no warmer or more lasting professional relationship than with Margaret Laurence. After reading the manuscript of her first novel, *This Side Jordan*, in 1959, he was sufficiently impressed to make Laurence an offer, conditional on finding a co-publisher in the United States or the United Kingdom. Rache Lovat Dickson at Macmillan shared McClelland's enthusiasm; they were joined by St. Martin's Press in New York after Knopf rejected the novel. Having been the catalyst for launching Laurence's career, McClelland wanted to oversee its advancement. He set Laurence up with a literary agent, providing her with an advocate for her financial interests while also benefiting M&S by enhancing her marketability abroad. After Laurence separated from her husband and moved to London with her children in 1962, McClelland wrote to his author Mordecai Richler, asking him to befriend a fellow Canadian writer. When Laurence's second novel, *The Stone Angel*, wasn't chosen for the 1964 Governor General's Award, McClelland exclaimed he was "mad as hell," even though the winning novel, Douglas LePan's *The Deserter*, had also been published by M&S.

McClelland had enormous faith in Laurence's talent. He told her in 1968, "You are the only writer I know who improves with each successive manuscript," and he called her "Canada's greatest novelist." Yet he wasn't uncritical: while applauding the strengths of *The Fire-Dwellers* in manuscript, he put his finger on what he considered the novel's soft spot and urged Laurence to eliminate it. Five years later, after he'd stayed up until 4 in the morning reading the manuscript of *The Diviners* and "ended up in tears during the last half hour," he extolled it to the skies, yet itemized a dozen aspects of the novel that needed revising.

In London Laurence was taken up by Alan Maclean, Dickson's successor at Macmillan. It was to Maclean, not her Canadian publisher, that she submitted an early draft of "Hagar," which would become *The Stone Angel*. Maclean was planning to bring out three of her books when McClelland wrote in alarm to Laurence, like a jealous suitor: "What in hell goes on at Macmillan's? Have they gone completely berserk? They are rushing the short stories into print. They are rushing the novel into print . . . Even if you were the second coming of Christ it would be foolish to publish three of your books in one season."

Laurence's reply was at once angry, funny, and poignant. "I resented your remark about the second coming of Christ so much that it was very fortunate for both of us that you were not present at the time, otherwise I would have clobbered you with the nearest solid object available. I do not imagine that HAGAR is without flaws, nor am I so lacking in critical perception that I delude myself about the quality of my writing . . . Please, Jack, do not ever imagine that I am at this point over-estimating my own abilities. My problem has always been the reverse."

Laurence's next vote of confidence came from the publisher who'd rejected her first book. Receiving three Laurence manuscripts from her agent, Alfred Knopf took the unprecedented step of publishing them all on the same day in 1964. Subsequently Laurence's fiction would be edited by a Knopf-M&S-Macmillan triad. The three-way arrangement typified McClelland's dealings with such internationally published novelists as Brian Moore, Mordecai Richler, and Margaret Atwood. M&S acquired only Canadian rights to their work. Although publishers usually prefer, if possible, to negotiate world rights, selling them off country by country or exporting manufactured books, McClelland was willing – to his own financial detriment – to forgo that return. He was satisfied if M&S benefited through increased visibility for the author and through lower manufacturing costs from a joint print run.

Laurence always stayed close to McClelland, whom she affectionately called "Boss," and he always stuck by her. But she didn't idealize him. In a 1971 letter to the poet Al Purdy, who had his own troubles with McClelland, she wrote: "There are many things about him which I don't like, and God knows I have had my difficulties with him, like every other writer he's ever published, but the fact remains that he has been until recently the *only* good publisher in Canada, the only one prepared to take any risks on new or different writers."

Margaret Laurence had provided a writer's definition of a good publisher. As the 1960s advanced, McClelland tried to be a good businessman

(1) **John Gray** personified the gentleman publisher of the old school, showing in this Ashley and Crippen portrait little trace of his years as a bon vivant and wartime counter-intelligence officer. Gray built Macmillan of Canada into the leading trade publisher of the 1950s, bolstered by educational publishing profits. (2) As head of Macmillan's school division, **Gladys Neale** was the industry's first prominent female executive.

(3) **Kildare Dobbs**, here sharing a laugh with **Beth Appeldoorn** of Toronto's Longhouse Bookshop, was among several Macmillan editors who were also accomplished authors. (4) During more than forty years at Oxford University Press, **William Toye** industriously combined the roles of author, editor, designer, production manager, anthologist, and encyclopedist.

(5) **Marsh Jeanneret** laid the foundations of scholarly publishing in Canada while directing the University of Toronto Press with a distinctly entrepreneurial flair. (6) Ontario's Royal Commission on Book Publishing exerted a strong influence on Canadian public policy. **Dalton Camp**, left, and **Richard Rohmer**, centre, had political clout, but Jeanneret, right, held the pen on the commission's reports.

Among Marsh Jeanneret's key associates at the University of Toronto Press were (7) the editor **Francess Halpenny** and (8) the business manager **Harald Bohne**, right, later director of the press, shown with his colleague **Harry van Ierssel**.

Prince of Publishers **Jack McClelland** was a magnet for both commercial and literary authors. (**9**) McClelland congratulates the popular print and broadcast journalist **Charles Templeton** on publication of his novel *Act of God*. (**10**) McClelland, centre, with two star poets whose reputations he helped create, **Leonard Cohen**, left, and **Irving Layton**.

McClelland & Stewart has been the proving ground for many leading figures in Canadian publishing. (11) **Hugh Kane**, left, Jack McClelland's right-hand man in the 1950s and '60s before moving to Macmillan, confers with **Jim Douglas**, later founder of Vancouver-based Douglas & McIntyre. (12) **Anna Porter** was M&S editor-in-chief in the 1970s before co-founding Key Porter Books. (13) **Peter Taylor** was McClelland's marketing genius.

(14) A lifetime in the publishing wars is etched on **Jack McClelland**'s face in this portrait by John Reeves. (15) McClelland shakes hands with **Avie Bennett** at the news conference announcing Bennett's purchase of McClelland & Stewart in 1985.

(16) **Stan Bevington**, "head coach" at Toronto's Coach House Press, collaborated with a wide range of poet-editors to instigate literary, design, and technological revolutions from the 1960s to the 1990s. (17) A few blocks away, poet **Dennis Lee** and co-founder Dave Godfrey influenced the canon and radicalized the politics of Canadian literature at House of Anansi Press.

too, balancing his risk-taking on fiction and poetry with more profitable non-fiction.

M&S set the gold standard for political bestsellers in 1963 with Peter C. Newman's *Renegade in Power: The Diefenbaker Years*. Then Ottawa correspondent for *Maclean's*, Newman produced a candid study of the defeated prime minister that represented a new genre for Canada. An insider's book, anecdotal and thoroughly savvy, its racy narrative exposed the fateful influence of character on politics. *Renegade* sold out its 28,000-copy first printing within weeks and went on to sell some 80,000 in hardcover, establishing the Ottawa political book as one of the strongest categories in the market. Such titles could also be influential politically. Some M&S books helped frame the terms of the national debate over the next few years: George Grant's deeply felt obituary for Canadian sovereignty, *Lament for a Nation* (1965), Walter Gordon's *A Choice for Canada: Independence or Colonial Status* (1966), René Lévesque's *An Option for Quebec* (1968), and Newman's *The Distemper of Our Times* (1968).

McClelland was always on the lookout for journalists who could write complete paragraphs and had something to say to a large audience. The paragon was Pierre Berton. Between 1959 and 1963, Berton's topical quick reads – *Just Add Water and Stir*, *Adventures of a Columnist*, *Fast Fast Fast Relief*, and *The Big Sell* – made money for M&S. So did his 1965 best-seller, *The Comfortable Pew*, subtitled *A Critical Look at Christianity and the Religious Establishment in the New Age*. It sold some 130,000 copies in trade paperback, although M&S had to share the profits with the Anglican Church of Canada, which had commissioned it. Berton's political tract *The Smug Minority*, used as a campaign tool by the New Democratic Party in the 1968 election, had a first paperback printing of 100,000.

Berton was a phenomenon: a fast-talking media commentator in a geeky bow tie who knew how to titillate his middle-class audience, both in print and on television. After Berton was fired from *Maclean's* for his column "Let's Stop Hoaxing the Kids About Sex," McClelland saw a chance to harness his star power to the M&S chariot. Berton's sales were already so important to the company that he owned a small percentage of M&S and sat on the board. Now McClelland appointed him editor-in-chief of a new entity, the M&S Illustrated Books Division. It was McClelland's first systematic attempt to treat books as product.

The division launched a series, jointly conceived by McClelland and Berton (who invested some of his own money), called the Canadian Centennial Library. In 1964 they signed a deal with *Weekend* magazine, the Saturday colour supplement distributed in numerous dailies across the country, to co-publish a series of lavishly illustrated, low-priced books about Canada's first century. Costs were shared equally, with M&S producing the books and *Weekend* providing the advertising and sales vehicle: splashy full-page ads with mail-in coupons. If mail-order merchandising worked for Charles Atlas, why not for McClelland and Berton?

Berton paired up with a managing editor, Ken Lefolii, also formerly of *Maclean's*, and Frank Newfeld, seconded from his job at M&S. Since Berton refused to drive out to the M&S offices on Hollinger Road, the team set up shop with a secretary in a downtown office above a garage and went to work. Their models were the successful Time-Life Books in the United States. Berton recruited high-quality authors for each title: William Kilbourn wrote *The Making of the Nation: A Century of Challenge*, Trent Frayne and Peter Gzowski shared the byline on *Great Canadian Sports Stories: A Century of Competition*, and Claude Bissell assembled *Great Canadian Writing: A Century of Imagination*.

Titles were released every two months from late 1965 through 1966. Each title had a 100,000-copy first printing, bound in unjacketed hard covers bordered with distinctive red bands. All sold out eventually, and the break-even point was 70,000 copies. However, since the retail price of the regular edition was $2.95 per copy, $3.95 for the deluxe edition, and revenues were shared with *Weekend*, profits were modest. McClelland and Berton had designed the scheme in consultation with a New York mail-order expert, but the model depended on even more massive print runs and made better economic sense in the American market.

The management of *Weekend* prudently called it quits in the mail-order bookselling game, but not McClelland. Believing he'd finally found the secret of making money in publishing, he plowed ahead, continuing the program under different names and advertising it by other means, principally direct mail. The immediate successor was the Canadian

Illustrated Library, launched in 1967 and featuring similar sorts of books: *The Inventors: Great Ideas in Canadian Enterprise* and so on. Berton again recruited respected authors: Robert Thomas Allen, Robert Fulford, Farley Mowat, even Hugh MacLennan, whose *The Colour of Canada* was one of the most successful books in the series.

The M&S illustrated titles soaked up their fair share of the cash Canadians shelled out for books published for the Centennial. Berton seriously doubted the economic wisdom of continuing the division, "but Jack was very enthusiastic. He thought he had the best idea going. He said, 'Oh, we can do everything – we can do butterflies, we can do birds.' I thought he priced the books too low, as he always did. Well, Jack flew by the seat of his pants. He never took a market survey in his life. I used to say, 'Jesus, Jack, let's look at the thing a little more deeply,' but he'd say, 'I'm sure it's going to work.' That was his Achilles heel."

Centennial Year was tailor-made for "The Canadian Publishers." It should have been the company's year of triumph, the vindication of McClelland's Canada-centred publishing strategy. Instead it triggered an avalanche of financial problems that nearly buried M&S.

McCLELLAND & STEWART

SEAL BOOKS

McCLELLAND & STEWART

7

SURVIVING PRINCE JACK

But I am *McClelland & Stewart.*

Jack McClelland (1983)

I n 1967 the M&S list hit a high of eighty-one titles. In addition to the illustrated books, they included entries in the New Canadian Library, the Canadian Centenary Series, the Canadian Best-Seller Library (mass-market paperbacks), and yet another paperback series, the Carleton Library, which reprinted Canadian works in history and the social sciences. Centennial Year also saw original fiction by Hubert Aquin, George Bowering, David Lewis Stein, Scott Symons, and Peter Taylor, and new poetry by Irving Layton, P.K. Page, and Al Purdy. It saw, briefly, the Canadian Book Preview Society, a short-lived book club whose subscribers received page proofs of M&S books in advance of publication. And when it was all over, Centennial Year was topped by an all-too-symbolic loss of $67,000 on M&S operations.

The company's financial health was threatened less by the operating loss than by debilitating demands on its capital, now tied up in a massive inventory of books. For years, Hugh Kane had been trying to apply the brakes to his boss's profligate ambition, but the battle was unequal. To some extent, Kane felt he'd lost it to Berton, whose influence on McClelland he considered excessive. After leaving in 1969 to become vice-president of Macmillan, Kane told the *Toronto Star* books editor Peter Sypnowich that M&S's financial crisis had begun when it doubled its sales volume within eighteen months, thanks partly to the illustrated books. Sales had ballooned, but profits hadn't materialized. "Any firm doing that without an infusion of capital is in serious trouble," Kane said.

A similar perspective came from Linda McKnight, hired as an educational editor at about the time Kane left. McKnight would become successively M&S managing editor, director of publishing, and president. On examining the company's financial statements, she said many years later, it was clear that "M&S had had good years and bad years. If they hadn't had the debt, they would have survived very nicely. But the debt was there forever, and it came from the audacious experiments around the Centennial."

Ironically, McClelland's efforts to act like a commercial publisher had landed him in bigger financial trouble than ever. He had no choice but to go in search of more working capital, in the form of either debt or equity. Having reached his borrowing limits, McClelland negotiated with the Bronfman interests to invest in a major publishing project, but Bronfman-owned Cemp Investments began talking about a cash investment in M&S itself. To sugar the deal, McClelland agreed to publish a book of poems called *Bitter Sweet Lemons and Love*, by an unknown Montreal writer named Sandra Kolber, who happened to be married to Leo Kolber (later a senator) of Cemp Investments. The book appeared with the author's portrait, Leonard Cohen–style, on the cover, and all the publicity materials printed for it were impregnated with the scent of lemons. Hollinger House reeked of essence of lemon oil for weeks afterwards.

During 1967 McClelland negotiated with Cemp and another Montreal investment firm, Starlaw (controlled by the McConnell family, owners of the *Montreal Star*), for a joint cash investment of $1.2 million. By signing the agreement, McClelland would have put himself in a position where he could be forced to give up control. At a meeting to close the deal, he was shocked by a demand that most of his senior management be replaced; Cemp and Starlaw also wanted to insert a financial officer just below him in the management structure. McClelland balked. As he told *Time Canada* four years later, "I got very emotional and dramatic, told them to stuff it and walked out on the deal without knowing where the hell the money I needed would be coming from."

In May 1968 John McClelland died at the age of ninety-one. Jack managed to carry on for another year with financing from the Royal Bank of Canada and the Toronto-Dominion Bank. But the company lost a further $123,000 and had to call in the accounting firm of Clarkson, Gordon to negotiate payment terms with its creditors. In desperation, McClelland turned once again to Cemp and Starlaw, and in spring 1969 the two companies backed M&S at the TD Bank for a total of $850,000 in loans.

The two investors insisted, once again, on installation of a financial watchdog. He was Larry Ritchie, a chartered accountant formerly with Clarkson, Gordon, whose role was to report regularly to Cemp and generally to keep McClelland's excesses in check. But the boss's dashing personal style and influence so pervaded M&S that within a few months, Ritchie had grown his hair out in a permed Afro and begun wearing coloured open-necked shirts.

And so there were two faces of M&S. The public saw the sophisticated, enterprising flagship of the industry, publishing some of the country's finest literary authors alongside bestsellers with soaring sales. But anyone with access behind the scenes saw a financially and at times morally compromised company, resorting to questionable schemes to stay alive. These included a biography of Sam Bronfman, by Terence Robertson, subsidized by the Bronfmans themselves; it remained unpublished after Robertson's suicide.

The second M&S wasn't a pretty sight, even to its owner: a bitter price to pay for having invested so heavily in Canadian writers. In a speech in October 1969, McClelland acknowledged that the future might lie with some of the young publishers nipping at his heels. And yet, to the eager, underpaid staff labouring within it, M&S was still the Great Cause. To Scott McIntyre, "working there, for a young man from Vancouver, was like dying and going to heaven." McIntyre, who would become a publisher himself in a few years, worked in the M&S advertising, promotion, and publicity department from 1967 to 1969. He considered the place "everything that the idealists and romantics tell you publishing is supposed to be. There was a sense of being in this great cauldron of extraordinary activity. Everyone who was anyone in the country came through the door. On the other hand, it was *that* close to bankruptcy all the time."

Catherine Wilson worked with McIntyre as a publicist after arriving at M&S in 1967. She was "absolutely blown away by what seemed to me to be the most glamorous profession in the world. It was exhausting and exhilarating in equal measure. I have never, ever had – before or since – so much fun in my life." The place generated spontaneous staff parties; it attracted famous authors who arrived from out of town and were often billeted in employees' homes. Margaret Laurence dropped by Wilson's office with a poster from China for her wall. Margaret Atwood read her Tarot.

The firm's 1969 fall catalogue announced a first novel called *The Edible Woman*, listed at $5.95 in hardcover and sharing a page with *The Pooh Cook Book*. Both listings were dwarfed by a full-page blurb announcing Ivan Shaffer's new novel, *The Midas Compulsion*, set among Wall Street and Bay Street "greed merchants." Shaffer seemed far likelier to have a big career ahead than the author of *The Edible Woman*, who was shown in a blurry photograph peering out warily from under a fur hat. She, after all, was merely a poet, albeit one who'd won a Governor General's Award. The book for which she'd won the award was misidentified in the catalogue.

Atwood had submitted her novel four years earlier. In spite of critical readings by Joyce Marshall ("interesting but not publishable") and John Robert Colombo ("I think the unconvincing narrative thread cripples it"), the author seemed promising enough that the editorial director, Jim Totton, had extended an offer in 1966. When Atwood received no follow-up for a year, she wrote, as she recalled, "several letters in spring '67 asking where it was; again silence." To her bafflement, she then received a letter from McClelland, who declared himself "enchanted" by a *Toronto Star* article about her and asked if by any chance she had an unpublished novel available. Informed that his firm not only had the novel in its possession but had already offered on it, McClelland sheepishly met with the author, guzzled Bloody Marys, and assured her that M&S was proceeding with publication. It took two more years for *The Edible Woman* to see the light of day.

McClelland blamed the farce on "the chaos and carelessness that existed for some time in our editorial department." Finally, as if to top himself, he wrote Atwood two years *after* publication, "I am told we lost a manuscript of yours for two years. Is this true? If it is, it is the first time that it has ever been drawn to my attention. What manuscript? When? And to whom did you complain?"

Atwood tried to settle him down: "I'm not mad at you for that, although it does make a good story." Responding to some of his more defensive remarks, she added, "I'm not 'bitter' about M&S. No one in Canada is bitter about them, because they have been a major publishing force, and I'm in favour of seeing that continue. But they are notorious in certain areas, and one discusses their failings as one discusses the failings of an eccentric aunt to whom one is, inevitably, related and committed."

Atwood stayed with McClelland despite the rocky start. Unlike some of his authors, however, she never became close to him: "He was my publisher, but he wasn't my best buddy," she explained in an interview. She ascribed this to several factors: a sense that she frightened him a little ("I think he thought I was nuts, and nuts in a way he couldn't really understand"); his touchiness about her second husband, Graeme Gibson (McClelland had rejected Gibson's novel *Five Legs*, then acted chagrined when it was successfully published by Anansi); and his preference for authors of his own generation, especially those who drank with him. As for her own tastes in friendship, Atwood acknowledged her publisher had his less endearing qualities: "He had a temper. He was a sulk. He would have hissy fits. He would get hurt. He would moan and complain, and all of that temperament he had."

Their professional relationship, however, prospered, especially after the acclaim for her second novel, *Surfacing*, which went through three printings at M&S in 1972. Anansi published her CanLit study, *Survival*, that year, and the unusual feat of having two celebrated books on store shelves simultaneously lent Atwood exceptional stature. She fascinated people, not only as a fresh and distinctive personality, with a face the camera loved, but as the standard-bearer for two movements approaching maximum force: feminism and Canadian cultural nationalism. She quickly became one of those authors to whom McClelland looked, frequently and desperately, for another big book. Her expectations of him were equally straightforward: "As for you and me, dear Jack, my major concern is that you be as stunning a publisher as possible. Far be it from me to wish to upset you except in ways conducive to that end."

Berton and Mowat were still vying with each other in the big-book category. Mowat, who published both *Owls in the Family* and the best-selling *Sibir* in 1970, was bigger internationally, Berton domestically. Berton told McClelland he didn't want to edit or write potboilers any more; he preferred to move on to "books of some substance." He stepped down from the Illustrated Books Division, cut back on his television work, and returned to his study to tackle the subject he'd been thinking about in the decade since his award-winning *Klondike*: the building of the Canadian Pacific Railway.

Berton treated the CPR story as the great national epic, casting it in heroic terms and focusing the narrative on the colourful personalities of politicians and tycoons. He'd tell the story in two volumes, to be published a year apart, and he took charge of more than the writing: he assembled his own team to research, edit, and design the books, and he entrusted publicity and rights to his long-time agent and business associate, Elsa Franklin. The project operated out of offices shared by Berton and Franklin in a Victorian brick house on Sackville Street in downtown Toronto. Practically all that remained for M&S was production, sales, and distribution. Berton felt he knew enough about the business to act as virtually his own publisher: "Jack wouldn't let anybody else do that. But I did it and it worked very well."

Yet for all that, Berton still needed M&S. Publication of the two-volume saga, *The National Dream: The Great Railway, 1871–1881* and *The Last Spike: The Great Railway, 1881–1885*, was the making of him as a serious author. Although he had his detractors among professional historians, Berton's railway history was enthusiastically received by the media and the public, and both volumes hit number one on the *Toronto Star*'s national bestseller list. When *The Last Spike* arrived on the list in 1971, *The National Dream* still occupied a spot, after twelve months, and the two resided side by side like inseparable twins for a year. They ended up selling about 130,000 copies each in Canada alone, a phenomenal quantity for hardcover titles.

A master recycler, Berton extended the books' lives by abridging them in one volume no fewer than three times: by a third for the 1972 American edition, *The Impossible Railway*, by two-thirds for a picture book, *The*

Great Railway Illustrated, and by half for a quality paperback, which sold another 175,000 copies. M&S illustrated the paperback edition with stills from the eight-hour CBC Television series based on the book, written by Timothy Findley and William Whitehead. And when the picture book was released in fall 1972, it joined the original hardcover editions and a revised edition of *Klondike* on the *Star*'s list, giving Berton – and M&S – four concurrent bestsellers.

On February 18, 1971, pursing dry lips, pushing back his hair, and lighting one cigarette after another, McClelland made a grim announcement – first to his staff, then to the media. He was putting M&S up for sale. Things were so bad that he couldn't rule out selling it to foreign interests.

Although it wouldn't have surprised McClelland's banker or accountant, the news shocked everyone else. It was as if some plague were scything through the industry: the previous fall, the sale of both Gage's book publishing division and the Ryerson Press to American publishers had shaken the book trade. Yet as disturbing as those takeovers had been, M&S was a whole other matter. People felt something more akin to nostalgia for Ryerson, whose best days were in the past, and had at most a vague idea of Gage's historic significance as a textbook publisher. But almost everyone knew about M&S and its importance to Canadian literature. The news seemed symptomatic of a culture in danger of annihilation.

In December, following the public outcry over Gage and Ryerson, the Ontario government had appointed the Royal Commission on Book Publishing. The M&S crisis fell into the commissioners' laps just as they were setting to work. A newspaper cartoon portrayed Rohmer, Camp, and Jeanneret facing the dilemma of having no Canadian publishers left to publish their findings on Canadian publishing.

Saying he needed to find a purchaser within two months, McClelland threw out an asking price of $1.5 million. As a leading figure in the Committee for an Independent Canada, the prominent nationalist lobby group founded a year earlier by Walter Gordon, Peter C. Newman, and Abraham Rotstein, he naturally didn't wish to see M&S bought by American interests; but, he declared, such an outcome was inevitable if Canadian investors didn't step forward. He'd sell to Americans only as a last resort: "This firm was not developed in order to be sold to foreign owners. It would be a negation of my whole career and all that this firm stands for."

In a 1971 *Saturday Night* feature by Silver Donald Cameron, McClelland ruminated on his publishing philosophy. Of course there was a way to make M&S profitable, he said: "All you have to do is fire all the editorial and design people, who cost $200,000 a year, keep one copy editor, publish ten or fifteen books already in the schedule, and milk that $2 million worth of backlist sales for all it's worth." But, McClelland explained, such an approach didn't interest him: "Money *doesn't* mean all that much to me, the books mean more to me than the money . . . And suddenly you discover, Oh God, if ten years ago I had followed the normal businessman's concern for a steadily increasing profit, then I'd be able to borrow money today. I wouldn't have the publishing house that I have today, and in fact I don't really believe that McClelland & Stewart would be as useful or as valuable to anybody. But you can't convince a Canadian banker of that."

"Jack was hard on money," Peter Newman said many years later. "It was not a discipline that he understood, or wanted to exercise. It was a burden. He always tried to find somebody who would take care of that burden for him, so he could get on with the real business of publishing."

For McClelland, the books were their own justification. Until his last day as a publisher, he'd persist in trying to be a Canadian Knopf. The trouble was that he also tried to be a Canadian Random House, with a commercial trade list; a Canadian Modern Library, building a classic reprint series; a Canadian New Directions, publishing poetry and literary translations; a Canadian Grove Press, issuing underground writing; and a Canadian Anchor or Signet Books, popularizing serious literature. M&S had managed to scrape together small profits in both 1969 and 1970: an encouraging sign, but it made hardly a dent in the nearly $2-million debt. McClelland's alternatives were selling the company, entering receivership, or finding an angel who bought into his philosophy of publishing and his view of M&S's importance. Miraculously, the Ontario government of Conservative premier William Davis sprouted wings.

A month after McClelland's announcement, the royal commission came to the same conclusion about the true value of his company. Issuing an interim report in March 1971, Rohmer, Jeanneret, and Camp told the Ontario government: "McClelland and Stewart represents an accumulated creative momentum in original Canadian publishing which could not quickly be replaced by other Canadian publishing enterprises should its program terminate or be sharply curtailed. We recognize the fact that part of the firm's present difficulties must be explained by the very scope of the program it has mounted, but that program is itself a national asset worthy of all reasonable public encouragement and support."

"A national asset": McClelland couldn't have asked for a finer encomium. Even better, the commissioners were prepared to put public money where their mouths were. They recommended that Ontario provide the firm with a ten-year debenture, or loan, worth nearly $1 million ($961,645, or one-third of M&S's reported assets). The loan should be interest-free for the first five years and made convertible to shares in the company. To safeguard its investment, the province should appoint directors to the board, and the federal government should be invited to share in the risk (the federal government declined).

At a time when almost no public support was available to publishers, the royal commission's proposal was unprecedented. The Davis government accepted the commission's advice, not only preserving M&S in McClelland's hands but ushering in a new era in Canadian public policy. Book publishing would no longer be regarded as a business like any other; it was a key cultural industry, producing what economists call "merit goods," things of intrinsic value to society that must not be abandoned to the mercies of the market. By throwing himself on the public's mercy, McClelland had judged the political mood with uncanny accuracy.

Two years before the Ontario rescue, a twenty-five-year-old named Anna Szigethy had turned up at M&S. Szigethy (later Anna Porter) had arrived in Toronto from Hungary, via New Zealand and the United Kingdom. In London she'd worked as a proofreader at Cassell and as a college sales rep at Macmillan; in Toronto she'd spent a little time at Collier-Macmillan, but as yet she didn't know much about Canada. Having heard that M&S was seeking a managing editor, she obtained "a very strange, short interview" with Frank Newfeld, whose sphere was design and production. The Czech-born Newfeld seemed primarily interested in her proficiency in French and German, and in the fact that "he was a foreigner and I was a foreigner." McClelland took her for lunch to his favourite haunt, the Westbury Hotel dining room, and asked her how many Canadian writers she'd read. Porter named Morley Callaghan and Leonard Cohen; belatedly she discovered that Margaret Laurence was Canadian too.

"After the interview, Jack wanted to go and look at a boat he was thinking about buying, so we drove downtown and walked about and found the boat, and somewhere around then he said, 'Well, I guess you're hired.' The condition was that I had to read all of the New Canadian Library within a week." McClelland didn't buy the boat but had found the employee who would be his editorial right hand for the next decade.

The following year, McClelland hired Peter Taylor. M&S had published Taylor's novel *Watcha Gonna Do Boy . . . Watcha Gonna Be?* in 1967, written when he was a young journalist. A New Brunswicker, Taylor worked then at the *Ottawa Citizen*, and one evening in Ottawa "over a hundred drinks," he'd gotten to know his publisher. He and McClelland discussed M&S's organizational problems, primarily the fact that the sales, publicity, and advertising departments lacked any coordinated strategy. Three years later, McClelland remembered he'd liked the young man's ideas for integrating the various marketing functions. Taylor, who had never worked in book publishing, suddenly became director of advertising, promotion, and publicity.

Before long, McClelland had given Taylor overall authority over trade marketing. Porter, meanwhile, had become editorial director. "Jack gave us titles instead of raises," was her recollection; later both became vice-presidents, with seats on the board. But their responsibilities were real enough: to help McClelland keep the leaky ship afloat throughout the 1970s.

Larry Ritchie, vice-president and general manager, tried to present a fiscally responsible face to the Ontario government, but it was Porter and Taylor and their teams who executed McClelland's creative vision. Their lineup of talent was impressive. Under Porter worked such editors as Linda McKnight, Pamela Fry, Lily Miller, John Newlove, Jennifer Glossop, James Marsh, and Patrick Crean. For his sales force, Taylor hired Allan MacDougall, later president of Raincoast Books in Vancouver, and John Neale, later president of Random House of Canada. Both became, successively, M&S trade sales managers. The college sales manager was Peter Milroy, who in later years would direct the University of British Columbia Press.

Everybody worked long hours. When Taylor packed up his briefcase to go home at 10 or 11 o'clock, he'd often pass Porter or McClelland, still working. Paul Audley, who was in the college department, said of McClelland, "I've never worked with anyone who worked harder. If you sent him a memo, he'd answer before he went home, even if he had to stay till midnight to do it. And he was decisive – if you'd given him enough information, you'd get a decision."

During that period, M&S became renowned for one-of-a-kind publicity gambits. The stunts often involved McClelland personally, and most were products of his and Taylor's fevered imaginations. Taylor liked to remember McClelland after hours, "two bottles of vodka on his desk, fingers going through his hair, and his shirt half off. He'd phone my wife at about 10:30 and say, 'Pat, you're a wonderful woman. Now, I really apologize for keeping Peter here. I know he said he'd be home for dinner, but we're just about finished.' Then he'd get me to phone Elizabeth and say I was in serious trouble and Jack had agreed to stay and help me out: 'Hate to screw up your plans for the evening.' We hatched some great schemes in those long evenings."

Some of the schemes are the stuff of publishing legend: McClelland in a billowing toga and snow boots, the novelist Sylvia Fraser in an off-the-shoulder silver gown, her blond locks crowned with laurels, launching *The Emperor's Virgin* in a March blizzard; McClelland climbing a rickety scaffold with Aritha van Herk to present the young author with a giant "cheque" for winning the first $50,000 Seal Book Award; shoeboxes delivered to the media to promote *The Snakes of Canada*, each supposedly containing a live reptile that had "escaped" through a ragged hole in the side. There was the "coat of many covers," a blazer printed with M&S jacket designs in which McClelland travelled the country, standing on street corners and giving away New Canadian Library titles to publicize a three-for-two sale. The then unknown novelist Tim Wynne-Jones worked incognito as a bartender at his own launch party, whipping off his white jacket to emerge as that year's Seal Book Award winner. Taylor once ordered construction of the world's biggest book, hauled by crane onto the roof of the newly opened World's Biggest Bookstore in Toronto. Even publicity-shy Margaret Laurence was inveigled to take part in theatrics: to celebrate publication of *The Diviners*, professional diviners doused for water in the pouring rain outside the Ontario Science Centre as Laurence hid behind the shrubbery, nervously swigging from a mickey concealed in Anna Porter's purse.

McClelland would do anything, no matter how outlandish, to sell M&S books. Taylor regarded the company as a family firm, except that instead of working for "the old man," you were working for "the bad kid." As the bad kid's hair turned from blond to white and the bags under his eyes deepened, his employees learned he could be complex and contradictory.

When M&S published a revised edition of *The Scalpel, the Sword*, a biography of Norman Bethune by Ted Allan and Sidney Gordon, the large print run was marred by a serious gaffe: Anna Porter had misspelled Allan's surname on the title page. When Allan received his author's copies, he phoned Porter to complain. "I told Ted all the books were bound and I didn't know what to do," Porter said. "He told me to put the call through to Jack's office, and by the time I rushed in there, I could hear Jack saying, 'Picky, picky, picky, Ted. I'd strongly recommend that the only possible solution is for you to change your name.'"

McClelland didn't take Porter to task, but to others he could be critical beyond reason. The company unveiled its fall list every year at the Westbury Hotel, and later at the Royal Canadian Yacht Club on Toronto Island. It was a festive occasion when the booze flowed, the food was plentiful, and Peter Taylor did his comedic best to keep the proceedings fun and upbeat. One year a series of glitches occurred. Finally McClelland rose to speak and, looking down pointedly at Taylor, told the assembled booksellers, media, and staff, "One of my biggest problems in life as a publisher, as you can see, is that I'm surrounded by fucking idiots."

Twenty years later, Taylor explained away the story, recalling in an interview that McClelland felt "an almost societal pressure" to come through for his star authors: "You had Harold Town breathing down your neck, you had Pierre, you had Farley. All these people who really matter.

They ran Jack with their demands, as much as Jack ran his staff. There was always a feeling that, you know, this is Sylvia Fraser, or this is Margaret Laurence, or this is Lenny Cohen, and you'd better not fuck up, because they're counting on Jack. Jack, in turn, is counting on Taylor. Taylor is counting on his staff. You were never quite sure who was driving who." Taylor preferred to remember how, when his conservative father offered to buy up all the copies of his novel for fear it would upset Taylor's mother, McClelland tactfully declined. He wrote to say that he didn't believe in censorship, and Taylor's parents ought to be proud of him.

Sylvia Fraser, for her part, observed that McClelland had "the forgiveness of the old sinner," which he extended to his employees when they needed a second chance. Some who worked at M&S, however, weren't so sure. John Robert Colombo, who freelanced for the firm for seven years, declined to go on staff because he felt McClelland showed more respect for people if he didn't employ them. The fate of Catherine Wilson was a case in point.

Wilson devoted five years to a job she loved, having succeeded Scott McIntyre as head of advertising, promotion, and publicity. But she was fired in 1972 when she inadvertently scheduled a launch party for the poet John Newlove's *Lies* on the same day as a gold-panning gimmick for the relaunch of Berton's *Klondike*. Since Berton's publicity was handled out of house by Elsa Franklin, Wilson hadn't been aware of the conflict, but Berton and Franklin saw red. To appease them, McClelland decided unilaterally that Wilson must go, then spent an evening with her at dinner in Montreal with Mordecai Richler and Louis and Rose Melzack of Classics Books, mentioning nothing to her about the imminent dismissal. "We said goodnight," Wilson recalled, "kiss, kiss, hug, hug, see you soon, and I went back to Toronto. The next morning, I got a call from Peter Taylor to meet him for breakfast." McClelland had given Taylor the job of firing her. "It was a terrible moment for both of us," Wilson said. "Worse for me." But she received moral and practical support from Berton's rival, Farley Mowat, and came out of the mess with a decent severance and other benefits.

Allan MacDougall remembered McClelland as equally capable of firing off vicious memos to his staff and of inspiring them to the heights. MacDougall was captivated by the climate of licence at M&S: the raucous editorial meetings, the long beery lunches, marathon sales conferences that ran on alcohol and sexual intrigue, the chalkboard in the boardroom where people scrawled witty or obscene slogans. He recalled his boss as a benign dictator. "When I was sales manager, I'd wake up sweating in the middle of the night thinking, 'This is Stalin I'm working for.' A man who could have you twisting and turning without even talking to you. Who demanded, without ever demanding. Who had this community of loyalty. Either you were with Jack or you were agin him. I loved working for him because he was, at the same time, a wonderful man."

New publishers kept emerging to compete with M&S for authors, media coverage, and retail space, yet McClelland continued to publish more books than ever. In 1973 his list surpassed 100 titles for the first time. In 1977, the year he created the Seal Books imprint, the list spiked at 127, with a record-high staff complement of 150, before settling into an average of about ninety books a year. From 1972 onward, the company benefited, like other publishers, from new grant programs at the Canada Council and the Ontario Arts Council. But while the grants made it more feasible to publish risky cultural titles, they also had a tendency to expand a publisher's output: a form of double jeopardy, since specializing in Canadian books, even subsidized ones, remained a shaky enterprise.

In 1975 Peter Newman provided M&S with some much-needed cash flow with the first volume of *The Canadian Establishment*. By then the editor of *Maclean's*, Newman had originally intended the book as a joint effort with his wife, Christina McCall; he would write about Canada's economic elite, she about the political elite. After their marriage ended, Newman proceeded with the business book, while she pursued the political angle by writing *Grits* for Macmillan. Volume I of *The Canadian Establishment*, *The Old Order*, would eventually sell 250,000 copies in all editions for M&S and be made into a CBC Television series. M&S published volume II, *The Acquisitors*, in 1981. While working on those books, Newman also wrote two bestselling offshoots: *Bronfman Dynasty: The Rothschilds of the New World*, published in 1978, and *The Establishment Man*, a biography of the young Conrad Black, released in 1982.

Newman's half-cheeky, half-fawning invasions of establishment privacy have been so successful over the years that in retrospect it seems a no-brainer to have published that first volume. But in fact, McClelland took a tremendous risk. The print run for the nearly 500-page hardcover came close to a record for a Canadian trade book: 75,000 copies, although pre-publication orders totalled just 35,000. McClelland committed himself to the huge run because the book was being released on November 1, and he knew there wouldn't be time to reprint before Christmas if the book took off. His gamble succeeded, but only after he'd averted a potentially ruinous lawsuit brought by the man Newman called the dean of the Canadian establishment, Paul Desmarais of Power Corporation. Desmarais sought an injunction to stop publication when the books had already rolled off the bindery line. Since Desmarais's complaint concerned a passage that was only ten lines long, McClelland struck an unusual deal: he had the ten lines rewritten, reset, and printed on a self-adhesive label, which M&S staff were called in over a weekend to stick onto page 74 of all 75,000 copies. The books arrived in the stores on schedule, buoyed by the kind of publicity money couldn't buy.

M&S profits on all Newman's establishment books were diminished somewhat by hefty legal fees. (The firm did enjoy access to one of the country's leading libel lawyers in Anna Porter's husband, Julian Porter.) Newman was grateful to McClelland for his readiness to brave that kind of pressure. He recalled McClelland phoning him at midnight to chortle over angry phone calls from members of Toronto's WASP establishment, often people who'd attended school with the publisher. "Jack was funny, he was fun," said Newman. "He was somebody you wanted to be with. Being part of Jack's stable was magic, because he was an author's publisher. You could talk to Jack about your personal life, you could talk to Jack about your health, and he really cared."

Newman's gratitude reached its practical limits in 1982, as he prepared to leave the financial security of *Maclean's* to embark on writing a three-volume history of the Hudson's Bay Company. Newman needed a large advance to finance the projected ten-year enterprise. His agent, the Toronto entertainment lawyer Michael Levine, knew McClelland didn't have the cash and negotiated a half-million-dollar package deal with Peter

Mayer, international CEO of Penguin, who was building a hardcover program in Canada. The advance was the largest for any Canadian author to that point. Newman's departure started a trend that would see many of the country's top authors, and many emerging writers as well, migrate from Canadian-owned publishers to the multinationals.

"Jack, to his credit," recalled Newman later, "saw it as something I should do. He advised me to go ahead, and he was nothing but a gentleman and very supportive." At Penguin, where he published thereafter, Newman found a different ethos. When Conrad Black took legal action against him and his publisher, Penguin's response was to print a retraction in the *Globe and Mail* and ask Newman to pay for it. McClelland would never have caved in like that, Newman believed: "Penguin is a very different house. It's a business. There's none of the excitement that there was with Jack, none of the midnight phone calls, none of the epiphanies that looked so great in the bar, drinking together, then vanishing with the morning sun."

As Newman's defection illustrated, Canadian publishing was outgrowing even Jack McClelland. Although he always worked on a bigger canvas than anyone else, his means couldn't keep pace with his ambitions. McClelland spread his resources so thin, inventing so many new formats and novel merchandising schemes, that it's surprising there was anything left for publishing books.

In 1977 alone, McClelland launched no fewer than three different product lines. *Magook* was his attempt to capitalize on the burgeoning field of Canadian children's literature. A hybrid creature, half magazine, half book, *Magook* featured appealing content by some of the country's best children's authors; it was sold, mass-market-style, in supermarkets and variety stores, but it lost money and was phased out in 1979 after eight issues. Canada's Illustrated Heritage was a fifteen-volume picture book series, with text by well-known authors, published between 1977 and 1979 by Natural Science of Canada, an M&S subsidiary, and sold by direct mail.

Seal Books was the most enduring of the three experiments. Canada still lacked mass-market paperback capability: a company to compete with lines such as Bantam, Avon, Dell, and New American Library. McClelland had tried it with the Canadian Best-Seller Library in the mid-1960s and found the economics of the mass-market distribution system prohibitive. A short sales cycle (a few weeks' rack exposure at most), monopolistic national and regional wholesalers, steep discounts, a returns rate often exceeding 50 percent, and the practice of returning unsold copies by sending back only the covers, while pulping the insides, make mass-market publishing a totally different business from traditional book publishing. The only way a Canadian publisher could participate in the system was to piggyback on an established American line.

An opportunity arose when the Trudeau government decided to use its Foreign Investment Review Agency to enlarge Canadian publishers' market share. In 1976 FIRA enabled General Publishing to purchase the Canadian branch of Pocket Books. Later that year, Bantam Books of Canada was undergoing a change of ownership, and Bantam's new owners agreed, as a condition of FIRA approval for their principal acquisition, to create a separate mass-market company as a joint venture under Canadian ownership. A partnership called McClelland & Stewart-Bantam Ltd., owned 51 percent by Jack McClelland, was announced in early 1977 to publish Canadian paperbacks under the Seal imprint.

In its first year, Seal's titles included low-priced editions of *The Canadian Establishment*, Atwood's novel *Lady Oracle*, Laurence's *A Jest of God*, Mowat's *The Snow Walker*, Brian Moore's *The Doctor's Wife*, and several others. It seemed, at the time, a great publishing breakthrough. But M&S lost money on the venture almost from the start. The mass-market paperback model, based on American demographics, wasn't truly viable in Canada. And Seal was paying Bantam more than it could afford in service fees. Although Anna Porter moved over from M&S to run Seal, control over pricing, distribution, and even cover design lay with the 49 percent partner. Despite the federal government's belief that it had driven a hard bargain, Sam Slick had triumphed again.

The Seal Book Award did stimulate the writing of a great deal of commercial fiction. Hundreds of would-be authors were enticed by the prospect of hardcover publication by M&S in Canada, by Little, Brown in the United States, and by André Deutsch in the United Kingdom, with subsequent paperback editions from Seal, Bantam, and Corgi, not to mention the $50,000 royalty guarantee. Over the years, Seal Books would undergo ownership changes until it came to belong, like so much of the industry worldwide, to Bertelsmann AG of Munich under the banner of Random House.

Among the most ill-fated of McClelland's 1970s schemes were two gorgeous doorstoppers about Iran by the photographer Roloff Beny. At first McClelland touted the projects, underwritten by Shah Reza Pahlavi, as "a licence to print money." But *Persia: Bridge of Turquoise* (1975) and *Iran: Elements of Destiny* (1978) ended up costing McClelland not only money but the respect, at least temporarily, of some of his admirers: Margaret Laurence, for one, by then a director of the company, considered it immoral to do business with the shah's repressive regime. Cost overruns resulting from Beny's various excesses, coupled with inadequate revenues from international co-editions, produced a deficit on the first title. McClelland hoped to recoup the loss on the second, but instead the shah's subsidy, along with thousands of finished books flown to Iran on two 747s, disappeared after Ayatollah Khomeini toppled the Pahlavi regime in 1979, leaving M&S holding the bag.

Reflecting on the disaster, McClelland regarded his only compensations as his trips to Tehran, where he was addressed as "Dr. McClelland" and sometimes enjoyed the company of Empress Farah, whom he termed "an enchantress." He recalled the conclusion of one meeting with the empress at her palace: "She was waiting to bid me good night. I suddenly became aware that her absolutely exquisite evening gown was absolutely transparent at the breast level. Here I had been with her for an hour and a half, but her face is so enchanting and entrancing that I had not noticed. I practically fainted on the way out."

McClelland had far better luck with a government-subsidized book of photographs closer to home. Canada's gift to the United States on its Bicentennial in 1976 was *Between Friends*, a sumptuous volume portraying life along the great undefended border, produced by Lorraine Monk of the National Film Board at a cost of $1 million. Rights to publish a trade edition were put out for tender. Knowing that Monk's Centennial opus,

Canada: A Year of the Land, had made a fortune for Copp Clark, McClelland trumped Macmillan and other bidders for *Between Friends* by committing M&S to printing twice as many copies as anyone else. This time his risk-taking paid enormous dividends: M&S is thought to have raked in, over the book's life, sales of close to $7 million.

M&S also published many books of enduring importance during that period: Ken Adachi's history of the Japanese Canadians, *The Enemy That Never Was*; Marian Engel's novel *Bear*; Alistair MacLeod's stories in *The Lost Salt Gift of Blood*; Walter Gordon's *A Political Memoir*; Gabrielle Roy's *Garden in the Wind*; Harold Town and David Silcox's *Tom Thomson: The Silence and the Storm*; Rudy Wiebe's *The Scorched-Wood People*. But only five years after receiving the Ontario loan, McClelland announced he was putting the company up for sale again.

As books editor and columnist at the *Toronto Star*, I was the journalist through whom McClelland floated that particular trial balloon. Even then, it struck me that he was fantasizing in public. Perhaps it was understandable: at fifty-four, he was homing in on his thirtieth year at M&S; if he was ever going to start a second career, that was the time. He seemed to yearn openly for a life after publishing, freedom from the relentless demand to fill the pipeline with new books, and from the endless claims of authors, employees, creditors, bankers. McClelland's public musings in the *Star* in 1976 resulted in discussions with various interested parties, including the newspaper's owner, Torstar, which had recently bought a vastly more lucrative Canadian publisher, the romance novel money-spinner Harlequin Books. But McClelland received only one concrete offer, which he rejected. Taking M&S off the market after six months, he told me the stumbling block had been his unwillingness to stay with the company under a new owner.

And yet McClelland spoke incessantly, publicly and privately, about unloading M&S. He even proposed selling it to a group of university student unions if they'd run it as a not-for-profit foundation for the good of Canadian culture. Other potential buyers to whom he talked, in addition to the Bronfmans and the McConnells, included the Loblaws grocery magnate Bertram Loeb, the Edmonton Oilers owner Peter Pocklington, the millionaire Australian-American novelist James Clavell, and the mining magnate Franc Joubin. None of the discussions led to anything.

Unable, or perhaps basically unwilling, to come to terms with investors, McClelland threw himself once more on the mercy of the Ontario government. By the late 1970s, he was into the provincial treasury for $2.9 million, including the original debenture. In 1981, he proposed that Ontario convert its loans to M&S into equity and become a part owner, but there was no deal. A senior government official close to the process said in an interview that McClelland's unending financial problems created a negative image of the publishing industry: "There was always a feeling in the Ontario government, I'm afraid, that Jack was a loser. You know, 'Why the hell do we need to be bombarded every year?' It was a very strong sentiment. It hurt the whole industry."

A sorry turn of events showed that McClelland had become desperate for every dollar. His old comrade-in-arms Hugh Kane had returned in 1976 to run the direct-mail program, Natural Science of Canada. In 1980, Kane turned seventy and decided it was time to retire. Back in 1956, he'd helped McClelland buy George Stewart's shares by forgoing part of his salary; now he wished to realize the value of the shares he'd acquired in exchange. His old pal Jake sadly informed him they were worthless.

As compensation, McClelland offered Kane, in recognition of four decades of service, a monthly pension of $1,000. Kane was understandably bitter; he told McClelland he'd unilaterally abrogated their agreement. But McClelland responded that they'd both tried to turn M&S around, and they'd both failed, and now there simply wasn't enough value in the company to let him do the right thing. Kane had little choice but to accept; he died four years later.

It was no secret that, in addition to a sixteen-hour workday and a two-to-three-pack-a-day smoking habit, McClelland drank to excess much of the time, except when episodes of near collapse forced him to go on the wagon. Anyone who dealt with him made the disconcerting discovery that after the first couple of pre-lunch vodkas, he was considerably less focused or coherent than before. By the end of 1981, in his sixtieth year, McClelland had reached a state of physical and mental exhaustion. People close to him ganged up to insist he cease his self-destructive ways.

The remarkable thing was that McClelland listened. At the beginning of 1982, he decided to become chairman of the board and to pass daily operations to "a more sane, conservative hand." Neither of the two likely successors was available: burned out, Peter Taylor was leaving to be a work-at-home dad, to be replaced as head of sales and marketing by John Neale; and Anna Porter had committed herself to running her own company, Key Porter Books. In any case, Porter recalled years later, "I didn't believe Jack was ready to have somebody else do that job. You can draw your own conclusions about whether I was right."

McClelland chose as his replacement Linda McKnight, who had succeeded Porter as M&S director of publishing. Pragmatic and down-to-earth, McKnight hadn't sought the presidency; she'd urged McClelland to hire someone from outside the firm. In retrospect, it seems likely McClelland chose McKnight for at least two reasons, apart from her innate capabilities. As an insider, she was a known quantity; and as a woman, she'd be easier, he assumed, to work with. Like John Gray, McClelland didn't like big timber to stand too close.

It was a rough period in which to operate a business. A major recession was battering the economy, and interest rates eventually rose into the high teens, costing M&S half a million dollars a year. For three years, McKnight made a brave and determined effort. "You were so busy coping with your particular alligator," she recalled, "you didn't even worry about the swamp. I didn't pretend to know what was in Jack's mind, ever. I think Jack is a very complex individual. And I think he was tired, and he wanted a change. But I don't think he wanted to get out of the business."

M&S turned a small profit in 1983, abetted by $600,000 raised in a fire sale of its inventory to the public, which angered booksellers. But the following year was dismal financially. Among the ninety-one titles published in 1984 were Michael Bliss's *Banting*, Matt Cohen's historical novel *The Spanish Doctor*, Sandra Gwyn's classic work of Canadian social history

The Private Capital, Farley Mowat's *Sea of Slaughter*, and Mordecai Richler's *Home Sweet Home*, yet the company suffered a loss of $2 million, its worst ever. Halfway through the year, an emergency offering raised $1.1 million from twenty-one private investors; they received shares and seats on the board, diluting McClelland's own shareholding to 64 percent. Raising new equity had been a condition imposed by the Ontario government for refinancing the firm's debt. Among the investors were the authors Atwood, Berton, and Mowat and a wealthy Toronto property developer named Avie Bennett.

At that point, McKnight provided McClelland with an astute, remarkably objective memo assessing the crisis facing the company. She told him he could no longer run M&S as he'd run it for thirty-two years, or it would die. McKnight had the courage to tell her boss *he* was part of the problem, and he had to go. She said that a team approach to running M&S by McClelland, herself, and the financial officer, Len Cummings, wasn't working, since "we lack the necessary degree of mutual trust and respect." She recommended that McClelland install new management in whom he had confidence, and then let go: "Allow that management authority without interference. Like Alfred Knopf Sr., say to authors, politicians, booksellers, the world, 'Alas, I am now emeritus and can only weep with you.'" She also offered her resignation.

McClelland neither accepted McKnight's resignation nor followed her advice, but in dysfunctional fashion, he continued making it impossible for her to do her job. He went over her head to sell paperback rights to several of M&S's Lucy Maud Montgomery titles to Seal Books. Here McClelland was in clear conflict of interest: not only was he pre-empting McKnight's plans to publish the books in paperback at M&S, but he now owned 75 percent of Seal *and* received royalties on the titles concerned (the result of a deal made years earlier with the Montgomery estate).

As McKnight told him in April 1985, this put her in an intolerable position. The next month, she learned Seal was offering what she considered unacceptably low advances for rights to other titles by some of M&S's most popular authors, apparently with McClelland's connivance. Since she was powerless to stop the transactions, and since her responsibility was to act in the best interests of the company and its shareholders, she did the honourable thing and resigned. McClelland felt aggrieved by the negative publicity that resulted.

In 1983 the lawyer Linda Davey had been trying to decide whether to sue M&S or McClelland personally over a disastrous goof: the loss of the distinguished biographer Phyllis Grosskurth's papers for her 1980 biography of Havelock Ellis, which the company had been storing. To answer the lawyer's question, McClelland told Davey, "But I *am* McClelland & Stewart." Such kingly hubris was understandable but, after so much of other people's money had been invested, unsustainable.

Several months after resuming the presidency in 1985, McClelland once again confronted an unforgiving financial reality. The Royal Bank, which had temporarily increased the company's line of credit, now expected to be repaid. McClelland had promised payment of a sizable amount, but when the deadline rolled around, he couldn't meet his commitment. He telephoned Avie Bennett, the board member who had assisted in arranging the financing, and Bennett recalled McClelland saying, "I promised the bank $300,000 this weekend but we're short of money. Avie, this business is driving me nuts. Can you help me with the bank?"

Bennett replied spontaneously, "Jack, are you interested in selling the business?"

McClelland said yes. Until then, Bennett hadn't known he wanted to be a publisher.

It didn't take them long to come to terms. Bennett paid McClelland $1 million for his shares, paid back his fellow investors at a cost of another $1 million, and assumed all the firm's obligations: a highly satisfactory outcome for authors, printers, banks, governments, and creditors alike. It might have been a happy resolution too for McClelland, except that he'd later write, "I don't regret a moment of my life except for the day I sold our company."

While Bennett publicly extolled McClelland for his outstanding contributions to Canadian literature, McClelland joked out loud that he'd finally "caught a live one": a buyer who could afford to own the "albatross" M&S had become. Their understanding was that McClelland, now sixty-three, would remain in a paid advisory capacity for five years, something Bennett considered inconvenient but necessary, since he lacked experience in the business and knew few of the authors. The new owner relocated the company to a prime downtown property he owned, the former Maclean-Hunter building at the corner of University and Dundas, renamed McClelland & Stewart House, and installed his staff on the top floor. McClelland took an office down the hall from Bennett's.

Soon Bennett and McClelland were openly disagreeing about how to do business. "They started fighting in our in-baskets," said Jan Walter, who had moved from Macmillan to become director of publishing at M&S. She recalled the surreal experience of receiving memos signed "J.G.M." followed immediately by contradictory directives from Bennett, and vice-versa. Walter and her colleague Peter Waldock, the former Penguin Books Canada president then in charge of M&S's sales and marketing, found it difficult to steer a middle course. "It was a period of great unease," Walter remembered. "It was clear they had a very uncomfortable relationship."

Part of the problem was their conflict over how much authority McClelland could exercise. Everyone, including McClelland himself, had assumed Bennett wouldn't involve himself in day-to-day operations. But Bennett was a creative problem-solver; he'd bought M&S because he wanted a challenge, and he wasn't about to act as some figurehead who merely signed the cheques. Consequently McClelland absented himself from the office more and more. A little over a year after the sale, Bennett offered to pay him out for the full five years if he preferred to depart.

McClelland announced he was leaving the arena where he'd fought almost his entire adult life. "I made a mistake," he told the *Toronto Star* books columnist Ken Adachi in February 1987. "If you no longer have complete control, you should get out."

As a parting shot, McClelland sold his 75 percent interest in Seal Books that same month, not to Bennett but to Anna Porter. Bennett had naturally been interested in owning Seal to achieve vertical integration with the M&S program. But McClelland would later say in an interview that Bantam had directed him to sell to Porter. Legally, Bantam owned only

25 percent of Seal, but effectively, it exercised almost complete control. The manoeuvre hardly endeared the two men to each other.

Jack McClelland was now settled financially, but without the power and influence conferred by being a publisher. If once he'd *been* McClelland & Stewart, who was he now? Needing something to do, he set himself up as a literary agent. His trusted secretary, the redoubtable Marge Hodgeman, stayed with him and became his business partner; two of his four daughters helped out with the agency. McClelland found congenial clients, such as the sportswriter Trent Frayne and the controversial former premier of New Brunswick, Richard Hatfield. The only problem was that he didn't enjoy himself. McClelland wasn't cut out to be a go-between for authors and publishers, a maker of other people's deals. "It's a lousy trade," he said succinctly.

In 1993, the year Marge Hodgeman died and McClelland turned seventy-one, he wound up the agency and stole away quietly into private life with Elizabeth. The Book Promoters Association of Canada created an annual award for excellence in book promotion and called it the Jack Award. Many hoped he'd capture his life and times in an autobiography. Seven times, by his own count, he began drafts of "My Rose Garden." One draft, he thought, was better than the others, but he lost it somewhere. He'd looked high and low, at his Florida condominium, at his cottage in Muskoka, at his apartment in Toronto, but somehow it had disappeared. His putative publisher, Anna Porter, perhaps the only M&S employee he'd ever admired unreservedly, commented, "I think he doesn't want to find it. For whatever reason, he feels his publishing life is over."

McClelland felt he'd given his all, and there was nothing left. Perhaps that was the reason he'd avoided the celebration in Guadalajara in 1996 and a similar heartfelt homage by friends, colleagues, and the public two years later in Toronto at the Harbourfront International Festival of Authors.

Just before her death by suicide, Margaret Laurence captured in a few poignant words McClelland's true significance as a publisher: "He is a Canadian pioneer. He has risked his life for us, Canadian authors. I think we have proved him right."

COACH HOUSE PRESS

HOUSE OF ANANSI PRESS

NEW PRESS

8

PRINTED IN CANADA BY MINDLESS ACID FREAKS

For I was drunk on the steady flood of talent,
the welter of manuscripts that kept
surfacing month after month and often
with lives attached . . .

Dennis Lee, "The Death of Harold Ladoo" (1979)

In 1966, while Jack McClelland was turning Canadian publishing upside down, a long-haired young poet was earning a modest living as a production assistant at Oxford University Press in Toronto. On the side, Victor Coleman was helping the poet Raymond Souster edit and produce *New Wave Canada*, an anthology to be published that year by Contact Press. Coleman's boss William Toye noticed him poring over proofs of the anthology and asked if he might read it. Toye showed the proofs to the veteran critic A.J.M. Smith, then in the throes of compiling *Modern Canadian Verse* for Oxford, and Smith was impressed enough to select poems by four unknowns, William Hawkins, Robert Hogg, George Jonas, and Michael Ondaatje, to cross-pollinate his own anthology. Toye obligingly designed the type for *New Wave Canada*'s cover and title page.

A few months later, Coleman left Oxford to work at Coach House Press. Although he'd always found Toye a supportive mentor, Oxford's propriety and Coleman's drug-tripping weekends were a less than perfect fit. Coleman's salary would fall to zero, but he'd get to collaborate with brilliant young writers and designers on some of the most exciting work ever published in Canada.

By 1967 the Coach House motto, "Printed in Canada by mindless acid freaks," began appearing inconspicuously on books, posters, and assorted print ephemera. For the generation of publishers just starting up, the objective wasn't merely to stake a professional claim, it was to reinvent the profession. They operated from an outlaw position, independent, unpaid if necessary, accountable to no one except (sometimes) their authors. Many of the new publishers were writers themselves.

They weren't the first Canadian writers to cross over into publishing. The small-press movement in English Canada had begun two decades earlier with another writer, John Sutherland, in Montreal. Merging his little magazine *First Statement* with its rival *Preview* to create *Northern Review* in 1945, Sutherland acquired a printing press and, from 1946 to 1951, produced a series of eight poetry books under the imprint First Statement Press. They included first collections by Patrick Anderson, Irving Layton, Raymond Souster, Miriam Waddington, and Anne Wilkinson, as well as the manifesto-like *Other Canadians: An Anthology of the New Poetry in Canada, 1940–46*. Sutherland published without grants, and with few patrons. He wrote in 1951, "I am sure there are more Canadians who have made speeches about the need for supporting Canadian literature than there will ever be subscribers to *Northern Review*."

One of the First Statement poets, Ray Souster, was a quiet, self-effacing man who toiled in a Toronto bank for over forty years while living another life as an accomplished practitioner of William Carlos Williams's poetics of everyday speech. Souster was befriended by a more politically engaged poet, Louis Dudek, who had spent eight years in New York. When Dudek returned home to Montreal in 1951, he and Souster became proselytizers of contemporary American verse. Souster began his mimeographed little magazine *Contact* in 1952, and he, Dudek, and Layton founded Contact Press. It would become the paradigm of the writers' press in English Canada.

In the first few years, all but three of Contact's thirteen titles were written by one or another of the principals. In 1956, for example, there were three books by Layton, two by Souster, and one by Dudek – but also *Let Us Compare Mythologies* by twenty-two-year-old Leonard Cohen, carrying the sub-imprint of Dudek's McGill Poetry Series. From then on, Contact looked eclectically outward.

Over the next decade, the press would produce first or early collections by Daryl Hine, D.G. Jones, Eli Mandel, Alden Nowlan, Al Purdy, Milton Acorn, Gwendolyn MacEwen, George Bowering, Frank Davey, John Newlove, and Margaret Atwood. Contact's three founders contributed money and shared the chores of production, while Souster kept the inventory and filled orders at his none-too-roomy Toronto home. Layton left Contact in 1959, the year of his triumph with *A Red Carpet for the Sun*, to be replaced by Peter Miller. A proper banker, who until then had practised poetry almost as a secret vice, Miller was surprised to discover that "in the same building where I was aggrandizing the profits of the Imperial Bank of Canada, a fellow-financier by the name of Raymond Souster doubled as a poet." Contact published Miller's first collection in 1958, his second a year later.

Before long, warehouse operations had moved to Miller's Rosedale apartment. The other two partners readily agreed to his proposal that he finance some books. Dudek wrote Miller, "You will be doing a very fine thing," joking that they really ought to find "some Communist millionaire" to act as patron.

Contact's poets also pitched in. Purdy promoted the list in Montreal; the Ottawa poet Harry Howith designed MacEwen's *The Rising Fire*. The new vogue for poetry readings in universities and candlelit coffee houses made Contact's books and writers better known. In Toronto, readings took place at the Isaacs Gallery and the Bohemian Embassy; in Ottawa at Le Hibou, a coffee house. Contact's print runs were normally 250 copies, plainly but professionally produced: 200 paperbacks selling at $2, fifty in hardcover for libraries. The press launched Newlove's first major collection, *Moving In Alone*, in 1965, and Atwood's first professionally published book, *The Circle Game*, the next year. Atwood turned to Contact, she said, because "it was the only log in the ocean."

Miller provided the press not just with cash but with commitment and energy. Relations between him and the two founders were friendly but businesslike, and communication took place mainly by letter. "This publishing house, unlike others of the period, resembled a monastic cell," Miller wrote in the literary periodical *Canadian Notes and Queries*. There was also the thorny question, much more prevalent in the days before grants, of whether to accept cash contributions from authors. Dudek considered the practice acceptable, as long as editorial standards were maintained. But Miller was adamantly opposed. "We are not a vanity press," he wrote to Dudek, "nor shall we be so long as I am involved." Souster, previously neutral on the issue, sided with Miller.

True to his mission of giving young poets a start, Souster sponsored and edited *New Wave Canada*, subtitled, with blithe disregard for mixed metaphors, *The New Explosion in Canadian Poetry*. It introduced the work of seventeen contributors, almost all in their twenties, from Daphne Buckle (later Marlatt) and David McFadden to bp Nichol and Victor Coleman. But when the anthology appeared, an accompanying flyer cited the three founders of Contact Press without mentioning Miller's involvement, and he was sufficiently hurt to resign. As he acknowledged many years later, "I had long struggled against the concept of a vanity press, but in the end I succumbed to my own vanity." Souster and Dudek had neither the will to persuade Miller to stay nor the resources to continue alone. After fifty-three titles issued over fifteen years, Contact Press shut down in 1967, going out in high style with a Governor General's Award for *The Circle Game*.

On joining Coach House Press at twenty-two, Victor Coleman was already an unusual man. Before Oxford he'd supported himself as a copy boy at the *Toronto Star*, forgoing university for an apprenticeship in Black Mountain poetics. During weekends in Detroit and Buffalo, where the American poets Charles Olson and Robert Creeley were teaching, he hung out with literary and political revolutionaries. He created and edited a little magazine, *Island* (after Ward's Island, where he was living), which mutated into *Is* (pronounced "eyes"), printed after hours on the back-shop press at Oxford.

Late in 1964, Coleman attended one of the literary soirees Earle Birney threw while teaching at the University of Toronto. Birney liked cultivating young writers and artists, and Coleman met the designer and printer Stan Bevington that night, beginning one of the most fruitful collaborations in Canadian publishing. Soft-spoken and enigmatic, Bevington was equally precocious. After working on small-town weeklies in Edson and Fairview, Alberta, he'd briefly attended the University of Toronto and the Ontario College of Art before launching his own design and job-printing venture. The impetus had come from Bevington's overnight success as a flag purveyor.

The summer of 1964 was a singular moment in the nation's life: the flag was up for grabs. Prime Minister Lester Pearson had announced that a made-in-Canada design should at last replace the British Union Jack and Red Ensign, and debate raged over what the new national emblem ought to look like. Bevington seized the entrepreneurial moment by creating small versions of the various designs under discussion, from a spray of three maple leaves flanked by two vertical bars, representing the Pacific and the Atlantic, to a design known as "nine beavers pissing on a frog." With an old-fashioned wood-and-brass bellows camera, Bevington photographed the images in his basement apartment, printed the results using a silkscreen process, and had them finished by seamstresses. He put them into the hands of his sales force, a ragtag bunch of art school friends and penniless hippies, who hawked them by the thousands on the streets of Yorkville, then emerging as headquarters of Toronto's counterculture. One summer generated enough cash to buy a used red Austin-Healey Sprite for dashing around town and an old hand-operated Challenge Gordon platen press – the same one that would become the logo for Coach House Press, which Bevington would launch a year later with a similar mixture of ingenuity and experimentation.

The coach house was a derelict Victorian structure on a back lane near the corner of Bathurst and Dundas Streets, which housed Bevington's home, studio, and printing shop. Bevington welcomed writers as creative partners. One was Dennis Reid, the future curator, who had known Bevington when they were undergraduates. Reid brought in the first trade title to bear the Coach House imprint, Wayne Clifford's *Man in a Window*.

Published in 1965, Clifford's poems were illustrated with Reid's sensual, photography-based illustrations and designed, hand-set, and printed by Bevington, working under the spell of Frank Newfeld's concept for *The Spice-Box of Earth*. Victor Coleman helped with distribution, and Bevington helped Coleman out by completing the printing of *New Wave Canada*, which for some forgotten reason the original printer had left unfinished.

Bevington bought an old Linotype machine and a new offset press – the beginning of his love of combining old and new technologies. While Bevington acquired design and printing jobs (for example, the cover and endpapers for Scott Symons's *Place d'Armes*, an M&S title), Coleman produced manuscripts that Wayne Clifford had acquired for Coach House and began soliciting more. The catch was that Coleman had to typeset them himself. "I taught Victor how to operate the Linotype machine," Bevington recalled, "not knowing he couldn't drive a car. So if he couldn't Linotype it, it didn't get published. That put a slight damper on his exuberance."

Each early Coach House title was memorable. Joe Rosenblatt's *LSD Leacock* and Henry Beissel's *New Wings for Icarus* were startling marriages of graphic and poetic imagery. Coach House's fourth title exploded the concepts of the poem and the book altogether. Written and conceived by bp Nichol, designed by Bevington, and produced by various hands, *Journeying and the Returns* incorporated a small, perfect-bound book along with other "poem objects" inside a blue and lavender cardboard case. The book had French flaps, unusual then in English Canada, and the long poem it contained was printed in coloured inks that emerged ghostlike from heavy grey stock. The case held printed samples of Nichol's playful concrete poems in various shapes, sizes, and media. These included an animated thumb-flip poem the size of a matchbox, a cutaway poem giving directions for its own destruction by fire, and *Borders*, a 45-rpm disk of Nichol chanting his sound poetry.

Nichol would become central to Coach House as both author and editorial conscience, but for the time being, Coleman was the prime "official/unofficial editor," as Nichol put it. Coleman's instinct for new poetic voices complemented Bevington's instinct for according each title its own look and feel. In Bevington's aesthetic, texture, shape, and colour were as important as illustration and typography. George Bowering's *Baseball: A Poem in the Magic Number Nine* was shaped like a pennant, with a grass-green felt cover. Coleman's own *One/Eye/Love* was elongated and adorned with swirling psychedelic drawings. The irregular size and shape of the early titles often made them sit awkwardly on the shelf, putting off booksellers and librarians. It was a problem to which the principals were cheerfully indifferent. Coach House produced *Nevertheless These Eyes*, poems by the West Coast painter Roy Kiyooka, with a mirror-like reflecting cover, and *The Dainty Monsters*, the first collection by twenty-three-year-old Michael Ondaatje, with an opulent, full-colour batik design.

In 1968, just as the press was hitting its stride, Bevington received notice that his coach house was to be demolished. Salvation arrived in the form of the poet and House of Anansi publisher Dennis Lee. Rochdale College was about to open at the corner of Bloor and Huron Streets, and Lee, one of its guiding lights, invited Bevington to become Rochdale's printer. Bevington and Coleman joined the horde of students and hangers-on moving into the still-unfinished high-rise. The plan was that Coach House would eventually take up residence there too, but for now the press found "temporary" digs in a crumbling two-storey brick building, a former stable, in a lane behind Rochdale.

Over the next few years, geography and ambition would link two of the most influential small presses in Canada's history. Sited within a few blocks of each other, Coach House Press and House of Anansi Press would share authors (Matt Cohen, Bowering, Ondaatje, Atwood) and even, on one occasion, produce a joint catalogue. As Cohen put it, both presses were "community centres for writers," where authors could sit around talking with their editors and one another, whether around the handmade pine table at Coach House or the Formica kitchen table at Anansi. But the differences between them ran deep, and Rochdale became the measure of those.

Dennis Lee, who had once considered entering the United Church ministry, had invested heavily in the Rochdale ideal. In his essay "Getting to Rochdale" in the 1968 Anansi anthology *The University Game*, Lee described his quest for a radically new kind of higher education. When Campus Co-op, a non-profit student housing cooperative, decided to build the twin towers of Rochdale and to graft an educational function onto a student residence, Lee became a principal architect of the process.

There would be no faculty, syllabus, or degree programs, and "resource persons" would take the place of professors. A Rochdale education would be what each student made it. It was a brave and exciting experiment that ultimately proved unworkable. Homeless young refugees from the drug culture, evicted from Yorkville by the police, found Rochdale's spacious lounges ideal for crashing; many were allowed to stay on for months since it would have been too "fascist" to make them leave. They were joined by those who wanted to sell them drugs, and by some who wanted to control that supply with dogs and guns. By spring 1969, it seemed there were as many unauthorized people living in the high-rise as students and resource persons. Rochdale's free clinic treated the fallout from bad trips, malnutrition, and venereal disease but couldn't prevent the deaths of several people who fell or jumped from upper floors.

Some thrived in that environment by embracing the chaos; others were repelled and overwhelmed. Seminars burned out after six to eight weeks. A professional potter set up a ceramic workshop, but "freaks" continually wrecked his equipment and left the place a shambles. And yet other creative pursuits bore fruit. The drama collective Theatre Passe Muraille was based at Rochdale for a time, most famously presenting its production of *Futz*, which resulted in the arrest of the producer, the director, and the entire undressed cast. People travelled nude on the elevators.

It was an environment that suited Coach House's bent for random spontaneity and artistic experimentation better than Lee's earnest intellectualism. Coleman offered a writing workshop on the serial poem, while down the lane Bevington and other Coach House designer-printers held graphic arts seminars at all hours. They were never so impractical, however, as to move their equipment into Rochdale. Instead Bevington patched up the leaking roof and rotting floorboards of the old stable, where his design and printing operations have remained.

Lee, meanwhile, was making such convoluted statements in the Rochdale *Daily* as "A minority with fairly desperate emotional needs . . . ties us into a syndrome of crisis/letdown which frustrates all the slower and more organic processes of education." At Rochdale's public meetings, pulling on his pipe and offering stern analysis of the residents' more harebrained notions, Lee began to seem like somebody's parent. He was nearing the age over which nobody could be trusted; he was almost thirty.

Occupying the middle of an experiment that police and civic officials were finding increasingly unacceptable, Lee got hit from both sides. In an "Apolitical Manifesto" in May 1969, Victor Coleman addressed their fellow Rochdalians: "Just about every piece of publicity Rochdale has received has had some statement from Dennis in it. I sincerely doubt we need such an apologist."

A few weeks later, Lee resigned, declaring Rochdale "an institution I can no longer live with." Years later he would say, "I still churn internally when I walk by the building." But it meant the House of Anansi would have his full attention.

In Dave Godfrey's sense of things, there were two reasons for starting Anansi. In 1966, scouting through the aisles of the University of Toronto Book Room, surrounded on all sides by American and British titles, Godfrey came to a startling realization: Canada was invisible. The second reason was that Dennis Lee had a manuscript that needed publishing.

Godfrey, then twenty-eight, had been away a long time. Before completing a two-year teaching stint in Ghana, he'd earned a B.A. from the University of Iowa, an M.A. from Stanford, and an M.F.A. from Iowa's famed creative writing program, where he'd met Clark Blaise. Godfrey's stories had been appearing back home in *The Tamarack Review*, but he'd refused an invitation to appear in an annual anthology of best American stories when the publisher wouldn't change the title to *Best American and Canadian Stories*. At the University of Toronto, first-year students were still studying Canadian literature as an end-of-term adjunct to the American literature course Godfrey had taken back in 1957. He asked Gordon Roper, who taught the course at Trinity College, when the university might introduce a dedicated CanLit program. "Maybe in ten years," Roper replied, "if the right people die."

Godfrey seethed with humiliation at being made to feel like a colonial in his own country. He shared his anger with Lee, then still teaching at Victoria College. Lee showed his poems to Godfrey, who declared they should be published right away. In spring 1967, when Lee's *Kingdom of Absence* appeared in an edition of 300 copies, the title page read "House of Ananse Press." The spelling would change on the next printing and all subsequent titles.

The name had originated with Godfrey's sojourn in west Africa. Anansi was a spider god who had created the world, then stuck around to play tricks on humans. The house logo was a stylized spider, a small but lethal-looking creature; the Anansi habitué Douglas (later George) Fetherling remembered that when the logo's designer was asked why her spider had only six legs, she explained demurely, "The other two are up its ass."

Until then, small-press publishing in Canada had meant poetry publishing, as exemplified by Contact, Coach House, Fiddlehead in Fredericton, and several presses just starting up in Vancouver, such as Talon Books and blewointment press. But from the beginning, Godfrey saw Anansi as operating in the public realm, beyond literature. Like Coach House, it would become an agent for change, but rather than revolutionizing the aesthetics of publishing, Anansi would radicalize its politics.

Godfrey attended a Vancouver meeting called by Peter Dwyer, the cosmopolitan former British spy who headed the Canada Council, to discuss how to encourage outlets for Canadian writing. The meeting sent a signal that the ten-year-old council, which had previously concentrated on the performing and visual arts, was open to funding publishing. Godfrey and Lee assembled a budget for four manuscripts and travelled to Ottawa to present it to a council arts officer, David Silcox. The books were eligible for assistance, Silcox told them, but he pointed out certain deficiencies in their budgeting, suggesting they go away and rework their figures. Crestfallen, Godfrey assumed they'd be leaving empty-handed. "No, no," Silcox assured him, "just go out the door, redo the numbers, and come back in." He wasn't supposed to rewrite his clients' applications but he did want to be helpful. A small contribution from the taxpayer augmented Anansi's start-up capital of $2,500, and Godfrey and Lee were in business.

Like a bar band cutting its first record, Anansi produced an initial fall list composed half of covers, half of new material. The original works were *The Absolute Smile*, a book of poems by George Jonas, and Godfrey's story collection *Death Goes Better with Coca-Cola*, which provoked the giant beverage corporation into making threatening noises about trademark infringement. The covers were reissues of Lee's collection and Atwood's *The Circle Game*, already out of print.

The partners' larger agenda took root the next year. *The University Game*, edited by Lee with Howard Adelman of Campus Co-op, fed a continent-wide hunger for educational reform, and the anthology soon had to be reprinted. Godfrey brought in *Manual for Draft-Age Immigrants to Canada*, a kind of draft dodger's *Whole Earth Almanac*, co-published with the Toronto Anti-Draft Program. In addition to selling many thousands of copies in Canada, Anansi shipped many thousands more to American campuses. Some copies became casualties of war, blocked by U.S. Customs and either confiscated or returned in damaged condition; others slipped through the lines. A slim paperback with drab brown covers, the manual sold far better than any other Anansi title of the 1960s, reaching 55,000 copies by 1970.

Also in 1968, Anansi published the first edition of Lee's *Civil Elegies*, a considerable poetic advance over his previous book; an expanded version of Al Purdy's *Poems for All the Annettes*, first issued by Contact; and *Airplane Dreams: Compositions from Journals*, by Allen Ginsberg. On Ginsberg's flying visit to Toronto to read at Hart House, his handler, Doug Fetherling, had persuaded him to leave behind enough journal material to make a forty-eight-page book. Although the work wasn't Ginsberg's finest, it provided the wherewithal for another political cause. Lee used it to challenge the notorious "manufacturing clause" in American copyright law. That provision effectively barred Canadian publishers from exporting books written by Americans into the United States by removing copyright protection from any book exported in more than 1,500 copies. Anansi defiantly proclaimed it was shipping 5,000 copies of *Airplane Dreams* to City Lights Books in San Francisco, Ginsberg's American publisher. The books were promptly confiscated, and Anansi made its point, at a cost it could scarcely afford. The clause was eventually rescinded as a result of industry lobbying.

Naturally all this rabble-rousing attracted media attention. The Toronto *Telegram*, the *Montreal Star*, and *Maclean's* ran features on Anansi. When they visited the press, reporters found a furtive cell operating literally underground. Arriving at the front door of Dave and Ellen Godfrey's rented brick house at 671 Spadina Avenue, an eccentric Victorian Gothic next door to a funeral chapel, they'd find a note directing them around the corner onto Sussex Avenue, down the second lane on the right and through a metal gate into the Godfreys' back garden. Passing a toy-filled sandbox, they'd enter by a rear door, duck their heads down a dark stairway, and emerge beyond the washing machine into Anansi's cockpit. Philip Sykes, writing in *Maclean's*, compared it to "a bunker in the siege of Stalingrad . . . Here guerrillas of the new writing plot daring forays. Here, at dawn, a young novelist rolls up his sleeping bag from the concrete floor of the furnace room and shouts that at last he understands his central character."

Writers did bed down in the furnace room in exchange for performing shipping duties, their privacy protected by a sooty blanket hung from the ceiling. The Anansi basement was dank and cold; whenever the Spadina bus braked to a stop outside, grit particles floated down onto the books and whoever was inhabiting the furnace room. Initially that was Fetherling, a refugee from Wheeling, West Virginia, via Manhattan, who became Anansi's first employee at $20 a week.

For Ellen Godfrey, having her husband's hobby/obsession/business invade their home while they raised young children was a mixed blessing. Long-haired strangers of both sexes wandered through the kitchen or up the stairs to the bathroom. When she retired to the bedroom, she'd find Anansi bills spread out across the bed. As the daughter of an entrepreneurial family from Chicago, Ellen Godfrey understood how out of character it was for her husband and Lee, both academics from middle-class Ontario professional families, to be in commerce. "People forget," she recalled, "that starting a business wasn't a normal thing for them to do." Nor was it normal for principals of other small presses, but Anansi was different; some of its books sold in large quantities, generating enough revenue that the founders had to cope with another unfamiliar problem – growth.

"One day, somebody took the unusual step of acquiring a postage meter," Lee remembered. "I just couldn't believe it. It suggested an institutional continuity that was kind of scary."

Godfrey was readier than Lee to adapt to the ways of business. He paid an assortment of students and writers in Anansi shares, a species of what he termed "communal capitalism." When the Royal Canadian Mounted Police, under pressure from the Federal Bureau of Investigation to find the source of *Manual for Draft-Age Immigrants to Canada*, arranged for a Revenue Canada auditor to visit Anansi, the accountant hung around a suspiciously long time. Ever the opportunist, Godfrey talked the man into teaching him basic accounting: "He helped us put our books together. Until then I hadn't realized inventory had a value."

When Godfrey moved to Provence during a sabbatical from Trinity, Lee took the helm, leading Anansi more deeply into fiction than any small Canadian press had gone before. During 1969–1970, Anansi produced an extraordinary group of titles that launched or advanced writing careers. These included Graeme Gibson's first novel, *Five Legs*; Matt Cohen's first novel, *Korsoniloff*; Peter Such's first novel, *Fallout*; Marian Engel's second novel, *The Honeyman Festival*; Michael Ondaatje's prose and poetry fusion, *The Collected Works of Billy the Kid*; Ray Smith's first story collection, *Cape Breton Is the Thought Control Centre of Canada*; and the first of many Quebec novels translated by Sheila Fischman, Roch Carrier's *La guerre, yes sir!* That was only part of Anansi's output during the period, which also included George Grant's important work of political philosophy *Technology and Empire*.

The Cohen and Such novels appeared in an experiment known as Spiderline Editions. In a blurb for the series in its fall 1969 catalogue, Anansi boldly attributed the "barrenness" of fiction in Canada to the conservatism of publishers wedded to mainstream realism. "We have one modest aim," Anansi immodestly declared: "to change the climate for Canadian fiction by letting the best young writers get into print, find an audience and get on with their next book."

There were five Spiderlines in all, published simultaneously and often reviewed as a group. They had uniform khaki paper covers and identical $1.95 price tags, made possible by using cheap typesetting and web-offset printing technologies. The other three novels were *The Telephone Pole*, by Russell Marois; *Eating Out*, by the American expatriate John Sandman; and an experiment within an experiment, *À perte de temps*, by Pierre Gravel, a novel of Quebec political terrorism, published in French.

Spiderline Editions didn't continue beyond 1969, but it positioned Anansi as the destination of choice for young novelists. Astonishingly, Anansi titles represented nearly a third of the original fiction issued in English Canada that year (in total, only about twenty-five titles). The press's output was all the more remarkable considering Dennis Lee's painstaking methods as editor.

"I found my way blindly to what I was doing," Lee remembered. "The kind of books I was good for [as editor] were by writers with a considerable talent who were still finding their way. I'd often make completely wingnut suggestions, but with some sense of what wasn't working. Even if the author didn't agree, it would catalyze him or her into seeing the work differently."

Before taking *Five Legs* to Lee, Graeme Gibson had sent the manuscript to the few Canadian publishers then handling fiction, an experience he found progressively more depressing. At Macmillan, he remembered, Jim Bacque had been interested in the novel. "The disconcerting thing," Gibson recalled, "was that every time I went to see Jim in his office, it was getting smaller. He had a big office and a big desk. Then I went to see him after he'd read it, and his office was half that size. Within weeks, he was sharing an office with somebody else, and then he turned down the book."

Dennis Lee didn't even have an office. The intensive editorial sessions between him and Gibson shifted from Lee's home to his room at Rochdale to Gibson's home, one constant being the dense fog from the pipes and cigarillos the two men smoked. Lee, Gibson thought, was "astonishing" as he immersed himself in the densely textured, difficult novel, on which Gibson had been working for eleven years: "Dennis approached the editing with the same sort of obsessive seriousness with which I'd approached the writing. He just pushed me and pushed me and forced me to really think about it." Lee told Gibson his novel was like an air mattress: the reader couldn't settle comfortably into it until they let some of the air out.

Since Anansi was broke, Lee had the book proofread for free, a few pages at a time, by denizens of Rochdale. Appearing in April 1969, *Five Legs* turned out to be Anansi's signature novel. Quirky, demanding, unnervingly comic, it was startlingly individual for its time and place, marked by the Upper Canadian angst of its guilt-deformed characters: a cultural specific that no other novelist had quite captured. The book sold well for an experimental novel, surpassing 3,000 copies in its first season and heralding, along with *Place d'Armes* by Gibson's friend Scott Symons, the arrival of a Canadian avant-garde. Even the phlegmatic literary columnist of the *Globe and Mail*, William French, wrote: "*Five Legs*, I have no hesitation in saying, is the most interesting first novel by a Canadian to be published in many years."

Lee replicated his deeply personal editorial involvement with other novels, but he knew his method didn't work for every author: "It could be a good thing for writers to do a book or two with me, then work with somebody else, after they didn't need that kind of midwife editing. I was camped in people's lives pretty centrally, and you don't want that to happen very often."

After receiving the Lee treatment on *Korsoniloff*, Matt Cohen came to a similar conclusion: "You saw in incredible detail how he saw your book. But you had to have the strength to stand up to him with an idea of your own." Lee rejected Cohen's second novel, *Johnny Crackle Sings*, after working extensively on the manuscript. He admitted to some confusion between editorial process and final product: "I have great trouble telling whether I like what is on the page or what has gone back and forth between us in discussion." Cohen took it hard but moved on to M&S.

Marian Engel travelled the opposite route, moving from a larger firm, Longman Canada, to Anansi, where she stayed for three books. In correspondence about her 1970 novel *The Honeyman Festival*, Engel fended Lee off in the manner prescribed by Cohen. She pointed out a basic difference between her intuitive approach and Lee's intellectual one, while appreciating his aesthetic and philosophical analysis of her fiction. The result of their collaboration was arguably Engel's best work until *Bear*, published six years later by M&S.

Lee didn't handle the list entirely on his own. He wrote to an old Victoria College classmate in England and asked her to sit on Anansi's board, which in practical terms meant contributing free editorial labour. And so, in spring 1970, Margaret Atwood took a hand in editing *The Collected Works of Billy the Kid*, urging Michael Ondaatje to tighten his book by cutting specified sequences. Coach House designed and produced *Billy the Kid*, making it Anansi's best-looking title to date.

The two houses tried cooperating on another level. A letter to bookstores and libraries at the beginning of 1969, typed on stationery featuring the spider and letterpress logos side by side, announced, "Two of Canada's liveliest presses have just gotten married . . . It isn't a legal union, but our first offspring has just appeared." Enclosed with the letter was a joint catalogue, Anansi starting from one end, Coach House from the other. Customers could order all the titles through Anansi, which promised "such bizarre customs as same-day shipping and tidy book-keeping." But the venture lasted only a few months, a victim, according to Stan Bevington, of Anansi's discomfort with Coach House's inveterate "playfulness": "It was a time when the choice between doing drugs or working included both, for me and the people who worked here. It was appalling to many people to think you could do both." Coach House people, highly productive in their own weird way, tended to view Anansi people as straight and graspingly commercial.

On Dave Godfrey's return from France, the momentum at Anansi clearly lay with Lee and others he'd brought into the press. Immersed in writing *The New Ancestors*, Godfrey was also busy co-founding another venture, New Press, and resuming his teaching. He soon distanced himself from Anansi, and vice versa.

Most of Lee's colleagues were women. Arden Ford (briefly Cohen, while married to Matt) had been working at the university's Student Printing Bureau and renting a room in Dennis and Donna Lee's house when Lee asked her, as a favour, to typeset *The University Game*. She also typeset and printed the first edition of *Civil Elegies*, collating it with Lee in the wee hours at the university. Ford moved to a dilapidated farmhouse near Algonquin Park with no telephone, electricity, or running water, but from time to time she'd emerge from the woods to work for Anansi, initially for shares whose value was entirely symbolic, later for cash, although never much of it. "In the beginning, we all worked there gratis," remembered Ford, later the business manager at McGill-Queen's University Press.

"People were living communally in one fashion or another, and one spent very little money. The material situation just wasn't the focus of our lives."

Ann Wall arrived at Anansi in fall 1968. Sickened by the Vietnam War, she and her husband, Byron Wall, emigrated from the United States and moved into Rochdale, where they kept running into Lee in the elevator. A month later, Ann Wall was working in the Spadina basement, proofreading, typing invoices, packing books, and generating sorely needed cash flow by mailing statements to bookstores. She worked for little more than a sense that it was all worthwhile. "What really struck me," she recalled, "was the quality of the writing that was all around. Here was this country, producing such fine writers but not publishing them, not even aware of them. Their work needed to get out there. Coming from the States, where everything seemed impossible, we saw Canada as a liberation."

Shirley Gibson arrived to promote her husband's novel in spring 1969. Having worked as the production manager at *Arts Canada* magazine, Gibson brought skills and contacts that Anansi lacked, and Lee asked her to stay on at $50 a week. She expanded media coverage of Anansi titles and improved their covers, commissioning work on a shoestring from hip young designers. She considered her specialty to be "working with small organizations, taking them out of the basement, tidying them up." Soon she was pressuring Lee to tidy up his drawn-out editing sessions, and the pair were striking sparks off each other. When Lee entertained the Canada Council's head of writing and publishing, Naim Kattan, Gibson greatly resented his introducing her and Ann Wall to Kattan as "staff." There was supposed to be no hierarchy at Anansi, but when the men went out for lunch, the women stayed behind.

Early in 1970, Anansi moved from the house on Spadina into a faded yellow brick mansion on Jarvis Street beside the Red Lion Pub. The press proceeded to publish a slew of titles that shaped the Canadian canon: more books by Cohen, Engel, Ondaatje (*Coming Through Slaughter*), and Graeme Gibson (*Communion*); new fiction by Austin Clarke and another writer from the Caribbean, Harold Sonny Ladoo; poetry by Atwood, Bowering, P.K. Page, Paulette Jiles, Patrick Lane, and John Thompson; translations of Quebec fiction by Hubert Aquin, Roch Carrier, and others; non-fiction by the University of Toronto historian James Eayrs, the *Globe and Mail* foreign correspondent Charles Taylor, and Northrop Frye (*The Bush Garden*).

Early in 1971, however, it seemed as if much of that publishing might never happen, at least not under the Anansi imprint. The press was still handling its own distribution, and the bulk of its inventory was stored in the basement of a five-storey brick warehouse. On a March morning when a three-alarm fire ravaged the old building, a hundred firefighters needed two hours to extinguish the blaze. Although untouched by fire, many of Anansi's 71,000 books suffered water damage. The inventory had a manufacturing replacement value of $40,000, but an out-of-date insurance policy covered only $9,000 of it.

Wading miserably through the flooded basement in rubber boots, Anansi staffers discovered that many of the trade paperbacks inside the soaked cartons needed only an airing to restore them to saleable condition. Meanwhile, the goodwill Anansi had generated during its four years of existence came to its rescue. Friends, writers, booksellers, suppliers, even other publishers volunteered to load books onto trucks supplied by Hunter-Rose, which did most of Anansi's printing. With the generosity for which he was known, the company's president, Guy Upjohn, cleared a large section of his plant, and damp books were spread out all over the floor to dry, saving about half the inventory. Booksellers helped out by paying their accounts early; even supposedly hard-hearted Jack Cole, president of the Coles chain, sent his cheque around by hand. Anansi was back in business eight days after the fire.

Ironically, the press had been trying to put out another sort of fire on the morning the blaze struck. Anansi, although vociferously nationalistic, kept attracting expatriate Americans who became central to its affairs. Ann Wall had happened along at just the right time. The cash-strapped press needed both volunteers and angels, and Wall was both, blessed with not only an American work ethic but an inheritance of old Virginia coal-mining money. In 1970, as Anansi's growing pains became acute, she began making small unsecured loans to the company and soon offered to invest directly, buying shares from the original principals as well as many small shareholders. The only condition of her friendly takeover was that everything, from editorial to personnel, remain the same.

But a *New York Times* article about Canadian publishing gave the situation a sinister twist. It said Anansi had been "sold in distress to a young American couple, Byron and Ann Wall, for less than $20,000," placing their purchase in the context of American takeovers and quoting what the Anansi principals considered a negative interpretation of the sale by Dave Godfrey. Since this was an extremely sensitive issue at the time, Anansi issued a statement to set the record straight: "One of our aims is to help make a country that will be our own. Ann and Byron Wall are working with native Canadians toward that goal."

Anansi closed ranks to resolve its difficulties, cutting back its 1971 list and trimming costs. But by the following year, personal burnout was taking a heavy toll on the press's collective psyche. One of the Spiderline novelists, twenty-six-year-old Russell Marois, committed suicide by lying down in front of a train. Harold Sonny Ladoo was murdered at twenty-eight on a visit home to Trinidad. The poet John Thompson died by his own hand a few years later, aged thirty-eight. In his remarkable, self-questioning long poem, "The Death of Harold Ladoo," Lee wrote about his relationship to the troubled generation of writers who revolved around Anansi. He described the conflicts among Anansi people in another poem, "Sibelius Park," as "the grim dudgeon" among "deep combative egos."

The press's internal politics were compounded by marital troubles. "Analyzing the interpersonal relationships took about as much time as the publishing," Arden Ford recalled. "Part of the reason I stopped working there was that it was such heavy going emotionally."

Shirley Gibson concurred: "There was a dark side to Anansi. More broken marriages than I can count." By the time Lee staggered away exhausted in 1972, his own marriage, as well as those of Atwood, the Gibsons, and the Walls, was disintegrating. Beginning her relationship with her future husband, Graeme Gibson, Atwood picked up some of the slack editorially. Unlike Lee's, her approach to Anansi manuscripts was swift and decisive. Atwood's ex-husband, the writer James Polk, was also on the scene and would soon become the press's chief editor, a post he'd fill with distinction for fifteen years.

Shirley Gibson replaced Lee at the head of Anansi's non-hierarchical hierarchy. "I think Dennis left because he sensed people were becoming impatient with him," she said in an interview before her death in 1997. "We gave him a schedule and asked him if he could meet it. He may have felt pushed." But first Lee would midwife Anansi's best-known title.

With its back perpetually to the wall, the press needed another money-maker. Earlier it had published two practical handbooks: *Law Law Law*, by the social activist lawyers Clayton Ruby and Paul Copeland, and *VD: The People-to-People Diseases*. The idea arose of adapting the handbook concept to teaching Canadian literature, and Atwood agreed to attempt it. "*Survival* was going to be the *VD* of Canadian literature," she recalled. "It was going to be a hundred pages long, and it was just going to be a hand-book. Because there wasn't one, and most people had been through school without ever having considered the existence of CanLit."

Atwood regarded *Survival: A Thematic Guide to Canadian Literature* as a community effort, since it benefited from so many contributions. The resources section at the back, compiled by Ann Wall and others, directed readers to a wide variety of information sources about Canadian books, art, music, drama, and film. Atwood had meant simply to synthesize the prevailing critical ideas about Canadian literature, adding her own slant. But Lee pushed her into enlarging her intuitions, until the book evolved into a pioneering thesis on the national gestalt. "Dennis got hold of it," she remembered, "and said, 'Well, this is a much bigger idea. Let's expand this. Let's consider that. Let's add this.' The manuscript pages are covered with tiny Dennis handwriting."

The public response to the book, published in 1972, stunned Atwood and everyone else at Anansi. People loved it or loathed it. Detractors took exception to Atwood's version of Canada's struggle to outgrow colonialism, as if the very word offended them. Some charged that she was overly nationalistic; others, objecting to her portrayal of Canadians as victims, that she wasn't nationalistic enough. Either way, *Survival* was wildly successful in achieving its aim: forcing Canadians to take a stand towards their literature.

Expected to sell 4,000 copies at most, enough to underwrite a few Anansi poetry titles or a first novel, *Survival* has been in demand ever since; by 2002, it had sold over 150,000 copies. *Survival*'s significance lay not just in its content or sales but in its political impact. It was therefore the sort of book that Coach House would not have published – but New Press would have.

After leaving Clarke, Irwin in 1968, I had occasion to hear more of Dave Godfrey's theories. One was that anyone could be a publisher. In Cape Coast, Ghana, Godfrey had visited a man of very limited means who printed his own books and bound them himself by hand. If that guy could be a publisher, Godfrey insisted, we all could. Another theory hit closer to home: "The model isn't Jack McClelland or John Gray," Godfrey would say, "it's Gérald Godin and Gaston Miron," naming two *indépendantiste* Quebec writers, both highly engaged politically, who had become publishers.

During his 1968–1969 sabbatical in France, Godfrey decided it was time that Anansi faced up to reality. It couldn't survive indefinitely on poetry, grants, and volunteer labour: the press would have to be run in a more businesslike fashion. It needed to become more professional, to publish more non-fiction to support the literary books. Godfrey felt he'd found in Europe the two people Anansi needed. One was Jim Bacque, with seven years' experience at Macmillan, who also was writing and living for a year in Provence. I was the other, becalmed with Suzette on the north coast of Crete after exploring the Continent by car.

Throughout a rainy Mediterranean winter, Godfrey, Bacque, and I exchanged exuberant letters about publishing strategies, book ideas, author possibilities. Being far from home had brought Canada into vivid and urgent focus, giving us a deeper feeling for the country's uniqueness, its importance to the world. Bacque and I assumed Godfrey had cleared the partnership idea with Dennis Lee. But back at Anansi, Godfrey's inspiration was shot down; when the notion of adding two more partners was put to a workers' vote, the collective decision was no.

Undeterred, Godfrey, Bacque, and I then resolved to start our own venture, naming it New Press. We wanted to provoke Canadians into discovering something resembling our shared epiphany after a year abroad. On our return to Toronto in summer 1969, we hit the ground running.

Our first title, *The Struggle for Canadian Universities*, proclaimed what New Press was about. The authors were Robin Mathews and James Steele,

Carleton University professors of English who'd been raising a ruckus about the domination of Canadian campuses by American professors and the resulting ascendancy of American content and viewpoints. Mathews and Steele were popping up everywhere, giving speeches, writing op-ed pieces, brandishing statistical proof that American academics had flooded the country in the 1960s, filled the top jobs, and hired their friends. *The Struggle for Canadian Universities* would be a compendium of polemics, certain to heap fresh fuel on the fire.

At twenty-five, I was the junior partner in New Press. And since Godfrey had his professorship, and Bacque his house in Moore Park, a cottage on Georgian Bay, and other assets, I would be the only one to receive a salary. In return I'd do the grunt work, starting with editing Mathews and Steele. They were a distinctly odd couple: Mathews charismatic and dogmatic, Steele dryly cerebral. Learning book production on the fly while editing their manuscript, I received help from James Bruce, a Hunter-Rose sales rep who conducted for me, as he did for many new publishers at the time, a veritable production workshop. When the cartons arrived containing 3,000 shiny red and white copies of *Struggle*, I parcelled up books to match the invoices I'd typed, weighed the packages, slapped on postage, and drove them to the post office. I was back in the warehouse.

To our amazement and delight, the book took off. We had to reprint immediately, and before Christmas 6,000 copies were in print and moving fast, especially out of college stores. We were sharing space with Anansi in the old house on Spadina beside the funeral home; the Godfreys, now living in Mississauga, sublet the place to the two presses. Down in the basement, Ann Wall offered me practical advice on invoicing, packing materials, and the care and feeding of the postage meter. A personable young writer named Mark Czarnecki had replaced Fetherling in the furnace room. Dennis Lee hung around, muttering ironic banter through pipe smoke. I couldn't tell whether Dennis enjoyed having an audience, or liked being surrounded by his editorial progeny, or just wanted to get away from the second floor, where Shirley Gibson reigned. From that floor there emanated a suspicion that the guys on the first floor were a little too commercial, a tad impure in spirit. New Press was to Anansi as Anansi was to Coach House.

Suspicion was directed especially towards Jim Bacque, who'd reached the unimaginable age of forty; worse, Bacque's Upper Canada College education cast him as a creature of privilege. Yet he'd be one of the first Canadian publishers to take up the causes of Aboriginal people and the environment, and his authors-to-be included Donald Chant, head of the newly formed Pollution Probe, and the Native activists Harvey McCue and Duke Redbird. Silver-haired Chant materialized in our doorway like Prospero without a cape, flourishing his manuscript. Bacque invited the brilliant young environmentalist David Suzuki for lunch to sound him out on doing a book; Suzuki accepted lunch but declined the book offer, too busy with his rising television career. Margaret Laurence appeared un-expectedly, gripping a cigarette between trembling fingers, determined to give Godfrey her feedback on the latest section of *The New Ancestors*, which she was reading as a work-in-progress. With my bent towards journalism, I signed up Margaret Daly of the *Toronto Star* to write an exposé of the Company of Young Canadians, the Trudeau government's version of the American Peace Corps, and Walter Stewart of *Maclean's* to do the same on Pierre Elliott Trudeau.

My partners were a slightly odd couple themselves. Bacque was smooth and rounded where Godfrey was sharp and angular, amiable where Godfrey was combative, sweetly funny where Godfrey was sardonic. As much as I liked them both, I soon realized they were oil and water. Editorially speaking, the tensions between them, and between them and me, were exciting and productive. We generated great book ideas in a spirit of creative competition. But the three-way partnership was also fraught with hidden frictions and complexities, and mutual comprehension was a constant challenge.

Our agreement was that each of us could put any title he wished on the list, subject to a limit of one-third of the production budget, and no more than one poetry title per year. Dave liked the loose arrangements, but he chafed under Jim's tendency to call him when he bent the rules. After only three months, a bitter dispute arose over Dave's delay in putting up his share of the collateral for our bank loan. I acted as the peacemaker, a role I'd find increasingly uncomfortable and thankless. New Press was saved, but at the price of our previous high spirits and trust in one another.

Early in 1970, we agreed to co-publish with Anansi an instant book on the hot local issue of the Spadina Expressway. A young academic couple, David and Nadine Nowlan, were writing a tract arguing why the express-way, if extended downtown, would ruin the urban core. The trick was to produce the book at record speed, since public opinion had to be rallied in time to influence a crucial vote at City Hall. Dennis would edit the book, I'd produce it, and New Press would handle money, sales, and distribution. The two of us agreed on a revenue-sharing formula.

Dennis came up with a brilliant title, *The Bad Trip: The Untold Story of the Spadina Expressway*. Working feverishly, he gave me a finished manu-script just under the wire. I spent all night in the typesetter's office proofreading the pages and rushed them at dawn to Peter Maher, the art director at Macmillan, who moonlighted for us on design and paste-up. Hunter-Rose manufactured the little paperback in time to allow us to fill several thousand back orders, reap fabulous publicity, and accelerate the Stop Spadina movement. The crucial vote was won: the expressway would not proceed.

Writing, editing, and producing *The Bad Trip* had taken only eight weeks, and Dennis and I claimed an unsubstantiated Canadian speed record, duly reported in *Quill & Quire*. *The Bad Trip* sold out and made a profit. But before long, a shadow fell across our victory; Dennis and I had neglected to write down the terms of our deal, and we remembered them differently. It was an honest difference of opinion, but we both felt wronged.

The Bad Trip's success was an affirmation nonetheless. The estab-lishment publishers would never have taken on such a book, for a whole host of reasons: obviously, changing times required a new generation of publishers. But being part of that generation was never simple. It was always one damn thing after another.

Fulfilling its manifest destiny by expanding westward, the University of Toronto bought 671 Spadina and evicted both Anansi and New Press. Jim Bacque persuaded Godfrey and me to make a small down payment on a three-storey house a couple of blocks west on Sussex Avenue, a funky corner property with gables, turrets, and balconies, situated among colourfully painted Portuguese homes. We invited our Anansi colleagues to move in with us, but they preferred to rent their own place on Jarvis Street.

Even before New Press had taken delivery of our first catalogue – a glossy black accordion-fold designed by Peter Maher, the cover portraying the three of us as Victorian gentlemen – we received a startling offer. With uncharacteristic recklessness, perhaps prompted by coverage in its own *Maclean's*, Maclean-Hunter proposed to buy a 30 percent interest in our company. Its executives wanted further buy-in options over the next three years until they held majority control. Meanwhile, they said, they'd back us at the bank for five times our initial capital.

As tempting as the offer was, it seemed out of the question. Why create a company based on our own ideas, only to surrender it to a bottom-line corporation? Even at 30 percent, Maclean-Hunter could exercise de facto control by holding the purse strings. But Bacque argued we'd be able to implement our publishing program much faster with Maclean-Hunter's financing; we could do more elaborate marketing, hire our own sales rep, publicist, and secretary; we could even afford to pay ourselves. Besides, he reasoned, Maclean-Hunter would be buying our publishing instincts, our links to the new youth culture, and it wasn't about to interfere with that.

Bacque was the conduit for the offer. This was natural enough since, two years earlier, he'd held informal talks with Maclean-Hunter executives about starting a new publishing house. Apprehensive but curious, Godfrey and I agreed to lunch in the Maclean-Hunter boardroom. Present were the chairman, Donald Hunter, the president, Donald Campbell, and the vice-president, Ronald McEachern, notorious for having provoked the resignations of *Maclean's* editors by meddling in their work. Gordon Rumgay, the magazine circulation wizard who'd brokered the proposal in the first place, was also there. Hunter and Campbell regarded us with benevolent shrewdness between mouthfuls of the best Alberta beef. They asked pointed questions about our business goals and sales projections and talked about "market share" and "product."

Hunter, an impassive man who lit a cigarette before the rest of us had finished eating, didn't say as much as Campbell, his CEO; Rumgay had told us Hunter was "Mr. Fifty-One" and would have to sign off on any transaction. It wasn't clear to me how little New Press would fit into the plans of a conglomerate operating cable television systems and trade magazines like *Canadian Bus and Truck*. But Campbell said he'd like to see a twelve-month cash-flow projection at our next meeting, which had somehow become scheduled for the following week, and I was just opening my mouth to ask what a cash flow was when Godfrey kicked me under the table. "It'll be ready," he replied briskly.

Once we were back on the sidewalk, I said, "Okay, so what's a cash flow?"

"Search me," Dave said, "but we'll know by next Friday."

A deal was struck. And so, with money filling our sails, New Press voyaged on. Peter Maher left Macmillan to become our designer and production manager. We hired Ingrid Cook, a young American émigré, as our editorial assistant, and Carole Orr (later Carole Jerome, the broadcaster and author) as our publicist. Mark Czarnecki came to do shipping for a while, before ascending to the post of *Maclean's* drama critic. We hired his friend John Bemrose straight out of the University of Toronto and put him, a poet disguised as a sales rep, into a leased Volkswagen Beetle to cover half the country, plus Boston and New York. And we rented out a room on the top floor of 84 Sussex to Mark and John's friend Marni Jackson, then an aspiring journalist. The New Press workday usually ended to the strains of her *Moondance* album filtering down the stairs.

The house became a hub of activity. Our authors Mel Watkins, Jim Laxer, Bruce Kidd, John Macfarlane, Teri McLuhan, Boyce Richardson, David Lewis Stein, Jim Lotz, and Eleanor Pelrine dropped by at all hours. Adrienne Clarkson edited a series for us on women's issues. Emissaries from *Guerrilla* and other underground papers arrived to sell us advertising, and in the narrow front hall piled high with boxes, hippie poets squeezed past suited printer's reps eager for a piece of the action: we had twenty-five new books scheduled. One was Dennis Lee's first children's book, *Wiggle to the Laundromat*, with illustrations by Charles Pachter. Christina Hartling, later a photo editor for *Quill & Quire*, took over the reception desk in the front room and taped a banner on the wall behind her, paraphrasing one of Dennis's lines: "In Smooth Rock Falls," it read, "I'll eat your balls."

It was bizarre to think that Maclean-Hunter money was behind all this: some of the earliest Red Power and anti-pollution books, Laxer's attack on continental energy corporations, future NDP leader Ed Broadbent's *The Liberal Rip-Off*, John Warnock's *Partner to Behemoth*, Margaret Daly's *The Revolution Game*, and Stein's novel *My Sexual and Other Revolutions*.

But there was no denying that New Press books made news and, occasionally, money. At a joint news conference to launch books by Laxer, Warnock, and Don Chant, the media turned out in force.

Nineteen-seventy was Dave Godfrey's banner year. The textual collage he created with Mel Watkins, *Gordon to Watkins to You: The Battle for Control of Our Economy*, termed "a political blockbuster" by the *Globe and Mail*, sold briskly on college campuses, and *The New Ancestors* carried off the Governor General's Award. The next year, New Press published several of the country's top political titles. Walter Stewart's first book, *Shrug: Trudeau in Power*, reached number two on the *Star* bestseller list behind *The Last Spike*. *Rumours of War*, by Ron Haggart and Aubrey Golden, demolished Trudeau's rationale for using the War Measures Act against Quebec dissidents in the October Crisis of 1970. Jim Bacque sold U.S. rights to both titles, a rare feat for Canadian political books. And New Press became part of a publishing coup that infuriated Ottawa.

Liberal MP Herb Gray had toiled for months on a study of foreign ownership, but the government was keeping it under wraps. Out of the blue, we received a confidential call from Abraham Rotstein, confidant of Walter Gordon and editor of *The Canadian Forum*; somehow Rotstein had come into possession of a bootleg copy of Gray's report, and the *Forum* was going to embarrass the Liberals by publishing it. But Rotstein knew the document would have wider impact if published in book form. He and his editorial board offered to let New Press reuse the *Forum*'s type if we could get the report into circulation quickly.

Both magazine and book versions had to be manufactured secretly, and fast. We reassembled the *Forum*'s type into book pages and produced *The Gray Report* as a $1.95 mass-market paperback. The response was considerable. We moved most of a 10,000-copy printing, although at that price we wouldn't make any money; the important thing was to get the thing out there. Justice Minister John Turner, lunching with Maclean-Hunter's Donald Campbell soon afterwards, asked Campbell, "Who are these guys, Don? You'd better tell them to withdraw that book or we'll prosecute under the Official Secrets Act." Nothing of the sort happened, and the Trudeau government did eventually adopt a more nationalistic, interventionist posture on the economy.

New Press produced good financial results for 1970 and 1971, posting a buoyant profit in the latter year. Maclean-Hunter exercised its next two options, bringing its stake to 49 percent. In 1972, however, our growth went wild; costs spiralled out of control, and we harvested a big loss for a company our size (we had over $300,000 in sales, equivalent to about $1.5 million today). We'd published too many titles, too soon; we were too hot not to cool down. As Diana Athill would observe in *Stet*, her memoir of working at André Deutsch in London, "It is not good for people to start a [publishing] venture with enough – not to mention too much – money."

We had great authors, a wonderful staff, including the editors Ruth Brouwer and Evelyn Ross, the sales manager David Stimpson, and the publicists Susan Helwig and Patricia Bowles, but the partners couldn't manage our own relationship. Maclean-Hunter nervously watched our wrangling but refused to take sides; it had bought itself a partnership and was bound and determined it should remain intact. Instead of a messy divorce, Maclean-Hunter demanded a civil separation, a reconfiguration of the company.

Bacque and Godfrey couldn't inhabit the same room, so Dave would work at a different location. Maclean-Hunter figured that, since he was a professor, Dave could operate an educational division to publish titles for the college market, while Jim and I could remain at Sussex to run the trade division. Without any research to determine the needs of the academic market, or how we could publish for it profitably, a separate office was established, duplicating staff and other overheads. As abrasive as Godfrey could be sometimes, I missed him in the office, missed his energy and insouciance as he bounded up the worn stairs crooning, "We've got to get ourselves back to the garden." The benefits of the three-way chemistry disappeared, along with the conflicts.

Maclean-Hunter bought Macmillan that year. In the name of making both publishers more efficient, the corporation replaced our manual systems of order fulfillment with a computerized system, operated from somewhere in the bowels of the Maclean-Hunter building. Both companies' reputation for customer service quickly deteriorated to become the worst in the industry. At New Press, the centre could not hold: there was no centre.

The unhappy situation came to a head in 1974. Despite attempts to save the company by dismissing most of our staff (a gut-wrenching process, producing my worst moments in publishing) and setting aside our core values to publish commercial titles, 1973 sales results had been bitterly disappointing. Maclean-Hunter refused to pick up its final option; worse, it refused to extend our bank guarantee. We couldn't, in all conscience, publish another title until we had our debts under control. We reprinted titles for which there was significant demand but began releasing authors from their contracts for forthcoming books. Other publishers, particularly Macmillan, picked up some excellent work.

Both Godfrey and Bacque left New Press's daily operations, and the educational division was closed. Godfrey was already committed to his third publishing house, Press Porcépic (later Beach Holme Publishing), then based in Erin, Ontario; and this time around he wisely avoided taking any partner except his wife, Ellen. I ran the New Press office on my own with a skeleton staff, our tasks melancholy and dispiriting compared with the adrenalin rush of publishing books. As agreed with my partners, I held our creditors at bay while seeking a buyer for the company.

In midsummer, Jack Stoddart Sr., owner of General Publishing, made an offer for our backlist, contracts, and other assets, committing himself to taking full responsibility for all New Press payables. It was an honourable resolution: the partners would get no money, but the authors and suppliers would receive 100 cents on the dollar, and writers with books on the backlist or still in the pipeline would be well published. New titles would keep appearing under the New Press imprint for another year or two, before the list was gradually subsumed within the General Publishing catalogue.

Stoddart offered Jim Bacque and me editorial positions with his firm. Jim accepted and stayed on for a year before devoting himself full-time to his writing. I wasn't ready to return to being someone else's editor. On the strength of a recommendation from Robert Fulford of *Saturday Night*, for whom I'd written reviews, the *Toronto Star* offered me the job of books editor and columnist. Fortunate to land on my feet, I said no thanks to Stoddart's decent offer and moved on.

PETER MARTIN ASSOCIATES

JAMES LORIMER & CO.

HARVEST HOUSE

9

ON THE BARRICADES

Books are weapons in the war of ideas.

David McFadden, *The Great Canadian Sonnet* (1970)

The bus was painted bright plum, its display lettering an equally disturbing shade of red. It rattled through the vast northern silences,
bringing books to the people.

Setting off from Parliament Hill on Canada Day 1972, the bus stopped
at Rideau Hall to receive the blessing of Governor General Roland
Michener, then continued east. The transmission was clunky, the body
antiquated; most of the seats had been removed. When the bus sighed to a
stop in shopping malls or parks in Moncton, Antigonish, Summerside,
or Corner Brook – its arrival announced, with luck, in the local media –
visitors climbed aboard to browse 2,500 Canadian titles: fiction, poetry,
drama, kids' books; biography, history, travel guides, cookbooks. Browsers
could place orders to be filled by their local bookseller, if any, or directly by
the publisher. Most of the cities and towns en route had no full-service
bookstore, and that was the whole point of the thing.

The book bus was the brainchild of the recently formed Independent
Publishers' Association, a renegade group operating outside the clubby
confines of the Canadian Book Publishers' Council. Publishers in the IPA,
unlike many in the older group, were all owned in Canada. Apart from a
few large members (Clarke, Irwin, General Publishing, University of

Toronto Press), the IPA comprised the new breed of small presses founded, like Coach House, Anansi, and New Press, in the previous few years: Peter Martin Associates; James, Lewis & Samuel; Black Rose Books; Delta Canada; Fiddlehead Poetry Books; Hurtig Publishers; Oberon Press; Sono Nis Press; Talon Books; Tundra Books. Most of them were run by writers or intellectuals. All were committed to originating Canadian-authored trade books, without the backing of schoolbooks or agency titles.

IPA members could be noisily, even obnoxiously assertive. Our favourite adjective to describe ourselves was "aggressive." In true 1960s style, the aggression was often turned against our elders – principally the "sellouts" managing the "branch plants," our pejorative term for the foreign-controlled subsidiary publishers – but also, at times, against Canadian colleagues whose main offence was living past forty. Jack McClelland, unchallenged as publishing's golden boy for a quarter-century, refused to join the IPA. Instead he sent Larry Ritchie to "observe" the meetings while advocating M&S positions. Heated debate ensued about whether this should be allowed. Those who admired McClelland insisted it should, since it gave him an inducement to join. McClelland had set our great experiment in motion, making possible new visions of what a publisher could be. And although he still had one foot in the old business model, his nerve and panache as a publisher had inspired many of us. Ritchie stayed, and M&S finally joined the association years later.

Like McClelland, we were ready to gamble everything on the home market. In IPA policy debates, James Lorimer of James, Lewis & Samuel declaimed vehemently, with relentless professorial logic, that pursuing international sales would be a misuse of our energies, since it detracted from our prime directive. He received little argument. Canada's bookstores, libraries, book clubs, educational curricula, and mass media were all so dominated by American books, and readers so programmed to follow the lead of *Time* and the Book of the Month Club, that extreme measures were needed to bring Canadian books above-ground. Margaret Atwood, in *Survival*, described Canada as "an unknown territory for the people who live in it." To address that void, Robert Fulford, Dave Godfrey, and Abraham Rotstein compiled *Read Canadian*, a hitchhiker's guide to the unknown galaxy of Canadian books, also released in 1972 by James, Lewis & Samuel. It sold 10,000 copies in its first ten months.

Flouting the convention that book publishing had to be done from Toronto, new presses soon sprang up like March crocuses where few, if any, had existed: on the West Coast and on the Prairies, in the Maritimes and in Newfoundland, primarily to publish authors from their regions. Ontario produced its share of new, often specialized publishers; some were dedicated to children's books, others to literary fiction, poetry, political issues, feminism.

The existence of so many new publishers achieved a critical mass. Canadians finally knew the pleasures of books in which their lives and localities became literature. University teachers agitated to establish CanLit as an academic subject. Thousands attended the annual Canada Days organized by Jim Foley, a teacher at Mohawk College in Hamilton, Ontario, to hear Canadian authors read. Magazines such as *Books in Canada*, *Canadian Fiction Magazine*, and *The Journal of Canadian Fiction* increased the outlets for critical coverage. *The Malahat Review*, *Descant*, *Grain*, and other literary journals provided feisty competition for *The Tamarack Review* and *Canadian Literature*. Stores opened to sell Canadian books only – first Longhouse Bookshop in Toronto and Books Canada in Ottawa in 1972, soon followed by the Double Hook in Montreal and A Pair of Trindles in Halifax. A heady ebullience filled the air, a belief that, despite the odds, anything was possible. As Matt Cohen wrote in his memoir, *Typing: A Life in 26 Keys*, "Those years were crucial, not because all the best books were written then (they weren't), but because the universe of Canadian literature mutated into a new existence."

The purple book bus, a manifestation of that new existence, was only the first of many cooperative promotion projects by Canadian publishers. After a final trip west, it was honourably retired in 1974, to be succeeded by more sober and sophisticated ventures.

Although the IPA had its practical side, it was first and foremost a political vehicle, founded by people who considered publishing books their contribution to the war effort. The principals at Coach House Press, however, felt otherwise. Coach House remained a writers' and artists' press, preoccupied with questions of aesthetics and craft. An internal disagreement in 1974 led to Victor Coleman's departure the next year; it arose, at least ostensibly, over whether to adopt electronic technology. Coleman saw Stan Bevington's embrace of computerized typesetting and design as dehumanizing. The technology was still new and, to many people in the arts, alien. Coleman (who later characterized his view as "rather naively myopic") began one of his periodic absences from the press, leaving to administer A Space, an artist-run gallery, and wouldn't return as an active Coach House editor until 1984. His editorial role was assumed by a fluid collective of people already associated with the press: the writers bp Nichol, Frank Davey, Michael Ondaatje, and David Young, variously complemented by Dennis Reid, David McFadden, Linda Davey, Sarah Sheard, the designer Rick/Simon, and others. The collective, naturally diverse in inclination, was untroubled by Bevington's fascination with what he called "the mix and match of technology."

As the main man in the Coach House matrix ("head coach" on his Canada Council applications), Bevington shunned industry politics. Nonetheless the press's agenda was implicitly political. Stan Dragland, a Coach House author and the founder of Brick Books, wrote: "Some might say that Coach House's only politics has been an undeclared anarchism, but that is to ignore the underlying motives for staying underground" – that is, subverting literary and cultural norms.

Anansi, on the other hand, plunged deeply into politics. In 1973 its landlords evicted the company from the Jarvis Street space, and Shirley Gibson found a natural fit with the tenants of the Egerton Ryerson Memorial Building, a shopworn brick structure in the low-rent industrial district around Queen and Sherbourne Streets. The building's name was a sardonic reference to the takeover of the Ryerson Press by McGraw-Hill, the event that had catapulted the IPA into being three years before. Besides Anansi, the tenants included the IPA itself and two companies instrumental in its founding, James, Lewis & Samuel and Peter Martin Associates. The three publishers pooled their sales and order fulfillment functions to create the Belford Book Distributing Company, named after the brothers who had pirated American editions in the 1870s.

Among the sales reps hired by Belford was a long-haired young man named Lionel Koffler, later the founder of Firefly Books. Koffler regarded Peter Martin as "a guy with drive and enthusiasm and a ready wit, who loved puns and Canadian history. Peter believed so strongly in his mission, many of us would have done almost anything for him." Martin had had a brief flirtation with distributing pornographic books to support that mission but dropped the venture when impolite competitors muscled in. His wife at the time, Carol Martin, later a publishing grants officer at the Canada Council, brought to their operation much-needed practicality and organizational skills.

Peter Martin and Jim Lorimer both served as IPA presidents in the early 1970s. Tall and imperious, Lorimer was the cooler head, the more strategic thinker and activist. But Martin, rumpled, garrulous, and impulsive, had started in the book business considerably earlier. In 1959 he and Carol Martin, as neophytes barely out of university, had taken a chance on starting something no one else had ever attempted: an all-Canadian book club.

The Martins had launched the Readers' Club of Canada while Peter was working for the Canadian Association for Adult Education in Toronto. Like the immensely popular Book of the Month Club, the Readers' Club sold memberships in return for an introductory package of titles; it offered main and alternate selections each month at discounted prices, employed the negative-option technique, and mailed out a well-written monthly brochure, *The Canadian Reader*. Unlike BOMC, however, the tiny Readers' Club had very little cash with which to advertise for members. It raised most of its start-up capital through an enthusiastic letter that Peter Martin's employer, the educator Roby Kidd, sent to a hundred of his friends and associates across the country, urging them to invest.

There was one other problem with the Martins' idea: although they'd decided to offer Canadian books only, there were relatively few new titles to choose from. As an inducement to join, they offered members a search service. The club would try to locate any Canadian title that members requested, in spite of the absence of bibliographic tools such as *Canadian Books in Print*, which wouldn't exist for another decade.

When the Martins approached publishers, John Gray tried to talk them out of the venture. He warned there were only a few thousand readers committed to buying Canadian books, and they'd have a tough time finding more. But the idealistic young couple felt they could reach beyond the converted and appeal to non-urban Canadians who lacked access to a bookstore. They succeeded in recruiting an impressive editorial board to choose their selections, in return for a monthly lunch: Robert Weaver of the CBC, Doris Anderson, editor of *Chatelaine*, and Arnold Edinborough, publisher of *Saturday Night*, where the club would often advertise.

The first selection, Mordecai Richler's *The Apprenticeship of Duddy Kravitz*, outsold the regular André Deutsch trade edition, distributed in Canada by M&S. Other early picks were Karsh's *Portraits of Greatness*, Peter Newman's *Flame of Power*, Robertson Davies's *A Mixture of Frailties*, and Farley Mowat's *The Desperate People*. In later years, Robert Fulford and Ramsay Cook joined the editorial board, and selections included *The National Dream* and *Surfacing*. Jack McClelland was among the club's strongest supporters, sometimes selling the Martins new books against the advice of his staff, while overdue invoices remained unpaid. Other publishers weren't so generous.

In the end, unfortunately, John Gray turned out to be right. Readers' Club memberships from small communities were few and far between, and the great majority of members came from the cities. The club, peaking at around 3,000 members, never did make money; it was an idea ahead of its time. But before all this became blindingly apparent, Peter and Carol Martin were seduced into becoming publishers by a deluge of unsolicited manuscripts. Testing the waters with a popular history of Gibson's Landing, British Columbia, they incorporated Peter Martin Associates. PMA would produce a small but diverse list of ten to a dozen titles a year, with an emphasis on Canadian politics, history, the North, and children's literature.

At first the Martins had no sales staff apart from themselves. To sell books outside Toronto, they relied on direct mail to stores and libraries and on their book club. But they believed a bigger market existed than they could reach, and since the Readers' Club gave them a bird's-eye view of all the publishing going on across Canada, they knew there were other small presses in the same boat. With the exception of Mel Hurtig, whose Edmonton bookstores linked him to the whole trade, the new publishers were isolated in their regions and scarcely knew one another.

On May 13, 1969, Peter Martin mailed four colleagues across the country a "shot-in-the-dark memo." Headed "Re: Selling Books," it went out to Hurtig, Gray Campbell of Gray's Publishing in Sidney, British Columbia, Michael Macklem of Oberon Press in Ottawa, and Maynard Gertler of Harvest House in Montreal. Martin proposed a scheme for joint national sales representation. Combining their lists, he argued, the five publishers could accumulate enough volume to support a full-time sales rep to cover Ontario and Quebec and "part-time, commission men" in other parts of the country. If other presses joined, such as Anansi, Western Producer Prairie Books in Saskatoon, and Mitchell Press in Vancouver, the consortium could have a hundred new titles a year, plus backlist – enough to afford biannual sales conferences, even an export catalogue.

Martin was laying out a blueprint for cooperative marketing projects that would emerge in the next decade. But the initial responses he received typified the contrarian spirit of small independent publishers. From the West Coast, Gray Campbell wrote: "We have decided to write off the rest of Canada. Why should we worry about east of Manitoba when anything we publish in our own orbit sells four to seventy thousand copies in the first year." From Ottawa, Michael Macklem replied that he and his wife, Anne Hardy, were already covering the country on their annual coast-to-coast sales trips; rather than take him up on the consortium, Macklem offered Martin an Oberon title for the Readers' Club.

Maynard Gertler was sympathetic to Martin's idea but believed it was even more urgent to participate in book displays at library and educational conferences. A well-to-do Montrealer, Gertler had founded Harvest House in 1960 with his wife, Ann Gertler, and they published a small list oriented to Quebec history and politics, as well as literary translations in the French

Writers of Canada series. Gertler told Martin the answer to greater professionalization lay in joining the big boys in the Canadian Book Publishers' Council. Since the CBPC's membership fees were prohibitively high, he proposed approaching the Canada Council to subsidize the cost.

Another Montreal publisher, fiery May Cutler of Tundra Books, joined the debate with a different idea. Cutler was ready to go war with the CBPC over misappropriation of nationality. She termed it the "'Canadian' Book Publishers' Council," since "most of them are not publishers at all – mostly jobbers for U.S. and English companies." She railed at the CBPC for monopolizing professional information and services, such as distribution of the new International Standard Book Numbers and the organization of the Canadian stand at the Frankfurt book fair, and decried the Canada Council for not being more helpful to small presses. In a letter written in response to Martin's original missive, Cutler even threw out a radical suggestion: "What about forming our own organization?"

Martin wasn't quite that ambitious yet. But as a budding nationalist, he wrote a guest column in the June 1969 *Quill & Quire* questioning foreign domination of Canadian publishing, at a time when such talk was considered impolite, if not imprudent. "Why has nobody noticed – or cared – that our book publishing industry is passing rapidly into American hands?" he asked. "Books are important to a nation's existence to a degree that is almost inversely proportionate to the audience they reach . . . If a people is going to control its own society, it should control its own book publishing."

Martin's proposal for a sales consortium was temporarily forgotten. An exchange of letters between Gertler and two CBPC presidents – Marsh Jeanneret and his successor, Campbell Hughes, president of the new Canadian subsidiary of Van Nostrand Reinhold – promoted the idea of subsidized CBPC membership for small Canadian-owned companies. At first Hughes worried that "policy could be dramatically altered if a group of new members were to come in representing a special area of interest," but eventually he and Gertler reached a tentative deal.

Informed of the terms, the Martins were dubious. Dennis Lee wrote Gertler to say that Anansi and "the chaps from New Press" wouldn't be joining the CBPC. "It's clear," Lee said, "that what is in the best interests of foreign head-offices which operate branches in this country, and what is in the best interests of indigenous Canadian publishing, writing and reading, are two distinct things." But the whole notion soon became moot: the Canadian publishing industry was about to change irrevocably.

In September 1970 W.J. Gage, a force in Canadian education for nearly a century, sold its publishing operations to its major American agency, Scott Foresman of Chicago. The next month, McGraw-Hill of New York, one of the biggest publishers in the world, took over the Ryerson Press.

Maclean-Hunter, anxious to acquire book publishing assets, had made an offer for Ryerson. In addition, a Ryerson employee group including Robin Farr had proposed raising the capital to buy it from the United Church of Canada. But the church was so desperate to stem the tide of losses from Ryerson's outdated printing operations that, rather than attempt to keep ownership in Canada, it accepted the highest bid.

Although the takeovers sent shock waves through the country, the Canadian Book Publishers' Council expressed no official concern. This was hardly surprising, since its president and most of its largest members represented American and British companies, one of which was McGraw-Hill of Canada.

On the day the Ryerson sale was announced, Peter Martin phoned several other small Toronto publishers, including Anansi, New Press, and James, Lewis & Samuel, to propose a joint response. To protest the takeovers, we created the ad hoc Emergency Committee of Canadian Publishers, which convened a news conference the next day at Anansi's Jarvis Street office, located conveniently up the street from the old CBC building. The committee demanded that the federal government disallow the sale of both publishers and prohibit all future foreign takeovers in the industry. The group also urged creation of a publishing development corporation, comparable to the Canadian Film Development Corporation (later Telefilm Canada). The media, including CBC Television's best-known correspondent, Norman DePoe, turned out for the news conference in force, giving the event national exposure.

The Emergency Committee discovered it had clout. A large crowd thronged to a protest rally in downtown Toronto. Meanwhile the CBPC authorized Ivon Owen of Oxford, chair of its Canadian Committee (the nomenclature was always good for a laugh), to offer special low rates for the new publishers to join. The diminutive chair, accompanied by the CBPC's well-tailored, mustachioed executive director, Toivo Roht, braved the young lions in New Press's front room on Sussex Avenue. Surrounded by a hostile audience, including the Martins, Dennis Lee, Shirley Gibson, Jim Lorimer, Dave Godfrey, Jim Bacque, and me, plus others now dimmed by memory, Owen stiffly offered well-meant, conciliatory phrases, and Roht read aloud Campbell Hughes's letter outlining the terms of the CBPC's offer. When Roht reached the end, there was a long silence. It was broken when Godfrey, who'd been seething throughout, muttered, "Cam Hughes is a Black driver on a segregated bus." That settled the matter.

On December 4, 1970, doing a little name appropriation of our own, Peter Martin, Lee, Bill Clarke, and I travelled to Ottawa to present a nine-teen-page brief I'd written on behalf of a group now calling itself the Interim Council of Canadian Publishers. Listed as signatories were nine firms: Clarke, Irwin; Griffin House; Harvest House; House of Anansi; Hurtig Publishers; James, Lewis & Samuel; New Press; Peter Martin Associates; and Progress Books. It was a motley crew, given that John Griffin was somewhere to the right of the Clarkes and Progress Books was the publisher for the Communist Party of Canada. But the Trudeau government, in the persons of Revenue Minister Herb Gray, Robert Stanbury, the minister for Information Canada, and their officials, listened solemnly as we made our arguments.

We stopped short of issuing "non-negotiable demands," in the rhetoric of the day. Instead we urged four "minimal first steps": creation of a federal loan program; federal and provincial programs for increased library purchasing of Canadian books; a threefold increase in Canada Council support for publishers *and* authors; and designation of book publishing as a "key industry," comparable to broadcasting and news-papers. This last measure – intended to prohibit foreign takeovers – we described as meaningless unless coupled with the first three. Our major

long-term proposal was for a federal publishing development corporation that would "invest jointly with publishers in costly projects." Far
from fearing government involvement in our industry, we embraced
Graham Spry's famous dictum when he and the Canadian Radio League
lobbied successfully for creation of the CBC in the 1930s: it was a choice
between "the State or the United States."

Later that month, the Ontario government established the Royal
Commission on Book Publishing. The state *was* paying attention. With
momentum behind it, the Interim Council of Canadian Publishers took
the natural step of constituting itself legally as a trade organization. The
Independent Publishers' Association emerged from a welter of debate at a
two-day founding meeting at Trinity College, University of Toronto, in
February 1971, attended by sixteen charter members and several
observers. Diplomatically represented at the oratory-filled meeting
by Harald Bohne and Hilary Marshall, with Marsh Jeanneret's silent
blessing, the University of Toronto Press was a significant addition to the
ranks, bestowing immediate credibility on the organization. Clarke,
Irwin's presence was equally important.

The IPA's constitution asserted that "a vigorous, Canadian-owned
and -controlled book publishing industry is essential to the educational,
cultural, social, and economic life of a united Canada." For the next thirty
years, that principle would guide the political and professional program of
the IPA and the organization into which it metamorphosed in 1976, the
Association of Canadian Publishers. It was a principle that would divide
the industry for a generation into two often adversarial camps. The fact
that the camps were never completely hostile or mutually exclusive
reflected the necessity to share the same market, lunch in the same restau-
rants, and drink in the same bars.

Peter Martin became the IPA's first president, a choice recognizing
his key role in the organizing process. But others would play larger parts
in years to come. Dennis Lee contributed principled reason and passionate language, particularly the rallying cry "Books of Our Own," which
would supply the name for a heavily attended ACP public forum in
Toronto in October 1976. Harald Bohne provided mature judgment and

knowledgeable counsel (not always taken), mixed with deep concern for the whole profession. Dave Godfrey, president during 1972, supplied conviction, guts, and reckless abandon. Bill Clarke, the 1973 president, bestowed *gravitas*: authority combined with intellectual rigour. And Jim Lorimer, president during 1974, presided behind the scenes, whatever his title, as chief ideologue, strategist, and agitator, driving both IPA and industry politics throughout the 1970s.

James Lorimer hadn't planned to become a publisher. The only hint of his future profession came when, as an undergraduate in economics at the University of Manitoba, he'd made money mimeographing and selling old exam papers, a business he bequeathed to his younger brother, Rowland, the future head of the Canadian Centre for Studies in Publishing at Simon Fraser University. Returning to Canada in 1966 from the London School of Economics, where he wrote his doctoral thesis on Adam Smith, Jim Lorimer saw himself as a writer; he was working on a book about poverty. He didn't particularly want to teach, either, but new universities were opening, old universities were expanding, and Canadian Ph.D.s were in short supply. Picking up a teaching gig at York University in Toronto almost as an afterthought, Lorimer taught social science courses combining economics, politics, and sociology.

Lorimer became involved in real-life poverty issues when he moved into Cabbagetown in working-class Toronto. His political instincts soon drew him into the community association's ultimately successful battle against a civic demolition project. That baptism in civic politics resulted in a close association with other urban activists, particularly a future councillor and mayor of Toronto, John Sewell. Lorimer began a sideline as a crusading civic affairs commentator in the *Globe and Mail*, exposing the excesses of developers and pro-development politicians.

Lorimer had a friend from college days, Heather Robertson, with whom he'd edited the University of Manitoba student newspaper. After Robertson took her M.A. at Columbia, she returned to Winnipeg to practise journalism and research a book on the struggles of Native communities on the Prairies.

She submitted a thick manuscript, *Reservations Are for Indians*, to McClelland & Stewart but, like other writers entrusting their work to M&S's overtaxed editorial department, received no response for ages.

Lorimer, meanwhile, read Robertson's manuscript, which graphically documented life in four Native communities, and found it stunningly powerful. He proposed his own work-in-progress on poverty to Maynard Gertler of Harvest House, who wasn't interested. Yet from his teaching experience, Lorimer knew that universities needed such books for burgeoning courses in urban and Native studies, particularly Canadian materials in paperback. In a conversation with a fellow neighbourhood activist, Alan Samuel, Lorimer observed that Canadian publishers didn't seem very enterprising. Samuel replied: "Well, I know how to be a publisher. I *am* a publisher."

A classics professor at the University of Toronto, Samuel was secretary of the American Society of Papyrologists, in charge of publishing the society's translations and transcripts of ancient Egyptian texts. As Lorimer recalled, "Alan said, 'You've got the ideas about content, and I know how to do production and marketing. So why don't we start a publishing company?' And I said, 'Sounds like a great idea to me.'" If Lorimer and Robertson couldn't get their work published elsewhere, he'd do it himself.

He and Samuel added a third partner, Bruce Lewis, a law student knowledgeable about business, accounting, and typesetting, and the three of them formed James, Lewis & Samuel. Their first list in fall 1970 consisted of five books: Lorimer's *Globe* articles, reworked as *The Real World of City Politics*; a trimmed-down version of *Reservations Are for Indians*; a report on the Biafra conflict then raging, by federal MPs Andrew Brewin (NDP) and David MacDonald (PC); *The Beds of Academe*, by Howard Adelman; and a study of university financing.

With less than $5,000 in start-up capital, JLS had to rely on credit from printers. But Robertson's hard-hitting, controversial book made an immediate impact, and Lorimer's own book sold well. Both had to be reprinted, and the company entered what Lorimer later called "that great virtuous cycle. You put the books out. The books sell. You get enough money from the bookstores to be able to pay the printers' bills and go back to press. Like everybody who gets into publishing, if your first book is successful, you keep going. If your first book's a flop, you don't."

James, Lewis & Samuel kept going. After several seasons, Lorimer shed his partners, being interested, as many of his employees can attest, in wielding sole authority and control; the firm became known as James Lorimer & Co. Lewis went on to law as planned. Samuel continued to teach and to publish papyrological studies and a variety of trade titles under the A.M. Hakkert and Samuel Stevens imprints.

Lorimer's company was firmly and conspicuously planted on the left, but with a sharp commercial edge. Its savvy, issue-oriented titles, some aimed primarily at the trade market, others at the academic market, spoke urgently to the times. Lorimer's authors included James Laxer and the economists Lukin Robinson and R.T. Naylor, writing on Canadian business; the political scientist Norman Penner, writing on the Winnipeg General Strike; and Marcel Rioux on Quebec separatism. Journalists included the CBC Television personality Larry Zolf, writing on federal politics and whatever else occurred to his unusual mind, as well as the young leftists who produced the feisty investigative newsmagazine *The Last Post*. They included the future Montreal city councillor Nick Auf Der Maur, Robert Chodos, Rae Murphy, and Mark Starowicz, later a CBC executive producer. The group proved adept at producing acerbic commentary on topics ranging from the failings of corporate Canada to the ascensions of prime ministers Joe Clark and Brian Mulroney.

Heather Robertson's next two books for Lorimer, *Grass Roots* and *Salt of the Earth*, established her as the pre-eminent social historian of the Prairies. They were succeeded by *A Terrible Beauty*, in which Robertson presented full-colour reproductions of Canadian war art. Toronto politics remained a strength of Lorimer's, as books appeared from Sewell and other civic reformers. Lorimer's own titles included *Working People*, combining text with photographs by Myfanwy Phillips (the novelist Hugh Garner called it "absolutely the best thing I have read about the urban Canadian working people"), and *The Developers*, which attacked the high rollers in Canada's property development industry and made the bestseller list in hardcover.

Lorimer proved more than once that small publishers could produce bestsellers. New Democratic Party leader David Lewis's *Louder Voices: The Corporate Welfare Bums*, a book that New Press allowed to get away, sold 20,000 copies during the 1972 election campaign. And in the mid-1970s, Lorimer, a man then seldom associated with humour, had tremendous success with *Frog Fables and Beaver Tales* and its successors: a series of zany but shrewd political satires by the CBC newsman Stanley Burke, illustrated by the Vancouver cartoonist Roy Peterson. The books depicted the adventures of an unruly gang of beavers and their foppish, buck-toothed leader, coexisting in a swamp with a bunch of frogs led by a weedy chain-smoker.

Even when his books were not overtly political, Lorimer's publishing decisions were implicitly so. When he ventured into cookbook publishing, it was with an assertively nationalistic cookbook written by Elizabeth Baird, couriered to the media along with a ripe acorn squash. When he began publishing children's literature, it was with Bill Freeman's historical tales of Canadian working people fighting exploitation by the bosses. In his only venture into adult fiction, Lorimer published Heather Robertson's historical trilogy *The King Years*, beginning with *Willie: A Romance*, a highly imaginative, hybrid form of political fantasy loosely based on the secret life and self-love of Mackenzie King.

Lorimer also had the chutzpah and sense of principle to pirate government documents, on the grounds that they should be in the public domain. In 1981, incensed at the way the Trudeau government had muffled the findings of the Bertrand inquiry into monopolistic practices in the oil industry, Lorimer had the commission's multi-volume report abridged and published in a clear, one-volume version titled *Canada's Oil Monopoly*. It sold briskly, vindicating his conviction that citizens have a right to easier access to their own government's research. But the Department of Justice disagreed. In a landmark case defining the extent of Crown copyright, the government successfully sued Lorimer, who was ordered to destroy all remaining copies.

In the 1980s Lorimer published ambitiously in a variety of genres, making adventurous forays into children's, educational, and regional books. He created a consortium to produce a grade nine social studies textbook for all three Maritime provinces. He started Goodread Biographies, a low-priced reprint series of Canadian biographies in paperback. He published magazines, including *Atlantic Insight* and the venerable *Canadian Forum*. Although he would grow more pragmatic with time, he acknowledged that he was motivated less by the business of publishing than by his political agenda: "I saw it as a political activity to publish books. I saw it as a political activity to publish a book that revealed how the land developers were screwing the Canadian public in sixteen different ways. And although I thought the company should be able to pay the people who worked for it, and to earn money for its authors, I didn't see that it was fundamental to the company that it should also be profitable and building up equity and growing in the way that businesses can grow."

Lorimer's values reflected a position shared by many of his IPA colleagues. The norms were cultural and political, not commercial. The goals were getting the books written, produced, and out among the people, not feeding the bottom line. And since publishers saw themselves as delivering essential public services, they didn't hesitate to pressure government to support those goals.

IPA lobbyists experienced early success in realizing some of their political objectives. In 1971 the Ontario government acted decisively on the first recommendations of its Royal Commission on Book Publishing, contained in three interim reports. One result was the emergency loan to McClelland & Stewart. Another was provincial legislation to preclude foreign-owned monopolies in the magazine and mass-market wholesale business. A third was a program of loan guarantees for Ontario book publishers, administered by the Ontario Development Corporation.

Access to bank financing has always been problematic for publishers; banks demand collateral in the form of capital assets, such as real estate or machinery, which most publishers don't own. The new Ontario program provided lending institutions with government guarantees, based on the discounted value of publishers' sales and inventories of Canadian books.

Although the program wasn't national (the IPA had sought a federal program), it would be a keystone of the large Ontario-based industry for nearly twenty-five years. The province also awarded participating publishers an interest rebate of half the prime rate on their loans, and the Ontario Arts Council began giving annual block grants to support literary books.

In the wake of Ontario's actions, Secretary of State Gérard Pelletier, a close confidant of Prime Minister Trudeau, announced in March 1972 the first federal measures for book publishing. Although these met only one of the publishers' "minimal first steps" from the December 1970 brief, they represented a significant political breakthrough. The government would substantially increase the Canada Council's modest support for publishing, making a total of $1.2 million available for block grants, translation grants, and book purchases. Pelletier also announced a further $500,000 for export promotion through the Department of Industry, Trade and Commerce. Pelletier's announcement flirted with designating book publishing as a "key industry" by describing Canadian ownership and control of publishing as "essential to the cultural development of Canadians." Moreover, Pelletier said his new measures were only the first steps to address "a situation the urgency and gravity of which are apparent to the government."

Jim Lorimer assumed the mission of ensuring that the federal government never forgot that "urgency and gravity," nor its promise to take further action. He editorialized in his spring 1973 catalogue that "while Canadian-owned book publishing seems to be flourishing in a relatively hostile economic situation, the federal government is still treating publishing as if it were some curious small-time anachronistic cultural activity. Instead of developing policies which will strengthen publishing, and help publishers increase their activities and reach larger audiences, it is offering them little handouts of $5,000 or $10,000 or $20,000." For years to come, Lorimer would hammer away – in IPA strategy sessions, at public conferences, in policy studies and government consultations, and through the media – at the inadequacy of what he termed "stopgap grants" and "culture welfare assistance." In their place, he pressed for "major structural measures" that would realize the dream of an economically healthy publishing industry under majority Canadian control. It was a dream that many in the 1970s, including politicians, talked about, but few – especially politicians – acted to achieve.

The term "structural measures," articulated most forcefully by Lorimer and the IPA's first executive director, Paul Audley, meant several things. It meant purchasing policies and regulations that would create a bigger presence for Canadian books in the distribution system, from public libraries to mass-market racks to book clubs. It meant regulation by each province to inject Canadian content into all levels of the educational system, and to require that those materials be published by Canadian-controlled firms. It meant equipping Canadian-owned publishers with the investment capital they needed to expand and grow. To complement and reinforce those measures, it meant legislation to enable Canadian publishers to displace foreign-owned subsidiaries and take control of the domestic market.

The Trudeau government failed to enact most of those ideas. But it did make a historic decision in 1974, a decision that was counterintuitive, given Pierre Trudeau's distaste for nationalism. Pelletier's successor as secretary of state, Hugh Faulkner, declared: "The Canadian government believes strongly that the major segment of the book publishing industry in Canada should be owned by Canadians. Canadian books and magazines are too important to the cultural and intellectual life of this country to be allowed to come completely under foreign control, however sympathetic and benign."

Putting teeth in that assertion, the government prohibited all foreign takeovers of Canadian-controlled publishers. It even went farther, empowering the Foreign Investment Review Agency to regulate and restrict "indirect" foreign investments in the book industry – that is, transactions where one foreign owner buys out another. Henceforth such transactions would be allowed only if FIRA determined that they provided "net benefit to Canada."

Those policy changes enlarged the habitable space for indigenous publishers and books. But like any good activists, Lorimer and the IPA praised them as positive first steps while demanding more forceful action for the long term. It was rather meaningless, after all, to prohibit Canadian-owned publishers from being sold to foreigners unless measures were taken to strengthen those publishers financially and assist them to compete with the multinationals. When Faulkner addressed a 1975 publishing conference at Trent University in Peterborough, Ontario, to announce a modest Canada Council program aiding book promotion and distribution, Lorimer, then IPA president, led a chorus of angry denunciations of the minister's "Band-Aid gesture." Faulkner retreated in disarray before the combined derision of Lorimer, Godfrey, Clarke, Audley, and Mel Hurtig. Only Hurtig, by then a lapsed Liberal, softened the attack by giving the government marks for sincerity and good intentions.

Lorimer would secure a wider platform within the book trade when he began writing a monthly column for *Quill & Quire* in 1979. Under the rubric "Cultural Politics," he subjected a wide range of industry issues, from media coverage of books to educational publishing to the half-realized federal publishing policy, to more sustained scrutiny than such matters normally receive. Writing in a compellingly logical style, Lorimer dissected the issues facing two successive culture ministers, Liberal secretary of state John Roberts and Progressive Conservative David MacDonald, and deluged them with advice, never hesitating to point the finger at empty promises or incompetent bureaucrats.

Lorimer's penchant for taking ad hominem verbal swipes at his adversaries often flustered the gentleman's profession. Years later, Ivon Owen remembered having an amiable chat with Shirley Gibson as a guest at an IPA anniversary lunch when Lorimer suddenly rose and burst out, "You have no right to be here!" Bill Hushion, a senior executive at a succession of foreign-owned subsidiaries and later head of his own distribution company, Hushion House, recalled the bitterness of being made to feel like "a branch plant whore."

Lorimer's confrontational style finally resulted in the loss of his *Quill & Quire* column when he provoked a publishing colleague once too often. Ron Besse was a former president of McGraw-Hill Ryerson and therefore identified with the foreign-owned subsidiaries and the takeover of the Ryerson Press; but by then he'd become a bona fide Canadian publisher, the owner of both Gage and Macmillan. Besse took serious exception to Lorimer's criticisms of the way educational publishers like himself were influencing provincial curricula. Although there was reason to doubt that Besse had a case to sue, he exerted enough legal pressure that *Quill & Quire* cancelled Lorimer's column after a run of eighteen months.

Lorimer's rigorous analysis of the structural problems of Canadian publishing was sound and left an indelible stamp on the policy debate. He generated political momentum that helped other members of the IPA and its successor body, the Association of Canadian Publishers, to secure additional support measures from Ottawa. The most significant of those measures was a new funding program, the Canadian Book Publishing Development Program, instituted in 1979. The program was launched under a Liberal minister, John Roberts, modified by David MacDonald, a Conservative minister during the short-lived Clark government, and confirmed by another Liberal, Minister of Communications Francis Fox, with a budget of $20 million over three years. Since the program was intended to strengthen the publishing business industrially by rewarding success in the marketplace (as opposed to the Canada Council's emphasis on cultural output), program funds were awarded according to a formula based on each applicant's sales of Canadian-authored books. Renamed the Book Publishing Industry Development Program and currently housed within the Department of Canadian Heritage, the program has contributed greatly over the years to sustaining Canadian publishers financially. Despite that fact, it wasn't a structural measure of the type that Lorimer, Audley, and their colleagues had envisaged.

Lorimer was among those who primed the IPA/ACP to become a more truly national body. By talking up the difficulties facing the growing ranks of regionally based houses – high production costs, distance from major markets, a lack of provincial support compared with Ontario's – he and others turned the association's attention to the needs of publishers throughout the country. Lorimer saw the political importance of an indigenous industry that flourished in every province. A regionalist as well as a nationalist, he was a Manitoban equally at home in Toronto's inner city and in Halifax, where he moved and acquired a second publishing house, Formac Publishing, in the early 1980s.

By that time, one of English-Canadian publishing's most singular qualities was its geographic and cultural reach. The range of fresh, innovative publishing practised in central Canada was being matched by energetic new publishers rising elsewhere, especially in the west. The Canadian industry's diversity and decentralization would stand in dramatic contrast to the tightening grip of conglomerate control elsewhere in the world.

HURTIG

GRAY'S PUBLISHING

DOUGLAS & McINTYRE

HURTIG PUBLISHERS

10

RISE OF THE WEST

It was all there, ready for the picking.

Gray Campbell on publishing in western Canada (1999)

I n 1955 Alberta and Saskatchewan marked fifty years in Confederation by publishing books: among them W.G. Hardy's *The Alberta Golden Jubilee Anthology* and J.F.C. Wright's *Saskatchewan: The History of a Province*, both published by McClelland & Stewart. In 1958 British Columbia observed the centennial of its founding with *British Columbia: A History*, by Margaret Ormsby, and *The Living Land*, by Roderick Haig-Brown, both from Macmillan, and Reginald Watters's *British Columbia: A Centennial Anthology*, from M&S. Just as Canada was a publishing colony of Britain and the United States, so was the west a publishing colony of Toronto.

That situation would be utterly transformed within a generation. Although the change was attributable to many factors, three publishers, each ruggedly independent in spirit and markedly different in background from the others, were crucial to the rise of publishing in the west.

Of all the unlikely start-ups in Canadian publishing, Gray Campbell's was the unlikeliest. Campbell was already fifty when he entered "this dodge," as he once called publishing. He'd been taking chances all his life. He left his native Ottawa to enlist in the RCMP at nineteen, concealing his age, and spent seven years stationed in southern Alberta. When war broke out in Europe, he joined Royal Air Force Bomber Command, piloting Lancasters over Germany during the Second World War and earning a Distinguished Flying Cross. Campbell and his English bride, Eleanor, moved to Alberta in 1946 with $80 in cash; with help from a veteran's loan and an anonymous benefactor, they bought a ranch at Squaw Butte in the Porcupine Hills and began raising four children. Campbell wrote an article about their ranching adventures for *Maclean's*, which led to a book-length version, *We Found Peace*, published by Thomas Allen in 1953. After twelve years of struggle, exhilaration, and pain, the family sold the ranch and moved to the gentler climate of Sidney on Vancouver Island. Campbell supported them all with freelance journalism: "I couldn't write," he said four decades later, "but I could sure tell a story."

The Campbells' island neighbours were a remarkable collection of back-to-the-landers and bohemians. Among them was a Second World War veteran, John Windsor, who'd been blinded in a tank attack in Italy. Campbell encouraged Windsor to commit his war experiences to paper, then tried to get the manuscript published for him back east. When Thomas Allen and another Toronto publisher rejected it, the Campbells decided to publish it themselves.

Their method of raising capital was unusual. Gray Campbell went on the live CBC Television program *Live a Borrowed Life*, forerunner of *Front Page Challenge*, to impersonate another neighbour, Donald MacLaren, one of Canada's fighter aces in the First World War. Campbell stumped the panel, won the top prize money, and turned it over to the Sidney newspaper editor who'd agreed to print the book. Windsor's *Blind Date*, run off four pages at a time on an old-fashioned flatbed press, appeared in 1962, the first of sixty titles from what would henceforth be known as Gray's Publishing.

A regionally published title was a rare bird in British Columbia, and the province's small book community lavished attention on Windsor's memoir. Jim Douglas offered Campbell tips about selling to the trade, confiding that he wanted to start a publishing house himself one day. Bill Duthie held an autographing session for Windsor at his Robson Street bookstore in Vancouver; he talked the book up to Jack Webster, who interviewed the author on his popular local radio show. That led to the

Vancouver Sun book editor Barry Broadfoot's review of *Blind Date*, and to coverage in the Victoria media.

Out of his affable nature and readiness to help others, Campbell had stumbled on a basic truth: British Columbians love to read books by their own. *Blind Date* sold out its initial run of 3,000 copies and had to be reprinted within a year. Unsolicited manuscripts started arriving on Campbell's doorstep. Everybody in British Columbia, it seemed, had a frontier story to tell, and before long Campbell found himself running a full-time publishing operation out of a converted chicken coop behind his home.

As he was the first to admit, Campbell needed help in almost every aspect of the business, and somehow that help always arrived. Another of his neighbours was the noted wilderness author R.M. Patterson; Gray's Publishing issued Patterson's narrative of pioneer homesteading in the Peace River country, *Far Pastures*, in 1963, and his *The Dangerous River* in 1966. Publishing Patterson, whose work had appeared in London and New York, raised the profile of Gray's and forced Campbell to bring his author contracts up to professional standards.

Selling American rights helped professionalize Gray's Publishing further. A Calgary nurse named Amy Wilson had written a book about saving lives in a harrowing cholera epidemic among Native people in the Yukon; after Wilson's manuscript was rejected several times in Toronto, the editor of *Chatelaine*, Doris Anderson, recommended that she try "that fella on Vancouver Island." Campbell published it in 1965 as *No Man Stands Alone* ("a terrible title," he admitted later), and Dodd, Mead bought U.S. rights the following year. Rather than simply reprinting Campbell's edition, the New York publisher re-edited the text, reset the type, and retitled the book *A Nurse in the Yukon*. Campbell found the American edition considerably superior to his own: "I learned from Dodd, Mead how to put a book together."

Strictly speaking, Gray Campbell wasn't British Columbia's first publisher. Mitchell Press, a Vancouver commercial printer, produced a few trade books each year, usually local histories and vanity titles. There were also private presses (private in the sense that they didn't market their books widely to the trade) in Vancouver: Klanak Press, founded in 1958 by the writers William C. and Alice McConnell, published small editions of

fiction and poetry; Discovery Press, a self-publishing venture by two pro-
fessors, G.P.V. and Helen Akrigg, produced the couple's books on early
British Columbia history; Periwinkle Press, operated by the visual artist
Takao Tanabe, printed fine limited editions and broadsides by letterpress.
The distinguished designer Robert R. Reid also made private editions and
collaborated with Tanabe in 1962 to produce John Newlove's collection
Grave Sirs, which the poet Robert Bringhurst, in a 1984 catalogue of British
Columbia literary books, called "the finest single example of literary pub-
lishing yet produced in B.C."

Nonetheless Gray's was the first general trade publisher to take root
west of Toronto. An abundant supply of manuscripts was close at hand, and
Campbell had the benefit of a cheap labour pool. Eleanor Campbell worked
on editorial and production. Two of the couple's sons handled sales and distribution, hitting the highway first by bus and then by van to sell the books
within a limited radius of Vancouver Island: the Lower Mainland, over the
Rockies into Alberta, and southward into the adjoining states.

Two of Gray's most celebrated titles arrived within a year of each
other. On a tip from a local schoolteacher, Campbell travelled up-island to
the Nootka reserve near Port Alberni to visit George Clutesi, an artist and
writer of the Sheshaht band. Clutesi was rumoured to have a manuscript
of tribal legends he'd been trying to get published for twenty years.
Campbell realized the stories of rejection by eastern publishers must be
true when Clutesi, on hearing Campbell was a publisher, refused to climb
down from his roof, where he was making repairs. Unfazed, Campbell
climbed up the ladder, sat for a while to chat, and scribbled his name and
phone number on a scrap of paper. A few months later, Clutesi phoned
and let him see the manuscript.

Campbell discovered he "couldn't make head or tail of it." He
entrusted the manuscript to an Englishwoman he knew with a deep
interest in Aboriginal cultures, Mary Gibbs, who worked closely with
Clutesi to address the difficulties of rendering the centuries-old Sheshaht
stories into English. The resulting book, *Son of Raven, Son of Deer*,
appeared at the same time that a Clutesi mural was drawing huge audiences at Expo 67. The book found an immediate audience, selling 4,000
copies in four weeks. Eventually, after major purchases by the provincial

Ministry of Education, there would be over 80,000 copies in print.

M. (for Muriel) Wylie Blanchet, yet another of Campbell's neighbours, had written a graceful account of sailing the coastal sounds and inlets with her five children, which had been published in the United Kingdom. Unhappy that her book had been poorly distributed in Canada ("It didn't even get west," Campbell recalled), Blanchet went to see him in the hope of escaping from her contract. She died soon afterwards, but her family succeeded in having the book rights reverted to the estate, and in 1969 Gray's brought out a Canadian edition of *The Curve of Time*. It would become a classic of West Coast literature, still widely read.

Campbell graduated from the old four-up press in Sidney to obtaining printing from the best firms in British Columbia. Evergreen Press of Vancouver worked with him, beginning with the R.M. Patterson books. In Victoria, Morriss Printing, which also did the elegant design and production of George Woodcock's *Canadian Literature*, took on George Clutesi's second book, *Potlatch*. In 1973 Evergreen produced Campbell's biggest and most ambitious title, Lewis J. Clark's *Wild Flowers of British Columbia*, a splendidly illustrated volume with 550 colour plates. Jim Douglas considered it "publishing of the highest quality," even though Campbell claimed with typical modesty that he "couldn't distinguish a daisy from a dandelion."

By the time he sold Gray's Publishing and retired in 1977, Campbell had successfully pioneered the regionally based publishing that now flourishes throughout English-speaking Canada. Several titles from Gray's backlist continue to sell actively, reissued by British Columbia houses such as Harbour Publishing and Whitecap Books. According to Harbour's publisher, Howard White, "Gray's editorial choices have stood up. They look better every year."

Recognizing the kick-start that Campbell had given their industry, the Association of Book Publishers of British Columbia created an award in his name to honour distinguished service to publishing in the province. At a banquet celebrating his career in 1999, Campbell savoured the recognition of his younger peers; he died a year later at eighty-eight.

If Gray Campbell was the consummate amateur of British Columbia publishing, Jim Douglas was the consummate pro. James Jardine Douglas had books in his blood, having grown up in an Edinburgh home where the children were permitted to read at the dinner table. Leaving school in 1939, he went straight into the book business. His first job was working as a "collector" for the Menzies bookstore chain, bicycling around the city to other stores to buy up out-of-stock titles ordered by customers.

During the war, Douglas joined Royal Air Force Aircrew, becoming a "wireless operational mechanic air-gunner" who flew in Liberator bombers. After service in the Far East, Douglas returned to Menzies; but when he realized the firm wouldn't make him a store manager until his forties, he left for a five-year commission as an RAF signals officer, acquiring two years of college education. On the day his commission ended in 1954, Douglas emigrated to Canada with his family, which by then included his daughter, Diana, future publisher of Vancouver's International Self-Counsel Press. Starting out in Toronto, the Douglas family made a second migration to the West Coast: "It was crazy to travel 5,000 miles and fetch up in a place you didn't want to be, so investing another 3,000 miles was better than going back."

Douglas earned his living in Vancouver as an electronics engineer, but he was desperate to return to his first love and sought out everyone in the local book trade. He became friends with Bill Duthie, then selling for Macmillan and M&S from the Coast to the Lakehead. Both men tried to buy Vancouver's leading bookstore at the time, Ireland and Allan, on different occasions; but Jimmy Allan, another Scot, stubbornly refused to sell to either of them and later went bankrupt. When Duthie took the plunge and opened his own store in 1957, Douglas took over Duthie's territory as a publisher's rep.

Duthie had worked on salary, but Douglas insisted on being his own boss. He started a western sales agency, negotiating commission deals with Hugh Kane at M&S, Donald Sutherland at Macmillan, and Hilary Marshall at the University of Toronto Press. "I always wanted to be a publisher," Douglas declared years later, "and that's why I started the agency. My plan was to turn it into a publishing house. I'm a long-term planner."

After a detour in 1962–1963 to serve as M&S's director of marketing in Toronto, Douglas reactivated the agency, now confining his travels to British Columbia. He built the business by paying meticulous attention to his customers and adding services to the sales function. Although M&S had always centralized its promotion out of Toronto, the head-office people didn't know the British Columbia media or bookstore scene; Douglas took over regional publicity for M&S and did the job so effectively that the company hired a string of similar reps across the west combining sales and publicity, dubbed "the prairie flowers" by Hugh Kane.

Douglas also became a wholesaler. Despite creation of the Cooperative Book Centre in Toronto, a publisher-owned library wholesaler, many British Columbia libraries continued to buy around Canadian publisher-agents by purchasing from American sources. Douglas started a regional wholesale operation specializing in children's books, opened a warehouse to hold both Macmillan and M&S stock, and did a brisk business for both companies.

Douglas even became a West Coast field editor. Jack McClelland offered him a commission on any book he found that M&S published. One title Douglas scouted, the journalist Simma Holt's book on the Sons of Freedom Doukhobors, *Terror in the Name of God*, sold so well that Douglas earned almost as much money as the author. He also sponsored Paul St. Pierre's *Chilcotin Holiday*, a collection of stories set among the cowboys of British Columbia's rugged interior. Douglas worked closely with the author to assemble the manuscript and illustrations, but M&S's handling of the book was "a complete shambles, a disaster." When finished copies arrived, both Douglas and St. Pierre reacted with horror: "The book was long and narrow, and it was *pink*," Douglas recalled. "It had a brooch in the centre, oval-shaped, with a drawing of a horse and a cowboy in it. It looked like a Valentine's card. I was embarrassed to take Paul his copies; the book was unsaleable."

Douglas knew he could do better.

Scott McIntyre walked into Douglas's wholesale business on Seymour Street one day in 1967 to propose a book for M&S, a collection of a friend's black and white photographs of Vancouver. Although Douglas judged the book idea wanting, "we got talking, and I liked Scott. He was energetic and bright and cheery and obviously fascinated by the whole idea of publishing."

Twenty years younger than Douglas, McIntyre had recently graduated from the University of British Columbia and taken a job in advertising. But he wanted to try publishing in Toronto, so Douglas recommended him to Hugh Kane. McIntyre worked at M&S for two years in advertising and promotion; after touring Europe with his wife, Corky, he returned to Vancouver, and the two men struck a bargain. Douglas would bring McIntyre into the sales agency at the beginning of 1970, selling him 40 percent of the business to be paid for out of earnings; if all went well, they'd start a publishing house together, also to be divided 60-40.

Within a year, Douglas was ready to make the switch to publishing. McIntyre had turned out to be "a first-class salesperson"; the agency was flourishing; and Douglas felt confident about leaving it in McIntyre's hands. They brought in Mark Stanton, another M&S alumnus, as a partner in the agency, which would become McIntyre & Stanton. Douglas sold the pair his remaining 60 percent and disposed of his wholesale company to the local competition, Harry Smith & Son. Equipped with the capital to start a publishing house, Douglas lacked only books; his commitments to M&S and Macmillan had prevented him from signing up any authors before going into business for himself.

As a result, Douglas gave up *Halfbreed*, the remarkable autobiography of the Saskatchewan Metis Maria Campbell, to M&S. The first catalogue from J.J. Douglas Ltd. in 1971 was simply a grab bag of titles for which he'd acquired distribution rights. His own books began appearing in 1972: a list running heavily to cookbooks and other practical titles, selected by a canny middle-aged bookman who didn't want to get in over his head, at least not yet. Titles like *Cooking for One* and *Sourdough Jack's Cookbook* (which came with a starter pack of sourdough) provided the fledgling company with cash flow to put it on its feet.

As the 1970s progressed, the sales agency once again expanded across the west to the Lakehead, and Scott McIntyre functioned as a silent partner in the publishing house. He couldn't be publicly associated with J.J. Douglas Ltd. since he was providing representation for a range of rival publishers, including Anansi, Hurtig, Lorimer, New Press, and Peter Martin Associates, in addition to M&S and Macmillan. But the partners conferred regularly, and McIntyre brought his market knowledge and eye for design to the table even before the house became known as Douglas & McIntyre. Basing their publishing program on what McIntyre called "the historic trading pattern of this province since the gold rush: regional first, international second, beyond the Rockies third," they tried consciously dividing their list among the three areas.

By far the strongest themes were regional. These would be mined again and again for the next thirty years, not only by Douglas & McIntyre but by many other British Columbia publishers: the rugged West Coast environment, the northwest Aboriginal cultures, provincial history. The company published *West Coast Trail*, *One Man's Gold Rush*, and *Looking at Indian Art of the Northwest Coast*, an introductory guide by Hilary Stewart that would continue selling steadily, reaching a quarter of a million copies by 2000. It published *How the West Coast Indians Lived*, which began as a stand-alone title for young readers and resulted in a series called How They Lived, introducing children to Native cultures in the various regions of Canada.

Of all the books he published, Jim Douglas considered *The Days of Augusta* his favourite. It arrived on a tip from a Vancouver Island woman who had tape-recorded the voice of eighty-six-year-old Mary Augusta Tappage, a Shuswap woman living in a tarpaper shack up in the Cariboo. Augusta recounted tales of her people and her own harsh life in a natural poetic diction that Douglas found exceptionally beautiful and moving. Scott McIntyre had the idea of sending a photographer to shoot images of her as she went about her daily routines, and the resulting book was a memorable and graphic record of a traditional way of life, co-published in the United States.

The northwest and Aboriginal themes provided a bridge to the desired international alliances. The most fruitful and lasting collaboration was with the University of Washington Press, which shared many of the same cultural interests as the Vancouver publisher. Douglas, McIntyre, and their editor Marilyn Sacks went to Seattle twice a year to discuss the two presses' forthcoming projects and determine which titles might travel successfully across the border. Washington bought for its imprint such JJD titles as *The*

Unknown Island, a picture book on the hidden beauties of Vancouver Island. Although the university press was eager to receive representation for its entire list in Canada, Douglas always declined, preferring to select only those Washington titles that made a good fit with his own trade list. Gradually Douglas acquired some two dozen agencies, mostly smaller trade houses from Canada, the United States, and Britain.

At a time of intense nationalism, Douglas believed in the importance of publishing internationally. In his opinion, "We could all learn to be better publishers, and part of that was internationalizing your books." He forged joint publishing ventures with David & Charles in England and Canongate Publishing in Edinburgh. And in 1975, when industry colleagues asked Douglas to become the first non-Ontario president of the Independent Publishers' Association (he'd served as founding president of the Association of Book Publishers of British Columbia the year before), he accepted the post on condition that the membership place greater priority on export. In subsequent years, he'd lead or participate in industry trade missions to the United Kingdom, China, Japan, Argentina, Australia, and New Zealand.

Since Douglas was also a fervent British Columbia regionalist, it was inevitable that the third wing of the company strategy, national publishing, would suffer by comparison. Douglas objected to what he saw as the excessively Canadian emphasis of so many publishers' lists: "Every damn title had 'Canada' in it." As an old-fashioned believer in self-sufficiency, he was no fan of subsidy; in 1976 he tried to return his block grant to the Canada Council, on the grounds that his firm had enjoyed a good year and could afford to repay the grant – only to be told, to his amusement, that the council had no mechanism for taking money back.

Arguably JJD's most important breakthroughs in the national market were children's picture books. *Johann's Gift to Christmas*, the tale of a music-loving mouse written by Jack Richards and illustrated by Len Norris, and Betty Waterton's *A Salmon for Simon*, illustrated by Ann Blades, were both extremely popular. They paved the way for a crucial alliance between the house that was about to become Douglas & McIntyre and a small press that would grow into one of Canada's most admired children's publishers, Groundwood Books of Toronto.

By the end of the 1970s, Jim Douglas was planning a phased with-drawal from the business. Replicating the process of eight years earlier, Scott McIntyre would move into the driver's seat of a company Douglas had founded, leaving the sales agency in the hands of Mark Stanton and his new partner, Allan MacDougall. Thus J.J. Douglas begat Douglas & McIntyre, which begat Stanton & MacDougall, which begat Raincoast Books, which begat the ultimate successor to the sales agency, Kate Walker & Associates. For D&M, serious challenges and hundreds of new books lay ahead. For Jim Douglas, who remained on the D&M board, and on the board of his daughter Diana Douglas's company, retirement would be neither as early nor as orderly as expected. But he'd be able to take pride in laying the foundations of a publishing house with style, substance, and staying power, a house that would attract many gifted writers and book people in the years ahead.

Before publishing books, Mel Hurtig too learned the discipline of the marketplace. He was a retail bookseller in Edmonton for sixteen years, the most successful on the Prairies. Unlike Gray Campbell or Jim Douglas, however, Hurtig's overriding goal as a publisher was to make an impact on the entire country. An irrepressible nationalist – he once headed the Committee for an Independent Canada and founded its suc-cessor, the Council of Canadians – he became the first English Canadian to build a major trade publishing house outside of Toronto. Hurtig dreamed on a grand scale, like Jack McClelland, whom he admired in-ordinately but emulated only selectively, and he too gambled heavily on fulfilling his dreams.

Hurtig's father, a Romanian immigrant, was a self-made Edmonton furrier. Hurtig didn't covet a future in the family firm, nor did he follow his brothers and friends into university; instead he went into business for himself. In 1956 Hurtig opened his first bookstore at the age of twenty-four. At 425 square feet, the store was tiny and cramped, but it had the field pretty much to itself; between Toronto and Vancouver, bookstores were few and far between. Although Hurtig's father co-signed the bank loan to begin the store, he had his doubts: "If it's such a good idea, how is it that no one has done it already?"

It seemed the only people cheering Hurtig on were his then wife and business partner, Eileen, and a sales rep who came calling. The night before Hurtig Books opened, Bill Duthie dropped by to wish the couple well, bearing a bottle of Rémy Martin, a pair of snifters, and a bouquet of flowers. A year later, he'd pay Hurtig the ultimate compliment by following his example and opening the first Duthie Books, where he'd soon be wearing a groove in the front counter with his belt buckle as he stood day after day, talking books with his customers and nipping from a bottle of rye.

Hurtig believed that he could tap into a growing appetite for books in Edmonton. Soon proving himself right, he moved into ever-larger premises and eventually opened two satellite stores. His flagship store on Jasper Avenue attracted the praise of visitors from André Deutsch to Nathan Cohen. It was a clean, well-lighted place, measuring 7,000 square feet: according to Hurtig, not only the biggest bookstore in Canada in the early 1960s, but the best. The store foreshadowed the consumer-friendly amenities introduced thirty years later by book superstores, boasting a coffee counter, tables and chairs for relaxing, and a space for author events. Customers and staff could consult several copies of *Books in Print* placed open on lecterns around the store. Hurtig's bookstores were profitable. Yet no matter how well they did, a prediction by his bank manager held true: each year, as Hurtig expanded, he had to borrow even more money.

When Hurtig branched out into distribution, he swore to provide his fellow booksellers with efficient service at reasonable cost. In 1962, over martinis in Japan, he persuaded Charles Tuttle, an American publisher who specialized in books on the Orient, to give him Canadian agency rights to the Tuttle Publishing list. Four years later, over brandies, Hurtig persuaded the chairman of the Guinness Corporation to transfer the rights to *The Guinness Book of Records* from Burns & MacEachern; Hurtig offered to double the order for Canada, and within three years he'd boosted the annual's Canadian sales from 1,000 copies to 7,500.

Having had an atypical taste of publishing, Hurtig felt encouraged to go on. He arranged with Tuttle to co-publish a series of handsome facsimile reproductions of out-of-print journals of early Canadian explorers, works in the public domain and therefore freely available. Hurtig commissioned scholarly introductions to each volume and chose the cover art, while Tuttle handled the printing in Japan. Without editorial, royalty, or typesetting costs, the two publishers were able to price the books cheaply and fill a demand from North American history buffs and libraries.

Hurtig continued to venture into the quicksands of publishing despite well-meant advice to the contrary, coming from a familiar source. Macmillan's John Gray stood on a wind-chilled sidewalk in downtown Edmonton one winter evening, telling Hurtig in his kindly way not to cash in his bookstores for a publishing career. "Don't do it. It would be a bad mistake," Hurtig remembered Gray saying. "All the best editors, printers, designers, the chain and department store buyers are in Toronto. It would be impossible to develop a national house successfully in Edmonton."

Hurtig, of course, didn't listen.

In 1968 a University of British Columbia graduate student named Susan Kent was supporting herself as a proofreader at Mitchell Press in Vancouver when she read a *Time Canada* article about Hurtig's plans to publish books. Kent, who came from a journalism family in Calgary (her brothers Peter and Arthur would become familiar faces on television), wrote to Hurtig saying she wasn't completely sure what a book editor was but thought she'd like to become one. Hurtig wrote back saying he wasn't sure, either, but she should fly to Edmonton to talk it over. During Kent's interview, Al Purdy blew in on a tour promoting his anti-American anthology *The New Romans*, Hurtig's first political book. The poet dedicated a copy "to Susan Kent, the newest employee and future head of the firm." Hurtig had assessed Kent's enthusiasm, seriousness, and intellectual sophistication, and by day's end she was hired.

Kent moved to Edmonton, living with the Hurtigs and their four daughters while starting her new job. For her first editing assignment, Hurtig handed her a copy of *The Chicago Manual of Style* and a thick manuscript that had been sitting around the office, *The Canadian Rockies: Early Travels and Explorations*, by the amateur historian Esther Fraser. "See what you can do with this," Hurtig told Kent. Over many months, she revised the manuscript extensively, teaching herself copy-editing and becoming friends with the author in the process. When Fraser's well-illustrated book appeared, it filled a gap in the market and went on to sell 32,000 copies in hardcover, a formidable quantity for any title. *The New Romans*, meanwhile, hit 35,000 in paperback in a shorter time span, becoming a number-one national bestseller.

Hurtig ran the publishing operation out of the back of his Jasper Avenue bookstore, in a raised, glass-fronted office from which he could survey the action on the floor below. Early staffers learned publishing as much by overhearing his telephone conversations and sharing his cigarette smoke as by any other means (he later gave up smoking but not the phone habit), and by sitting in on frequent visits from authors, politicians, and customers. Jan Walter, later of Macmillan, M&S, and Macfarlane Walter & Ross, had her first editorial job with Hurtig, succeeding Susan Kent, who moved on to work for André Deutsch in London. "Any literary figure who came through Edmonton had to stop at Mel's," Walter recalled. "You'd be sitting in the third chair in that office, so you got to eavesdrop and be part of it." Walter Gordon, Margaret Laurence, Peter Newman, Abe Rotstein, Jack McClelland, Leonard Cohen, and Eric Kierans were a few who wafted through the door, en route to Hurtig's comfortable home for a drink or dinner. They'd begun visiting when he was a bookseller and continued visiting after he became a publisher and, briefly, an unsuccessful Liberal candidate in the 1972 federal election.

Hurtig's two major concerns as a publisher, national politics and Alberta culture, were combined in his influential 1971 bestseller, Harold Cardinal's *The Unjust Society: The Tragedy of Canada's Indians*. Cardinal was a Cree who was already head of the Alberta Indian Association at age twenty-four. According to Hurtig, Cardinal practically had to be locked in a hotel room with a ghost writer to get the book finished and out on time, but when they emerged, Cardinal had delivered himself of a scathingly effective denunciation of Department of Indian Affairs bureaucrats in Ottawa and a federal White Paper on Aboriginal policy. The book, its title parodying Pierre Trudeau's 1968 election catchphrase, reportedly made Trudeau angry, and his Indian affairs minister even angrier; one reviewer wrote that the book accused Jean Chrétien of "arrogance and deceit" and dismissed him as "a pawn of the bureaucrats."

Hurtig reaped satisfaction from the government's discomfiture, since his own earlier attempt to get Trudeau's attention with a paper on Aboriginal policy had been ignored. Hurtig had pursued Cardinal knowing the young firebrand's "poised, self-confident, proud, angry and articulate" personality would capture the attention of the public and politicians as he never could himself. Since he was at odds with so many other Liberal policies, from foreign ownership to taxation, it was all the more curious that Hurtig would run for office as a Liberal. In any case, publishing well was the best revenge. *The Unjust Society* moved nearly 80,000 copies and became Hurtig's second number-one seller.

One of the many traits that distinguished Hurtig from other Canadian publishers was his faith in print advertising. Then as now, most publishers considered newspaper and magazine ads too expensive, given the number of books they were likely to sell. But Hurtig began reserving pages 3 and 5 of *Quill & Quire* every month for full-page ads boosting his books, and reached the public through newspapers ads covered by each title's hefty marketing budget. Hurtig combined a strong focus on marketing with highly selective publishing and detailed, cost-conscious budgeting. He claimed that each of the first fifteen books he published was profitable, as were many that followed, such as *Alberta: A Natural History*, which sold a phenomenal 73,000 copies; Andy Russell's *The Rockies*; *The Real Poverty Report*, a renegade document by Ian Adams, Bill Cameron, and two other writers who'd resigned in disgust from the staff of the Senate Committee on Poverty; and a surprise bestseller, *You Can't Print THAT!*, by the Southam political columnist Charles Lynch.

In 1972 Hurtig crossed his Rubicon. To generate capital for his expanding publishing operation, he sold his bookstores. The buyer was the same Vancouver wholesaler, Buddy Smith, who had bought Jim Douglas's wholesale business. Although the stores didn't flourish under Smith's absentee ownership, the main store metamorphosed into Audrey's Books, which remained one of the best independents in Canada.

Hurtig moved the publishing company into a nondescript, low-overhead warehouse tucked beneath the Fifth Street overpass in downtown

Edmonton. In 1973 sales surpassed half a million dollars, making the company the most substantial mid-size publisher in Canada. Hurtig was now ready to make his largest investment to date in a single book, a precursor of megaprojects to come.

Among the 140-and-counting titles he has written or edited under his own name, the one-man publishing industry John Robert Colombo – poet, Canadianist, anthologist, trivia buff, "master gatherer," literary magpie – is most famous for a book he published with Hurtig in 1974. Hurtig obtained the rights in part because he was willing to include Colombo's name in the title: a case of one large ego saluting another. (Visitors to Hurtig's office under the overpass found themselves surrounded by his wall of fame, papered with photographs and clippings of his exploits, speeches, and meetings with the famous.)

Colombo had previously signed a contract with the Toronto educational publisher Fitzhenry & Whiteside to compile a reference work of quotations from Canadian history and literature. In the course of the project, Robert Fitzhenry informed Colombo that he didn't want to use the working title, "Colombo's Canadian Quotations," and preferred to call the book "Quotations Canada." Not wishing to be associated with something that sounded like a government agency, Colombo cancelled the contract and returned the $5,000 advance to Fitzhenry. As luck would have it, Hurtig phoned the next day and, upon hearing the story, asked to see the manuscript. Hurtig was staggered by its sheer bulk but five days later mailed Colombo a contract proposing a $10,000 advance, the company's largest to date.

"What do you want to call it?" Colombo enquired mischievously. " 'Hurtig's Canadian Quotations'?"

No, Hurtig was happy with the title as it was. He went ahead with plans to print 20,000 copies of the 735-page hardcover: a total investment of $125,000, a very large amount for the time, representing 80 percent of the company's line of credit. Jan Walter was given responsibility for the massive editing job. Still new to the profession, she was apprehensive about her readiness for the task. Hurtig reassured her, saying, "Very little work to do here, Jan. John's a professional. Knows his stuff cold. Done this kind of thing many times. Not a problem."

"At that point," Walter remembered, "I was still pretty green and couldn't bring any overarching sense of discernment to the project. Of course I knew there was a lot riding on it. Mel was writing letters to book-sellers and the media, putting on the big push. Once again it was going to be the best book we'd ever published. Every book – every season – we'd have the best book we'd ever published."

When the massive *Colombo's Canadian Quotations* duly appeared, it was reviewed in the *Globe and Mail* under the headline "Quotations Book Needs Good Editor." Walter's heart sank; reading on, she learned that the reviewer, Morris Wolfe, had found errors in the text. Walter prepared to offer her resignation. Her publishing career was over. She saw the headline engraved on her tombstone. But Hurtig was patient, understanding; he asked her, as he had on other occasions, "So, Jan, what did you learn from this?" And they carried on. It's easy to understand why she called him "an ideal employer."

There were other, more favourable reviews, and by Christmas 1974, *Colombo's* had sold three-quarters of its run and was into the black. It was joined on the *Toronto Star* bestseller list by another Hurtig book with the author's name in the title, *Peter Gzowski's Book About This Country in the Morning*. Gzowski had left *This Country in the Morning*, the popular forerunner of *Morningside* on CBC Radio, and the oversized paperback, consisting of interview transcripts, recipes, and other items from the program, tapped into national nostalgia for the show. Brilliantly art-directed by the M&S designer David Shaw, who moonlighted for Hurtig from his Toronto base, it sold 44,000 copies when all was said and done. The success of the two books earned Hurtig the Canadian Booksellers Association's Publisher of the Year award in 1975.

But the biggest and brightest of all the big ideas in Hurtig's career came when he found himself in a school library in Swift Current, Saskatchewan. He was about to give a speech on Canadian sovereignty, and as he surveyed the library shelves, Hurtig saw that all the reference books and encyclopedias were American. Whenever they researched an essay, he realized, the students would learn about American history, American heroes, American values.

By late 1975, having discovered the same anomaly in other schools across the country, Hurtig was convinced that the lack of reference material about Canada was a national disgrace. Even the most recent edition of the ten-volume *Encyclopedia Canadiana*, originally published in 1957 by Grolier, was seriously outdated and inaccurate. Hurtig met in Toronto with Morris Wolfe and Ivon Owen, who had once condemned the Grolier encyclopedia in *The Tamarack Review* as "a great national disaster," to discuss preparing a completely new Canadian encyclopedia. Owen, by then freelancing, would be executive editor, Wolfe general editor. It would be ten years, and a voyage of Ulyssean proportions, before *The Canadian Encyclopedia* sailed safely into harbour.

It all began in orderly, well-planned fashion. With Owen and Wolfe ready to serve, and the University of Toronto primed to provide office space and library privileges, Hurtig submitted a minutely detailed, forty-two-page prospectus and funding proposal to the Canada Council. The proposed encyclopedia would draw on the most recent scholarship and present its material in lively, jargon-free language for a broad readership. Hurtig had mustered a blue-ribbon advisory committee and had solicited endorsement letters from dozens of eminent Canadians, from Northrop Frye to Premier William Davis of Ontario. He even offered to award French-language rights free of charge to a Quebec publisher.

Sympathetic to the idea, the Canada Council nevertheless responded by imposing costly conditions. It would support Hurtig's project only if he agreed to establish a parallel French-language editorial office and ensure that the French edition appeared at the same time and price as the English. In effect, the council sought a structure similar to the one Marsh Jeanneret had finessed for the *Dictionary of Canadian Biography* with the advice of Cardinal Léger. The Catch-22, as Hurtig called it, was that the council didn't ante up any additional funding for the additional expenses.

But Hurtig didn't abandon hope. Three years later, Alberta was deciding how to spend $75 million of its taxpayers' money to celebrate the province's seventy-fifth anniversary in 1980. Despite his public disagreements with Premier Peter Lougheed, and his political unpopularity with the governing Tories, Hurtig wrote Lougheed proposing that Alberta mark the event by making "a gift to Canada," in the form of a $2-million contribution to the encyclopedia's development costs. Part of the gift would cover the purchase, at cost, of copies to be donated to every school, library, and post-secondary institution in the country.

Galloping inflation had driven the project's budget far above the original estimate. Hurtig proposed making Alberta's support conditional on a matching amount from the federal government, figuring that would pressure Ottawa into kicking in another $2 million. As a further incentive for the Lougheed government, Hurtig committed himself to basing the encyclopedia's operations at the University of Alberta.

After a long wait, the cabinet minister in charge of anniversary celebrations phoned Hurtig: Alberta wouldn't be contributing $2 million, the minister reported; the government preferred that Hurtig receive no help at all from Ottawa and would provide the whole $4 million. Hurtig was astonished. Alberta's contribution would consist of $3.4 million for research and development, and $600,000 to underwrite 25,000 copies to be presented to libraries and schools throughout Canada. If it hadn't been for Peter Lougheed, Hurtig said later, there would have been no *Canadian Encyclopedia*.

The race was on, and the stakes were huge. Even with $4 million in funding, Hurtig needed to borrow an equivalent amount to finance production and marketing. If the encyclopedia was going to achieve wide public acceptance, its contents would have to be comprehensive in scope, knowledgeably selected, authoritatively written, and impeccably edited. And if it was going to succeed in financial terms, its physical production would have to be rigorously costed and controlled. The necessary coordination among advisory boards, writers, editors, staff, and suppliers was mind-boggling.

Increasingly busy with his political commitments, Hurtig needed professionals capable of turning his dream into reality. His decision to opt for a made-in-Alberta project meant he lost his first choices for the senior editorial positions; neither Owen nor Wolfe was prepared to move to Edmonton. Hurtig approached his friend William Thorsell, an editor with the *Edmonton Journal* and later editor-in-chief of the *Globe and Mail*. When Thorsell proved unavailable, Hurtig advertised the position across the country. The man he hired would make *The Canadian Encyclopedia* his life's work.

James Marsh had been toiling away in happy obscurity for a decade at Ottawa's Carleton University, editing the Carleton Library for M&S. Ironically, Marsh had dropped out of university himself in the 1960s to become an editor at Holt, Rinehart & Winston, where he handled history and social studies texts and even wrote a book in a social studies series. He moved on to Collier-Macmillan, where he succeeded Anna Porter. Two years later, Porter hired him for the Carleton Library.

Working out of Carleton's Institute of Canadian Studies, Marsh attended interdisciplinary seminars organized by the institute's distinguished director, Pauline Jewett, and collaborated with leading scholars on editing works in the series. He thus acquired the qualifications necessary for editing Hurtig's encyclopedia: a knowledge of Canada and its history that was both broad and deep, and a familiarity with academic editorial boards, with their propensity for time-consuming intellectual wrangling.

Hurtig signed Marsh to a contract spelling out his obligations to bring in the encyclopedia on budget and on time, and offering a considerable financial bonus as an incentive. Moving to Edmonton in 1980, Marsh began to work closely with the managing director, Frank McGuire, "a tough, hard-working Scot," in Hurtig's words, who had been the Queen's Printer for Alberta and a provincial director of communications. McGuire would oversee the logistical, financial, and, to some extent, political aspects of the project. He and Marsh would clash frequently over spending, but Marsh later acknowledged that McGuire's management skills were invaluable in shepherding the project past numerous obstacles. Among those was the visceral dislike some people in the Alberta government felt for Mel Hurtig and his politics.

Marsh proved a tough character in his own right, even downright ornery when pushed. He visited the operations of the Encyclopaedia Britannica Company in Chicago and Columbia University Press, publishers of *The Columbia Encyclopedia*, in New York; he conferred with Francess Halpenny of the *DCB* and Helmut Kallmann at UTP's *Encyclopedia of Music in Canada*. From those discussions, Marsh learned much about the organizational complexities and structural pitfalls of major editorial projects. He concluded that relying on input from numerous academics invited chaos and required centralized command and control.

Hurtig had appointed a national advisory committee of prominent academics under Harry Gunning, president of the University of Alberta. Gunning was instrumental in providing the encyclopedia with office space, access to the university's excellent library, and use of its computer facilities, highly sophisticated for the time; but Marsh knew that, if the advisory board had too much sway, it would be impossible to meet Hurtig's goals. With the support of Davidson Dunton, president of Carleton University and an advisory board member, Marsh decided "to pull the teeth of that board. The first thing I had to do – and it was very hard and delicate – was to tell these people, 'I'm running this thing, not you.'" The process would be no more democratic than getting a movie made. Hurtig was the producer and McGuire the assistant producer, but Marsh was the director.

Marsh did draw on the advisory board's expertise in assembling some 300 specialized consultants who helped decide which topics should be covered and by whom; the consultants also evaluated articles as they came in. From 1980 to 1984, Marsh ended up assigning, in round numbers, 8,000 articles from 3,000 different contributors, totalling over 3 million words. Many articles had to be redrafted or reassigned. Contributors were late, sometimes by as much as a year; some submitted 5,000 words when 500 were needed. Other articles were drafted in-house by Marsh or his staff, then submitted to experts for revision. The aim was to generate, as Hurtig put it, a text that an intelligent high school student could use.

By 1983 more than two dozen editors and researchers were working under Marsh's direction in two old houses near the university. Six senior editors were responsible for major subject areas. Staff based in other cities included three former UTP editors, Mary McDougall Maude and Rosemary Shipton in Toronto and Dan Francis in Vancouver. The chief designer, David Shaw, worked out of Toronto. "I fought with my own

THE PERILOUS TRADE | 240

senior editors quite a bit," Marsh acknowledged many years later. "One of the senior editors objected to the way I controlled things. She mustered a rebellion among some of the other senior editors, contending that I was imposing my intellectual view on the encyclopedia, and it ought to be determined by the academic community. I put it to Mel that this was his choice, and he chose that I was in control of things. That editor was fired."

Like previous editors at Hurtig Publishers, Marsh had nothing but praise for the boss: "People have assumed that Mel interfered or somehow directed the editorial work of the encyclopedia. He did not. He had this amazing ability to trust people, to really put himself in their hands." Hurtig read the manuscript and made suggestions, which Marsh could take or leave. The only time Hurtig ever imposed a content decision was when he insisted that there be no entry on himself.

Hurtig recalled that, for a time, Marsh was working eighteen-hour days and looking "exhausted, haggard, and thin, with big black circles around his eyes." There were running disagreements between Marsh and Frank McGuire. Hurtig asked UTP's director, Harald Bohne, to assess the problem and make recommendations, and Bohne's report helped clarify the respective roles of the general editor and the general manager, allowing the project to go forward.

McGuire's domain, physical production, was also of paramount importance. Hurtig wanted high-end quality combined with user appeal. The original plan to produce a single volume was changed when a dummy book was manufactured and proved too cumbersome. Hurtig was also committed to manufacturing the encyclopedia entirely in Canada – not for him the usual resort to cheaper printers in Hong Kong or Singapore for illustrated books. But no Canadian bindery could handle such a thick spine. Hurtig resolved the dilemma by publishing the work as a three-volume set; it would be casebound in gold-stamped, midnight blue linen, and enclosed in a natural-linen-covered slipcase. After *The Random House Encyclopedia* appeared in the United States with colour illustrations, Hurtig scrapped his plan to run the illustrations in black and white and went ahead with full colour.

On Friday, May 13, 1983, all Hurtig's arduous preparations suddenly seemed for naught. Throughout his business career, he had banked at the

Canadian Imperial Bank of Commerce; now the bank informed him it was calling his entire loan, which at that point stood at $700,000, and giving him a mere two weeks to pay it off. "The blackest day of my life," Hurtig called it. "With no warning, the bank was quite prepared to wipe us out – not only Hurtig Publishers but *The Canadian Encyclopedia* with it . . . Everything I had been working for over the space of twenty-seven years would be lost."

Hurtig's response was to threaten that he'd embarrass the hell out of the CIBC by blaming it for the death of "the largest-ever project in the history of Canadian studies": an embarrassment that would be particularly acute since the bank's chairman was the lead fundraiser for the new John Robarts Chair in Canadian Studies at York University. The threat obtained immediate cancellation of the loan call, giving Hurtig enough time to make other arrangements. He moved to the new, Edmonton-based Canadian Commercial Bank; but that bank collapsed on Labour Day 1985, jeopardizing the encyclopedia's survival yet again, until the Bank of Montreal stepped in.

Even then Hurtig's perils weren't over. Having championed the project, the Alberta government panicked when the magazine *Alberta Report* alleged that the encyclopedia would reflect a left-wing interpretation of Canada. The provincial cabinet instructed the culture minister to review all the articles and report on their political bias. Jim Marsh was dead set against turning over the manuscript for official scrutiny, but Hurtig, facing the termination of his funding, had little choice. He struck a compromise, proposing that Peter Meekison, vice-president of the University of Alberta and a prominent Conservative sympathetic to the project, should examine the material. Meekison's report to the government was positive, and there were no more threats of political cleansing.

Before going to the printer, Marsh had to make a final round of cuts for reasons of length. The edited manuscript was well over the 3-million-word limit decreed by the production budget. Sitting with the proofs for two and a half months, trying to find 400,000 words to eliminate, was probably the hardest job Marsh had ever done. It was also physically demanding; the proofs were processed with ammonia, and the fumes made his nasal passages bleed as he worked.

When *The Canadian Encyclopedia* finally reached the manufacturing stage, twenty-seven different Canadian firms were involved. The paper was made in Quebec, the cover cloth in Ontario; the colour separations were done in Vancouver and the printing in Montreal, with work subcontracted to a plant in Edmonton. In all, printing, binding, and packaging the gigantic run of 150,000 sets of the encyclopedia (450,000 volumes, plus overruns) took nearly a year. The quantity was based on advance orders from booksellers (bought as 50 percent returnable, instead of the usual 100 percent), which reached 105,000 as early as May 1984. It was unquestionably the largest book printing contract ever undertaken in Canada. Tough penalty clauses encouraged suppliers to deliver finished copies well in advance of the September 1985 publication date.

Hurtig had made a judgment call to sell the encyclopedia through retail bookstores. Executives at Encyclopaedia Britannica in Chicago, who had offered to buy the whole project (Hurtig wasn't interested), had advised against it, warning about the danger of booksellers' price cutting. But as a former bookseller, Hurtig felt he could hardly leave the stores out of the action. He also wanted Canadians across the country to be able to visit their local bookstores and walk out with their national encyclopedia. It would cost them $175, or $125 if they placed an order in advance of publication. The prepublication savings, and Hurtig's insistence that there would be only one printing, created an incentive for customers to order right away; it was a stratagem that boosted advance sales, the size of the print run, and his profit margin.

The encyclopedia was a hit from the start. Sets flew out of the stores, many at the prepublication price, and four days after publication Hurtig had shipped every last set. Reviews praised the encyclopedia as an invaluable, authoritative reference and a handsome piece of book-making. The public demand continued unabated. By November orders had arrived for another 40,000 sets, but Hurtig stuck by his promise that there would be no additional printing: an astute marketing decision, since it stimulated demand for an updated second edition.

After total costs of $12 million, Hurtig reaped a profit of $2 million, which sat in the bank collecting interest. "For the first time since I opened my tiny bookstore twenty-nine years earlier," he exulted, "we were entirely debt free. Debt free!"

It was a moment to savour. *The Canadian Encyclopedia* was unquestionably a triumph, primarily because of Hurtig's dedication. No other publisher in the country possessed his combination of vision, guts, political savvy, publishing knowledge, marketing skills, financial smarts, and personal energy, all needed to implement such a project and surmount the obstacles. Not the least of those obstacles were certain aspects of the culture Hurtig sought to celebrate. It had been his own banker, after all, who had asked, "Why do we need a Canadian encyclopedia anyway, when there's already so many encyclopedias on the market?"

After his triumph, Hurtig took a pass on offers for his company that would have allowed him to retire in comfort. He elected instead to keep his proven team intact under Marsh and McGuire and to publish a revised version in 1988, the year of the election fought over free trade between Canada and the United States, which Hurtig and the Council of Canadians opposed fiercely. The second edition of *The Canadian Encyclopedia* would contain 1,800 new articles, three-quarters of a million new words, and hundreds of new illustrations and maps, and would run to four volumes. More than 60 percent of the articles from the previous edition would be expanded or updated. Errors and omissions would be corrected. All the profits from the first edition, calculated after substantial bonuses had been paid, would be invested in the new version, and Hurtig would go back to the bank for an additional $5 million in financing. He was riding the crest of a wave. He was obsessed.

The 1988 edition, bound this time in scarlet cloth with gold stamping, showed there was still prodigious demand. Consumers could again save $50 by ordering early. A new marketing wrinkle allowed purchasers of the first edition to trade it in for a $100 discount, resulting in a net cost of only $125: the same as the 1985 prepublication price. Hurtig would donate the used sets to underprivileged families. The scheme should have worked like a charm. It almost did.

Véhicule Press

NEW STAR BOOKS

TURNSTONE PRESS

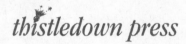

thistledown press

COTEAU BOOKS
WWW.COTEAUBOOKS.COM

VÉHICULE PRESS| NEWEST PRESS | GOOSE LANE EDITIONS | HARBOUR PUBLISHING

NEW STAR BOOKS | FIDDLEHEAD POETRY BOOKS | PORCUPINE'S QUILL

CORMORANT BOOKS | OOLICHAN BOOKS | TURNSTONE PRESS

ARSENAL PULP PRESS | TALON BOOKS | BREAKWATER BOOKS | PRESS PORCÉPIC | OBERON PRESS

THISTLEDOWN PRESS | COTEAU BOOKS

11

A CLUTCH OF DREAMERS

Guerrilla armies live amid the people who sustain them
and for whom they struggle. So do book publishers.

Jason Epstein, *Book Business* (2001)

From being a handful scattered across Canada in the 1960s, small presses became a concerted movement in the 1970s. Anansi and Coach House showed the way, but so did Gray Campbell, Jim Douglas, and Mel Hurtig. If it was possible to publish books from Sidney, Vancouver, or Edmonton, why not Saskatoon? St. John's? Madeira Park? That was the revolutionary message. Writers no longer waited to be recognized in Toronto, New York, or London; anyone could publish, right now, right here – *wherever* here was.

Some small presses are better described as microscopic, employing only one or two people including the proprietor, and releasing as few as four or five titles a year. But most of the country's literary authors and movements have emerged from small presses. They are the shock troops of Canadian literature. Without them and their work, the landscape would be unrecognizable.

Michael Ondaatje's route to McClelland & Stewart, the Booker Prize, and international acclaim started from Coach House Press and the House of Anansi. Before her Governor General's and National Book Critics Circle Awards, before her Pulitzer and Orange Prizes, Carol Shields published three titles with tiny Borealis Press of Ottawa. Jane Urquhart published her early poetry and short fiction at the Porcupine's Quill in Erin, Ontario. Sharon Butala and Bonnie Burnard brought out their first story collections with Coteau Books of Regina. Thomas Wharton launched his international career with NeWest Press in Edmonton.

It's a cliché to portray small presses as the farm teams of the industry. In reality, they represent the heartland of Canadian literature. They not only inhabit every region but live among the people in a manner not possible for a Toronto-based multinational like Random House of Canada or a large Canadian-owned company like M&S or Key Porter. Small presses occupy the front lines, spotting young talent before it surfaces elsewhere, egging on and launching new writers. Their ethos was captured by one of the founders of Turnstone Press in Winnipeg, the novelist Wayne Tefs, when reflecting on his origins as a publisher:

> It's twenty years ago, and you're sitting in a pub on Pembina Highway in Fort Garry and a clutch of dreamers is dreaming words, words in ink and cut pages and covers. You're dreaming the book, the tangible, tactile object. You haven't heard yet of perfect binding, of dingbats, of saddle stitching, Corel, Ventura, fulfillment, or financial statements. You have no notion that you're looking down the dangerous end of a telescope at more than two hundred published books, at Governor General's Awards, at GG nominations, First Novel Prize nominations . . . the delighted faces of dozens of first-time authors. You certainly are not contemplating twenty years of labour, of screening twenty thousand manuscripts, of Editorial Board meetings, conferences with writers, proofreading, copy-editing, launches, grant applications, Literary Press Group, the ACP, conference calls . . . No, you are in love with words, with story, with song, and you are doing nothing more than dreaming the book – a simple thing, a good thing, a thing that carries and sustains what you are and what the place you live in may become.

Tefs was introducing an anthology that exemplifies the small-press gift for cooperation. It was a co-publication by Turnstone, Coteau, and

NeWest, all marking, or about to mark, their twentieth anniversaries in 1996. To celebrate, they collaborated on *Due West: 30 Great Stories from Alberta, Saskatchewan and Manitoba*, each deputizing a writer-editor to select ten stories for the book. The project made explicit statements about pride in the excellence of Prairie writing, and implicit statements about sharing resources instead of competing: a value long held on the prairies, and typical of the small-press movement.

Once ignited, that movement spread like wildfire. In 1970 English-language firms with fifty or more Canadian-authored titles in print numbered just thirty-two; by 1980 they'd nearly tripled, to eighty-nine. Nearly all the newcomers were indigenous. In 1970 only fourteen of the companies – fewer than half – were Canadian-owned, but by 1980 their number had grown to sixty-eight, representing three-quarters of firms with enough staying power to build a substantial backlist. Twenty-two of them were based outside Ontario, compared with three in 1970. The impact of these developments, on not only the growth but the diversity of Canadian literature, was incalculable.

The Independent Publishers' Association and its successor, the Association of Canadian Publishers, would fall short of their objective of a federal publishing development corporation; and they would fail to achieve structural measures such as restricting provincial purchasing of educational materials to Canadian-owned firms. Yet their success in obtaining grant programs, beginning in 1972, transformed the publishing scene. Grants equipped small presses with working capital that they couldn't have obtained otherwise, except from an angel or a winning lottery ticket.

Paradoxically for people who've relied, in part, on public support, few business people are more independent of spirit or contrarian of mind than small-press publishers. As one veteran of the movement, Anne Hardy of Oberon Press in Ottawa, commented, "We don't make any money out of publishing, so we might as well do it our own way."

Small presses invent their own mandates, based on the passions and proclivities of their owners. Living on the margins, for the reward of publishing books that matter to them, they confound economists and con-sultants hired by government to advise on the industry. With the odd exception, small-press publishers have been immune to exhortations from well-meaning MBAs to change their business practices, to publish in more lucrative areas, to give the market what it wants. Such advice ignores the reasons why they play the game in the first place.

Once there was a time before grants, when dreaming the small-press dream was even more difficult. Three of Canada's oldest small presses have survived into the present with the tenacity of pine trees growing out of rock.

The earliest of the three, located in Fredericton, New Brunswick, began as the labour of one man. Back in 1954, while editing the University of New Brunswick quarterly *The Fiddlehead*, the indefatigable poet, critic, and translator Fred Cogswell persuaded the university to finance a book a year. The manuscripts were to be chosen by an editorial board, but after three years Cogswell broke with his board to publish, on a hunch, a collection of poems with the curious title *Emu, Remember*, by an unknown named Al Purdy. The next year, the university withdrew its support.

Cogswell funded Fiddlehead Poetry Books personally for the next twenty-four years on a professor's salary. From his cluttered office in the university's English department, assisted only by the occasional volunteer, he sent forth a constant stream of slim chapbooks, uneven in quality and often indifferently designed but providing a badly needed outlet for promising new poets. Those whose first books appeared from Fiddlehead include Alden Nowlan (1958), Joy Kogawa (1967), Don Gutteridge (1971), and Roo Borson (1977). The advent of Canada Council block grants simply increased Cogswell's prodigious capacity to publish; in 1973 he somehow found the time to issue an astonishing total of forty-four titles in twelve months.

On his retirement in 1981, Cogswell passed Fiddlehead Poetry Books to a fellow writer, Peter Thomas. Moving the press to a garden shed on Fredericton's Goose Lane, Thomas added fiction and non-fiction under the imprint Goose Lane Editions. Several years later, he hired a young intern named Susanne Alexander, who did everything from word processing to bill collecting in return for a third of the salary she'd been earning as a New Brunswick arts bureaucrat.

Although the press couldn't afford to pay Alexander until its Canada Council grant arrived, she loved the work so much that in 1989 she and her fellow employee Julie Scriver purchased the press from Thomas. They brought in Laurel Boone, a journalist and freelance editor, to take charge of the editorial side, and the three women built up the Goose Lane list in areas that excited them, principally fiction and art books. They discovered the Miramichi novelist Herb Curtis and published fiction by two authors serving as writers-in-residence at the University of New Brunswick, Helen Weinzweig and Douglas Glover. After the latter two were nominated for Governor General's Awards, Goose Lane began attracting manuscripts from outside the region and became an admired presence on the national scene.

At the other end of the country, Talon Books originated in Vancouver in equally modest circumstances, with a mimeographed magazine started by poetry-drunk students at Magee Secondary School. Moving with its founders to the University of British Columbia in 1964, *Talon* came to be edited principally by an intense, soft-spoken young man named David Robinson. The magazine intersected with two other embryonic ventures in the West Coast poetry scene, Very Stone House and blewointment press.

Very Stone House, the creation of the poets Patrick Lane, Seymour Mayne, bill bissett, and Jim Brown, a co-editor of *Talon*, published two memorable British Columbia poets who died tragically and young: Red Lane (Patrick's brother) and Pat Lowther. Bissett, an original in ways more far-reaching than his eccentric orthography, had been publishing his poetry magazine *blewointment* since 1963 – every copy was different, containing various strange items stapled inside – and he began producing books under the blewointment press imprint in 1967. That same year, Robinson and Brown decided to move in the same direction, and Talonbooks, as it was first styled, co-published three chapbooks with Very Stone House.

Talon remained a poetry press for a few years, publishing the editors of Vancouver's *Tish* magazine, George Bowering, Frank Davey, Jamie Reid, and Fred Wah, as well as Coach House authors such as bp Nichol and Victor Coleman. Talon's most ambitious early titles were the thick anthology *West Coast Seen* and Phyllis Webb's *Selected Poems, 1954–1965*.

As designer, Robinson gave the books' black and white covers a gritty, urban quality, reminiscent of New Directions Paperbooks; the press did its own printing, handled by Gordon Fidler.

Talon's editorial scope began to widen after Robinson met Peter Hay, a Hungarian Canadian who taught drama at the new Simon Fraser University in Burnaby. Contemporary theatre was beginning to blossom, and Hay had obtained publishing rights to several play scripts. Robinson seized the chance to enter a field where other publishers feared to tread, on the usually correct assumption that there was no money in it. In 1970 Talon issued George Ryga's *The Ecstasy of Rita Joe*, which would become Canada's best-selling play. The drama list eventually embraced playwrights from every part of the country, from Michael Cook, David French, David Fennario, and Wendy Lill to Linda Griffiths, Ken Mitchell, John Murrell, John Gray, and Sharon Pollock. By far the most substantial literary press west of Toronto, Talon also published Quebec authors in translation, led by the prolific Michel Tremblay, who would make it his English-language publisher for both drama and fiction.

Fiction writers west of the Rockies gravitated to the nervy little press, and Talon published its first novel, Audrey Thomas's *Songs My Mother Taught Me*, in 1973. Thomas would be joined by another American expatriate, Jane Rule, the septuagenarian novelist Howard O'Hagan, and a range of younger West Coast talents, among them Brian Fawcett. Thomas, who had already published three books in New York, produced four more titles with Talon before moving on to Penguin in Toronto. She fondly remembered the early years at the press for their "madhouse, Monty Python atmosphere" and Robinson's infectious enthusiasm.

In 1974 Robinson applied for a federal Local Initiatives Program grant to hire a business manager and a promotion person. The grant didn't come through, but the tall, leonine young man who'd served for four months as business manager without pay agreed to stay anyway. Then in his late twenties, Karl Siegler wasn't exactly a fount of business experience – he'd studied physics in Germany and literature at Simon Fraser and had planned an academic career – but publishing's addictive allure had entered his blood. By sheer force of personality, Siegler would become synonymous with Talon.

Finding the press virtually bankrupt, Siegler established a more rigorous bookkeeping system and pricing policy. "We were still doing our own printing then," he remembered, "and I developed a docket system that could follow jobs around, so we could do real costing. I repriced every-thing. I did all those classic things you do when you're trying to reorganize a company. But at the same time, I went after grant money."

Remarkably, Siegler succeeded with British Columbia's right-wing Social Credit government, which awarded the press a special grant in 1975 to help it back on its feet. This was all the more surprising since the province would have no grant program for publishing until fifteen years later. Talon rented the cheapest office it could find, a walk-up in an indus-trial slum overlooking the prostitutes on East Cordova. The partners posed for photographs peering existentially out of derelict cars in the auto dump across the street. Publishing fifteen to eighteen titles a year, they increased their sales to $100,000, but another economic crunch hit in 1979, as it did for much of the industry, and the next year Siegler announced darkly that Talon would have to close unless it received immediate financial assistance. He drew up an elaborate brief, single-spaced without margins, and fired it off to governments in Ottawa and Victoria.

Siegler's plea worked. The Canada Council went against procedure and approved a one-time emergency grant of $20,000, in addition to the press's block grant. Shrewdly, the council made its help conditional on the province's matching that amount. Backed against the wall, British Columbia reluctantly agreed.

Siegler had resorted to dramatic measures to ensure Talon's survival; but Robinson, weary of the financial strain, took a different tack. He pro-duced *Mama Never Cooked Like This*, by Susan Mendelson, a well-known local caterer and CBC Radio personality, then *The Umberto Menghi Cookbook*, by the celebrated Vancouver restaurateur. In 1984 Robinson told Siegler he'd reached the end of his tether with literary publishing and wanted to publish books with some promise of financial return. It was Siegler, ironically, who insisted that Talon must remain true to its founding principles. Seventeen years after starting the firm, six years after *Quill & Quire* had described the pair as "a marriage of true minds," Robinson walked away, never to return.

Although he wouldn't buy out his partner for another eight years, Siegler took sole control. He continued building the list in the established genres, adding non-fiction on subjects that reflected his political commitments: the Japanese-Canadian internment, the environment, Aboriginal issues, British Columbia history. At times it could be difficult to separate Talon's program from its publisher, especially when Siegler issued dire pronouncements about the imminent end of Canadian publishing or denounced the treasons of politicians and bureaucrats in Ottawa. But he considered his involvement in industry politics a stark economic necessity.

"I always knew the job of building a literary culture in this country was not just finding the authors, editing them, then marketing them in Canada and abroad," Siegler recounted. "No matter how well we did that, it would never be enough, not as long as we were selling our books at [unrealistically low] American prices. A lot of people ask me, 'Why did you spend that much time on the publishing associations?' I sat on every committee the ACP has ever had. I was president a couple of times. But the reason was not because I wanted to play government, or because I thought my colleagues were particularly interesting or exciting. I never wanted to be a social butterfly. I just knew that no matter how efficient you were, part of your job was working on public policy in an ongoing way."

Events proved Siegler right. Funding measures were instrumental to his ability to continue, with his wife and business partner, Christy Siegler, pulling Talon through a succession of financial scrapes. Finally, in 2000, the Sieglers moved the press's editorial office from east-side Vancouver and achieved a measure of tranquillity in the pulp and paper community of Powell River.

A very different house from the early small-press era has had an equally strong influence on the country's literature. Oberon Press has been based in Ottawa since its founding in 1966; the nation's capital just happened to be where Michael Macklem, an Upper Canada College alumnus and former Yale English teacher, and his wife, Anne Hardy, lived. Macklem wrote Oberon's first title, a scholarly life of John Fisher, Bishop of Rochester, and the text for some attractive children's picture books, but they were atypical of the press's output. Oberon distinguished itself by launching the careers of a brilliant array of new fiction writers.

Oberon's discoveries came from throughout the country. They included, from the Atlantic region, David Adams Richards (who remained with the press for his first five books) and Wayne Johnston (two books); from the west, W.P. Kinsella, W.D. Valgardson (three books apiece), and Keath Fraser; and from Ontario, Margaret Gibson, Bronwen Wallace, and Isabel Huggan. Among the writers introduced in Oberon's annual story anthologies, *Coming Attractions* and *Best Canadian Stories*, were the future Booker nominee Rohinton Mistry and the future Giller winner Bonnie Burnard. On the press's backlist of nearly 600 titles, writers of the calibre of Hugh Hood, Gwendolyn MacEwen, Tom Marshall, David Helwig, Norman Levine, John Metcalf, Leon Rooke, and Diane Schoemperlen appear with striking frequency.

Macklem and Hardy couldn't have done it all alone. Their editorial vision was greatly magnified by writers who assisted them as anthologizers and, occasionally, acquiring editors: principally Helwig and Metcalf. Metcalf's friends Rooke and Clark Blaise, as well as Sandra Martin, Maggie Helwig, Douglas Glover, and others also pitched in. For the rest, the press has stayed very much within the family.

Macklem and Hardy ran Oberon quietly for eleven years out of the family home on a maple-lined street in affluent Rockcliffe Park – Linotype machine, shipping room, and all. When an *Ottawa Citizen* article inadvertently revealed their location, the municipality forced them to move to more expensive offices with commercial zoning. Even so, Oberon remained almost reclusive at times, as if operating inside a bubble. Macklem, who designs the books, has continued to set poetry in hot-metal type; and although Oberon's prose titles are being set from computer files, he still prepares all the display type for covers, title pages, and headings from his collection of hand-set fonts. A passion for typography gives Macklem a strong affinity with other craftsmen-publishers such as Coach House's Stan Bevington, who has been Oberon's printer since the 1983 demise of Hunter-Rose.

In addition to handsome book-making, Oberon has long been known for idiosyncratic trade practices, particularly a refusal to accept returns. The founders dropped out of the ACP early on, fed up with what they considered its internecine politics. Rather than use commissioned sales reps, they criss-cross the country every fall to sell their list personally; the trips not only furnish restaurant reviews for Hardy's annual *Where to Eat in Canada* but propel them into needed contact with booksellers and librarians. To work with them, the couple brought their son Nicholas Macklem into the firm as general manager, and their daughter-in-law Dilshad Engineer as editor-in-chief. The Macklem clan probably wouldn't know, much less care, which Toronto literary schmoozefests to attend.

There are as many ways to start a small press as there are presses themselves. New Star Books and Arsenal Pulp Press evolved in different ways out of Vancouver's hippie culture, mutating into more structured operations to become veterans of the dynamic British Columbia publishing industry.

New Star originated in *The Georgia Straight* when it was still a communal underground newspaper at the end of the 1960s. After the paper went private, several of its writers reconstituted themselves as Vancouver Community Press. Maoist and Trotskyist influences competed for control, and in 1973 the press's name was changed to New Star Books, reflecting the ascendancy of the Maoists. Further schisms led to the conclusion that publishing itself was a bourgeois affectation and the press should be liquidated.

Two members of the collective disagreed. The political activist Lanny Beckman and Stan Persky, a poet and teacher who'd arrived from San Francisco, incorporated New Star in 1978 and ran it from their Kitsilano home with a mission to influence the province's political debate. New Star published a succession of hard-hitting books on poverty, labour history, Aboriginal issues, and regional culture. It hired young Rolf Maurer from the British Columbia Teachers' Federation in 1981 and pursued North American publicity and sales. But New Star made its biggest impact by hitting local targets. Persky's instant book, *Son of Socred*, a mass-market paperback exposé of the provincial Social Credit premier, Bill Bennett, and Russell Kelly's *Pattison: Portrait of a Capitalist Superstar*, an unflattering biography of the powerful British Columbia businessman Jimmy Pattison, sold "ridiculously well," as Maurer put it, in that polarized political climate.

Eventually Maurer assumed management of New Star and moved it to Vancouver's east side, bringing fiction and poetry back to the list while retaining the core commitments to social justice, British Columbia culture, and the environment – notably in the widely admired writings of Terry Glavin, editor of the press's Transmontanus imprint. Under Maurer, New Star has stayed small but principled.

Pulp Press always took a more anarchic, high-spirited view of the world. Founded in 1971 by Stephen Osborne and several of his fellow students at the University of British Columbia, including the fiction writer D.M. Fraser, the Pulp collective issued pamphlets and broadside poems, which it posted free around the city, in addition to books. It produced a semi-monthly magazine, *3¢ Pulp*, consisting of "poems, stories, spoofs and provocations." Pulp was renowned for its Three-Day Novel Contest, a writing marathon held every Labour Day weekend (once won by bp Nichol), and kept itself alive with job typesetting and printing.

By 1978 Pulp was receiving a small Canada Council block grant. A ruckus had erupted in Parliament over council funding for blewointment press, particularly its collection containing bill bissett's poem "A Warm Place to Shit." A Vancouver Conservative MP considered Pulp's grant equally appalling, since the press was distributing a Brazilian title in translation, *Manual of the Urban Guerrilla*, published by a radical press in San Francisco. Council officials had an interesting time explaining to Parliament and the media that they funded only Pulp's Canadian publishing, not its imports; it was too fine a distinction for some. The furor resulted in the collective's telephone being tapped by the RCMP but also helped Pulp land a national distributor. The latter went bankrupt in 1982, however, with the result that Pulp lost its receivables and had to sell off its printing operation to cover its debts.

Reincorporating as Arsenal Pulp Press, the house engaged an industrious young intern from the University of Victoria named Brian Lam. But publishing fatigue had set in, and by 1985 long-term members of the collective were saying it was time to find real jobs. Only Stephen Osborne and Lam wanted to keep the press going. The pair took responsibility for Arsenal Pulp with a shared determination, as Lam phrased it, "to stay subversive, but in a way that we could make a living."

Osborne and Lam put more effort into marketing and eventually ceded the Three-Day Novel Contest to up-and-coming Anvil Press of Vancouver. Still, they didn't expunge all the old wackiness. During Social Credit premier Bill Vander Zalm's time in power, Arsenal Pulp collected the funniest of the premier's malapropisms and in 1988 published *Quotations from Chairman Zalm* as a three-by-four-inch mini-paperback. The satire-vérité caught the public fancy and sold 30,000 copies in three months, spawning a long-running series of Little Red Books covering subjects as various as garden slugs, UFOs, and Don Cherry. Although not all the press's titles have been so lighthearted – *Stoney Creek Woman*, a biography of a Carrier elder, was acclaimed as a work of Native history from the female perspective – Arsenal Pulp has helped CanLit to take itself a little less seriously.

Like the founders of New Star and Arsenal Pulp, the "clutch of dreamers" who started Turnstone Press in 1976 were writers. They and their counterparts at Coteau Books in Regina, Thistledown Press in Saskatoon, and NeWest Press in Edmonton have all run variations on the editorial collective. David Arnason, a fiction writer, poet, and teacher at the University of Manitoba, recalled that when Turnstone started up, publishing was much in the air in Winnipeg: "Joan Parr was publishing fiction at Queenston House, Dorothy Livesay was at the university starting her magazine *CV/II*, I was editing *The Journal of Canadian Fiction* with John Moss. We got talking about the need for chapbooks. There were a lot of good poets around who were having trouble getting published."

Arnason and the press's other founders, Dennis Cooley, Wayne Tefs, and Robert Enright, published poetry by many hands, including collections by the novelists Robert Kroetsch and W.D. Valgardson, before moving into literary criticism, fiction, and non-fiction. Turnstone would eventually hit its stride at ten to twelve titles a year, and some Turnstone authors would burst into national, even international prominence: among them Sandra Birdsell, David Bergen, Margaret Sweatman, Lawrence Hill, and Michelle Berry. The press published *Touch the Dragon*, twenty-four-year-old Karen Connelly's memorable account of her year as an exchange student in Thailand, after the manuscript had been turned down by a dozen publishers; it received a Governor General's Award in 1993, making Connelly the youngest writer ever to win the prize.

Turnstone has seldom been able to afford more than two or three low-paid staff, working under a volunteer editorial board. Similar arrangements have obtained at Coteau Books and Thistledown Press, both of which also specialized in poetry before trying other genres. Founded in 1975, Coteau published the award-winning poet Anne Szumigalski, eventually branching into fiction and children's books. In 1988 it released Bonnie Burnard's story collection *Women of Influence*, which won a Commonwealth Writers' Prize for best first book, the first time a Canadian had taken the honour. Six years later, Burnard was nominated for the Giller Prize, and five years later she won it for *The Good House* from HarperCollins.

Meanwhile Glen Sorestad, later to become Saskatchewan's first poet laureate, and three colleagues started Thistledown as a Prairie poetry press. It too expanded its list, originating fiction for adults and young adults, then non-fiction on nature and spirituality. Thistledown's best-known book has been Jeffrey Moore's unusual novel, *Prisoner in a Red-Rose Chain*, with foreign rights sold in many countries.

Edmonton's NeWest Press has roots in the influential cultural periodical *NeWest Review*, started by George Melnyk. The press's large volunteer board, which reads the manuscripts and selects the list jointly, has included many of Alberta's most eminent writers: the novelists Rudy Wiebe, Aritha van Herk, and Robert Kroetsch, the critic Diane Bessai, the poet Douglas Barbour. (With Stephen Scobie and Shirley Neuman, Barbour also operated the adventurous Edmonton literary imprint Longspoon Press from 1980 to 1986.) NeWest has published in several genres, from western history and social issues to poetry and drama, including plays by the celebrated Alberta playwrights Sharon Pollock and Brad Fraser. Its novels *A Chorus of Mushrooms*, by Hiromi Goto, and *Icefields*, by Thomas Wharton, have both won Commonwealth Writers' Prizes.

By having different writers on their boards and a revolving professional staff, some presses broadened their editorial range while deepening their regional impulses. Diverse management also helped them avoid burnout, a problem more acute for single-owner houses.

On the other hand, sole proprietors are freer to develop a personal publishing signature. While sharing ownership of Press Porcépic with Ellen Godfrey, Dave Godfrey was less encumbered by business partners on his third time around – able, for instance, to indulge a taste for the exotic poetry of Joe Rosenblatt, and to move the press from Erin, Ontario, to British Columbia when personal circumstances dictated. The writer and publisher Barry Callaghan of Exile Editions could finance translations of obscure (in English Canada) Québécois or Israeli or Serbian poets from his winnings at Toronto racetracks. Ron Smith, a writer operating Oolichan Books out of little Lantzville, Vancouver Island, and Beverly and Don Daurio, running Mercury Press from Stratford, Ontario, and later Toronto, have fashioned literary presses offering their own unexpected pleasures.

It takes courage, if not outright heroism, to tackle the aggregate demands of even the smallest small press: plowing through the avalanche of manuscripts, dealing with disgruntled and demanding authors, selecting and editing the fortunate few, arranging for the books' design and pro-duction, overseeing their sales and marketing and distribution, and trying to reconcile those very disparate activities with an ability, at the end of the day, to make the other kind of books balance. Small-press publishers must assume each of the tasks accomplished by separate departments in a large publishing company, and all for little or no financial return.

To reduce overheads enough to make a small press viable, even with grants, a publisher may find it necessary to bring the house into the home. Simon Dardick and Nancy Marrelli, a Concordia University archivist, moved Véhicule Press into their narrow row house in Montreal's bustling Plateau quarter, after a co-op running the press fell apart in 1973. Dardick, a painter, had been part of the group of visual artists, printers and poets working out of an artist-run space called Véhicule Art on St. Catherine Street. He and Marrelli continued Véhicule's main thrust of publishing poetry and created a sub-imprint, Signal Editions, under the editorship of Michael Harris, which has issued more than fifty titles over the years:

translations of Marie-Claire Blais and Gérald Godin, work by Don Coles, Gary Geddes, David Solway, and Stephanie Bolster. But the new owners also endowed the press with a broader vision, coloured by personal enthusiasms for Montreal's cosmopolitan social and cultural history.

Véhicule has originated fiction by writers such as Kenneth Radu and David Manicom and urbane, visually attractive non-fiction on art, jazz, literature, the Jewish community, sports, sex, and eating out – even a valuable brief history of publishing in Anglo Quebec. But it has largely avoided the great subject that divides Montrealers, politics. Instead Dardick and Marrelli have preferred to publish in a nostalgic and celebratory mode, as reflected by Véhicule's exuberantly sophisticated Web site featuring its own titles and Montreal's literary landmarks. When the press celebrated its twenty-fifth anniversary in 1998, some 500 guests descended on the Atwater Library to toast Véhicule's importance to the city's literary life.

Jan Geddes operated Cormorant Books from a far more secluded location: her 1830s farmhouse on a lonely stretch of highway near Dunvegan, Ontario, halfway between Montreal and Ottawa. Her husband, Gary Geddes, the poet, critic, and Concordia English professor, had attempted a short-lived press named Quadrant Editions, which had tried to solve the problems of sales and distribution by offering titles on subscription, like a magazine or book club. When that experiment didn't pan out, the couple began Cormorant in 1986 to publish books the conventional way. Jan Geddes, who had previously done editing and promotion for the erstwhile Ottawa trade publisher Deneau & Greenberg, assumed sole direction of Cormorant after three years, phasing out poetry to concentrate on her first love, fiction.

The book that made Cormorant's national reputation is a moving, gemlike story of a little boy and his pregnant mother who set out on a hazardous journey to Canada from the mountains of Italy. After several Toronto publishers turned down Nino Ricci's *Lives of the Saints*, Cormorant released the novel in 1990; it was greeted with the combination of ecstatic critical praise and commercial success that writers and publishers dream of, winning a Governor General's Award and remaining on bestseller lists for over a year. Ricci would move on to McClelland &

Stewart and Doubleday Canada for his later novels. But Jan Geddes, rather than acceding to offers from richer publishers, tenaciously held on to rights to *Lives of the Saints*, since the ongoing revenue was vital to her ability to publish other new talents.

Among these were Elizabeth Hay, Carol Bruneau, and two highly praised first novelists, Patrick Kavanagh (*Gaff Topsails*, with rights sold to leading American and British publishers) and Peter Oliva (*Drowning in Darkness*). *The Oxford Companion to Canadian Literature* identified the Kavanagh and Oliva titles as two of the most technically and imaginatively accomplished novels released in the period 1983–1996. In the latter year, Stoddart Publishing bought a 40 percent interest in Cormorant, and Geddes was able to continue her work with greater financial security. Although she found a rare freedom to publish books she believed in, the downside was "the ongoing process of disillusionment" whenever publishing reality failed to meet expectations, and when encouraging reviews or decent sales eluded deserving books. At such times, she said evenly, "your focus just had to be getting the books out – and remembering how damned important it is."

Another press with sensibility and nerve similarly originated outstanding fiction far from the pressures of the city. Initially adopting the Coach House Press model of original publishing combined with job printing, the Porcupine's Quill would ultimately emerge as Canada's pre-eminent literary press.

Tim and Elke Inkster founded the Porcupine's Quill in 1974 in the sleepy southern Ontario town of Erin. With no formal training apart from a two-hour workshop at Coach House, Tim Inkster had taught himself design, typesetting, and printing while working as a pressman at Press Porcépic, and Elke Inkster had become an accomplished bookbinder. The couple bought the storefront building across the street from Porcépic, started a printing and publishing business downstairs, and moved in above it. By providing design and printing to more than a dozen small presses, the Inksters supported themselves and raised the production standards of other publishers' books.

Tim Inkster, a poet himself, edited the small but eclectic Porcupine's Quill list, including poetry by several authors who later became known for other things – the *Maclean's* film critic Brian D. Johnson, the publishing executive Ed Carson, the novelist Jane Urquhart – as well as Urquhart's early story collection *Storm Glass*. Inkster gave his books a well-made, elegant look: printed on antique laid paper, with pages sewn into signatures in the traditional manner. Porcupine's Quill books have received some of the book world's most prestigious design awards in competitions at the Leipzig International Book Fair, the Art Directors Club of New York, the American Institute of Graphic Arts, and the Vancouver-based Alcuin Society.

After fifteen years, Inkster surrendered editorial direction to the writer John Metcalf, by then based in Ottawa after teaching English in Montreal and living in rural Ontario. As Metcalf's demanding personal aesthetic took hold, the press grew, and Inkster was able to drop much of the job printing and focus on design, production, and management. Metcalf's own aspirations for the Porcupine's Quill came out of his long experience as an author, critic, and freelance editor. Along the way, he'd absorbed lessons in how *not* to get published.

Stan Bevington had once agreed to publish Metcalf's stories as an early Coach House title. "I got very excited about it," Metcalf recalled, "then I didn't hear anything for about three months. I phoned Stan and said, 'So, what's happening? What's happening with my book?' And Stan said, 'Don't worry. We're working on it.' And then I didn't hear anything for about six months, so I phoned him again and said, 'What's happening with my book, Stan?' And he said, 'Look, man, if you're going to harass me, I'm not going to do it.'"

The stories ended up at Clarke, Irwin, appearing in *New Canadian Writing 1969* and as part of a full-length collection, *The Lady Who Sold Furniture*. Metcalf moved to M&S for his first novel, *Going Down Slow*, but found it "the worst company I published with in terms of promotion, contact between editor and author, and general civility." The neglect suggested to him that the M&S dictum about publishing authors, not books, extended mainly to Jack McClelland's inner circle. Metcalf found a more welcoming environment at Oberon Press, where he published two collections of his own short fiction while editing *Best Canadian Stories* from 1976 to 1982 and launching the *Coming Attractions* anthologies, initially titled *First Impressions*.

After operating as a one-man anthology factory for publishers as various as Macmillan and ECW Press, proselytizing on behalf of his literary vision, Metcalf settled at the Porcupine's Quill in 1989. He seized the opportunity to turn it into primarily a fiction house with a sizable ambition: to pursue "the conscious intention of changing the nature and shape of short fiction in Canada." In addition to authors he's been championing indefatigably over the years – Hugh Hood, Norman Levine, Clark Blaise, Leon Rooke, Ray Smith, John Mills – Metcalf has published story collections by his latest discoveries: Andrew Pyper, Caroline Adderson, Terry Griggs, Steven Heighton, Elise Levine, Michael Winter, and others. In the novel, Metcalf's taste has ranged from the complex (Keath Fraser's *Popular Anatomy*) to the intelligently mainstream (Cynthia Holz's *Onlyville*) and the commercially hip (Russell Smith's *How Insensitive*, which has sold over 7,000 copies). Metcalf has had no hesitation in declaring his writers the most accomplished of their generation, and the Porcupine's Quill "the best literary press in Canada." The only problem with the boast is that it is largely true.

In the process, Metcalf has assembled a national network of writers and teachers who act as his critical eyes and ears. He heard about one of his finds, Annabel Lyon, from the writer and teacher Linda Svendsen, in the University of British Columbia creative writing department: "Linda said, 'You should look at this girl. She's fabulous.' From all over the country I'm getting suggestions." Young writers who have published with him have undergone an apprenticeship with an insightful but exacting mentor willing to take infinite pains with their work, provided they were too. Sometimes Metcalf would suggest that an author rewrite a story, and if that didn't correct the problem, "I'll write the scene myself and say, 'This is what I mean. Now I want you to throw away what I've done and take from it the idea I'm getting at and do it yourself.' If I were not a writer myself, I couldn't do that. And then there are writers I don't touch at all, because they don't need it."

A writer's signature energy and use of language are what arouse him: "I can still remember the excitement of first reading Keath Fraser or Terry Griggs. When you read the opening paragraph, I mean, it's like being punched between the eyes. You're just clouted with the full power of a new writer, and you say, 'Yes, this is it. This is what we want.'"

Because writing is conducted in isolation, Metcalf has tried to foster a sense of community among Porcupine's Quill authors. Writers need one another, he explained: "I think they desperately need to feel they are part of something larger than themselves. This gives them a certain kind of strength to go on, to work harder." In critical broadsides such as *Kicking Against the Pricks* and *Freedom from Culture*, he's been notoriously dyspeptic in decrying writing grants as a stimulus to mediocrity in Canadian literature; yet Metcalf has more recently acknowledged that the Porcupine's Quill couldn't function without federal and provincial funding. For most titles, there simply isn't a big enough domestic readership to support the costs of literary publishing.

Like many another small press in recent years, the Porcupine's Quill has seen its authors get reviewed glowingly, then gobbled up by large publishers for big advances. In the most extreme example, an agent obtained half a million dollars for international rights to Andrew Pyper's first novel, *Lost Girls*, after Porcupine's Quill had published Pyper's accomplished but far less commercial short stories. Metcalf acknowledged frankly, "I have to be honest: I sometimes feel a twinge of resentment when that happens. On the other hand, I realize they have to live. We can give them reputation and in some cases even fame, but we can't give them money, because we haven't got any." And he too, while working gratis for the press, benefits from the exchange: "I get paid as an editor in that a succession of extraordinary young people allow me to share in the passion of their lives."

Such are the accommodations that small presses must make. Simon Dardick has preferred to see the loss of Véhicule authors as tributes to his press's perspicacity. Manuela Dias of Turnstone Press observed, shortly before her untimely death in 2001, that she was happy for authors lured away by bigger publishers, "because it's really difficult to be a writer."

At the same time, literary presses need to find more reliable revenue sources than poetry or a succession of first books. Hence Turnstone's Ravenstone imprint, specializing in mystery and Gothic novels. And hence

Goose Lane's strategy of diversifying into other genres. Susanne Alexander and her partners introduced some impressive literary authors – Alan Cumyn, Shauna Singh Baldwin, Rabindranath Maharaj, Lynn Coady – only to see them wooed away by competitors with fatter chequebooks. Although its editing is professional, its design stylish, and its marketing well conceived, Goose Lane lacks the cash up front for either swell royalty advances or splashy advertising. And so the press has resorted to creative alliances with institutions: collaborating with the Beaverbrook Art Gallery in Fredericton to publish a full-colour book on the painter Mary Pratt, and co-publishing with the Art Gallery of Nova Scotia and the Canadian Museum of Civilization. It has also partnered with the CBC to launch the audio book series Between the Covers, drawn from the radio program of the same name and marketed in the States as well as Canada.

Goose Lane's alliances illustrate the strategic moves a regional press can make to operate on a national, or even international, level. Trying to achieve something similar from tiny Prince Edward Island proved a long struggle for Ragweed Press.

The fact that the province boasted a publishing house at all was something of a miracle. It started with a writer of Indian, Malay, Scots, French, and Persian descent named Réshard Gool, who arrived to teach at the University of Prince Edward Island, became a dedicated Islander, and stayed on to found Square Deal Press. With sheer sweat equity, supplemented by the occasional grant, the charming and voluble Gool produced a lively mixture of literary and regional books during the 1970s. By the time he wound up operations in 1980, Square Deal had produced thirty-three titles, including Gool's own novel, *The Nemesis Casket*.

Square Deal's niche was assumed almost immediately by Ragweed Press, whose publisher, Libby Oughton, was also an émigré – in her case, from Toronto, where she'd worked at the ACP. Oughton bought a house on the island, published Maritime poets, and made forays into local history, young adult fiction, and children's picture books. Eventually she established an imprint called gynergy to publish feminist literature. One title immediately put gynergy on the map: *Don't: A Woman's Word*, by Elly Danica, a memoir of childhood sexual abuse, made a powerful impact on publication in 1988.

By that time, Oughton felt she'd fought long enough to keep a marginal operation going; but Ragweed had seized the imagination of another newcomer, Louise Fleming, a federal civil servant transferred from Ottawa. With a master's in French-Canadian literature and a background in lesbian activism, Fleming acquired the publishing house in 1989. Her partner, Sibyl Frei, formerly manager of a regional economic development program in Yukon, joined her in the business, which grew until it occupied most of their house in Charlottetown.

Fleming and Frei built an ambitious and wide-ranging list that embraced but also transcended the region. Under the Ragweed imprint, they produced non-fiction about Island life, historical novels set in the Maritimes for both adults and younger readers, and picture books for ages five to eight with strong, active girl characters. Under gynergy, they published serious feminist and lesbian scholarship for an international audience. Pragmatically, they subsidized their list with guides to Island birds, wildflowers, and nature walks, and, of course, the settings of *Anne of Green Gables*, marketing the guides through gift shops serving the local tourist trade.

Fleming and Frei did many things right, particularly considering that neither had a background in publishing. But after a decade, gynergy was losing ground in the North American feminist market, the press's American distributor had gone out of business, and the challenges of running a multi-faceted publishing house from such an isolated location had become overwhelming. Ultimately the partners sold their company to Balmur Entertainment and Stoddart Publishing, which moved it to Toronto.

Another island with deeply rooted traditions, Newfoundland, was undergoing a cultural renaissance when Breakwater Books started up in 1973. At the time, only a little Newfoundland writing had appeared from Toronto publishers: Harold Horwood's fiction from Doubleday Canada, Percy Janes's from M&S. Clyde Rose and four partners invented

Breakwater over drinks at a St. John's pub, determined to combat what Rose termed "the total disregard for Newfoundland literature," not only in central Canada but within the province. The bearded Rose, with his grizzled sea dog's face and pirate's temper, soon became the driving force behind the press: a flamboyant, often embattled figure in the publishing industry and in Newfoundland itself.

One of Rose's marketing trademarks was promoting his authors by breaking out the screech and bringing in old-time fiddlers to make merry at conferences and book launches. But behind the blarney and ballyhoo, he and his partners had three serious, interconnected aims: to conserve Newfoundland history, tradition, and folklore; to publish contemporary Newfoundland writing; and to inject Newfoundland content into the provincial school curriculum. A former English teacher, Rose would publish the writing – the poetry of Al Pittman and Tom Dawe (both Breakwater partners), the novels of Helen Fogwill Porter and Bernice Morgan, the journalism of Ray Guy, a folklore series, a children's program that included Pittman's classic *Down by Jim Long's Stage* – then demand it receive its due in the educational system.

Rose anthologized the authors he'd published, and worked to blast the anthologies into the schools. Provincial ministers and education bureaucrats were not amused by his style or tactics, which ran to denunciations aired by the media. In the early going, he remembered, government officials were "unwilling partners" in his crusade: "It was open battle, you know. And basically, I fought the battle through the public press. I paid for it, mind you – I was not very popular. But I believed in what I was doing, and I had a lot of support behind me."

Breakwater moved on to develop books for environmental and social studies courses but lacked the capital necessary to compete with Toronto-based textbook publishers by developing major series. There were years when Breakwater's revenues surpassed $1 million, putting it well beyond the small-press level, with educational sales accounting for up to 70 percent of the total. But as in the cod fishery, bountiful times were followed by lean years. Other publishers emerged in St. John's to compete with Breakwater for trade authors, principally Creative Book Publishing, with its literary imprint Killick Press, and Harry Cuff Publications.

Although Breakwater enjoyed some successes off the Rock – the popularity of Ray Guy's humour, the international appeal of Bernice Morgan's historical novel *Random Passage*, made into a television mini-series – and exported some of its fiction as far away as Germany, Rose found it nearly impossible to make money on trade books. By the turn of the millennium, he was wondering whether a new generation would have the stomach to continue his struggle. But with his usual ebullience, he believed he had created something of enduring value to pass on. "What Breakwater has done," Rose asserted, "is to bring a generation of Newfoundlanders to a recognition that we have tremendous writing talent here in our own community. You can never turn back the clock on that now."

Presses specializing in regional non-fiction have a presumed advantage: the big Toronto companies don't usually go after their market or their authors. But if that market is scarcely over 500,000 people, like Newfoundland's, publishing for it is seldom profitable. British Columbia, on the other hand, with eight times that population, is large enough that one regional house has grown well beyond the small-press scale.

Before starting Harbour Publishing, Howard White was a poet and a journalist; and before that, he supported himself by operating bulldozers in his hometown of Pender Harbour, a logging and fishing community perched on a ledge of the Sunshine Coast. At the University of British Columbia, White came under the influence of Warren Tallman, the American literature professor who had organized the seminal 1963 poetry conference and was a mentor for the *Tish* poets and Karl Siegler. White absorbed Tallman's teachings about rooting literature in the vernacular and the local. As both poet and publisher, he would apply that principle to his own time and place: "It helped me come back to this coast and see the loggers and fishermen and pioneers as literary subjects. I took it as licence to start writing about those people in their own language."

White unsuspectingly launched a publishing career when, in Pender Harbour between earthmoving jobs, he became outraged by police intimidation of hippies and draft dodgers in the area during the Vietnam War. White and his wife, Mary, decided to rally public opinion by publishing a weekly paper, *The Peninsula Voice*; they bought an old offset press that had been used to print rock concert posters in Vancouver, and White taught himself how to operate it. In addition to news, the paper ran historical features about life in the rain-soaked inlets and misty mountains of the coast, old-timers' reminiscences in their own words. The material found a large popular readership: "People here have a sense of their uniqueness, a sense that their story has been left out of the official history of Canada, so they have to write it themselves."

Having created a genre of coastal literature, the Whites decided to devote a magazine to it. They were aided by a federal Local Initiatives Program grant and the serendipitous discovery that one long-haired newcomer, the future filmmaker Cal Bailey, had magazine experience in New York. Bailey masterminded the design, layout, and printing of the magazine, complete with comic strips and line drawings, and the first issue of *Raincoast Chronicles* appeared in 1972. Printed in sepia ink, with the homespun flavour beloved of the times, the issue quickly sold out 3,000 copies. A second issue sold 5,000, a third 10,000. Whenever the printing bills arrived, White took off in his bulldozer and cleared a few driveways or building lots to raise the money.

The success of *Raincoast Chronicles* propelled White into publishing books. One of the magazine's writers was the logger and poet Peter Trower, and in 1974 Trower's *Between Sky and Splinters* became Harbour Publishing's first title. Another contributor, a logger named Bus Griffiths, drew strange comic book panels portraying life in the forestry industry; Griffiths produced *Now You're Logging*, described by Alan Twigg, the founder of *B.C. Bookworld* magazine, as "a cartoon novel designed as a textbook on logging as well as a comic romance and adventure story."

Continuing demand for earlier issues of the magazine prompted the Whites to reprint issues one to five between hard covers. Before long, there were two *Raincoast Chronicles* collections (the first has sold over 70,000 copies), followed by books on the history of coastal settlement, lighthouses, and legendary heroes. There were also late works by the novelist and poet Hubert Evans, forgotten by most Canadians but not by White, who obtained rights to Evans's final writings when the author was eighty-seven. And there was poetry by Patrick Lane, Tom Wayman, David Zieroth, and others.

Over 80 percent of Harbour's market has always been in British Columbia and the American Pacific Northwest. "I get a lot of manuscripts from back east," White once said, "some of which are really good, but I send them all back." The exceptions are writers from elsewhere who have made the coast their home. A *New Yorker* writer, Edith Iglauer, published her celebrated memoir *Fishing with John* with Harbour. And in the 1990s, after Al Purdy moved to Vancouver Island, Harbour became his publisher of choice for new work as well as his autobiography, *Reaching for the Beaufort Sea*, and his collected poems, *Beyond Remembering*.

Undoubtedly the apogee of White's remarkable career was *The Encyclopedia of British Columbia*. It took him ten years to wrestle that single-volume, 824-page project into print, amid labours similar to Mel Hurtig's in birthing *The Canadian Encyclopedia*. White engaged the historian Dan Francis, a former senior editor on the Hurtig project, as the editor. Francis not only had the requisite experience but, White said, "might be the one person who wouldn't think I was crazy." The issue of sanity arose because of mammoth editorial and design problems resulting from commissioning 4,000 entries and obtaining 1,500 illustrations, and the matter of incurring a $500,000 printing bill.

Since White was financing the encyclopedia out of Harbour's cash flow, the project moved slowly at first. Corporate donations began arriving only after he heeded calls to make the encyclopedia more high-tech by including a CD-ROM with the print version. But when *The Encyclopedia of British Columbia* finally hit the stores in 2000, media coverage was ecstatic. The break-even first printing of 15,000 sold out within weeks, and a second printing soon started earning a profit. It was the achievement of a lifetime for a publisher who'd stumbled into the profession by accident. And it meant Harbour would never again be a small press, by any definition.

When Peter Martin first proposed in 1969 that small presses unite to sell their books, he was showing a pragmatism that would be intrinsic to the movement's success. Martin's approach was adapted by Belford Book Distributing and by various cooperative projects spun off by the ACP after the retirement of the book bus in 1974: the Canadian Book Information Centre, for one, which promoted publishers' titles collectively, and Canadabooks, which marketed books to educators. But it was the Literary Press Group, another offshoot of the ACP, that most closely embodied Martin's idea.

The LPG emerged in 1975 from the ACP's growing membership, which spanned increasingly broad variations in size, vocation, and market. Since small literary presses had needs different from those of large trade or scholarly publishers, creating their own organization made eminent sense. Regional publishers' associations were also forming at that time.

During the first dozen years of its existence, the LPG launched a series of joint marketing ventures. The first was known, with conscious self-satire, as Cloudland: a direct-mail project aimed at the individual book buyer. "Everyone loves Cloudland!" declared one LPG flyer, but sales were disappointingly low. Successive schemes became increasingly market-savvy, culminating in the creation of the LPG sales consortium, a network of part-time commissioned reps based in all regions. This would prove the most cost-effective method for establishing literary press titles in the national market. The LPG reps worked particularly well with independent bookstores committed to carrying small-press titles, and the efforts of both were reinforced by increasing interest by the mainstream media in Canadian books, coverage in national review periodicals such as *Books in Canada*, and the regional book tabloids. With the success of *B.C. Bookworld*, similar free tabloids appeared in the Atlantic region, the Prairies, and English-speaking Montreal.

In 1987 a breakthrough occurred when fifteen LPG presses collectively contracted with University of Toronto Press Distribution for order fulfillment and customer accounting. For UTP, then enlarging its warehouse, the additional volume of business was welcome. But it was also expensive business to service, since the presses' sales were low, their orders often for one or two copies at a time. The lack of economies of scale was offset, at first, by grants allowing the project to go forward.

Funding support also allowed the LPG to hire a part-time executive director and a full-time sales manager. In the first season of the new arrangements in 1988, group sales hit six figures, and the LPG began growing by leaps and bounds. Membership surpassed thirty presses, then forty. When the energetic and enterprising Marc Coté arrived as executive director, he proved adept at accelerating the organization's growth through imaginative promotion and grantsmanship. The increasingly autonomous LPG began to lobby politically for its members' interests outside the confines of the ACP. The dreamers of the small-press movement were coming of age, taking their place in the world. And by then another publishing movement, equally driven by passion and idealism, had launched its own revolution.

TUNDRA BOOKS | WOMEN'S PRESS

ANNICK PRESS

GROUNDWOOD BOOKS | OWL BOOKS

FIREFLY BOOKS

THEYTUS BOOKS | TREE FROG PRESS

KIDS CAN PRESS

12

THE MAVERICKS OF KIDLIT

I'd sooner publish Peter Rabbit *than* Das Kapital, *and I consider* Das Kapital *quite important.*

May Cutler of Tundra Books (*Quill & Quire*, April 1985)

"Where Are the Books for Canadian Children?"
That headline ran in the November 1971 *Quill & Quire*, introducing an eloquent brief submitted to the Ontario Royal Commission on Book Publishing. Written by Margaret Tyson, who described herself as a Peterborough, Ontario, housewife and mother of two young daughters, the brief was a *cri de coeur* from a parent who yearned for books to read to her kids about their own country.

Tyson knowledgeably outlined the kinds of books that Canadian children were not getting: picture books evoking the Canadian landscape ("I don't want my children to fall into the trap of expecting an English spring in their own backyard . . . [but] to be familiar enough with their land that they can appreciate her beauty"); ABC books ("you would be amazed at the amount of propaganda in foreign ABCs"); stories about Canadian children's everyday experiences; and stories set in Canada's cities.

When Tyson had been planning a holiday with her family in the west, she'd asked her librarian for storybooks set in Edmonton or Vancouver. There weren't any. What made her especially angry was that, even when good Canadian kids' books existed, information about them was hard to come by. She cited *Sally Go Round the Sun*, the folklorist Edith Fowke's collection of Canadian songs, games, and rhymes for children, colourfully illustrated by Carlos Marchiori and published by M&S. "No book has given my children and me more pleasure," she wrote, yet she'd never seen it advertised or discussed in the media, and had stumbled across it only accidentally. On the other hand, she knew all about Golden Books, Dr. Seuss, and hundreds of other American children's titles because, "good, bad or mediocre, they are so relentlessly promoted that to the average consumer there seems to be nothing else on the market . . . We have the ridiculous situation in which poor books sell because they are well known, and good ones are ignored."

Only a few Canadian titles were then regarded as children's classics: the works of Lucy Maud Montgomery, the wilderness epics of Farley Mowat, Roderick Haig-Brown, and James Houston, the picture books of Elizabeth Cleaver. Some librarians, the gatekeepers of children's literature, disdained the rest of Canadian children's publishing. Others urged action to remedy the lack of quality.

Sheila Egoff, a professor at the University of British Columbia School of Librarianship and author of *The Republic of Childhood*, wrote a trenchant paper for the Ontario royal commission pointing out the disparities between Canada and other English-speaking countries. In 1968, Egoff reported, American publishers had issued 3,874 children's titles and British publishers 2,075; Canadian publishers had produced 47. That figure was equal to only 1.2 percent of the American total, in contrast to the numbers for school textbooks, of which Canada had produced 207 compared with the Americans' 2,210, or nearly 10 percent, a closer reflection of the difference in population. In fact, Egoff pointed out, Canada was the only country of the three that published more textbooks than children's books.

Egoff was sympathetic to the practical problems underlying those statistics. She'd canvassed English-Canadian publishers and heard their "basic unhappiness" with the economics of the genre, even "notes of sadness, puzzlement, and frustration." Publishers had told her that they *wanted* to produce kids' books but had pointed to obstacles ranging from a lack of good manuscripts and the smallness of the domestic market to the tendency of librarians to bemoan the lack of Canadian materials while preferring imports.

Egoff's prognosis was gloomy. She didn't foresee that the domestic market would grow significantly; she predicted that publishers would continue having to subsidize their children's titles out of other revenues but suspected they'd eventually tire of losing money and give up. Reinforcing the gloom, the October 1972 *Quill & Quire* featured an article by Doug Gibson, then a young trade editor at Doubleday Canada, explaining why Canadian children's publishing was at best a marginal business: "If all publishers are born gamblers," Gibson wrote, "the men and women who publish children's books are the sort of people who jump out of tenth-story windows in the hope that an open truckload of mattresses will be going by." Children's publishing multiplied the difficulties that Canadian books normally faced. The high costs of illustration, colour printing, quality paper, and durable binding compounded the usual problem of pricing books low enough to meet foreign competition. Even then the Canadian product would generally be ignored by the media and ordered in tiny quantities by bookstores.

In the same *Q&Q*, Irma McDonough declared "a serious emergency" in children's publishing. McDonough, editor of *In Review*, an Ontario library quarterly that reviewed all Canadian children's titles, wrote, "We cannot allow Canadian children's literature to disappear by default." She proposed a countermeasure: establishment of a "dynamic Centre for Canadian Children's Books" to conduct promotional programs aimed at librarians, teachers, parents, and grandparents. Presciently, McDonough argued that a greater commitment to both producing and promoting children's books would lead to a higher-quality product: "Librarians find many Canadian books wanting. Of course not all imports are the best either, but volume in publishing discovers the best, and an author grows with every book he or she publishes."

Around that time, the first children's editor in Canadian publishing was appointed. Clarke, Irwin announced it was hiring Janet Lunn, herself a recognized author, to plan a dedicated program. Lunn's appointment signified a rare commitment and an understanding that publishing children's books wasn't a spare-time activity for editors with other priorities.

Taking that recognition to the next level would require publishers ready to devote their entire list to children's books. And it would require not the sweetness and light associated with Peter Cottontail but enough bloody-mindedness to confound the naysayers. Fortunately the godmother of all mavericks in the children's book industry had just materialized.

"If you can survive childhood, the rest is easy," May Cutler once told an audience. Seventy-five at the time, Cutler was delivering the annual Hugh MacLennan Lecture at McGill University, and her subject was "Fear of the Original: A Canadian Phobia."

Cutler alluded to her own troubled childhood: "Enormous creativity is required of the child trapped by obsessive, erratic and violent parents. He must use all the imagination he can summon to puzzle through confusing human behaviour . . . Originality starts with new ways of feeling, thinking and reacting to life itself and a passionate courage to put order into chaos. That order often takes the form of art, but it begins with living."

Cutler thus briefly cast a light on the origins of her groundbreaking career as founder of Tundra Books: a career distinguished by fierce dedication to children's publishing, empathy for the marginalized and persecuted, and a fighter's instinct. Cutler herself was an original, certainly, as anyone who came into contact with her soon discovered.

May Ebbitt Cutler first made an impact publicly in 1943–1944 when, as features editor for the *McGill Daily*, she fought against the imposition of quotas on Jewish and foreign students entering the university. She went on to study journalism at Columbia University and developed her taste in art by haunting the New York galleries. After a stint at the old *Montreal Herald*, where Mavis Gallant also worked, Cutler left the paper to start a family with her husband, Philip Cutler, a lawyer. By the time she began Tundra Books in 1967, renting a downtown Montreal office for $30 a month, her business experience had come from running a restaurant; it provided, she said, good training in deficit financing.

Tundra was a child of the Centennial. Its first titles were a series of paperback guides to Expo 67, retailing at a dollar apiece, and Cutler's own young adult novel, *I Once Knew an Indian Woman*, which won a Centennial book prize and was published in the United States by Houghton Mifflin as *The Last Noble Savage*. At first Tundra's list consisted

mainly of adult non-fiction. It was an interesting mix, leaning towards architecture (Moshe Safdie on his Habitat project in Montreal; an illustrated book
on Arthur Erickson), politics (an account of the riots-and-racism controversy at Sir George Williams University in Montreal in 1969), and Canadian
history (a Sir John A. Macdonald album).

But Cutler's publishing instincts quickened when she received the
manuscript of *Mary of Mile 18*, a picture-storybook set in northern British
Columbia. She responded with delight to nineteen-year-old Ann Blades's
direct, unaffected draftsmanship and fresh colour sense. "There was such
a lovely feeling about it," Cutler recalled. She couldn't afford full-colour
printing while still pricing the book at an acceptable level, so she applied
for a project grant from the Canada Council, which was then evaluating
books individually.

The council's rejection infuriated Cutler. Based on outside assessment
of the manuscript, the negative response triggered her long-running
"war with the Canada Council," as she called it. "They said, 'Isn't it a pity
that with so few Canadian children's books, we can't do any better than
this?' And I said, 'I'm not submitting another thing to you people!'"

When Cutler published *Mary of Mile 18* in colour without subsidy, it
won the Canadian Library Association medal as children's book of the year
for 1971. Her belief in the book pushed her to sell foreign editions, while
the domestic edition eventually surpassed 60,000 copies. *Mary of Mile 18*
became a landmark title and pointed Cutler even more clearly in the direction she wanted to go.

Later that year Tundra published its second picture-storybook,
Shizuye Takashima's *A Child in Prison Camp*, its poignant watercolours
documenting the wartime internment of Japanese Canadians through a
little girl's eyes. It was the only book Takashima ever produced, and it has
had a lasting influence as one of the earliest books dealing with that sor-
rowful episode. Tundra has kept it in print ever since.

Cutler's evolution into an all-children's book publisher took another
three years. In 1973 she published a second Ann Blades, *A Boy of Taché*, and
showcased the autobiographical art of William Kurelek in *A Prairie Boy's
Winter*. This much-honoured title, co-published in nine countries, was the
first of several books by the Ukrainian-Canadian painter, followed by

Lumberjack (1974), *A Prairie Boy's Summer* (1975), and *A Northern Nativity: Christmas Dreams of a Prairie Boy* (1976).

Cutler fashioned her own aesthetic of children's publishing: high-end production of full-colour picture books on multicultural themes. Using "primitive," naive, or magic realist art styles, Tundra's artist-authors captured the social and emotional struggles of children from ethnic minorities growing up in communities across Canada. During the decade 1976 to 1985, Tundra titles included John Lim's *At Grandmother's House* and *Merchants of the Mysterious East*, Sing Lim's *West Coast Chinese Boy*, and Ted Harrison's *Children of the Yukon* and *A Northern Alphabet*. Warabé Aska's *Who Goes to the Park* and Allan Moak's *A Big City ABC* were both set in Toronto, and Miyuki Tanobe's *Québec je t'aime/I Love You* and Stéphane Poulin's *Ah! Belle cité!/A Beautiful City ABC* were set in Quebec City and Montreal, respectively.

Although explicitly rooted in the Canadian experience, Tundra's books held a strong appeal for publishers abroad. Attending the Frankfurt International Book Fair and the Bologna Children's Book Fair, Cutler was able to sell rights to many of her titles and showed the way for younger colleagues who soon followed. Tundra titles also won international recognition for design, including citations by the American Library Association and the *New York Times*, and awards from the World's Most Beautiful Books competition in Leipzig. "I would have closed down Tundra and given up on several occasions," Cutler recalled, "if it were not that the foreign publishers whose illustrated books I most admired admired mine, and Tundra received international awards given for the first time to Canadian books."

Cutler began calling Tundra's program "Canadian Children's Books as Works of Art." In her study *Modern Canadian Children's Books*, Judith Saltman observed that Tundra's output was oriented as much towards the art market as towards children. "Many of the Tundra productions," Saltman wrote, "combine sophisticated, stunning art work with thin, weak, minimal, or adult-oriented texts. And, although the books are splendid works of art, they do not tell gripping stories." No doubt Cutler would take issue with such statements, arguing that Tundra authors such as Roch Carrier in *The Hockey Sweater* or Dayal Kaur Khalsa, Stéphane Poulin, or

Gilles Tibo speak directly to kids in vivid images and stories. Cutler was always taking issue with someone.

When the Canada Council introduced block grants in 1972, Tundra became a recipient of the annual formula-based funding, which dispensed with the subjective judging Cutler had found so objectionable. Nonetheless, she protested, her grants still failed to reflect the high costs of children's publishing. Denouncing what she considered the council's excessive power and "incestuous" dealings with the arts community, she blamed the organization's short-sightedness for her 1980 decision (later revoked) to get out of publishing children's books altogether.

Cutler had originally advocated creation of a group such as the Association of Canadian Publishers, and she was one of the association's sixteen charter members. But sitting with her colleagues in a collective body, painstakingly seeking consensus and negotiating compromise, was foreign to Cutler's temperament. She was quick to take umbrage at policies she disagreed with and resigned from the ACP twice, objecting to its strongly nationalistic positions. "The creative process is an individual one," she once declared, "and nationalism carried on too long – no matter how enlivening it may be initially – becomes self-defeating and self-destructive."

Wanting to belong to *some* publishers' group, Cutler joined the Association nationale des éditeurs du livre under her company's French name, Les Livres Toundra. (Some of her titles appeared in both official languages.) From a base in that hotbed of Quebec nationalism, ironically, she fought the Quebec government for not funding the province's English-language publishers. Eventually she'd pour her protean energies into politics as mayor of the anglophone city of Westmount, meanwhile continuing to publish as vigorously as ever. In 1995, after nearly three decades in the profession, Cutler sold Tundra Books to Avie Bennett of McClelland & Stewart. The imprint continued to bear the stamp of her creative vision.

May Cutler's every act as a publisher was driven by utter conviction, a quality that epitomizes the industry she pioneered. Perhaps the intended readership explains the zeal and idealism that drive children's publishers, their unshakeable belief in the importance of their work. Certainly idealism motivated Women's Press; early in the 1970s, it began publishing books that pushed Canadian children's literature in a radically new direction.

A feminist collective, the Canadian Women's Educational Press started in Toronto in 1971 on a grant from the Trudeau government's Opportunities for Youth program. The press's raison d'être was producing books that male-owned and -managed publishing houses (virtually all of them at the time, except for Tundra) weren't publishing: books on daycare, the politics of housework, sexual abuse, and women's social history. Women's Press was atypical in other ways. Its editorial policy required manuscript approval by all members of the collective. Embodying their opposition to hierarchy, members rotated jobs every few weeks and did their own typing. "We decided not to hire somebody to do our shitwork," one member explained at the time.

The press's top seller was *Everywoman's Almanac*, a datebook crammed with interviews and facts reflecting a feminist reading of Canadian life. Meanwhile the collective's two-colour books for children, basic in design and no-frills in production, radiated an unpretentious simplicity in developing what a former member, Margie Wolfe, called "a new kind of children's literature." The stories depicted life as many urban kids experienced it, featuring single-parent families, sibling rivalry, poverty, or racism, while presenting characters free of racial and gender stereotypes.

The press's kids' books had a frankly didactic purpose, but they were also innovative and offbeat. Titles such as *Fresh Fish and Chips*, by Jan Andrews, and the humorous Ms. Beaver series, by Rosemary Allison, featuring a feisty social activist heroine with a large tail, found their audience and sold strongly. Women's Press also encouraged kids to write for other kids, an approach that resulted in *Come with Us*, a book in which inner-city children spoke about their own lives.

By the end of the 1970s, other creative young publishers had come to the fore, and their vitality and dedication built a children's industry where none had existed. Some, such as Patsy Aldana of Groundwood Books, had passed through Women's Press. Kids Can Press was another collective, before becoming privately owned. The not-for-profit house Books by Kids evolved into Annick Press. Owl Books grew out of the children's magazine

(1) **Roy MacSkimming**, right, poses for *Maclean's* with his partners **Dave Godfrey**, left, and **James Bacque** during the start-up of New Press on Spadina Avenue in Toronto, 1969. (2) **James Lorimer**, shown in his customary garb as a nationalist advocate with the Independent Publishers' Association, drove industry politics during the 1970s.

(3) First as an Edmonton bookseller (standing, with the author **W.O. Mitchell**) and (4) later as publisher of *The Canadian Encyclopedia*, **Mel Hurtig** was a book trade pioneer. (5) The presidents of the largest publishing companies in British Columbia, **Allan MacDougall**, left, of Raincoast Books and **Scott McIntyre** of Douglas & McIntyre, have emerged as major players in the Canadian-owned industry.

Literary presses coast to coast:
(**6**) Principals of Talon Books flaunt their low overheads in east Vancouver during the late 1970s. (**7**) The poet, designer, printer, and publisher **Tim Inkster** runs the Porcupine's Quill in Erin, Ontario. (**8**) **Susanne Alexander** of Fredericton's Goose Lane Editions has added CBC audio books to her literary list. (**9**) **Clyde Rose** takes a stand outside Breakwater Books in St. John's.

Canadian children's publishers have achieved both cultural and business success, growing from tiny start-ups to substantial companies while reaping international recognition. (**10**) **Anne Millyard** and **Rick Wilks** co-founded Annick Press. (**11**) **Patsy Aldana**, seated (with her colleague **Kelly Mitchell**), created Groundwood Books. (**12**) The partners **Valerie Hussey**, right, and **Ricky Englander** built Kids Can Press into a profitable asset.

(13) **Bill Clarke** was the second-generation publisher at Clarke, Irwin, the firm co-founded by his parents in 1930. (14) **Malcolm Lester** and **Louise Dennys** are shown during happy times at Lester & Orpen Dennys. The demise of both firms was emblematic of what one observer termed "a very difficult business."

(15) Two generations of **Stoddarts**, **Jack Jr.** and **Jack Sr.**, turned General Publishing, later Stoddart Publishing, into the largest Canadian-owned general book company before it collapsed under massive returns and other stresses in 2002. (16) **Ron Besse**, owner of Gage and later Macmillan, steered clear of dangerous waters and made money.

The largest trade publishing companies in Canada all deploy outstanding editor/publishers: **(17) Phyllis Bruce** of HarperCollins Canada; **(18) Doug Gibson** of McClelland & Stewart; **(19) Cynthia Good**, formerly of Penguin Canada; **(20) Ellen Seligman**, M&S fiction publisher, with the author **Michael Ondaatje**; **(21) Diane Martin**, left, and **Louise Dennys** of Knopf Canada, with the literary agent **Bruce Westwood.**

Knowledgeable, community-based booksellers were critical to the rise of Canadian publishing. **(22) Bill Duthie**, shown in his Vancouver store during the 1960s, and **(23)** the **Britnell** family's store on Yonge Street in Toronto were mainstays of independent bookselling for decades. But Britnell's and nine out of ten Duthie Books outlets succumbed to the power of the Chapters superstore chain at the end of the 1990s.

Owl, published by the Young Naturalists Foundation. Together with Tundra and Women's Press, these imprints represented the first full generation of English-Canadian children's publishers.

Industry veterans saw the newcomers, who wanted to publish children's titles exclusively, as brave but foolhardy. How long could they possibly last? But the kids' presses were soon feeding a voracious demand as the baby boom generation discovered the joys of parenthood. During the high times of the 1980s, boomer parents equipped their children with every consumable advantage to succeed in a competitive world, including the best in books. Affluent adults flooded bookstores seeking quality; and for the first time in history, much of the best available quality was Canadian.

Simultaneously another new phenomenon emerged, in the form of bookstores dedicated to kidlit. They were led by the Children's Bookstore, opened in Toronto by Judy and Hy Sarick in 1974, and within a decade dozens of children's-only stores followed, from Woozles in Halifax to Vancouver Kidsbooks. The better independents, such as Duthie's, Britnell's, Audrey's, and Shirley Leishman's, also kept well-stocked children's sections. A healthy market boosted the annual output of Canadian titles to about 200 in the 1980s and nearly 400 in the '90s. As Sheila Egoff noted in an updated edition of her classic study, co-authored with Judith Saltman and issued in 1990 as *The New Republic of Childhood*, more children's books were published in Canada during the 1980s than in the previous 150 years combined.

Helping to promote those books was an organization of the kind earlier advocated by Irma McDonough. In 1976 McDonough and others founded the Canadian Children's Book Centre to raise awareness among librarians, teachers, booksellers, parents, and kids themselves. Under the leadership of its dynamic first executive director, Phyllis Yaffe, and her successors, the centre created a receptive climate for Canadian children's literature by publishing the selection guide *Our Choice*, organizing author and illustrator tours, producing colourful brochures and posters, and assembling a reference collection. The centre also brought young readers face to face with authors and illustrators by organizing Canadian Children's Book Week: seven days of celebratory events and activities across the country every November. Like its French-language counterpart,

Communication-Jeunesse, the Children's Book Centre has been an essential ally for publishers and authors.

The visionaries of Canadian children's publishing were mostly women. One exception to that rule, other than William Toye, was Rick Wilks.

Wilks and his business partner, Anne Millyard, hadn't really meant to start a publishing company. "Being a publisher was the farthest thing from my mind," Wilks recalled twenty-five years later. "We just thought, 'Let's try publishing a book.' Presumably there was nothing to lose. There was a *lot* to lose, but I didn't quite perceive that."

Although neither of them knew much about publishing, Millyard and Wilks shared strong convictions about children's literature and the child's right to be listened to and supported. "The prejudice against the child as a person, and what he is saying, is mind-boggling," Millyard said in the 1970s. From her experience of working in a Toronto free school, she saw parents as basically unwilling to accept their children's ideas and creativity. Wilks agreed, believing kids' books too often projected restrictive attitudes that stifled children's natural curiosity, creativity, and independence.

In 1974 the pair obtained government funding to undertake a study of reading in Ontario schools, analyzing the materials available and how children related to them. The results showed that children responded especially well to writings by their peers and identified positively with other kids' thoughts and emotions. That discovery prompted Millyard and Wilks to start collecting children's writing and artwork; from there it was a short step to publishing some of it, in an illustrated 1975 anthology called *Wordsandwich*. A sympathetic printer tutored them in book production, showing them how to lay out pages using an aquarium as a light table, and suddenly they were publishers with a non-profit entity called Books by Kids.

The unassuming freshness of *Wordsandwich* caught the fancy of adults, who buy the majority of children's books, and it sold out a small first printing. "We reprinted in three weeks," Wilks remembered, "and reprinted in another six weeks, and went on the radio and had national publicity, and I just thought, 'This publishing is a breeze. What's everybody whining about?'"

A quiet man with an acute sense of humour, Wilks was only twenty-three at the time, barely out of university. Millyard was forty-six, with two children. As Wilks acknowledged, they were "the odd couple" of Canadian publishing, family friends (Millyard and her husband were friends of Wilks's parents) who enjoyed working together. The two weren't frightened off when their bookkeeper explained they were technically bankrupt. "We were nowhere near making it," Wilks recalled, "but we liked the experience, so we thought we'd try another book. It was like teaching yourself to fly an airplane or do brain surgery."

Their next titles were *The Thing in Exile*, a collection of poems by three sixteen-year-old boys, and *Making Waves*, which won a design award in 1976. Both books contained invitations to kids to mail in their stories and artwork. Inevitably the partners received hundreds of manuscripts, and Millyard and Wilks read them all, submitting the best to a panel of children before deciding which to publish in two more editions of *Wordsandwich*.

By then, Millyard and Wilks had also become excited about publishing children's books by adults, and Annick Press was born. For the first six years, the pair didn't write themselves a regular paycheque. They ate food grown in Millyard's garden and got by with a grant here, a grant there, in addition to their sales. "In those days, if there wasn't a grant for it, we didn't do it," Wilks said. It would take several years before Annick could fly on its own, but Millyard and Wilks were fortunate in coming across two individuals who helped them get it off the ground.

After leaving Belford Book Distributing, Lionel Koffler started representing American counterculture publishers and smaller American university presses, eventually founding Firefly Books. In 1979 Rick Wilks overheard Koffler pitching the buyer at the Can-Do Bookstore in Toronto. "It blew me away," Wilks recalled. "Lionel was just great." The Annick partners had been about to move their distribution from Burns & MacEachern to Macmillan, which had offered to invest in their publishing program; but when Koffler told them, "I understand what your books are all about and I'd like to add them to my list," Wilks and Millyard sensed he'd make a better match. Their intuition was sound. Sold by Maclean-Hunter the next year, Macmillan dumped its agencies, whereas agency representation remained a core business for Firefly.

Throughout the 1980s and '90s, Annick and Firefly grew together, stretching the limits of the Canadian market while tapping into the enormous potential of the United States. Koffler built up American sales for Annick and his other clients through sheer attention to detail, going after the 7,000 public libraries and the 100,000 school libraries in the United States as well as the retail trade. His network of regional sales reps attended every state library conference and assiduously sold books one copy at a time. Firefly became one of the country's largest domestically owned publisher-distributors, with Annick as its biggest Canadian client.

Not long after signing with Firefly, Annick received an envelope containing four children's manuscripts. The author had mailed them to seven publishers, but the other six, including Clarke, Irwin, had replied with rejections. Millyard and Wilks read the stories and immediately telephoned the author to say a contract was in the mail. Robert Munsch, a former American who taught at the University of Guelph, Ontario, responded, "Oh, fine," thinking it would be nice to have his work published.

Millyard and Wilks needed an illustrator for Munsch. Encountering Michael Martchenko's work in an art exhibition, they suspected his sensibility might be wacky enough to accompany Munsch's tales. Although he'd never illustrated children's books before, Martchenko happily accepted the assignment, and in 1979, Annick published two of the stories, *The Mud Puddle* and *The Dark*. A third, *The Paper Bag Princess*, appeared in 1980. The child appeal of the Munsch-Martchenko duo was enormous. *The Paper Bag Princess* has rolled on to more than forty printings and sales of a cool 1.5 million copies in Canada and the United States. Along with later Munsch titles, such as *Mortimer, Thomas' Snowsuit, I Have to Go!*, and *Pigs*, all illustrated by Martchenko, Munsch's books have generated total sales for Annick of several million copies.

Young audiences loved Munsch's exuberant flouting of authority and his depictions of kids expressing themselves loudly and uninhibitedly. Judith Saltman described the books' appeal in *Modern Canadian Children's Books*: Munsch's "tongue-in-cheek child satires," she wrote, "show brave and plucky kids surviving absurd adventures, ingeniously extending the limits of their freedom while thwarting authority figures such as arrogant demons, pompous mayors, curmudgeonly teachers and principals, and cold technology. Munsch's style is comfortably collo-quial, fast-paced, and rich in sound patterns . . . that invite the child to participate in the telling."

Annick published Munsch in hardcover first, but sales soared after his books were reprinted as thin, staple-bound paperbacks selling at $4.95. Despite the low retail price, they sold in such quantities that they became quite profitable, especially since their uniform eight-by-eight-inch format allowed them to be reprinted together. Their success opened many doors in the bookstore, library, and school markets throughout North America. Millyard and Wilks started paying themselves a salary.

In 1986 the two turned down Munsch's highly emotional tale of a mother and her son, *Love You Forever*, considering it out of character with Munsch's other work, its theme too adult for young children. But Koffler picked it up for Firefly. As of 2002, *Love You Forever* had sold the aston-ishing quantity, surely unprecedented for a Canadian-authored title in any genre, of 17 million copies, mainly in the United States. Although Annick lost Munsch as an author after rejecting this manuscript (he eventually signed with Scholastic Canada), Millyard and Wilks have republished his titles in various formats and pursued readers in the same age group through other authors' work.

Annick persisted with books for younger children – a niche it continues to fill with the wildly successful Mole Sisters series by Roslyn Schwartz – but adventurously tried out new formats. It produced a variety of sturdy, brightly illustrated board books for toddlers. And it coined a term, "Annikins," for a publishing format new to North America: three-by-three-inch paperbacks, in which existing titles by Munsch and other Annick authors are reproduced in miniature. Millyard borrowed the concept after receiving professional mentoring from a children's publisher in Germany. Selling for 99 cents, then $1.25, Annikins were first released in the mid-1980s, finding a hugely receptive market as impulse buys beside cash registers in book and toy stores; by 2002 they had sold 9 million copies. More recently Annick branched out to publish some of its titles in French. And in 1998, with Millyard's retirement imminent, the firm opened a West Coast office and engaged Colleen MacMillan, an experienced editor formerly with Western Producer Prairie Books in Saskatoon and Whitecap Books in Vancouver, to acquire fiction and non-fiction for older children and teenagers.

Another Firefly client, Owl Books, contrasted with Annick's whimsical storytelling by carving a distinct identity as an information-based non-fiction publisher. Owned by Key Publishers, Michael de Pencier's Toronto-based magazine empire, Owl Books was first directed by Annabel Slaight, editor of *Owl* magazine. Slaight drew her books' contents largely from the magazine, published for ages eight to twelve and covering nature, science, and technology in inventive, interactive ways. The dozen or so titles that Owl Books publishes each year have stuck with that approach: the Strange Science series, for example, dealing with vampires, UFOs, and other paranormal phenomena, the Wow Canada! series, and *Cybersurfer: The Owl Internet Guide for Kids*.

With its link to the magazine, Owl Books once enjoyed the advantage of cross-media marketing of its books. Slaight created a character named Dr. Zed, an eccentric white-haired scientist who taught kids science through do-it-yourself experiments. When she went into Toronto schools looking for a real-life scientist to play the character, Slaight found him in a teacher named Gordon Penrose, who even looked the part with his halo of white hair. Penrose starred as Dr. Zed in public appearances and on the *Owl-TV* program, introducing the books to a wider audience. The program was picked up by PBS in the United States, and the Dr. Zed series sold some 500,000 books over fifteen years.

After receiving distribution through Key Porter Books, Owl found a better fit with Lionel Koffler, alongside Annick's list and Firefly's own children's program. Owl's domestic and American sales zoomed. Diane Davy, a former president of Owl who later became president of Key Porter, termed Koffler "a consummate marketer, who has put time and money into understanding the American market and learning how it works: how to get children's books reviewed, how to reach school libraries." Davy characterized Koffler as a tough negotiator: "Lionel is a very dogged businessman with firm convictions, who's right 90 percent of the time and believes he's right 100 percent of the time." No longer directly associated with the magazine, which passed into other hands, Owl Books has stuck profitably to its original market niche, while publishing under the trade name Maple Tree Press.

For Groundwood Books of Toronto, a strategic alliance for marketing and distribution would be equally critical to the firm's early growth and success.

Groundwood has always been first and foremost its founder, Patsy Aldana. Recognized on three continents as a superb children's publisher, Aldana has produced a wide range of remarkably original work, distinguished by sophisticated text and art and amply honoured by a long list of national and international awards over a quarter-century. While growing up in Guatemala with an American mother and a Guatemalan father, Aldana devoured English-language books: "Reading children's books was my main contact with the English language. I've always had a passion for them." After studying at Stanford and Bryn Mawr, she emigrated to Canada with her first husband in 1971 and acquired a varied background in the practical side of publishing by retailing books at the Toy Shop in Toronto, working at Women's Press, and managing sales for Belford Book Distributing.

Like Jim Douglas, Aldana was a long-term planner. She studied the great tradition of British and American children's books stretching back to the 1930s, read the critical literature, and incubated her vision of a contemporary children's publishing, distinct from the more traditional approaches of large Canadian houses. She foresaw plenty of room for new kinds of books, a sense reinforced by early visits to Bologna, where she witnessed the expanding international market for the genre.

Rather than expressing her leftist, feminist, and nationalist values by publishing books that would compete with existing presses, Aldana set her sights on creating a children's-only publishing program, an act she considered wholly political: "If you don't have a children's culture, you really don't have a national culture. Every other Anglo-Saxon country but ours had developed a children's literature. I don't think there's any contradiction between children's issues and being interested in politics."

Aldana knew exactly the kinds of books she wanted to publish. They'd be marked by strong stories and characters, challenging illustrations, high-end production values: "I felt very strongly that picture books should be text-driven, not just beautiful for their own sake." She released the first three Groundwood titles at a splashy Toronto launch in fall 1978. Some in the book trade looked askance at her as an upstart – an ambitious thirty-one-year-old single mother wearing jeans and long hair, with radical politics and little capital – until they examined her books more closely. Two striking, full-colour picture-storybooks – *Giranimal Daddy Lion*, by Francesca Vivenza, designed by Frank Newfeld, and Blair Drawson's *Flying Dimitri* – were bold in conception and accomplished in execution. A funny, realistic young adult novel, titled *Hey, Dad*, by Brian Doyle, then an unknown Ottawa high school teacher, received an enthusiastic reception from reviewers and the public and became the first in a succession of robust Doyle novels. The following year, Aldana published *The Orchestra*, by Mark Rubin, a picture book that would go through ten printings; a translation of a classic novel by a Québécoise, Suzanne Martel's *The King's Daughter*, which two decades later was still selling 4,000 copies a year; and another Doyle, *You Can Pick Me Up at Peggy's Cove*.

From the start, Aldana arranged for marketing and distribution services from Douglas & McIntyre. After testing their alliance for two years, the companies forged a somewhat atypical partnership in 1980: D&M would capitalize Groundwood's operations and own its inventory, but Groundwood would remain a separate company under Aldana's control, owning rights to the books. She became a minority partner in D&M, doubling as the firm's eastern marketing manager and running its Toronto office. Aldana said that without Scott McIntyre's enthusiastic support, Groundwood would not have succeeded as it did. But the alliance conferred distinct advantages on the Vancouver-based partner as well: D&M acquired a physical presence in the critical Toronto and Ontario markets, a major enlargement of its publishing program, which already included some children's titles, and a greater ability to attract foreign agencies.

Groundwood has published abundantly across many categories and age groups. It became renowned early for its picture-storybooks and its fiction for middle readers (ages eight to eleven) and young adults (twelve and up). Its program has included many of Canada's kidlit stars. Indeed, Groundwood authors have carried off so many prizes that rivals began referring sardonically to the Governor General's Awards for children's literature as "the Groundwood awards." Tim Wynne-Jones, multi-talented author of the Zoom picture book series and several critically acclaimed young adult novels, shared the stage at SkyDome in Toronto with J.K. Rowling, author of the Harry Potter books, at a mass reading in 2001. The illustrator Ian Wallace, celebrated for the sensual beauty of his work, has been a Groundwood author, as has Marie-Louise Gay, author/illustrator of *Stella, Star of the Sea* and other international bestsellers. The press's writers have included Teddy Jam (Aldana's husband, Matt Cohen, writing under a pseudonym); Paul Yee, one of whose books, *Ghost Train*, was chosen by a Swiss children's jury as best book of the year; the popular novelists Martha Brooks, Sarah Ellis, Welwyn Wilton Katz, Celia Lottridge, and Diana Wieler; Ann Blades, who moved over to Groundwood from Tundra and D&M in the 1980s; and of course Doyle, translated into various languages and shortlisted in 1999 for the prestigious Hans Christian Andersen Prize, known as "the little Nobel."

Children's publishers have worked alongside their industry colleagues to fight for the interests of the Canadian-owned sector, and none more actively than Aldana. Combining May Cutler's combativeness with her own acute political instincts, she devoted energies to lobbying for the Association of Canadian Publishers, including two terms as president, in addition to serving on the boards of the Canadian Children's Book Centre and the International Board on Books for Young People. Aldana authored a comprehensive ACP policy paper in 1980 seeking that elusive quarry, a federal publishing policy, at a time when the association still hoped to secure long-range structural measures to complement grants.

In 1990 Aldana was instrumental in organizing a landmark exhibition of Canadian children's book illustration at the Bologna fair. Nonetheless she has found that Canadian picture books travel less successfully to Europe than to the United States, largely because of differences in visual sensibility. Canadian young adult fiction, on the other hand, is more popular in European countries. "We could sell three times as many novelists into Germany as we have to sell," according to Aldana. "It's incredible. The Germans say Canadian books are much better than anything coming out of the States. I think that's because we've been publisher-driven for the most part, our publishers are still relatively small, and we've had an editorial vision and high editorial standards."

Knowing the domestic market isn't big enough to sustain that vision, Aldana formed close ties with American, European, and Latin American publishers and built an extensive international network. As the 1990s wore on, however, changing market conditions back home would pose dangers to children's and adult publishers alike. Aldana's cosmopolitanism would soon be a prerequisite for survival.

Another children's publisher who adopted Canada also brought a vibrantly international outlook. Coming of age in and around New York during the 1960s, Valerie Hussey had marched against the Vietnam War and demonstrated for the Equal Rights Amendment. Practical by nature, she trained as a teacher, but she went into educational publishing instead, with short stints at Westinghouse Learning Corporation, Harcourt Brace, and Macmillan.

Hussey arrived in Toronto, having met her future husband, a Canadian, while travelling in Greece. She looked up "Publishers" in the Yellow Pages. Making a cold call at the Egerton Ryerson Memorial Building, where she'd noticed three different publishers had their offices, Hussey presented herself at the front desk of arch-nationalist James Lorimer and announced, "I've just arrived from New York." Instead of being ushered in to see Lorimer, she met his business partner at the time, Catherine Wilson, the former publicist at M&S. Wilson generously provided her with a detailed overview of the Toronto publishing scene, complete with names, addresses, and telephone numbers. "Go see this person," Wilson told Hussey, "and use my name. Go see that person, but don't use my name, they can't stand me."

Hussey spent two years in the educational division of General Publishing. She dropped into Women's Press but didn't stay long, because she wasn't a collectivist in her bones: "I'm too strong-willed." When she made her way to Kids Can Press in 1979, it wasn't the press's collective aspect that appealed to her as much as the publishing opportunity it represented.

Kids Can had been created in 1973 by a small band of aspiring writers and artists, many of them American expatriates, to publish non-sexist children's books. Financed with seed money from the federal Opportunities for Youth and Local Initiatives Programs, its early titles were written and illustrated by members of the collective, printed on Gestetner mimeograph machines, and staple-bound with two-colour covers. Some of them retold the folk tales of immigrant communities in Canada. Angela Wood collaborated with Ian Wallace to create *The Sandwich*, one of the first Canadian picture books portraying children in an ethnically mixed urban classroom.

In 1979 Kids Can was selling about $17,000 worth of books, less than the total value of its grants. It was run by one person, Priscilla Carrier, when Valerie Hussey came calling, hoping to find a way into trade publishing. After Hussey wrote an impressive reader's report on a manuscript, Carrier gave her a novel to edit, then suggested they work together. Hussey agreed, but only if Carrier was willing to put Kids Can on a more professional basis: "I said I didn't care how much it was, but we had to pay ourselves."

Hussey's ambition resulted in a clash with Carrier, who left in 1981 after Hussey presented a personal vision for Kids Can to the collective's board. The board approved the plan and, remarkably, decided to dissolve itself. By that time, Hussey recalled, most of the members had lost interest and were willing to turn management over to her: "I think the board understood that if something was going to happen, somebody had to make it happen. So I just ran the press, at that point, as if I owned it."

She brought in a colleague, Ricky Englander, a librarian working at the Canadian Children's Book Centre whose knowledge of children's literature and the marketplace complemented Hussey's publishing and pedagogical background. Their combination of skills would make them a potent team. They decided to emulate an American children's publishing model, developing a full-range program across genres. Like Owl Books, they'd focus on non-fiction with a child-centred, hands-on approach, developing books that could be used as supplementary curriculum materials and classroom resources. "In that part of the list," Hussey said, "we were really publishing for the librarian, for the teacher, for the parent, more than for the child." But they also published picture-storybooks, sitting across a table from each other as they edited manuscripts page by page.

One day Englander saw Camilla Gryski demonstrating the string game known as cat's cradle and asked her to write a book about it; the resulting Cat's Cradle titles have sold hundreds of thousands of copies in Canada and the United States. Englander and Hussey also approached the Ontario Science Centre and walked out with an agreement to co-publish *Scienceworks*, experiments for children using the science centre's interactive methodology. "At that point, we'd done almost nothing," Hussey recalled. "But we talked our way in, and they gave us a chance. It was chutzpah as much as anything."

They saw such institutional alliances as their way forward. Foreign editions of *Scienceworks* were eventually published in a dozen countries, from the United States to Thailand. Kids Can Press went on to co-publish with the Royal Ontario Museum, the National Gallery of Canada, the Art Gallery of Ontario, and the Federation of Ontario Naturalists. Hussey and Englander didn't ask the institutions to invest in the books, only to contribute their expertise and imprimatur in return for a royalty. The institutional connection gave the books instant credibility with adult buyers and boosted sales in Canada and abroad.

The partners divided marketing duties, with Englander responsible for domestic sales, Hussey for international deals. It gave Hussey real pleasure to go to Bologna and negotiate on an equal basis with senior New York editors who, in the past, might have been her bosses: "As an American expatriate, I wanted to bring what I was doing home. That was exciting. I saw the international marketplace as critical from the beginning, both from a learning standpoint and as a key to financial success."

Kids Can built links to American publishers during the 1980s, selling rights or finished books to William Morrow, Viking, Little, Brown, and Scholastic. The partners struck a deal with Addison-Wesley, supplying the American company with its entire children's non-fiction program. Addison-Wesley paid development fees in addition to royalties, which helped capitalize Kids Can's operations; it might have bought the Canadian firm, if not for federal regulations prohibiting foreign takeovers.

By 1986, after five years of running the press, Hussey and Englander had transformed it utterly from the days of the collective. They arranged to purchase Kids Can's assets and convert them into a privately held company, in which they were equal partners. That was a decisive year: it also marked publication of a picture book about a green, small-boy-like turtle named Franklin, who would introduce the notion of branding into Canadian publishing.

Like those first Robert Munsch manuscripts at Annick Press, the first Franklin manuscript arrived unsolicited. Its author, Paulette Bourgeois, was a Toronto journalist awaiting the arrival of her first baby; she'd decided to try her hand at writing a children's story. She submitted it to Kids Can under the title "A Turtle Called Chicken," after being turned down by six other publishers. Hussey and Englander accepted the manuscript, changed the title to *Franklin in the Dark*, and made the all-important matchup with the illustrator Brenda Clark, who had worked for them previously. When the book was complete, it sold about 10,000 copies in Canada in the first year – encouraging, but not fantastic – and was bought by Scholastic for the United States.

Bourgeois and Clark didn't meet until after publication of *Franklin in the Dark*; it took them three more years to create another Franklin story. But once he got going, Franklin triggered an astonishing flood of revenue, particularly in U.S. dollars. More than thirty Franklin titles have appeared to date, with rights sold to more than thirty countries; about 40 million copies are in print. But book-related income would be only part of the tidal wave of revenue that flowed from Franklin's genial self as he metamorphosed from storybook character to brand, inspiring a television series, a line of plush toys, and a line of clothing. Franklin transcended children's literature to attain that apogee, children's merchandising, and Kids Can Press became a very profitable enterprise.

Kids Can remained far more than Franklin. The company has been publishing about forty-five titles a year: picture books, young adult fiction, even poetry, as well as non-fiction dealing with Canadian subjects such as the national anthem, the flag, and the country's natural resources. In 1997 Kids Can began a major push into the States, selling most of its list there directly except for Franklin, whose American book rights remain licensed to Scholastic. Originally Hussey and Englander had expected American sales would exceed Canadian within five years. As usual, they were ahead of projections.

It was unquestionably Franklin that attracted Nelvana, the large Toronto-based animation company that had produced *A Cosmic Christmas*, *Babar*, and much other admired children's programming. In 1995 Nelvana licensed not only Franklin's film and video rights but the merchandising rights as well, which would allow it to cash in, if and when Franklin became a superstar. Nelvana also wanted to buy Kids Can outright. According to Hussey, she and Englander replied, "How flattering. Thank you very much. Let's see if we like each other."

The firms dated for three years, while Nelvana proceeded with a Franklin television show. It became one of the top-rated series on American cable, and in 1998 the two companies tied the knot. By that time, Kids Can had hit $10 million in revenues. Nelvana paid $7 million for the once tiny press, and in 1999 it launched another television series based on a Kids Can character, Elliot Moose.

After seventeen years with the company, Englander had been looking for an exit strategy; the deal met her need nicely. But Hussey wanted to stay with the business, and Nelvana wanted her to stay, knowing it needed a knowledgeable publisher at the helm. Excited to be learning a new business in mid-life, Hussey enjoyed the buzz surrounding electronic media and merchandising deals and felt comfortable in Nelvana's entrepreneurial culture. "I define luck," she said, "as being in the right place at the right time, and knowing it."

Hussey had long been thinking strategically, seeking mutually beneficial partnerships. Even before the Nelvana deal, the press had signed a lucrative deal with Irwin Toys, which sold craft kits based on Kids Can titles with a copy of the book included. "With every business relationship we entered into," Hussey recounted, "I would look and ask, How far can this go? How can we make ourselves more valuable to somebody else? Could we position ourselves to sell to that company?"

In the process, Hussey and Englander did some fine children's publishing. And they flouted the cliché that nobody makes money publishing Canadian books.

Few Canadian publishers have strategized as successfully as the Kids Can principals. By building a robust children's publishing industry, they and their colleagues in other houses spawned followers among large and small firms across the country.

Regional strengths have emerged in this as in other genres, and talented children's authors and illustrators have found their way onto the lists of publishers doing other kinds of books. Although relatively few companies have based their entire program on kids' titles, many have produced strong material for children, often with regional settings or historical backgrounds. Among these have been Breakwater Books in Newfoundland; Ragweed Press on Prince Edward Island; Formac Publishing and Nimbus Publishing in Nova Scotia; Hyperion Press, Peguis Publishing, and Pemmican Publications in Manitoba; Coteau Books and Thistledown Press in Saskatchewan; Tree Frog Press in Alberta; and Beach Holme Publishing, Harbour Publishing, Polestar Book Publishers, Raincoast Books, Theytus Books, and Whitecap Books in British Columbia. Pemmican and Theytus are Aboriginal presses, producing original children's material by Native authors.

The 1990s saw several small to mid-sized publishers begin to specialize in children's books in a serious way, cresting a second wave of the movement. Orca Book Publishers in Victoria, Calgary-based Red Deer Press, Second Story Press in Toronto, and Lobster Press of Montreal all scored some impressive triumphs. And once they saw Canadian kids' books breaking out, it didn't take long for large companies, both domestic and foreign-owned, to move in on the action. Key Porter, Stoddart Kids, Penguin, Doubleday Canada, and HarperCollins all committed themselves to substantial children's programs, drawing on an abundant pool of writing and illustrating talent to seek a piece of a buoyant market.

Yet that market couldn't expand indefinitely. The climate for children's books was scarcely immune to the upheavals that imperilled the domestic book industry from the late 1990s onward. The children's sector, in fact, would prove particularly vulnerable.

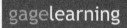 

McGRAW-HILL RYERSON | LESTER & ORPEN DENNYS

GAGE LEARNING CORPORATION | DENEAU PUBLISHING

13

A VERY DIFFICULT BUSINESS

If the domain of ideas is surrendered to those who want to make the most money, then the debate that is so essential for a functioning democracy will not take place.

André Schiffrin, *The Business of Books* (2000)

As they prepared to launch Annick Press in 1975, Anne Millyard and Rick Wilks asked Bill Clarke, "How do you start a small publishing house in Canada?"

"Oh, it's easy," Clarke replied. "You just start a large one and wait."

At a time when so many new publishers were struggling to find their feet, Clarke, Irwin was a symbol of continuity: a link to the days of Hugh Eayrs and Lorne Pierce, an embodiment of the traditional Canadian model. The nineteenth-century notion that a single text could capture all that a well-taught pupil ought to know had kept the company prosperous, long after W.H. Clarke's premature death in 1955. Its agency business had flourished. Its trade list lent a certain prestige. It had history, stability, an air of permanence. All of that would change with withering rapidity.

After Gage and Ryerson came under American ownership in 1970, Clarke, Irwin was the largest Canadian-owned textbook publisher left. Drastic changes to Ontario's school system, so populous that it determined the health of educational publishing in English Canada, soon ensured that the industry would become the preserve of multinationals.

Ontario's amalgamation of its school boards in 1969 convulsed administrative structures and threw textbook purchasing into limbo. Even more important, the province removed its textbook stimulation grants, which for many years had provided school boards with a set amount per pupil to be spent on books. Free to allocate their budgets as they wished, the reconstituted boards found other priorities. At the same time, changes in educational philosophy were moving away from the core text and towards multiple resources in the classroom.

For Clarke, Irwin and similar firms, the combined effect of the changes was devastating. Print runs of 50,000 copies became 5,000 or less by 1970, or more likely were simply cancelled. Bill Clarke, by then managing the company as executive vice-president, remembered attending a gathering of educational publishers in Macmillan's Bond Street boardroom. He likened it to a Quaker meeting: after the usual hearty greetings, everyone sat in sober silence. Finally someone felt moved to say, "So, we're not seeing very much business this year." Someone else replied, "No, we aren't, are we?" And a third burst out, "There isn't *any* business."

Clarke, Irwin had just printed 30,000 copies of a French reader, on indications from the Ontario Ministry of Education that the books would be required. The company had also invested heavily in a full-colour elementary science series. Suddenly there was no money in the system to purchase the books, and they became the publisher's nemesis, dead inventory.

Before long a changing economy also created difficulties in the agency system. The devaluation of the Canadian dollar delivered a triple whammy, raising the costs of book importation, which increased the cover prices of American and British titles in Canada, which increased buying around by booksellers and librarians. Clarke, Irwin's agency business shrank. As Bill Clarke later publicly acknowledged, the company lost money for the first seven years of the 1970s.

The changes decreed by Ontario education bureaucrats had been unilateral, made without adequate consultation with publishers who, for decades, had been meeting the province's and the country's need for texts. "The ministry did all this without any regard for the consequences," Clarke recalled years later. "I don't think they recognized the impact. It also reflected their lack of interest in Canadian books." And, he might have added, in the survival of Canadian publishers.

Foreign-owned subsidiaries suffered too; but they were cushioned from the worst effects of the ministry's actions by their ready access to learning materials researched, tested, and manufactured by their parent companies, whose investment had already been covered in the American market. Subsidiaries could Canadianize that content if need be (although in some subjects, that wasn't required) and still sell it at a profit. As curriculums across Canada changed under the influence of a liberalized, child-centred pedagogy, the subsidiaries of Ginn, McGraw-Hill, Prentice-Hall, Holt, Rinehart & Winston, Addison-Wesley, D.C. Heath, and others enjoyed a growing economic advantage. In time the pedagogical changes would benefit Canada's emerging children's publishers too, by opening the school market to their titles; but firms built on the traditional textbook faltered. It was no coincidence that ownership of Gage and Ryerson went south at this time.

Bill Clarke threw himself into reshaping the company his parents had created. He and his staff of ninety-five had to learn a different kind of publishing, and fast. Having found more than forty educational projects in the pipeline when he arrived in 1966, Clarke jettisoned most of those remaining after 1970. To replace lost revenues, he turned in desperation to trade books. Within three years, Clarke, Irwin's sales volume went from being 75 percent educational, 25 percent trade, to the reverse.

The children's program under Janet Lunn built on the firm's backlist and agency strength, particularly the Dutton list, publishing Jean Little and Barbara Smucker and introducing the young novelist Kevin Major. Clarke, Irwin won the Canada Council Children's Literature Award for three consecutive years, 1977, 1978, and 1979. On the adult side, Bill Clarke hired an array of new editorial talent, including the future publisher Louise Dennys, the future Writers' Union lawyer Marion Hebb, and the future Doubleday Canada publisher John Pearce. Two writers, Elaine Dewar and Stephen Williams, were hired as editors on the same day as Pearce in 1976.

Clarke, Irwin made its most important literary contribution since the 1950s when it relaunched Timothy Findley's career. Findley's third and, some feel, best novel, *The Wars*, was released in 1977, followed by *Famous*

Last Words. The company threw a memorable dinner party for *The Wars* at the Park Plaza Hotel in Toronto, a surprisingly stylish event thanks to Catherine Wilson, the publicist, with Pearce playing First World War tunes on the piano and the tables adorned with poppies.

Richard Rohmer, chair of the Ontario Royal Commission on Book Publishing, began his unlikely second career as a commercial novelist with Clarke, Irwin; *Ultimatum* kicked off his string of successful potboilers with one-word titles and stick-man characters. In non-fiction, the firm originated such titles as Bruce Litteljohn's *Wilderness Canada*, Rick Butler's historic photography album, *Vanishing Canada*, and *No Safe Place*, Warner Troyer's exposé of mercury poisoning in northern Ontario.

But it wasn't easy to make a dowager dance like a teenager. Clarke, Irwin was still top-heavy with tradition, its payroll weighed down by family retainers whom Clarke couldn't bring himself to fire. The trade program never quite took off, hobbled as it was by a shortage of cash. As Clarke put it, "Scurrying around, looking for markets wherever they existed, was the order of the day." He needed to borrow more and more money from the bank; he conceeded that he could never have secured the necessary financing without provincial loan guarantees from the Ontario Development Corporation.

Clarke also sought business solutions. He arranged to provide order fulfillment for other Canadian publishers, taking on growing clients such as Douglas & McIntyre, James Lorimer & Co., Kids Can Press, and the Canadian subsidiary of Allyn & Bacon, an American educational firm. He moved the company's warehouse out of Clarwin House and into a bigger facility near the airport. He made a major commitment to a new computer system, which, with his background in math and science, he'd find irresistibly, even fatally absorbing.

By 1980, the year of its fiftieth anniversary, Clarke, Irwin seemed poised for transition to a more viable state. Several of the industry's best minds lent a hand. Jim Douglas advised Clarke on managing the company's difficulties. Robin Farr left his position as publishing adviser to the Ontario Ministry of Culture and Recreation to come on board as executive vice-president. On her retirement from Macmillan, Gladys Neale arrived to rebuild Clarke, Irwin's educational program. Arden Ford came via Anansi and the ACP to work on the management side. But all the king's horses, it seemed, and all the king's men and women couldn't put Clarke, Irwin together again. In the end, they weren't given a chance.

The bank debt had hit $1.6 million, and the Ontario government was nervous about its guarantee. Robin Farr found it frustratingly difficult to keep Clarke's mind concentrated on the bigger picture. Clarke had become preoccupied with personally fixing a computer system that proved unfixable. "He focused on that," Farr remembered, "and we just went down and down."

Gladys Neale had entertained high hopes for her educational projects. But one evening in 1983 when she was working late in her office, auditors arrived and changed the locks on the doors. "Another girl was also working late, and she and I were the first to know that Clarke, Irwin had gone into receivership. It was terrible. I can remember saying to this man, 'But how are we going to get into the building in the morning?' 'Oh,' he said, 'we'll make sure people can get in.' It was a shock. If they [the bank and the provincial government] had just left Clarke, Irwin alone for another year, we could have pulled it out of its difficulties. But for all intents and purposes, they shut us down."

Given that serious efforts were being made to save the embattled company, it was tragically unnecessary for Ontario to pull its loan guarantee. For Bill Clarke, the government's action was a bitter blow: "The first quarter of 1983, which is when Clarke, Irwin was put down, was the largest first quarter in our history." Knowing the Davis government was unhappy with its liability, Clarke had been actively raising capital to pay off the bank. He'd already lined up $1 million but was never given time to complete the refinancing. Why?

There were many reasons, some intertwined with the political and economic climate of the day. Bill Clarke offered two specifics. The company was beginning to publish books that made the reigning Tories uncomfortable; one was Troyer's *No Safe Place*, which implicated the government in the mercury poisoning crisis. More fundamentally, the Ontario government was fed up with the publishing industry's inability to solve its financial problems, ten years after the royal commission. "Publishing has lost its sex appeal," Dalton Camp told Clarke.

The two largest liabilities under the ODC loan guarantee program were McClelland & Stewart and Clarke, Irwin, and at the bottom of the 1982–1983 recession, Ontario wanted to put an end to its exposure. "The government was inclined to issue a fairly strong lesson," Clarke opined. "It wasn't prepared to do so through M&S, but it was through Clarke, Irwin."

He might have added that a contributing factor was Clarke, Irwin's purchase of the Fleet Books backlist. Fleet was the former trade program of Van Nostrand Reinhold's Canadian subsidiary, which the Canadian-owned Thomson organization had bought as part of its acquisition of VNR in the United States. When Thomson decided to get out of trade publishing (it was more profitably involved on the educational side through ownership of Thomas Nelson), it sold the Fleet line to Clarke, Irwin. To Ontario government officials, that was a sign of bad business judgment on Clarke's part; with his own program seriously undercapitalized, he was stretching his resources too thin.

After the initial shock of receivership, John Pearce remembered, there was a lull as the receivers asked staff to carry on business as usual, the better to assist them in appraising Clarke, Irwin's assets. A month later, all employees were dismissed when it was announced that the assets had been sold. In an ironic twist of fate, Clarke, Irwin's backlist and inventory went to the Book Society of Canada, the firm founded by the late John C.W. Irwin; the owner was now John Irwin the younger, Bill Clarke's cousin.

John Irwin engaged several Clarke, Irwin staff members, including Pearce and Neale, whose projects meshed with the Book Society's ongoing educational business. In 1984 the new proprietor renamed the integrated company Irwin Publishing, in what could only be seen as the denouement of a four-decade family disagreement. John Irwin issued some of Clarke, Irwin's works-in-progress, and four years later he sold Irwin Publishing to another second-generation firm, Stoddart Publishing.

Bill Clarke took at least some consolation from knowing that the Clarke, Irwin legacy remained. As he told his employees on the day the fifty-three-year-old company closed its doors, "There's one thing you have to remember: the books are out there. They can never take that back."

One of Clarke's former employees, meanwhile, was heading for greater things. Clarke, Irwin's fate showed that publishing tradition wasn't enough without vision; and vision was something Lester & Orpen Dennys always had plenty of.

Known first as Lester & Orpen, the company began in Toronto in 1973. Malcolm Lester, a former rabbinical student, and Eve Orpen, originally from Vienna, resembled Rick Wilks and Anne Millyard in being a younger man and an older woman who became partners in publishing. In Lester's case, seven years as an editor at Holt, Rinehart & Winston, followed by a stint overseeing Coles Notes and the Coles Canadiana Collection, had made him eager to originate his own titles. For Orpen, working in marketing at General Publishing, Collier-Macmillan, and Thomas Nelson's Australian branch had kindled an ambition to find international markets for Canadian books. The pair considered their experience and temperaments – his introverted, hers extroverted – complementary. Their first title was a bestseller. After that it got harder.

Remarkably, the bestseller was poetry, of a sort. In Australia, Orpen had promoted the wildly popular writings of Rod McKuen, a strong-but-sensitive American versifier, and she considered Terry Rowe a Canadian McKuen. She wasn't far off: Rowe's *To You with Love* sold 20,000 copies. After that euphoric start, the house published a small list mixing popular fiction and serious non-fiction. L&O published two bestselling novelists of the mid-1970s, the folksy storyteller Morley Torgov, whose *A Good Place to Come From* was filmed for television, and the pseudonymous Philippe Van Rjndt, author of sophisticated, internationally successful thrillers.

When Eve Orpen's cancer, which had been in remission, returned in 1976, she and Lester soberly discussed their company's future and agreed he should think about finding another business partner. Together they met with an energetic, striking young Englishwoman with preternaturally large eyes, and after a long talk over lunch, they agreed Louise Dennys could be the one. "Eve was quite taken with Louise," Lester recalled. "She said, 'If something happens to me, you should pursue the conversation.'" After losing her only son to Hodgkin's disease, Orpen herself succumbed to cancer in 1978 at fifty-two.

Dennys joined the firm. As Graham Greene's niece and a distant cousin of Robert Louis Stevenson, she had a literary birthright; she'd attended Oxford, trained as a bookseller, and managed the Oxford University Press bookshop in London. She emigrated to Toronto in 1972, sponsored by Louis Melzack, owner of the Classics chain, who wanted her to manage his branch in the Colonnade, an elegant shopping concourse in midtown. But breaking into publishing was Dennys's real goal, and when she was offered a junior position at Clarke, Irwin, Melzack advised her to accept.

At Clarke, Irwin, Dennys did a little of everything ("I was assistant to the assistant") and worked with her first author, Alden Nowlan. She credited Bill Clarke with encouraging and mentoring her, "although Bill was by then deeply involved in the whole computerization of the company, and a lot of the time he was down in the basement somewhere." Eager to begin acquiring manuscripts, Dennys came across two that she felt demanded to be published: a collection of metaphysical poetry by Richard Outram, and two novellas in translation by the Czech émigré Josef Skvorecky, whose Sixty-Eight Publishers, based in Toronto, was the leading publisher of Czech dissidents after the Soviet invasion. Clarke told Dennys the firm couldn't afford to publish either book, however worthy; both were certain to lose money. She insisted she'd make them affordable by finding co-publishers.

Figuring she should start at the top, Dennys travelled to New York on borrowed money and took the manuscripts to the people at Knopf, who eventually accepted Skvorecky's *The Bass Saxophone*. And on a trip home to England to visit her parents, she went to the Hogarth Press, a Clarke, Irwin agency. "It was the best Christmas of my life," Dennys remembered; Hogarth's editor, the poet D.J. Enright, offered to publish both manuscripts.

Returning triumphant to Toronto, Dennys found she still couldn't persuade Clarke to take the leap. But one of Outram's friends, the Toronto antiquarian bookseller Hugh Anson-Cartwright, was prepared to help her publish both books. Dennys edited the manuscripts in the dusty back room of Anson-Cartwright's store, the typesetting and printing were done at Sixty-Eight Publishers, and the two titles appeared under the imprint Anson-Cartwright Editions. Louise Dennys had become a publisher.

Both books were well received. Anson-Cartwright Editions continued to issue the occasional title, but it couldn't afford to pay Dennys a salary, and she accepted Malcolm Lester's offer to work with him. After she joined Lester and his only employee, the novelist-in-the-making Barbara Gowdy, they worked towards a vision of Lester & Orpen Dennys, as the firm would be called. Previously Lester had done all the editing, Orpen all the marketing. But both Lester and Dennys were editors, and so they agreed she would specialize in fiction, he in non-fiction; she'd be responsible for an aggressive international marketing strategy, he for managing L&OD's finances. Before making a commitment to any title, they'd both have to feel enthusiastic about doing it.

To sell foreign editions of their books, they believed, it would be necessary to reciprocate by buying Canadian rights to international titles. That would mean persuading American and British publishers to break out rights for Canada instead of lumping them in with Commonwealth or North American rights, trading the Canadian market back and forth as if they owned it. "We were a bone caught between two dogs," as Dennys put it. The other challenge was "an impression in New York and London that Canadian books were boring – which we fought with great passion."

In 1980 she and Lester introduced their International Fiction List, a quality paperback line with distinctive typographic cover designs featuring the initial paragraph of each text. The first title was Skvorecky's *The Bass Saxophone*, the second a translation, *Deaf to the City*, by Marie-Claire Blais, and the third was Joy Kogawa's novel of the Japanese-Canadian internment, *Obasan*, one of the books Dennys is proudest to have published. The list had "international" in the title, but it wasn't easy to change attitudes abroad. Dennys went to London in 1982 as head of an ACP trade mission, and she and the other Canadians had to twist arms even to get meetings with the British. When Dennys appeared on a panel before an audience of British literary agents, she told them that if they made Canadian rights available, their authors would benefit from being marketed properly in this country and receiving a full royalty, instead of the usual reduced export royalty. Afterwards, P.D. James's agent approached Dennys; James's critically admired crime novels had been selling only about 2,500 copies in hardcover through their Canadian distributor, and would L&OD be interested in publishing her next one? Dennys conferred with Lester by phone, and they signed up Canadian rights to *The Skull Beneath the Skin*.

American publishers were also resistant. The hard-nosed president of Simon & Schuster, Dick Snyder, didn't take kindly to L&OD's approaching his author Joan Didion. Although Didion was interested in being published in Canada, Lester recalled, "Snyder didn't want this because Canada was part of his traditional market. He threatened some sort of reprisal if she signed with us, then threw up his hands and told her, 'I don't know why you want to sell off Canadian rights anyway! I feel very patriotic about Canada.'"

L&OD's glittering string of international signings began with Italo Calvino's *If on a Winter's Night a Traveller* and eventually included Didion's *Democracy*. The International Fiction List came to comprise a mix of Canadians, Italians, Czechs, Irish, British, and Americans. Graham Greene, D.M. Thomas, Ian McEwan, John Irving, William Trevor, Thomas Keneally, and Kazuo Ishiguro appeared alongside Morley Callaghan, Barry Callaghan, Jane Rule, Matt Cohen, Antonine Maillet, and Alberto Manguel.

Some titles, however, came at a hefty price; the royalty advances L&OD agreed to offer weren't always justified by Canadian sales. The company was no better capitalized than most domestic trade publishers and relied on federal and Ontario grants and a provincial loan guarantee. In non-fiction, meanwhile, Lester originated books on baseball, reflecting his personal passion for the sport, and on Canadian politics and history. The company published *None Is Too Many*, Irving Abella and Howard Troper's important and disturbing account of Canada's pre-war refusal to accept Jewish refugees from Germany; *The Illustrated History of Canada*, edited by R. Craig Brown; and Patrick Watson's *The Struggle for Democracy*, based on an international television series.

By 1988 L&OD's sales had reached $1.5 million. Nonetheless, "cash was always a worry," recalled Lester. "I didn't want to lurch from crisis to crisis and barely get by. I was confident we could survive, but I felt we needed some financial stability." The company had created a distribution partner-ship with Deneau Publishing, which had moved from Ottawa (where it had been Deneau & Greenberg) to Toronto; but rather than improving their financial situations, both firms had to be bailed out by the Ontario government. L&OD's revenues weren't keeping pace with the capital needs of its publishing program. Lester was feeling burned out. As debt rose around them like water, he and Dennys decided to capitalize on their glowing literary reputation and seek a buyer.

They received expressions of interest from two wealthy suitors. Avie Bennett, who had bought M&S three years earlier, seemed to Dennys interested more in absorbing a competitor than in harnessing the two principals' creativity. Christopher Ondaatje, on the other hand, a financier whose brother Michael had edited a short-fiction anthology for L&OD and was a friend of Dennys's, offered them a dream deal: Lester and Dennys could remain as president and publisher, respectively, with all the autonomy they needed; they'd receive the security of a $1.3-million bank guarantee and over $100,000 apiece for their shares. Ondaatje flew Lester and Dennys down to his Bermuda estate to plan their future together. It was all too good to be true: "I would say the honeymoon lasted maybe fifteen, twenty minutes," Lester remembered.

On the eve of their announcement at the Park Plaza's Roof Bar in August 1988, misunderstandings emerged, particularly over editorial autonomy. But the partners went ahead anyway, Ondaatje telling the media he was taking his brother's advice "to just leave them alone." And Christopher Ondaatje proceeded to do exactly that. He evinced so little interest in the firm that he even passed up book launches. The abrupt cold shoulder was puzzling. Four months later, the mercurial investor announced he was selling L&OD, along with the rest of Pagurian Corporation, his highly profitable holding company, to Hees International Bank Corp., part of the multibillion-dollar Edper conglomerate of Peter and Edward Bronfman. Then began what Dennys called the "awful, Kafka-esque nightmare."

Although Christopher Ondaatje remained chair of L&OD, his main interest seemed to lie in the firm's publication of his own book, *Leopard in the Afternoon*, about his journey to photograph wildlife in the Serengeti. Only a month after the book appeared in fall 1989, he resigned as chair, abandoning his erstwhile partners to a painful relationship with Hees. Two years later, Ondaatje explained himself to the journalist Don Gillmor in a feature in *Saturday Night*: "I love Malcolm and Louise, especially Louise. She is one of the most talented people in publishing. She has great taste, you can't buy taste. But they didn't want me, they just wanted my money. I didn't need to get much back but they didn't give me anything. It was a disaster."

What Ondaatje walked away from was certainly a disaster. Hees had never wanted to own a publishing house. The corporation's bloodless accounting mentality was antithetical to the intuitive, romantic culture of L&OD. Hees took a hard look at the balance sheet in mid-1990, and its spokesmen, quoted in the *Saturday Night* article, uttered the ultimate euphemism about Canadian publishing: "It became evident after we saw those numbers that it really was a very difficult business."

After a misguided attempt to improve L&OD's cash flow by withholding authors' royalties, which provoked an outraged letter from John Irving to Peter Bronfman, Hees put the publishing house up for sale. At least four serious offers emerged during 1990: from Penguin Canada, Stoddart Publishing, Key Porter Books, and Lester and Dennys themselves, in concert with private investors. Penguin's offer went nowhere since its international CEO, Peter Mayer, was unwilling to accept a 49 percent position in a joint venture, as required by federal ownership regulations. The other three offers all had the disadvantage, from Hees's point of view, of leaving it to cover the $1.3-million bank debt. Not that the conglomerate couldn't have afforded it. As Dennys told Peter Bronfman in a last-ditch personal appeal, the paintings on his wall were worth more than the cost of letting L&OD go.

If the demise of Clarke, Irwin had been unnecessary, Hees's execution of L&OD in early 1991 was unforgivable. Lester was understandably furious when Hees paid less than 100 cents on the dollar to some creditors, particularly printers (although not to authors, interestingly). The cost of settling the debts in full would have been equivalent to the conglomerate's rounding up its petty cash. But legally, Hees didn't have to accept the responsibility; L&OD was separately incorporated. Once again, the attempted marriage of book publishing and corporate Canada ended in divorce.

As in any divorce, there were assets to dispose of, which in L&OD's case were attractive. Hees sold the contracts and inventory to Key Porter, which had been a 10 percent partner in L&OD, pre-Ondaatje. Anna Porter offered Lester and Dennys an opportunity to renew their partnership in alliance with her. Lester said yes, Dennys no.

Doubting that her high-end literary publishing would make a comfortable fit with the more pragmatic and commercial Key Porter culture, Dennys decided to seek backers for an imprint of her own. Even when Sonny Mehta, the head of Knopf in New York, invited her to set up a Canadian branch, Dennys replied that she wanted to take a shot at independence. She drew up a business plan and spoke with possible investors, including Avie Bennett, who offered her a position as M&S rights director; but nothing else materialized. The economy was in recession again, the recently imposed goods and services tax was chilling domestic book sales, and a publishing start-up didn't look like the season's best idea. When Mehta came calling again, Dennys found his offer "irresistible, especially after I'd done what I could. There was no Canadian publisher making that call, so it was wonderful. Sonny was saying, 'Do what you've been doing for the last ten years, but do it with us.'"

Mehta knew he was getting one of the finest literary publishers in Canada. And since Knopf was wholly owned by Random House, there was no problem with federal foreign investment rules; Dennys would simply be heading up a new imprint within an existing subsidiary. The only drawback was that she couldn't imagine moving to Mississauga, the sprawling suburb west of Toronto where Random House of Canada was located: "I said, 'I just have to be downtown. This is how I live.' So I ran Knopf Canada out of my apartment, which isn't all that big, until Random House got a downtown office a year later. It was one other person and I, then two others and I. Literally with my husband putting on his socks in the next room."

With access to Random House of Canada's marketing power, along with bigger editorial and advertising budgets than she'd ever known, Dennys was able to spread her wings as a publisher. Since 1991 she's directed one of the strongest and most critically successful trade lists in Canada, headlined by her "New Faces of Fiction" program.

Lester, meanwhile, pursued a career path that would have its occasional crescendos before subsiding into a sustained diminuendo. He became an equal partner with Key Porter in a new company, Lester Publishing, which allowed him too to continue doing what he'd done so well: building a quality non-fiction list, starting with works-in-progress from L&OD. In 1992 Lester produced the award-winning *The Story of Canada*, a children's version of L&OD's *Illustrated History of Canada*, with text by Janet Lunn and Christopher Moore; Lester considered it the most successful book he'd ever published, with sales of over 100,000 copies. Lester's children's program, edited by Kathy Lowinger, published the popular *Beethoven Lives Upstairs* and two Governor General's Award–winning young adult novels by Julie Johnston. Lester also published *The Will to Win*, the first instalment in *Chrétien*, a projected two-volume biography of Prime Minister Jean Chrétien by Lawrence Martin.

Despite those successes, the Lester imprint was plagued, as L&OD had been, by financial and partnership problems. In 1995 the right-wing Conservative government of Mike Harris cancelled Ontario's long-standing loan guarantee program: a body blow to the publishing industry. Termination of Lester Publishing's bank guarantee compounded the company's difficulties, exacerbating differences between Lester and Porter. In 1996, five years after beginning the firm, Lester moved on.

Following a year's sabbatical, Lester started his third publishing venture. Some may have considered this the ultimate act of masochism, but he saw it as a case of publishing running through his veins: "It's what I know how to do. And what I love to do. What really got me going again was a number of friends saying, 'We think you should go back into publishing. We'd be willing to support you.'"

With fourteen investors backing him, Lester returned to the trade with Malcolm Lester Books: a small, select list specializing in history, biography, and Judaica. It was, Lester admitted, the worst of times to begin a publishing house. The recently created Chapters chain was increasingly monopolizing the retail book market and would soon make life hell for publishers. But despite the difficulties, Lester persevered, ruefully recalling Jack McClelland's rake analogy and replacing it with his own: "I feel like Sisyphus rolling the stone up the hill. Never quite get it over the top. Just keep rolling it up and rolling it up."

In 2001 Malcolm Lester Books suspended operations.

Mel Hurtig was as stubborn and dedicated as Lester, and no more likely
to quit when he was ahead. His stunning critical and financial success with
the first edition of *The Canadian Encyclopedia* in 1985 had led his fellow
publisher Ron Besse, owner of Gage and Macmillan, to offer Hurtig
$3 million for his company and a commitment to keep *The Canadian
Encyclopedia* updated in future editions. "Anyone with any brains would
have accepted," Hurtig wrote in his memoirs. "With $2 million [in profit]
already, I could retire [he was fifty-four], write, paint, hike, golf, and above
all devote more time and money to the Council of Canadians."

Instead Hurtig embarked on the four-volume second edition. Retailers
pre-ordered about 80,000 sets, or nearly three-quarters of the 113,000-
copy printing. The launch party took place in September 1988 at Toronto's
historic St. Lawrence Hall, with servers dressed as Sir John A. Macdonald,
Louis Riel, Barbara Ann Scott, and other figures from Canada's past. The
next morning, Coles bookstores greeted the encyclopedia's arrival by
slashing the publisher's suggested retail price from $225 to $99. The rival
W.H. Smith chain immediately followed suit.

Although the price war appeared a bonanza for consumers, independent booksellers felt sideswiped. Since they received smaller discounts on
their smaller orders, starting at 40 percent off the retail price, they would
have lost too much money if they'd tried to match the chains' price. The
chains' buying power qualified them to receive a discount allowing them
to approach break-even at $99, while diverting customers by the thousands
into their stores.

Angry independent booksellers, who then represented about 60 percent of English Canada's retail market, began returning their sets to Hurtig
for credit and blaming him for the situation. Some faulted him for offering
the differential discount, even though it had long been standard practice
in the trade. An Ottawa independent, Food for Thought Books, hung a sign
in its window headlined "Don't Buy This Book," telling customers they
should purchase the encyclopedia from a nearby W.H. Smith outlet
and urging them to phone Hurtig's toll-free number to complain. The
Canadian Booksellers Association called on its members to react reasonably; it reminded them that the debacle was damaging Hurtig's company
even more than theirs.

Legally, Hurtig couldn't prevent the chains' price-cutting, any more than Jack McClelland could when Coles and W.H. Smith had heavily discounted bestsellers by Pierre Berton and Peter Newman in the 1970s. The federal Competition Act, after all, actively encourages price competition. But as Joanne Thibeault, an independent Winnipeg bookseller, said, the behaviour of Coles and Smiths was "not illegal, but immoral."

At the end of 1988, some 23,000 sets of the second edition remained unsold, representing over $2 million in lost revenue for Hurtig. And yet reviews were again glowing: the *Globe and Mail* considered the new edition "superior to its predecessor"; *The Canadian Library Journal* and *The American Review of Canadian Studies* both called it "a remarkable achievement." Although Hurtig was still able to show a profit of $750,000, the seeds had been sown for an altogether surprising downfall.

Hurtig's original motive in publishing *The Canadian Encyclopedia* had been to provide high school students with a deeper knowledge of their country. Now he chose to persevere with a project equally close to his heart. With his encyclopedia staff still in place, he announced a children's version, *The Junior Encyclopedia of Canada*, to be published in fall 1990.

The *Junior* was planned not as a dumbed-down version of the existing text but as a brand new work. Articles and illustrations were carefully selected for young readers. Hurtig, who saw the children's encyclopedia as a major step towards a "national school curriculum," had a thousand articles classroom-tested to ensure they were curriculum-suitable. The federal government agreed to a special grant of $950,000 from the Department of Communications, provided Hurtig could locate a matching grant, and he came up with a similar amount from the Charles Bronfman family's CRB Foundation. Hurtig Publishers itself would invest $3 million, with the remaining $7 million to come as a bank loan.

Encyclopaedia Britannica officials were so impressed by Hurtig's sample pages that they offered to buy exclusive marketing rights to the *Junior Encyclopedia*, which they estimated would outsell the adult version. Accepting Britannica's offer would have eliminated Hurtig's financial risk and guaranteed him a healthy profit. But once again he elected to proceed independently. As if in response to that act of hubris, or perhaps because he had transgressed the edict that provincial jurisdiction over education is forever sacred, the gods now punished Mel Hurtig.

Rather than provoke another ruinous retail price war, Hurtig decided to sell the *Junior* directly to families, schools, and libraries. He devised a carefully orchestrated advertising and promotion campaign, supported by a $3-million marketing budget. The best Hurtig would warily offer his former confreres in bookselling was a commission on any orders they generated and passed on for fulfillment; to encourage their participation, he offered free floor displays and sample sets for customer browsing.

The centrepiece of Hurtig's marketing campaign was a mass mailing featuring a promotional brochure, a pre-publication discount offer, and a response card; enthusiastic letters were enclosed from the publisher and the editor, along with encomiums from famous Canadians. Hurtig used the services of a savvy Toronto marketing firm, which based the campaign on the results of preliminary test mailings. Probably no Canadian book publisher had ever resorted so thoroughly to market research.

The response was bitterly disappointing. By pub date, a mere 10,000 sets of the *Junior Encyclopedia* had been ordered. Only 35,000 would ultimately be sold: a high figure for a conventional title, but far from enough to pay the bank and other creditors on such a costly project. After all Hurtig's success, he faced the appalling prospect of bankruptcy.

From late 1990 until spring 1991, with increasing desperation, Hurtig tried all reasonable measures to save his company. He cut back on overheads. He cancelled future titles and laid off employees. He turned to potential sources of support in both the private and the public sectors, seeking short-term assistance from the governments of Ontario and Alberta; both turned him down. Influential supporters, such as Bob Blair of Nova Corporation and the *Globe and Mail*'s publisher, Roy Megarry, intervened with the bank to buy him time. But in the end, as Hurtig told *Quill & Quire*, "We either have to sell the company, come up with new equity investors, or rob a bank."

The last option would have held the most appeal, given Hurtig's distaste for bankers. But like Jack McClelland, whom he'd admired as a publisher and surpassed as a businessman, Hurtig finally sold his company to Avie Bennett. A Maecenas with the courage of his convictions and the money to back them up, Bennett committed his firm to keeping *The Canadian Encyclopedia* not only updated but renewed in electronic form. At a Toronto news conference in May 1991, when he and Hurtig announced the folding of Hurtig Publishers and its backlist into McClelland & Stewart, the respect between the two men was evident. "It must be a perfect deal," Hurtig managed to joke, "because Avie thinks he didn't pay enough, and I think he paid too much."

Later that year, M&S issued the first CD-ROM version of the encyclopedia. Over the next decade, the CD-ROM was updated each year by James Marsh and his Edmonton-based team of researchers, resulting in cumulative sales of over 250,000 copies: a singular accomplishment, particularly since American CD-ROM encyclopedias were being bundled free with computer sales. A French-language adaptation was funded by the Department of Canadian Heritage. In 2000, using new technology to subsidize the old, M&S adapted the electronic version back into print form and published a mammoth unabridged edition in one volume; containing 2,640 pages and over four million words, it was the largest single book ever published in Canada. Later in 2000, under the auspices of the Historica Foundation, all 26,000 articles were made accessible on-line. Bennett had kept faith with Hurtig's dream that the encyclopedia must have an ongoing place in Canadian life.

Although losing his company was painful, Hurtig had always done exactly what he wanted, and he'd continue to do so. Immediately following the sale, he signed a contract with Jack Stoddart Jr., another publisher who had been interested in buying his firm, to write his first book: a thoroughly documented, uncompromising attack on free trade, the business establishment, and the Mulroney government. *The Betrayal of Canada* was published in fall 1991, mere months after Hurtig's exit from publishing. It topped bestseller lists all the way into early 1992 and sold nearly 50,000 copies. It was a book that, written by someone else, Hurtig would have loved to publish. If publishing well is the best revenge, writing well is even better.

Ron Besse is a rarity: someone who not only has made money in Canadian publishing but flies his own airplane. A player in some of the industry's most critical deals, Besse has been key to the fate of three of Canada's oldest publishers, Ryerson, Gage, and Macmillan. And yet he hardly seemed predestined to be a book publisher. Growing up in the small town of Stayner, Ontario, Besse moved to Toronto to take a business program at Ryerson Polytechnical Institute, planning a career in sales. Every other kind of professional has taken a shot at being a Canadian publisher, from ministers, poets, and professors to bulldozer operators and astrophysicists; perhaps it was a salesman's turn.

Graduating in 1960, Besse was recruited on campus by the Canadian branch of McGraw-Hill, one of the world's largest educational, scientific, and professional publishers. Every fall he travelled to the Atlantic provinces, and in the winter and spring to the west. He travelled by air, at a time when most other publishers' reps were still taking the train. McGraw-Hill was expanding rapidly in Canada, relocating to a new facility in Scarborough, at the eastern edge of Toronto, and before long Besse was promoted to sales manager for the territory from Yonge Street to the West Coast. After two more years, he was general manager for national school operations, kindergarten through high school.

In 1966 McGraw-Hill opened a Quebec branch, and Besse, although not bilingual, was sent to Montreal to manage it. He liked the Québécois, found the Quiet Revolution stimulating, and had the thick skin necessary to withstand attacks from *indépendantistes* objecting to an American company publishing for Quebec schools and colleges. "My challenge to them was: if we weren't doing it right, help us get it right. We tried to correct the problems. And by never being defensive or fighting back, we eventually became quite successful."

Besse returned to Toronto at thirty as McGraw's vice-president and general manager. In 1970, having been identified as a high flyer by the parent organization, he was transferred to Mexico City as managing director of the Mexican branch and editorial director for Latin America. For four years, Besse travelled throughout Central and South America, from Panama to Chile, arranging for publication of Spanish translations of McGraw-Hill's scientific and technical books. He accessed financing from American aid programs, obtaining assistance from trade officers at American embassies. Business grew so fast that Besse was given responsibility for starting McGraw-Hill's branches in Spain and Portugal.

A year before he returned home for good, Besse flew to Toronto for a weekend meeting with John Gray and Hugh Kane. They wined and dined the thirty-four-year-old, interviewing him for the position of president of Macmillan. Gray was heading into retirement, and Kane clearly wasn't being tapped to succeed him; they felt that Besse, with his international publishing experience, would be preferable to some Maclean-Hunter apparatchik who might be imposed on the firm. Besse was tempted but immediately saw the problems inherent in a book publisher being owned by a magazine publisher. And although he elected to stay with McGraw-Hill, the Macmillan offer would play a part in his future.

When Besse returned to Toronto in 1974, he leapfrogged over more senior colleagues to become McGraw-Hill's president in Canada. The firm had a different name now: McGraw-Hill Ryerson. Four years earlier, Besse had played a role in the takeover of English Canada's oldest publishing house. Between his stints in Quebec and Latin America, he'd teamed up with William Darnell, McGraw-Hill's veteran editorial director, to evaluate the Ryerson backlist; they'd gone into the ornate Ryerson building on Queen Street (now home to City-TV) and recorded each title's five-year sales history, projecting sales forward on a three-to-five-year forecast. In the process, Besse had absorbed some valuable lessons. One was that a publisher shouldn't also be a printer: Ryerson's printing losses were obliterating its publishing profits. Another was "Buy assets, not shares": as a company, the Ryerson Press wasn't worth much to anybody, not even the United Church, which had owned it for 141 years; but as intellectual property, its backlist and contracts were golden to McGraw-Hill.

"What we learned," reflected Besse, "was that here you had a very successful book publishing operation in both trade and education. It also had an unbelievable brand name in Ryerson, which is why we eventually renamed our company. Ryerson was rich in wonderful products like the Lucy Maud Montgomery, the Alice Munro, all kinds. And it really gave McGraw-Hill in Canada a tremendous boost to bring that product in. But to make it profitable, we had to take it out of their culture and put it into ours."

By the time Besse left MHR in 1976, he'd honed an ability to see value where it was invisible to others, a crucial talent in a takeover artist. And he'd begun to think about applying that talent for his own benefit: "I was convinced that if I could own my own publishing company, I could run it as well as McGraw-Hill had taught me to run theirs."

Besse was uncomfortable knowing there was then little honour for a subsidiary publisher in his homeland: "I always felt I was somehow walking around wrapped in the Stars and Stripes." He remembered an industry meeting where disparaging comments were made about foreign-controlled publishers. "I got up in that meeting and said, 'I'm sitting here as a Canadian and I grew up in Stayner and went to Ryerson and work in Canada. I happen to be employed by an American publisher. But I'm sitting here today feeling like a second-class citizen, listening to you people talk. Do you have no sense of how you make a Canadian feel? Like a traitor.'"

Besse was ready to put his money where his mouth was, except that he didn't have much money. Instead he'd persistently leverage other people's. In 1976 he became president and CEO of Consolidated Graphics, a Canadian printing and packaging conglomerate that was experiencing difficulties. Besse was hired by the aging majority owner, Miller Alloway, to turn the company around; if a book publishing operation became available, they'd consider buying it. Within a year, Besse was in negotiation for Gage Educational Publishing (later Gage Learning Corporation).

Scott Foresman, the Chicago-based educational publisher that had acquired Gage seven years earlier, was open to selling. The American firm liked the idea of an experienced publisher like Besse being in charge of marketing its books in Canada. Orchestrating the purchase of Gage for Consolidated Graphics, Besse repatriated the venerable house.

Alloway had sold 20 percent of Consolidated to Besse, but the two men clashed. Displeased with Besse's headstrong approach, the owner fired him from Consolidated *and* from Gage, which Besse was managing. Gage was Besse's real interest; he had no difficulty persuading Scott Foresman's CEO, Gordon Hjalmarson, that the American company's Canadian business was in jeopardy without himself at the helm.

Scott Foresman made a deal with Besse. It threatened legal action against Consolidated for not protecting its interests as a minority shareholder, then lent Besse the money to buy a majority interest in Gage. By 1978 Besse had control, at least on paper. He proceeded to run Gage so profitably that he paid back the loan out of earnings within five years and acquired more of Scott Foresman's shares, to the point of owning all but 22 percent of the company. In 1989, when Scott Foresman was swallowed by HarperCollins in the States, he acquired the rest.

Soon after pulling off that coup, Besse engineered another. He received a phone call in 1980 from the chairman of Maclean-Hunter, Donald Campbell. Maclean-Hunter had concluded that Macmillan was too small to be profitable, Campbell said (revenues were then about $7 million), and he wanted to bulk it up by merging it with another publisher. Campbell proposed buying Gage, integrating it with Macmillan, and installing Besse as a minority partner to run the merged operation.

Besse responded, "Don, I'd be interested in buying Macmillan."

Within a month, the deal was done, although not without controversy – so much of it, you'd have thought Besse had engineered another foreign takeover. Various stakeholders, including the Writers' Union of Canada, the Association of Canadian Publishers, and even the Canada Council, publicly voiced concerns about the cultural implications of Besse's acquisition. Mistrust of Besse was exacerbated by his fondness for the term "profit centre." Jim Lorimer attacked the deal in *Quill & Quire*, and both the *Globe and Mail* and the *Toronto Star* editorialized that, given Macmillan's central importance to Canadian literature, more was at stake than a private business transaction.

At issue was the future of Macmillan's illustrious trade list. Bridging the older generation of Callaghan, MacLennan, Creighton, Davies, and Gallant, and the younger one of Richard Wright, Jack Hodgins, Guy Vanderhaeghe, Roy MacGregor, and Dennis Lee, the Macmillan list rivalled the M&S program in significance if not size. Would Besse merely strip all the el-hi and college business out of Macmillan to strengthen Gage? Would he neglect the trade list, leaving it to die? Or sell it off piecemeal to the highest bidder? But Besse was too smart to ignore the assets in Macmillan's trade list, or the potential in future books from the authors under contract. He wanted to own Macmillan for much the same reasons he'd urged McGraw-Hill to buy Ryerson a decade earlier. What's more, his critics didn't know he'd been aware of Macmillan's potential since 1973, when he'd been asked to run it.

In dealing for Macmillan, Besse followed his two takeover maxims: buy assets, not shares, and use the other guy's money. He didn't buy the company, which had become integrated as a division of Maclean-Hunter, since he had no interest in assuming its liabilities: "I saw a lot of Maclean-Hunter overheads being put onto Macmillan. They were moving overheads around and making the company look bad." Instead Besse cherry-picked the Macmillan backlist, as his critics had warned he would, shunning many titles he didn't consider worth owning. Second, he didn't pay cash. Maclean-Hunter financed the deal, worth a reported $3 million, by taking Gage shares, which Besse would buy back out of earnings. And just as he'd foreseen, the merged Gage-Macmillan operation, called Canada Publishing Corporation, was extremely profitable.

While the controversy was still at its peak, the Liberal minister of communications, Francis Fox, called Besse to Ottawa to discuss the uproar and the demands that Fox 'do something. Besse explained to Fox that everyone was worried about the backlist; he admitted he was prepared to buy the whole thing if he could have the less desirable titles for a cent a copy. Fox's publishing official, Georges Laberge, phoned Cam Fellman, a Maclean-Hunter executive who had taken over responsibility for Macmillan from the well-liked Bill Baker, and asked Fellman if he'd agree to Besse's offer. Fellman said yes. With that settled, Fox, Besse, and Laberge went on to enjoy a good lunch, accompanied by a fine wine.

On the other question of whether Besse would continue Macmillan's original trade program, public pressure had an impact. Although his natural inclination was to rationalize operations and maximize profits, Besse didn't believe in antagonizing people unnecessarily. To answer his critics, and because it never hurts to get your company's name in the news, Besse held a media conference in Toronto to reveal his intentions. Accompanying him was Doug Gibson, Macmillan's trade editorial director since 1974, now seen as a symbolic link to the "old" Macmillan. "Maybe in hindsight, I needed to see the response to the takeover," Besse conceded before the crowded room. He announced that, after two weeks of discussion, he'd appointed Gibson publisher of the trade list. Gibson stepped up to the mike and added, "I will say unreservedly to all authors, 'If you felt at home at the old Macmillan, you'll feel at home at the new Macmillan.'"

Instead of merging the trade program with Gage's trade division at his Scarborough headquarters, Besse would re-establish Macmillan as a distinct imprint in a separate office downtown: a significant symbol to some Macmillan authors, who weren't keen on visiting the Gage building on Commander Boulevard. Gage's trade editor, Colleen Dimson, would move to Macmillan. The changes succeeded in selling the takeover to skeptical writers, publishers, and editorialists. In today's era of deregulation and privatization, it will seem extraordinary that the collectivity believed it had a right to call Besse to account.

Besse retained about thirty of Macmillan's ninety employees. As its operations were gradually integrated with Gage's, more and more staff moved out of 70 Bond Street, until only the trade division was left. Jan Walter, who had arrived two years earlier from Edmonton, remembered the eerie sensation of huddling with her colleagues on the top floor of the historic building. The lower floors were vacant, the furniture had been auctioned off, the elevator had stopped. When the day arrived for the trade personnel to depart for their new offices on Front Street, a ceremony was held to mourn the passing of an era. Staff, authors, and well-wishers gathered to bid farewell to the building, surrounding the front steps that John Gray had first bounded up fifty years earlier. Gibson made a speech, shouting to be heard above a passing truck, and a piper skirled a last lament.

Besse would do other publishing deals, but none so dramatic. He'd buy a music publisher, G.V. Thompson, an American business publisher, Forkner, and again insert himself where angels feared to tread, in Quebec. He built the distributor and publisher Diffulivre out of the Montreal subsidiary of the French firm Bordas – the second foreign-owned publisher he'd patriated in his career – and hired the knowledgeable Georges Laberge away from the government to become his minority partner. Besse regarded the Quebec book market, with its high retail prices, healthy profit margins, and relative lack of foreign competition, as an excellent place to make money.

Besse operated Gage profitably too. His target for every "profit centre" was 20 percent before taxes, with the exception of trade, where he allowed he'd accept 5 percent. Gage proved more able than Clarke, Irwin at adapting to the changes in educational publishing, and Macmillan's educational list made a handsome contribution to Gage's earnings. As Macmillan titles were reprinted, Besse placed the Gage imprint on them, distressing Gladys Neale, who felt their parentage had been erased.

Before Doug Gibson's departure for M&S in 1986, Besse moved Macmillan into a building he'd purchased on midtown Birch Avenue and began spending more time there, personally managing the company and reassessing its viability. The essential unprofitability of Canadian trade publishing, especially in fiction, hit home when he examined sales of *What's Bred in the Bone*, the second volume in Robertson Davies's Cornish Trilogy. The first hardcover printing of 30,000 had sold out soon after publication in fall 1985, and the company had printed another 7,500 to fill new orders; eventually, however, it received 15,000 as returns. If that was the price of publishing the country's leading novelist, Besse decided, he'd better get out of fiction altogether.

"I really don't like to be in a business that doesn't make a profit," he said years later. "And yet here we had some of the best authors. So I did a lot of business analysis of trade publishing, and I drew the conclusion that it was almost impossible to build a profitable business around fiction."

From then on, under a succession of publishers beginning with the former M&S president Linda McKnight, Macmillan's trade list became gradually narrower, its quality more diluted. By the early 1990s, a once-great literary imprint was producing almost exclusively cookbooks, sports books, business books, and self-help books. But the trade seemed to have forgotten how worried it had been about the fate of Macmillan. It had other worries now.

As a newcomer to the industry in 1985, Avie Bennett soon realized there was no magic solution to becoming a successful publisher. The trade demanded creativity, hard work, and attention to detail, all things he was good at. Drawn to the challenge, he began living and breathing M&S,

putting in long days at the office with his staff. People skills and personal connections were essential too, and at first the shy, somewhat socially awkward Bennett thought he could annex those by retaining Jack McClelland. When that didn't work out, he brought in Adrienne Clarkson, after the former CBC Television host and producer had completed a stint as Ontario's first official representative in Paris. Bennett felt Clarkson's intelligence, knowledge of Canadian society, and abundant poise and charm would make her a great asset as publisher of M&S; she'd also published two novels with the firm.

But Clarkson had no more hands-on experience of the profession than Bennett. One former M&S staffer remembered the future governor general's first meeting with the editorial staff in 1987: "She sat us down in the boardroom," he recalled, "and gave us a flag-waving pep talk about the cultural importance of M&S. Some of us had been there for years and didn't need to be lectured. She had no interest in listening, and it caught up with her pretty fast." Clarkson and Bennett also made the tactical error of letting key employees go, such as Jan Walter and the vice-president of sales and marketing, Peter Waldock, who became a successful book wholesaler. Clarkson herself was gone the next year.

Bennett then promoted Doug Gibson to the post of publisher. Early in 1986, Gibson had been Bennett's first major hire, scooped from Macmillan to begin a small, select trade list under the Douglas Gibson Books imprint. It was the first time a Canadian editor had been given a personal imprint within a larger firm. By acquiring Gibson, Bennett would also acquire many of the extraordinary fiction writers with whom Gibson had worked at Macmillan. Robertson Davies, Alice Munro, Mavis Gallant, W.O. Mitchell, Jack Hodgins, and Guy Vanderhaeghe were among those who gradually followed their editor to M&S, and the imprint's first title was Munro's *The Progress of Love*. The transplanted authors added lustre to M&S's already star-studded list and buoyed its financial performance.

Once appointed publisher, Gibson oversaw the company's entire trade list while continuing to edit his own authors under his imprint. The overall program of seventy to eighty new titles a year was handled by a seasoned editorial staff, pre-eminent among them the esteemed fiction editor Ellen

Seligman, whose authors have included Margaret Atwood, Michael Ondaatje, Jane Urquhart, Rohinton Mistry, and Anne Michaels.

Bennett hired the publishing veteran Bill Hushion as vice-president of sales and marketing; Hushion rebuilt the company's agency list by acquiring numerous British and American lines as ballast against the uncertainty of original publishing. Also coming on board was Chris Keen, with a fund of retail experience from the venerable Britnell's bookstore. Bennett urged his executives to be more adventurous in experimenting with business approaches outside publishing convention, but he also respected their judgment. At editorial board meetings, his vote was one of five or six. In customarily blunt style, he once told an M&S author, "I was against publishing your book, but I got outvoted by my staff."

Bennett acquired another publishing house when May Cutler put Tundra Books up for sale. He felt M&S needed an outstanding children's program, and although Cutler's expectations of Tundra's value were high, she and Bennett managed to come to terms late in 1995. Bennett moved the company from Montreal the next year, keeping Tundra's name intact and bringing its public relations and rights manager, Catherine Mitchell, to Toronto. He also hired the children's editor Kathy Lowinger, formerly with Lester Publishing, to ensure the continuing vitality of the list. Tundra has stayed at the forefront of Canadian children's publishing, producing books of quality and marketing them with vigour.

At M&S, Bennett emphasized quality. His personal pride made him determined to enhance the company's standing in Canadian culture. Like his predecessor, he was interested primarily in trade publishing, and he sold off M&S's college list to Oxford in 1996. What really excited him was publishing prestigious, high-profile titles such as the two-volume political epic by Christina McCall and Stephen Clarkson, *Trudeau and Our Times*, and Trudeau's own *Memoirs*. Bennett's readiness to continue plowing his own cash into M&S meant the company could travel first class; it was understood in the trade that he covered annual operating losses of $1 to $2 million, particularly in the early years. Bennett even generously acknowledged in *Quill & Quire* that, in a tough profession, Jack McClelland had been a better businessman than everyone had thought.

 GREY STONE
BOOKS

KEY PORTER BOOKS

FITZHENRY & WHITESIDE | GREYSTONE BOOKS

KEY PORTER BOOKS

STODDART PUBLISHING | MACFARLANE WALTER & ROSS

GENERAL PUBLISHING

14

NET BENEFIT

The Government of Canada has just, for the first time,
adopted a clear and precise policy on the question of
foreign investment in the critical sector of book publishing
and distribution ... The government acknowledges that
publishing, like broadcasting and the press, is an element
essential to our identity and our cultural sovereignty.

Marcel Masse, minister of communications (July 1985)

During the 1991 recession, Canadian publishing re-entered crisis mode. In addition to Lester & Orpen Dennys and Hurtig, two more publishers ceased operation. An admired non-fiction publisher in Toronto, Summerhill Books, succumbed following the death in the previous year of its founder, Gordon Montador. And the largest remaining publisher in the Prairies, Western Producer Prairie Books of Saskatoon, announced it was putting its assets on the block. Worsening the industry's chronic fragility were the harsh economic downturn and the newly imposed goods and services tax, both biting deep into purchases by consumers, libraries, schools, and universities, and creating an estimated drop in book sales of up to 30 percent. The industry was demoralized. Unless decisive action were taken, further business failures seemed inevitable.

In the increasingly anxious climate, the Association of Canadian Publishers looked to the only federal politician who seemed to care about publishing, indeed about Canadian culture in general: the tough-minded minister of communications, Marcel Masse. A handsome, exceptionally intense man, Masse was an unusual figure in Prime Minister Brian Mulroney's Conservative cabinet. He was a Quebec nationalist whose English was barely comprehensible, an ambitious activist who seemed angry all the time – at the Americans, at his fellow ministers, at his own bureaucrats; yet his commitment to Canada's broader cultural interests was genuine. While in office, he took his ministerial responsibilities with deep seriousness and acted with greater concern for the survival of English-Canadian culture than most English Canadians. His political courage would embroil him in conflict with his own government.

Masse believed it was only "normal," by which he meant "healthy," for a sovereign state to enjoy a vigorous cultural life of its own. To do so, the nation must exercise control not only over the industries that originate cultural products but over the markets for those products. When Masse looked at Canada's cultural industries – book and magazine publishing, film, sound recording, broadcasting – he saw an abnormal situation everywhere but in broadcasting. There, at least, strong structural measures had been in place for many years, and regulation had carved out space for Canadian content. That space was enforced by a body whose powers were legally binding, the Canadian Radio-television and Telecommunications Commission, and reinforced (as in the newspaper industry) by stringent Canadian ownership requirements. But in less regulated cultural industries, the market was thoroughly dominated by American distribution networks and products; and although public investment had increased production of Canadian content, it had failed to solve the problem of market access. It was a colonial situation, and Masse didn't like it.

Masse saw his job as using the state to patriate the cultural industries. In that respect, he resembled the French culture ministers André Malraux and Jack Lang, or a Red Tory of the kind who'd built the CPR or written *Lament for a Nation*. Masse's position set him squarely against the grain of his own government's Thatcherite, free market ideology of deregulation and privatization. In 1986 he commissioned a public discussion paper, *Vital Links: Canadian Cultural Industries*; he liked to call it "my answer to Murphy," referring to the chief American negotiator in the Canada-U.S. free trade talks, Peter Murphy.

Masse knew his ideas were unpopular with his cabinet colleagues, especially Finance Minister Michael Wilson and the prime minister, who were fixated on signing a free trade agreement with the States. So Masse worked within their agenda. He took the line that, in order to sell its trade goals to Canadians, the government had to address the public's fears about losing economic and political sovereignty. The most effective way to do that, he argued, was to strengthen Canada's cultural identity. Masse's strategy succeeded for a time in pushing some tough measures through cabinet. Ultimately the most contentious was a structural measure to strengthen Canadian control of book publishing: the so-called Baie-Comeau policy.

Masse's brainchild was an extension of ownership and investment regulations adopted in 1974 by the Trudeau government. Secretary of State Hugh Faulkner's previously quoted assertion that "Canadian books and magazines are too important to the cultural and intellectual life of this country to be allowed to come completely under foreign control, however sympathetic and benign," had been enforced, however fitfully, by the Foreign Investment Review Agency. In addition to prohibiting foreign takeovers of Canadian-owned publishers and disallowing start-ups by foreign-controlled firms, the government had instructed FIRA to review "indirect acquisitions": those in which a foreign-controlled publishing subsidiary in Canada changes hands through a takeover outside the country. Each time an indirect takeover occurred, FIRA was to assess the transaction's impact in cultural and economic terms. The transaction would be approved only if deemed "of net benefit" to Canada.

The two most visible outcomes of the Liberal policy occurred soon after its adoption. In 1976 the American resource conglomerate Gulf + Western (later Paramount, later still Viacom) bought the New York publisher Simon & Schuster, including its paperback arm, Pocket Books. FIRA rejected the Canadian aspect of the takeover, since the new owners were planning to switch Simon & Schuster's lucrative Canadian business from General Publishing, under Jack Stoddart Sr., to their wholly owned asset, Pocket Books of Canada. Such a move would have represented a major loss of revenue for General. As a result of FIRA's ruling, General was able to retain the Simon & Schuster agency *and* acquire Pocket Books of Canada, enlarging its own operations as well as the market share under Canadian control. The following year saw the policy's other major result: the new owners of Bantam Books in the United States were permitted to complete the Canadian part of their takeover only after Bantam agreed to the partnership with Jack McClelland that created Seal Books, increasing the presence of Canadian-authored paperbacks in the mass market.

After the Mulroney government took over in 1984, FIRA was replaced by Investment Canada, whose mandate was to *encourage* foreign investment. And yet, amazingly, in July 1985, Marcel Masse persuaded his colleagues at a cabinet meeting in Baie-Comeau, Quebec, not merely to keep the Liberals' ownership rules for the book industry but to go much farther. Foreign investors would be welcome in book publishing, distribution, and retailing, the Baie-Comeau policy stated – but only in joint ventures, with Canadians holding majority control.

The policy's intended application was even bolder. Whenever an indirect takeover occurred, a majority interest in the subsidiary would have to be sold to Canadians within two years, at fair market value. In Masse's mind, the strategy would work like some cultural hydroelectric project, redirecting revenue flows from the most lucrative parts of the industry – educational publishing and agency distribution – into the hands of Canadian publishers.

If implemented, the Baie-Comeau policy would certainly have succeeded in strengthening Canadian-owned publishing dramatically. It would even have achieved Faulkner's stated goal of bringing the major segment of the industry under Canadian control. A wave of mergers and acquisitions rolled through international publishing from the mid-1980s through the 1990s, creating numerous opportunities to patriate large foreign-controlled subsidiaries. But whenever those opportunities occurred, the Mulroneyites deliberately fumbled the ball.

Their first chance to enact the policy arose immediately, since Gulf + Western was continuing to vacuum up publishers. Faced with the requirement of divesting itself of its latest acquisition, Prentice-Hall of Canada, G+W informed Canada's ambassador to the United States, Allan Gotlieb, that it would pursue a "scorched-earth response." The exact nature of the threat was never spelled out publicly, but it was enough for the government to beat a hasty and ignominious retreat. The Prentice-Hall transaction was grandfathered under Baie-Comeau, on the grounds that it predated adoption of the policy. The government then had no choice but to extend the same privilege to Pearson PLC, the British-based owner of Viking Penguin, which had just acquired Pitman PLC, owners of Copp Clark in Canada since 1963.

Only once, in fact, did the Mulroney government enforce its own policy. Again G+W was involved. Later in 1985, the conglomerate bought two educational publishers with Canadian branches, Ginn and General Learning Corporation. After combining the two companies, Paramount Communications, as the corporation was known by then, reluctantly complied with Baie-Comeau by going through the motions of issuing a prospectus for selling 51 percent of Ginn/GLC to Canadians. But the terms it demanded, such as a majority of directors on the board, were so unappealing that the offer, as the ACP declared, was "designed to fail." Despite keen interest in purchasing the company by Ron Besse of Gage, Robert Fitzhenry of Fitzhenry & Whiteside, and other Canadians, Paramount was uncooperative to the point of obstructiveness.

By the time the Mulroney cabinet took action on the Ginn/GLC case in 1989, four years had passed. By then the government had bound itself hand and foot with the Canada-U.S. Free Trade Agreement. Canada's negotiators had accepted the insertion of clause 1607, designed to compensate American investors for any assets "expropriated" under Canadian policy. The clause effectively required the Canadian government itself to purchase "at fair open market value" any American company divested under Baie-Comeau. This was interpreted as meaning international, not Canadian, market value. And so when Paramount disingenuously claimed there were no acceptable Canadian offers for Ginn/GLC, the government agreed to purchase – through the Canada Development Investment Corporation – 51 percent of the company at the inflated price of $10.3 million. Even then the CDIC didn't get effective control. Paramount insisted on retaining control over major operational decisions; and although the government vowed to resell the 51 percent to

Canadians as soon as possible, thus realizing the potential of Marcel Masse's strategy, the CDIC actually gave Paramount a veto over any sale.

Such absurd, conflicted conduct resulted from the fact that the minister who had formulated the Baie-Comeau policy lacked the authority to enforce it. That power belonged to Investment Canada, another arrangement that was designed to fail. The Department of Finance, horrified at the prospect of having to buy foreign-owned publishing subsidiaries whenever they changed hands, let Investment Canada know that it was unhappy about its exposure. Finance estimated that Baie-Comeau could cost the taxpayer up to $40 million a year over the next ten years. Subsequently all of Investment Canada's rulings fudged, obfuscated, or delayed enforcement of the policy.

Pearson, through Penguin Books, was allowed to take over the Canadian branch of New American Library in 1988. The following year, Rupert Murdoch's giant News International was allowed to take over William Collins and merge it with Harper & Row to create HarperCollins, even though the deal gutted the revenues of Harper's Canadian-owned agent, Fitzhenry & Whiteside, and deprived Gage of agency revenue from Scott Foresman, which HarperCollins had acquired. In neither case was any significant benefit obtained for Canada.

By 1990 the Baie-Comeau policy had become a bad joke, embarrassing proof of the government's hypocrisy in claiming culture had been kept "off the table" during the free trade talks. Masse had tried to get other strong measures adopted by cabinet: an investment bank to finance growth in the cultural industries through strategic investments, modelled on a similar agency in Quebec; a cultural investment review agency housed within the CRTC, with powers to enforce federal ownership regulations; a refundable investment tax credit for book publishers. Masse retained as a consultant Paul Audley, the former ACP executive director, to help him develop a policy rationale for the tax credit; it would have levelled the playing field with imported books by reducing Canadian publishers' high costs of development and marketing. All these measures were blocked, sooner or later, by Finance.

In fall 1990 the ACP engaged me to advocate its members' cause in Ottawa. Since leaving the *Toronto Star*, I'd been a Canada Council official, a policy adviser to the Federal Cultural Policy Review Committee co-chaired by Louis Applebaum and Jacques Hébert, and an Ottawa-based consultant – work that had included a stretch with Masse and his assistant deputy minister, Jeremy Kinsman, writing the cultural industries paper *Vital Links*. Subsequently Masse had commissioned a study from Price Waterhouse showing that the six largest Canadian-owned, English-language publishers had suffered aggregated losses of 3 to 6 percent of revenues in 1987, 1988, and 1989. The study documented the ACP's case that action to sustain the industry was urgently needed.

Early in 1991, I attended a meeting between Masse and representatives of five of the publishers in the Price Waterhouse study (the sixth was Lester & Orpen Dennys, by then defunct). Compared with the haughty yet ebullient minister I'd known a few years earlier, Masse looked shrunken and deflated, even depressed. He knew what bad shape some of the companies were in; he'd seen their numbers. During his years in the portfolio (out of which he'd been yanked twice, whenever he was becoming too effective), he'd done what he could to help them; but he held out little hope that the tax credit he'd been advocating would be implemented. "They don't care," he said of his anglophone cabinet colleagues with a disconsolate shrug. "They just don't care."

The companies represented at the meeting amounted to a roll call of the Canadian majors. Ron Besse, Jack E. Stoddart (son of the previous owner of General Publishing), Scott McIntyre, and Anna Porter were present in person; Avie Bennett was represented by Bill Hushion. Without their firms in a healthy state, the indigenous industry in English Canada would consist mainly of small to medium-sized publishers who lacked the resources to compete with the multinationals in our own market.

At its AGM in April 1991, the ACP membership set aside a proposed slate of twenty nominees and instead elected a small, seasoned executive to serve for twelve months with a single overriding mandate: to obtain a new commitment from Ottawa to strengthen Canadian-owned publishing. Members of the six-person "junta," as it became known, were Porter, McIntyre, Karl Siegler of Talon Books, Philip Cercone of McGill-Queen's

University Press, Louise Fleming of Ragweed Press, and Randy Morse of Reidmore Books, an Edmonton educational publisher. I was appointed interim director, with the job of coordinating the ACP's political campaign and keeping pressure on the government.

On the very day the ACP elected its new executive, Marcel Masse was replaced at Communications by Perrin Beatty, the former minister of national defence. Two days later, Beatty was on the phone to me and a couple of dozen other cultural lobbyists. The phone blitz succeeded in starting the new minister off on the right foot with the cultural community. But Beatty and his senior officials would see and hear a lot from us in the next twelve months, probably too much for their liking.

The senior departmental bureaucrat on the publishing file was Assistant Deputy Minister Paul Racine, a former Quebec journalist who seemed to fancy himself a *philosophe* in a pinstriped suit. Racine appeared to view publishers with a mixture of disdain and irritation; in meetings, he'd lean back in his chair, pyramid his fingertips, and close his eyes while others spoke, as if contemplating higher things. Racine's second-in-command was the director general for cultural industries, Adam Ostry. Barely over thirty at the time, Ostry was the son of the high-placed economist Sylvia Ostry and the department's first deputy minister, Bernard Ostry, who had moved on to head TVOntario. Wearing even sharper suits than his boss, the younger Ostry conducted himself on public occasions with uncivil arrogance for a civil servant; his style was frequently autocratic and at times confrontational, notably when he insulted senior publishing figures to their faces. Neither Racine nor Ostry appeared to have much use for Paul Audley, who, as Masse's special adviser on publishing, threatened their influence in the departmental hierarchy.

In that unpromising climate, the ACP team bent our efforts to helping Beatty achieve the tax credit that Masse and Audley had devised. We lobbied other departments, such as Industry and Foreign Affairs, seeking their support for the proposal; but we concentrated on Finance, where fiscal policy is made and resistance to the credit was greatest. We met with tax and social policy officials, with Finance Minister Michael Wilson's officials, with Deputy Minister of Finance Fred Gorbet. Over and over we argued the political case for supporting publishers, books, and authors, and we passed the department's responses back to the Department of Communications – which, we soon discovered, wasn't held in terribly high esteem by fellow bureaucrats.

At last we had an all-morning conclave between our council and the senior assistant deputy minister of finance, Ian Bennett, surrounded by half a dozen of his officials armed with laptops and calculators. For three hours, we listened to the departmental mantra that, in an era of tax reform, the tax system couldn't be used for cultural ends. By noon, it was clear that only one argument carried any weight with the Finance mandarins. Although the tax credit was definitely a dead duck, the department seemed seized by the damage being done to the book industry, and to the higher cause of literacy, by the goods and services tax. We heard unmistakable hints that Finance was prepared to entertain a substantial increase in direct funding to publishers to offset damage from the politically unpopular GST.

We rushed off to see Perrin Beatty, tracking him down in the corridors of the Centre Block. After question period, we rode with the minister and the discomfited Paul Racine on one of the little green buses that scoot around Parliament Hill trundling officials to their destinations. Hanging from the handstraps, we described the morning at Finance and assured Beatty and his ADM that the publishing industry would stop pushing for the tax credit if it received major funding to sustain it through the current crisis. Bringing his departmental program up from $8 million to $35 or $40 million, we thought, should do the job. Beatty seemed keen to work with us towards that objective.

Of course, Finance needed a quid pro quo. To obtain the new funding, publishers would have to forgo not only the tax credit but the benefits – purely theoretical, by that time – of the central provision of the Baie-Comeau policy: the divestiture requirement, and the resulting obligation to compensate American investors. According to the government's calculations, that could save up to $40 million right there.

And so, in January 1992, Perrin Beatty stood before television cameras at a crowded Toronto news conference to announce a major new package for book publishing. The centrepiece was a 300 percent increase in funding for the Book Publishing Industry Development Program, to a level of about $25 million a year over the next five years. Supplementing that, the $60-million program that subsidized postal rates for books would be replaced by the $25-million Publications Distribution Assistance Program, a move that would net a substantial savings for the taxpayer while more directly targeting assistance to both publishers and book-sellers for their distribution and marketing costs.

There was more. Beatty promised to address the age-old problem of buying around; he'd be proceeding with amendments to the Copyright Act to create a legal requirement that the book trade obtain imported titles from their authorized Canadian distributors. This was a measure long sought by the large, mostly foreign-owned firms in the Canadian Book Publishers' Council, through their hard-working executive director, Jacqueline Hushion; the ACP had no problem supporting it. In a new spirit of rapprochement, we'd backed their goal while receiving reciprocal support for the funding increase for Canadian-owned publishers.

Beatty also announced an end to the Baie-Comeau divestiture provisions and a return to the looser "net benefit" requirement for indirect takeovers. Moreover, net benefit should accrue, he said, not only to Canada but to the Canadian-controlled sector of the industry. The other ownership measures from the Trudeau era all remained in place. New foreign-controlled start-ups in publishing or bookselling were still prohibited, and direct foreign takeovers were still disallowed, although with one loophole we hadn't expected: a Canadian-owned company in dire financial straits could now sell to foreigners, provided it had first been offered to Canadians but had received no reasonable offers.

A few critics, some from within the association itself, attacked the ACP for selling out principle for a mess of pottage. But the government had con-sistently shown it had no stomach whatsoever for enforcing Baie-Comeau. If politics is the art of the possible, we'd extracted the best deal possible under the circumstances. We also had Perrin Beatty's commitment that we could negotiate the terms under which the new money would be spent. This too was a victory; it resulted, after many testy meetings in which Karl Siegler butted heads with Adam Ostry, in improving the funding formula in favour of smaller presses. Ron Besse's Canada Publishing and the other two large Canadian-owned publishers, Stoddart Publishing and M&S,

acknowledged that it was chiefly ACP lobbying that had achieved the new measures, and they left the CBPC to join our association.

As for Marcel Masse, who departed federal politics in 1993, he'd later write: "I tried, when I was in Ottawa, to fight for the things that I believed were important to a nation's self-worth. I often failed."

One member of the ACP junta, Anna Porter, possessed not only a glamorous public profile but serious political connections. Although Porter was conspicuously not a team player, her social and business contacts (including, ironically, Conrad Black) helped give the ACP an edge in Mulroney's Ottawa. When we were getting nowhere with Finance, Porter had played her insider card, arranging a Saturday meeting with the finance minister. Michael Wilson had once said that Canadian publishers suck and blow at the same time, but he still had to return Anna Porter's phone calls.

Porter was the only publisher to succeed, for a time, in obtaining leverage from the Baie-Comeau policy. It was another coup in what has seemed a charmed career. But Porter achieved her success with dogged perseverance and productive networking. She'd been Jack McClelland's first choice for M&S president when he kicked himself upstairs, but she'd known well enough not to accept the position, having run Seal Books for him – a job that had left her "bored witless." She wanted time to be with her baby daughter and write her mystery novels. And besides, she'd already started a publishing company.

By Porter's own account, the firm's origins were a haphazard process, a result of her friend Michael de Pencier's lending her an office in 1980 among the magazines housed at Key Publishers. She and de Pencier first produced a handsome art book by the Newfoundland painter Christopher Pratt. Following it with a collection of Allan Fotheringham's gossipy political journalism, they coined the imprint Key Porter Books: a fifty-fifty partnership, with a ready-made infrastructure in de Pencier's rabbit warren of a building deep in downtown Toronto.

De Pencier was a relatively silent partner; it was up to Porter to make the company fly. She had no stable of authors or backlog of works-in-progress to build on. She'd promised Jack McClelland she wouldn't raid

M&S, and it was a promise she kept, even when former authors came calling with manuscripts or book ideas. Porter made it easier for herself by announcing a no-fiction policy; that eliminated many authors, as well as protecting her from a risky side of the business. "After years of working for someone else," she remembered, "I was determined to build something that wasn't going to get into financial difficulties. I didn't want to have to go through the kinds of things that Jack went through."

When Clarke, Irwin went into receivership in 1983, the Fleet Books inventory came on the market, and Porter bought it, including numerous photographic titles on nature, furniture, and crafts that were an ideal fit with her plans to co-publish internationally. Porter acquired marketable authors such as the canoeing authority Bill Mason and the nature photographer Freeman Patterson. Even more important, she acquired Phyllis Bruce, who would remain her editor-in-chief for the next ten years and would be intrinsic to Key Porter's early success.

Originally an educational editor with Nelson and Copp Clark, Bruce had moved into trade books at Van Nostrand Reinhold and brought to Key Porter a wealth of experience and author contacts. Later she went to HarperCollins, where she has been widely regarded as a superb editor, one of a tiny elite with a personal imprint. But when she joined Key Porter in 1983, the company was shoehorned into a space shared with de Pencier's flagship magazine, *Toronto Life*. "Anna and I had to share an office with a bookcase in the middle," Bruce recalled. "She worked on one side of the bookcase and I worked on the other, without a door. So if I wanted to visit the washroom, and she was talking to an author, I'd have to emerge from behind the bookcase and step over this writer. It was very much a seat-of-your-pants kind of operation. It was chaotic but exhilarating. The staff went from four people to twenty-five while I was there."

An unlikely bestseller shot Key Porter to national recognition in 1985: the memoir of a washed-up politician. Jean Chrétien had lost the Liberal Party leadership to John Turner two years earlier and returned to private life. Chrétien's autobiography, *Straight from the Heart*, ghost-written by Ron Graham, rocked the trade by selling 120,000 copies in hardcover before going into paperback with Seal and helping position the author for another run at the leadership. "Anna's idea of doing a book with Chrétien was a stroke of genius," Phyllis Bruce remembered. "Others, who shall remain nameless, said, 'What a dumb idea. Why would you do that?' But she just went for it. It was the breakthrough book that put Key Porter on the map."

With her instinct for a deal, Porter sought bigger challenges. A rare opportunity presented itself in 1986 when the huge German media conglomerate Bertelsmann, which had just bought Bantam Doubleday Dell in the United States, took the Canadian government at its word on Baie-Comeau: Bertelsmann decided to comply with the policy by divesting itself of majority ownership in Doubleday Canada. In their search for an acceptable Canadian partner, Bertelsmann executives, who knew Porter from her years of wheeling and dealing at the Frankfurt International Book Fair, decided to entrust her with the presidency of their newly acquired subsidiary.

Porter in effect borrowed the money from Bertelsmann and became CEO of Doubleday Canada as the 51 percent partner. She divided her time between directing the company and running Key Porter. It was a huge stretch, but other publishers noticed positive changes resulting from the new ownership. There was a marked increase in the number of Canadian titles selected by Doubleday's book clubs, particularly the Literary Guild, a practical demonstration of how the Baie-Comeau strategy could affect the business reality of publishing. The following year, Jack McClelland made his final exit from M&S and sold his majority interest in Seal Books, where he was a partner with Bantam, to Porter instead of Avie Bennett. Now Porter was running three companies, two of them in partnership with Bertelsmann interests.

The details of what happened between Porter and the president of Doubleday in the States, Alberto Vitale (characterized by the publisher André Schiffrin in *The Business of Books* as "an illiterate businessman" with "a thuggish disposition and a thoroughly anti-intellectual attitude"), may have to wait for Porter's memoirs. The farthest she'd go in an interview was to call it a case of mismatched expectations: "When two partners decide to marry, and they both go into the marriage with totally different expectations, they're generally both disappointed. I'm sure they were as disappointed with me as I was in them . . . Alberto and his people from BDD basically underestimated my devotion to Key Porter."

Porter acknowledged that Bantam Doubleday Dell had expected her to function as "a well-paid ambassador," building a stronger Canadian list for Doubleday, buying titles for the book clubs, and dropping Key Porter. She, on the other hand, "thought it was a brilliant opportunity to roll Key Porter and Doubleday together." In her scheme, Key Porter would become the Canadian publishing arm of Doubleday, while the bigger company would provide Key Porter with marketing and distribution clout; sales of its huge American list would underwrite her program. But Doubleday's head office and its German owners had other aims in mind.

Even before Vitale moved on to head Random House in 1989, Porter realized she'd have been wise to negotiate an ironclad agreement guaranteeing her exclusive Canadian agency rights to Doubleday's lists. Without such an agreement, she owned a controlling interest in what could easily have become a shell: "They could have at any moment said, and in fact they pointed this out very smartly, 'Okay, you can keep owning this, but we're going to sell our books into Canada direct [from the United States]. So your 51 percent is not worth a hell of a lot.'"

Meanwhile Doubleday's masters downgraded Canadian content in the book clubs by eliminating a separate Canadian buyer. In 1991, five years after getting hitched, Porter invoked the partners' "buy-sell" agreement, whereby, if one party made an offer that wasn't accepted, the other had to counter-offer. She was bought out and left the partnership financially intact.

"We parted amicably," Porter observed. "Even in the days of our divorce, they did not treat me in any way but professionally and exceedingly fairly." In the end, Bertelsmann got the kind of deal it wanted. It replaced Porter with a 51 percent paper partner, a retired Winnipeg businessman named Abraham Simkin, who lived in Florida and had little contact with the company; this satisfied the Mulroney government that control had been divested to a Canadian citizen.

Porter's ownership of Seal came to a similarly unceremonious conclusion the next year. With Baie-Comeau consigned to the dustbin of history, Bertelsmann wanted Porter out of the way. Asked in an interview why she sold her majority interest in Seal to "my Germans," as she'd once called them, Porter replied, "For the same reason I gave up skiing. It wasn't going to get any better. The Seal experiment didn't work for Jack, and it didn't work for me. By comparison to Bantam Doubleday Dell, we were like fleas on a large dog's back."

Porter readdressed herself to the Key Porter program. With McClelland retired, she felt free to poach M&S authors and acquired Farley Mowat for her list. She purchased the L&OD backlist and began her partnership with Malcolm Lester. Eventually Phyllis Bruce moved on to HarperCollins, to be succeeded by Susan Renouf, formerly of Douglas & McIntyre.

In 1995 Key Porter suffered what Porter called "our one totally dreadful year" – to that point, at least – an experience shared by dozens of other Canadian publishers. Ironically, it came at the hands of one of her own authors. In its first term in office, Jean Chrétien's government showed itself no particular friend of Canadian publishing. First it negated the one apparent accomplishment of the Baie-Comeau policy; then it broke faith with the entire Canadian-owned sector.

In 1994 the Liberals sold the CDIC's 51 percent interest in Ginn/GLC back to Paramount/Viacom, taking a loss on the taxpayers' investment by accepting exactly what the Mulroney government had paid for the company five years earlier. The Chrétien government alleged it was bound by a secret, unwritten deal between the Conservatives and Paramount that, if Baie-Comeau were ever dissolved, Paramount could repurchase the shares. The secret deal at least explained why the CDIC had never attempted to resell its interest to Canadians as promised. Ironically, it was left to the official opposition under Bloc Québécois leader Lucien Bouchard – a Stoddart author – to raise a stink in the House over both the ruling parties' mendacity.

Michel Dupuy, the new Liberal minister of Canadian Heritage (the department that had subsumed Communications), appeared naive and ineffectual as he stumbled through the Ginn controversy. That impression was confirmed a year later when Finance Minister Paul Martin told each department to offer up spending programs as sacrificial lambs in his slash-and-burn federal budget. After Dupuy privately assured the ACP that publishing programs would be protected, his department clawed back over half the money committed to the book industry three years earlier. Without any warning, the Book Publishing Industry Development Program was cut by a third, and the Publications Distribution Assistance Program was eliminated completely over two years.

The Liberals would eventually restore the BPIDP funding, and then some, under the next heritage minister, Sheila Copps. But in the meantime, publishers who had based their business plans on the 1992 federal commitments, committing themselves in turn to authors, employees, suppliers, and bankers, were hung out to dry. As Karl Siegler put it, "Had this kind of 'business' dealing been carried out in the private sector, the government players would now be facing the courts on charges of fraud, conspiracy, and entrapment."

Like the rest of the Canadian-owned sector, Anna Porter suddenly found herself overextended. "That's when we hit the wall," she related. "It was a very tough, tough year. I had to raise additional money for the company and put in my own, not to mention begging our suppliers to wait to get paid, and all those wonderful things one does."

During that survival year, Porter was forced to rethink her publishing strategy. She redefined her basic operating principles: "One, we'd never put all our eggs – not even most of our eggs – into any single basket. Second, we'd strive to do about 50 percent of our business on a non-returnable basis. And third, we'd aim to hit a fifty-fifty split in our net income between Canada and the outside."

Export became the cornerstone of the company. Sales of rights were stepped up to a dozen or more countries, with emphasis on direct selling into the United States through a series of distributors. Non-returnable selling meant "special sales" that bypassed the bookstores: selling promotional books in bulk to corporations, producing commissioned books, packaging books for retailers' own imprints, such as Chapters' Prospero brand. Porter summarized her unapologetically pragmatic approach: "We sell books to anybody who is willing to buy books and has the money. We sell them to brokers and banks. We sell them to Kresge's and Wal-Mart and Woolworth's and Marks and Spencer's in England and door-to-door companies up and down the East Coast and the West Coast and the centre. You name it."

The strategy isn't romantic, but it pays Key Porter's bills, some of which are now for Canadian fiction, since Porter removed her ban on that genre. "It's not that my heart and soul happen to be in the next home repair guide, although we will do a home repair guide if it's guaranteed cash," Porter explained. "It's that you have to hedge your bets. You go out and make money and keep the business thriving to pay for the next Tim Wynveen or Erika Ritter or Zsuzsi Gartner," she said, naming three fiction writers she had published. After playing with the multinationals and living to tell the tale, Porter's was the mordant voice of realism in the twenty-first century.

For years, Key Porter and Douglas & McIntyre were mentioned in the same breath. Certainly there were similarities between the two companies. Both were expanding, Canadian-owned, editorially diverse trade houses. They were comparable in size: about $10 million in annual revenues by the late 1990s, mostly in Canadian-authored titles. Both firms were best known for their non-fiction, particularly illustrated books. Both co-published with institutions such as museums and art galleries and pursued exports as a key to survival. And, like Anna Porter, Jim Douglas and Scott McIntyre had worked at M&S.

But in other respects, the companies have become markedly different. Headquartered in Vancouver, D&M has always specialized in West Coast and First Nations subjects. It has become the country's leading publisher of art books. Its affiliation with Groundwood Books gives it one of Canada's major children's programs (although Key Porter also publishes for children). In company culture, Key Porter has been a more or less benevolent dictatorship, whereas D&M has practised cooperative federalism.

The Douglas & McIntyre Publishing Group comprises three autonomous lists, as of early 2003. Patsy Aldana runs Groundwood out of Toronto. Rob Sanders operates the Greystone Books imprint at the

company's Vancouver office, his list focused on natural history, the outdoors, sports, and popular culture. And McIntyre publishes, under the
D&M imprint, books on art, history, politics, food, and what he has called
"the voices and culture of this place," meaning British Columbia. The
firm's decentralized output reflects the genial McIntyre's flexibility, his
respect for his colleagues' publishing strengths, and his lifelong "love of the
process of making books, the physical artifacts."

A readiness to collaborate was evident early, and not only in the
alliance with Groundwood. After D&M moved its eastern order fulfillment
to Clarke, Irwin, those two firms also worked closely together for several
years. D&M's first Toronto office was located in the Clarke, Irwin building,
and Douglas frequently "went off on his charger," as McIntyre put it, to
assist Bill Clarke. The companies took the unusual step of co-publishing
an expensive art book: a full-colour volume on Emily Carr, whose writings
Clarke, Irwin had first published in the 1940s. Released in 1979, the art historian Doris Shadbolt's *The Art of Emily Carr* sold out its 30,000-copy first
printing within six weeks at $40, a high cover price for those days.

The next year, D&M took an initiative that would prove crucial for its
survival. Hope still lingered in the early 1980s that smaller Canadian publishers could break into the school market. When the chance came to
tender on a contract for the British Columbia social studies curriculum,
both Douglas and McIntyre decided to make a concerted bid. It was a huge
challenge for a company their size: a linked series of social studies textbooks for grades one through six, with teachers' guides, to meet the
specifications of a new curriculum. McIntyre's skill set gave him the edge in
handling the project, and Douglas returned to manage the company, just as
he'd been heading off into retirement. At one point, more than sixty people
– teacher-advisers, writers, editors, translators, designers, photographers,
illustrators – were working on the proposal and presentation pages under
McIntyre and his project adviser, Carol Langford; many of them worked
gratis pending a successful bid. Since they couldn't all fit into the
company's tight little offices in an industrial building on Venables Street, a
"war-room" was established to coordinate the far-flung activities.

D&M was up against Copp Clark, Prentice-Hall, and other competitors
with decades of experience and connections in the field. McIntyre recalled

how it played out: "We were the only western company. And everyone, of course, thought it was a put-up deal, under the table. But we were simply better. We won cleanly and honestly because we produced the best stuff. We blew our brains out. I'll never forget one of our competitors from Toronto who stood up and said, 'It's not fair. You spent too much money. You made it impossible for us to compete.' But there was no money from the government. We just did it."

After incurring major debt and a massive investment of sweat equity, the profits were sweet. With print runs of between 30,000 and 60,000 copies per title, Douglas & McIntyre Educational, a separate entity, later won purchases from most of the other provinces, and even an adaptation from Australia. Producing books for six grade levels over five years, 1981 to 1986, the firm grossed upwards of $15 million. Some of the net profit went into D&M proper, a shareholder in the educational entity – a fortunate outcome since, as McIntyre put it, "That's the only reason Douglas & McIntyre survived the Clarke, Irwin receivership."

When the locks were clapped on the doors at Clarwin House in 1983, D&M's inventory and receivables were trapped inside. With Clarke, Irwin suddenly on the brink of bankruptcy, so was D&M. The company appealed to three governments – Ontario, which had precipitated the receivership; British Columbia, since D&M was the largest publisher in that province; and the federal government – to prevent its becoming collateral damage. After weeks of desperation, the appeals were successful.

D&M considered taking on other educational projects, but as curriculum and buying patterns changed, it became clear the company wasn't sufficiently capitalized to stay in the field. In 1989 it accepted an offer from Thomas Nelson – Canadian-owned because it was held by the Thomson organization – to sell its educational operation for a "fair" price, according to McIntyre. By then, D&M's trade sales had grown substantially, more than taking up the slack, and Greystone Books was on the horizon.

Rob Sanders had arrived at D&M in 1987 after twelve years of building Western Producer Prairie Books, the book publishing program of the *Western Producer* newspaper, owned by the Saskatchewan Wheat Pool. With a background as an English teacher and a western sales rep for Holt,

Rinehart & Winston, Sanders had created a sturdy regional press in Saskatoon with a growing national reputation for its non-fiction. By the time he left Western Producer, it had become the largest Prairie publisher after Hurtig.

At D&M, Sanders was publisher of the trade list while McIntyre ran the educational wing. But with that company sold, McIntyre wanted back into trade, and the two colleagues redefined their respective roles. The Wheat Pool put Western Producer Prairie Books on the block in 1991, and D&M purchased its assets with a loan from the Federal Business Development Bank. Sanders took charge of his former program, culled the backlist, and made it the foundation of Greystone Books.

Greystone's mandate wasn't merely to impersonate a Prairie press out of Vancouver. Instead Sanders combined titles on western Canadian culture with illustrated books on wildlife and the environment. Since his photographic nature titles were too costly to publish for the Canadian market alone, he ensured they had the content and design quality to become international co-editions. His Nature titles (*The Nature of Wolves*, *The Nature of Sea Otters*) lent themselves to that model: edited, designed, and produced in-house, each was pre-sold to publishers in four or five other countries. "The strategy," Sanders explained, "is to get enough publishers together, each taking 5,000, 10,000, 20,000 copies, so that the book works for everyone." Many years of attending Frankfurt enabled him to build an international network of publishing relationships, and he has co-published with some of the major firms in France, Germany, Sweden, Britain, and the United States. Greystone's other main export thrust has been American distribution of its wider list, especially titles on hockey and men's health, through Sterling Publishing in New York.

All three D&M publishers seem to agree that a wise publisher, as McIntyre has often said, has three eyes: one on the writer, another on the reader, and the third fixed on the cash register. If one imprint has a bad year, another makes up for it. Just the same, McIntyre wondered at times if he'd practised too much "innate Celtic caution: certainly some people think we have." The company has seldom participated in costly book auctions, conducted by literary agents to drive up their authors' advances. The highest advance to a D&M author for quite some time was the $50,000 paid for General Lewis MacKenzie's 1993 memoirs, *Peacekeeper: The Road to Sarajevo.*

If he cared to, however, McIntyre could have cited the fair share of risks his company has taken over the years: the educational gamble; the sumptuous volumes on Tom Thomson, Bill Reid, Jack Shadbolt, Betty Goodwin, and other artists; the small but distinguished fiction list edited by Aldana, including works by Monique Proulx, Fred Stenson, and Wayson Choy (*The Jade Peony*); and the occasional idealistic "folly." McIntyre pointed to the 1999 D&M title *A Story as Sharp as a Knife: The Classical Haida Mythtellers and Their World*, a monumental, 527-page, annotated translation of Haida oral literature by the poet and linguist Robert Bringhurst. "That book," McIntyre observed, "is one of those follies that reconfirm why you do this. I don't think it'll sell worth a damn in the short term. But twenty years from now, it will be regarded as the most important book we've ever published."

Both Douglas & McIntyre and Key Porter were distributed in the late 1990s by General Distribution Services, part of the Stoddart Publishing empire. Jack Stoddart, known as Jack E. or Jack Jr. while his father was still alive, also purchased a 10 percent ownership stake in both rival firms as an adjunct to the distribution deals. Like Ron Besse, Stoddart always contended that Canada needed not more publishers but larger, stronger, more competitive ones.

Stoddart practised what he preached. During the 1980s and 1990s, he bought up or invested in a wide range of publishers. Sometimes he followed his father's example of picking up bargains, but he also made some acquisitions with the simple intent of preserving an important literary program. Stoddart's ultimate goal appeared to be creation of a diversified Canadian-owned publisher on a scale to compete on more equal terms with the multinationals. By the late 1980s, his group of companies had become the largest Canadian-owned book publisher after Thomas Nelson and the multinational romance publisher Harlequin Books.

The firm's aggressive acquisition strategy stretched back over four decades, ever since the elder Stoddart had purchased a small book importer grandly named General Publishing in 1957. Operating above a downtown Toronto greasy spoon, General had been founded by a bachelor of modest means named Norman Wittet, who had originally called it Imperial Publishing. Nearing retirement, Wittet approached Jack Stoddart Sr., then the trade sales manager at Macmillan, and proposed that the younger man buy him out.

Stoddart was still in his late thirties, having joined Macmillan out of high school in Shelburne, Ontario, in 1936. His aunt, Ellen Elliott, who was Hugh Eayrs's assistant at the time, had suggested he apply for a job as a back order clerk. Always a spiffy dresser with a shine on his shoes, Stoddart became Eayrs's chauffeur of choice after John Gray grew too busy for the role. Eayrs had a habit of falling asleep in the car while talking with authors or visiting publishers, and Stoddart would carry on the conversation until Eayrs awoke.

After serving in the RCAF during wartime, Stoddart became a traveller selling Macmillan trade books in Ontario and the west. Industrious and outgoing, he was the natural choice for trade sales manager when the position fell open. But his ambitions were frustrated by Macmillan's traditionalism and social snobbery. According to his successor, Donald Sutherland, Stoddart wanted to be a director of the firm, "but John Gray and Frank Upjohn felt he wasn't really out of the right drawer." Stoddart purchased General after Wittet died of a heart attack while lugging sample cases along Front Street in Toronto. John Gray is said to have told a mutual friend: "I'm really very worried about what Jack has decided to do. I'm sure he's put all his money into that little rundown company, and I'm afraid he'll lose the whole thing."

Stoddart built up the little rundown company, whose sales for 1957 had been $115,000, with deft sure-handedness. After obtaining several agencies with good prospects, such as Dover Publications and Sunset Books, the company moved into a former clothing factory on Adelaide Street. In 1965, with sales surpassing $1 million, Stoddart leased a new facility built to his specifications in suburban Don Mills. The move was the first in a publishing migration to the Lesmill Road area; before the 1960s were out, Harlequin, William Collins, and Fitzhenry & Whiteside would all relocate there.

Stoddart continued to accumulate agencies and make astute take-overs. The Musson Book Company, which dated from 1896, had once published the likes of the poet Pauline Johnson, but it had subsided into the mould of an agency house after becoming the distributor for Simon & Schuster in the 1930s. Eventually Musson atrophied, and one of its British agencies, Hodder & Stoughton, bought it for a dollar in 1963. Hodder was relieved to unload Musson to Stoddart in 1967, along with Canadian distribution of its own books: "Jack Stoddart was the only Canadian with the courage and competence to take over the [Hodder] Trade representation," wrote John Attenborough in his history of the British publisher.

Stoddart turned Musson into a money-maker in no time. The Simon & Schuster agency alone boasted tremendously profitable authors such as Jacqueline Susann, Harold Robbins, and Carlos Castaneda; and Hodder & Stoughton's paperback line, Coronet Books, gave General immediate access to the mass market. Using the specialized sales force that marketed Coronet, Stoddart could now put Canadian titles into mass-market distribution.

So far, Stoddart had done little original publishing. But acquiring paperback rights to hardcover titles was a relatively safe way to publish Canadian authors with a track record. Stoddart started his own paperback line, dubbed PaperJacks; one of its earliest titles, purchased from M&S, was Margaret Atwood's *Surfacing*. As the list grew, PaperJacks competed for rights against other reprint houses such as Penguin, Bantam, New American Library of Canada, Collins's Totem Books, and later Seal Books.

When New Press became available in 1974, Stoddart bought it as a backlist resource and a tax write-off. A far bigger deal was the purchase two years later of Pocket Books of Canada. Stoddart acquired an established money-spinner with a warehouse in nearby Markham and a proven sales force under the veteran book marketer James Smallwood. Pocket Books churned out sixteen mass-market titles a month, reaping $1 million in pre-tax profits. The purchase was a textbook case of the Trudeau government's foreign investment regulations achieving their objective: General would use the profits to create a significant Canadian publishing program. At the same time, the company reaped continuing profits from its agency lines, holding rights to such mega-sellers as *The Joy of Sex*, which sold over 300,000 copies in Canada.

In strategy and style, General was marked by its origins as an importer, and even more deeply by the business values of its founder. Jack Stoddart Sr. mistrusted any publishing done without *both* eyes on the cash register. The company acquired an image, which it would never entirely shake, as square, unimaginative, a bit philistine. It would take generational change at the helm to modify that perception.

"I'd never wanted to be in the publishing business. I was a musician. I just needed a job afterwards. And I started working in the warehouse and stayed around and learned a bit about it as I went along."

He was so publicly identified with the firm for two decades that it was startling to hear those words from the younger Jack Stoddart. In the early 1960s, while playing guitar with Robbie Lane and the Disciples, he became ill; his replacement in the band was the future guitar legend Domenic Troiano, and suddenly Stoddart was out of work. Like it or not, he found himself in the family business: "I did my time in the warehouse and in the accounting office and in sales and management. I was in the middle of it all, but I didn't have control, and that was fine with me. Because, you see, I never wanted it. I never really wanted promotions."

Not having trained for any other career, Stoddart came to like the book trade. The only part he disliked was educational sales, but he put that behind him as fast as he could, moving over to manage Musson in 1967. A few years later, Stoddart's father wanted him to move up to president so that he could "retire." Jack Jr. declined the presidency two years running, not believing the boss was ready to let go: "I knew he was never going to retire. I'd worked with him a long time, and we'd had the odd argument. At the end of the day, it was his company, not mine. I'd argue for what I thought was right, then tell him to make up his own mind. Whether he wanted to do it the way I was suggesting or the way he wanted, it didn't matter to me."

Despite the disclaimer, Stoddart would exhibit plenty of his father's wilfulness and stubbornness in the years ahead. In 1977, when he finally accepted the presidency, it was with his eyes open: he saw himself as, in effect, an executive vice-president working for the owner. But at the same time he gathered around him a team of like-minded younger executives, such as Nelson Doucet in trade sales, Bob Wagner in merchandising, Lloyd Klinck in operations, and Bill Hanna in editorial: unpretentious, practical, hard-working men who'd risen through the ranks. "It wasn't us against them," Stoddart recalled, "but they were far more my age than Dad's. We developed a team approach and a good working relationship through the 1970s and '80s."

The young president was preparing for the day when he'd take over for real. His younger sister, Susan Stoddart, rejoined the firm in 1982 after an absence due to illness, but the siblings didn't get along: "We were a world apart in some ways." Their father suffered a mild stroke, then another, and his formidable memory began failing. In 1984, certain he could never work with his sister after their father was gone (Jack Sr. died in 1988), the younger Stoddart proposed splitting up the company.

In partnership with Doucet and Wagner, he financed a buyout of the publishing side of the business, along with most of its trade agencies, while Susan Stoddart took control of the PaperJacks/Pocket Books operation, renaming it Distican in 1989. Later she also wrested the Simon & Schuster agency away from her brother, which did nothing for family relations. But Distican would remain a distributor, whereas for Jack, developing a strong publishing program became a top priority: "The other [mass-market] side of the business was just being a kind of wholesaler, and it didn't interest me in the least, except as a way of making a lot of money. So it may have been one of those dumb decisions, but now I had an interesting career."

In addition to its considerable agency business, General was selling about $1 million a year of its own trade books under Hanna and the associate publisher, Ed Carson. But the Canadian program was scattered among various imprints: some of the titles appeared from General, others from Musson or New Press Canadian Classics or George J. McLeod, purchased in 1978. To endow their list with a more coherent identity, Stoddart and his team regrouped the disparate brands under the name Stoddart Publishing.

When Carson left to start an original trade program at Random House of Canada, Stoddart opted not to replace him. Instead he relied on General's traditional editorial approach, decision-making by committee. A publishing board consisting of Stoddart and his senior staff ensured that input from sales and marketing would always factor heavily into publishing decisions – the key decision-makers being Stoddart and his lieutenant and minority partner, Nelson Doucet. That structure meant the company never quite shed Jack Sr.'s personality. A trace of the founder's Macmillan years also remained: signs demarcating the boundary of the warehouse reminded those entering the executive offices, "No cups without saucers beyond this point."

Stoddart's other goal was to add an educational publishing program. In 1988, with John Irwin ready to sell Irwin Publishing, Stoddart bought him out, becoming heir to the Clarke, Irwin legacy as well as the Peter Martin Associates backlist, which John Irwin had purchased seven years earlier. Now Stoddart's holdings had greater diversification and balance. Irwin Publishing – under its president, Brian O'Donnell, and the vice-president, Michael Davis – continued to grow into a strong and profitable educational publisher. With a program focused on special education, mental health, and teaching resources, Irwin's dollar volume would approach the sales level of the Stoddart trade list by the turn of the millennium.

The Stoddart program grew through a combination of original publishing, agency business, purchasing rights to such imports as *Spycatcher*, the huge British bestseller of the late 1980s, and the continuing purchase of small companies. Stoddart, like Avie Bennett, became a busy acquisitor. He used his economic clout to associate himself with some of the most admired lists in Canadian publishing, sometimes as sole owner, sometimes as partner.

House of Anansi's owner, Ann Wall, had first put her struggling press up for sale in 1975, following Shirley Gibson's departure. Wall had wanted a buyer who appreciated what Anansi stood for and would uphold its literary list. She received expressions of interest from many industry players, including Michael Macklem and Malcolm Lester, but no offers she couldn't refuse. When Hugh Kane of Macmillan offered to pay a dollar for her shares and take Anansi off her hands, it was the last straw: "I decided I'd bought this toy," Wall recalled, "and everybody else had had a turn running it, so now it was my turn."

With more than $50,000 of her inheritance tied up in the company ("She'd have made a better return putting it into Mongolian bonds," said Dave Godfrey), Wall ran Anansi for the next fourteen years in collaboration with her editor, Jim Polk. The pair kept the press close to its literary and philosophical roots, with occasional counsel from the veteran publishers Barney Sandwell and Harald Bohne, who joined their board. Editorially, "the Anansi themes were there, and they seemed to us to work," Polk said. In addition to poetry from new writers such as Erin Mouré, Kristjana Gunnars, and Don Domanski, Polk and Wall published fiction by Jacques Brault, Roch Carrier, David Williams, and Rachel Wyatt, prose by Northrop Frye, George Grant, the journalist Charles Taylor, and Margaret Atwood (although they couldn't persuade her to revise *Survival*), and a history of Rochdale College.

But in the changing publishing climate of the mid-1980s, Anansi began to struggle once more. With many small presses entering the scene, furthering the literary renaissance that Anansi had launched, and with agents pushing advances through the roof, the cash-poor press was at a growing disadvantage. Its most successful authors had long since moved on to bigger companies. Again Wall decided to sell, and this time she was adamant. The buyer, in 1989, was Jack Stoddart.

Stoddart committed himself to keeping Anansi as autonomous as possible. He termed it "a small press running within a big company," using the parent firm's resources to publish a new generation of writers. "It would have been fundamentally wrong to let Anansi go out of business," Stoddart commented. "You should never let a good publishing house die. The inventory gets sold off, the books get separated from the contracts, and an important asset gets broken up and lost."

The new Anansi got its own publishing board, composed of writers and critics under the chairmanship of David Arnason. It racked up a Governor General's Award for John Ralston Saul's *The Unconscious Civilization* and won several GG nominations and a Giller Prize nomination. In the late 1990s, recognizing that publishing by committee doesn't work in literary publishing, Stoddart began giving Anansi's youthful and energetic editor, Martha Sharpe, more freedom to build the list.

Stoddart also took minority positions in two other literary presses, Quarry Press of Kingston, Ontario, and Cormorant Books, investing to keep their publishing programs alive and providing both with sales and marketing. And in 1992 he acquired the Ontario regional house of Boston Mills Press, based in Erin, retaining its publisher, John Dennison, to direct the list of illustrated books on railways, boating, and local history. With additional capital, Boston Mills was able to broaden its program and grow considerably. Stoddart's most enterprising strategic investment, however, was his partnership with a dynamic new publisher on the Canadian scene.

Stoddart recognized the creative potential of three talented partners whose combined expertise made them a potent team. John Macfarlane had been editor of *Weekend* magazine and publisher of *Saturday Night* before becoming editor of *Toronto Life*. Jan Walter had been director of publishing at M&S for five years after her stints at Hurtig and Macmillan. And Gary Ross was an accomplished author and editor, an associate of Macfarlane's at *Weekend* and *Saturday Night*. In Macfarlane Walter & Ross, the partners had conceived a boutique publisher dedicated to high-quality non-fiction, small enough to let them work closely with authors producing innovative trade books on politics, society, and culture. In 1988 they pitched their concept to three Toronto publishers who might provide them with financing, marketing, and distribution: Morton Mint at Penguin, David Kent at Collins, and Stoddart.

MW&R chose Stoddart over the others, Jan Walter said, "because, when we sat across the table from Jack, we knew we were dealing with the person who made the final decisions, who would have our fate in his hands. And he was prepared to invest, and to offer us comfortable shareholding arrangements." With Stoddart taking 49 percent and the other three 51 percent, MW&R was established with Walter as managing director and "The Art of Non-Fiction" as its motto. The three principals brainstormed book ideas, reaching agreement among themselves before conferring with Stoddart and his publishing board – who would not unreasonably withhold consent if MW&R felt strongly about a project. It was an arrangement Walter had observed working well in Holland, which she'd visited with an ACP trade mission: "You could have autonomy in the areas that were important to you – acquisition and editorial development and design – while still cooperating with your competitors in areas where it made sense to cooperate – sales, warehousing, order fulfillment, and financial services."

MW&R published its first title in 1989: *One Hundred Monkeys*, by Robert Mason Lee, an intelligent and entertaining disquisition on Canadian politics. The firm later enjoyed well-deserved critical success with *The Mother Zone*, by Marni Jackson, *Road Games*, by Roy MacGregor, and *An Acre of Time*, by Phil Jenkins. *Mulroney: The Politics of Ambition*, by John Sawatsky, was the company's first big seller, with hardcover sales topping 30,000. At the five-year mark, when they reviewed their arrangements, the three principals sold additional shares to Stoddart, whose holding rose to 85 percent.

MW&R's second five years were marked by two enormously successful titles. The muckraking journalist Stevie Cameron's *On the Take: Crime, Corruption and Greed in the Mulroney Years* was the hottest political book of the decade, hitting 100,000 copies in hardcover before selling a similar quantity as a Seal paperback. And *Boom, Bust & Echo*, by the demographer David Foot and the journalist Daniel Stoffman, became the best-selling Canadian hardcover ever, surpassing 250,000 copies. MW&R had an unprecedented four number-one bestsellers on the *Globe and Mail*'s annual bestseller list in consecutive years, 1994, 1995, 1996, and 1997.

The founding partners used their share of the earnings to buy back shares from Stoddart, raising their combined holdings to 45 percent. But in 1999, by mutual consent, all four principals chose not to renew their arrangement for a third five-year period; instead they sold 100 percent of the company to Avie Bennett. Although M&S would now exercise control while providing similar services to Stoddart's, MW&R remained a distinct, semi-autonomous house with its own offices. MW&R did not, however, take into M&S *On the Take, Boom, Bust & Echo*, or several other top money-makers. Stoddart insisted on holding onto those books as part of his price for striking a deal.

Jack Stoddart's acquisitions alone would have made him the dominant player in Canadian-owned publishing during the 1990s. But at the same time, his company's distribution arm, General Distribution Services, became critical to the sector's economic health. Eventually providing order fulfillment for sixty-two Canadian publishers, from Key Porter and D&M to some forty small firms in the Literary Press Group, Stoddart acted as the linchpin between his colleagues and their domestic customers.

Reinforcing that powerful position, Stoddart, an avowed Liberal supporter, also acted as the industry's nationalist standard-bearer, serving as ACP president for three consecutive terms from 1996 to 1999. Assisted by the ACP's executive director, Paul Davidson, he led a successful campaign to persuade Heritage Minister Sheila Copps not only to restore but ultimately to increase the BPIDP funding that had been cut in the 1995 budget, and to introduce measures such as a loan guarantee program. Stoddart's major disappointment was an inability to persuade the government to enact his policy of choice: a tax credit for investors in Canadian-owned publishing companies. Unlike the earlier tax credit proposal, that measure would have rebated a percentage of investments in company equity, rather than in new book production.

From the standpoint of his own firm, Stoddart's numerous extra-curricular involvements produced mixed results. Industry politics frequently took him away from managing company affairs. And his investments in other houses meant that fewer financial and human resources were available to build the program at Stoddart Publishing itself, or to plan a long-term, integrated corporate strategy.

Although it issued close to 150 titles a year, the Stoddart imprint still lacked a compelling identity. One seldom thought of Stoddart authors in the sense that one thought of Anansi authors or M&S authors or Knopf Canada authors. The reason lay partly in the fact that Stoddart had never developed a strong fiction program, and most of the stars in Canadian literature today are novelists; the company had once published Carol Shields and Leon Rooke, but let them get away to other publishers. Stoddart's successful authors were more likely to come from the firm's extensive list of business and personal finance titles, such as David Chilton's *The Wealthy Barber*, a 1.5-million-copy seller, first self-published by the author. And although Stoddart produced illustrated books by the post-M&S Pierre Berton (*Pierre Berton's Canada*, *Pierre Berton's Seacoasts*), they were a far cry from the author's most interesting titles.

Where the company did excel was in issue-oriented books: titles on politics and society dealing with vital questions of national purpose and sovereignty. Stoddart was David Suzuki's publisher, issuing a dozen titles by the influential environmentalist and social philosopher. The company originated Senator Keith Davey's *The Rainmaker*, Mel Hurtig's *The Betrayal of Canada*, Marci McDonald's *Yankee Doodle Dandy: Brian Mulroney and the American Agenda*, and substantial books by Hugh Segal, Judy Rebick, Walter Stewart, Murray Dobbin, and Marq de Villiers. It issued essential critiques of globalization by Maude Barlow, writing with Tony Clarke. Without books like these, the political debate of the 1990s would have been even more bereft of ideas and alternatives and even more dangerously one-sided, especially given the continentalist tilt of the media after Conrad Black's purchase of Southam Newspapers and Black's conversion of the *Financial Post* into the even more right-wing *National Post*. Jack Stoddart's most enduring accomplishment would be his authors' contributions to Canadian democratic discourse.

HarperCollins*PublishersLtd*

ECW PRESS

PENGUIN BOOKS CANADA | WHITECAP BOOKS

RANDOM HOUSE OF CANADA

McARTHUR & COMPANY | DOUBLEDAY CANADA

HARPER COLLINS CANADA

KNOPF CANADA | ECW PRESS

15

WARS OF SUCCESSION

*To achieve the survival of one great Canadian institution,
I have given it into the care of another great Canadian
institution.*

Avie Bennett, on donating 75 percent of McClelland &
Stewart to the University of Toronto (June 2000)

To understand Canadian publishing at the turn of the millennium, it is necessary to visit the United States: to survey the floor at the Los Angeles Convention Center in May 1999, or at Chicago's McCormick Place in May 2000 and 2001, or at the Jacob K. Javits Center in New York City in 2002. All were sites of BookExpo America, the massive annual trade show of the American Booksellers Association.

Sprawling over several halls, the shows feature aisle upon aisle of eye-popping displays pitched at thousands of retailers. Like believers at Lourdes, the booksellers swarm the floor under gaudy banners and brilliant lights, moving from one publisher's stand to another to witness the latest miracles. Some stands are so spacious and lavishly appointed they feel like model homes. Booksellers linger long enough among the easy chairs to exchange a few words with the Time Warner or Random House or HarperCollins reps and haul off complimentary book bags stuffed with catalogues, posters, calendars, pens, buttons, and reading copies of next season's surefire bestsellers. And each year, inconspicuous amid the crowds, with no stigmata to identify them as alien, forty to fifty Canadian publishers are beavering away on the show floor. They write up orders, sell rights, cheer on their American distributors. The largest firms typically boast their own stands; smaller presses operate from the booths of their American representatives, or from the official Canada stand.

Competing with celebrity authors and glitzy convention parties, the Canadians are there to capture a piece of the $20-billion (U.S.) book market. Even a few crumbs from such a rich table would add substantially to their revenues. But one secret they've all discovered is to appear as un-Canadian as possible: to masquerade, in fact, as Americans.

M&S packages its titles in a catalogue decorated with a stylized Stars and Stripes, emblazoned "McClelland & Stewart U.S." University of Toronto Press positions itself in an aisle where it assumes the coloration of its neighbours Yale, Stanford, and Chicago. Smaller houses adopt similar camouflage. Arsenal Pulp Press's American sales are pushing 40 percent of its dollar volume. Orca Book Publishers of Victoria has increased its American business from a third of total sales to a half. Quarry Press has exceeded that level since it began publishing on pop music and health. Even publishers whose lists may appear too regional or specialized for export are finding a niche in the United States. Clyde Rose of Breakwater Books trolls for customers for his tales of Newfoundland whalers and sealers. Dimitri Roussopoulos has found a radical American readership for the backlist of his Montreal anarchist press, Black Rose Books.

Penetrating the American marketplace means adopting an American orientation. Whitecap Books of Vancouver wows them with its full-colour books on Arizona, New Mexico, and the Rockies; printed in Canada with the benefit of the low dollar and sold at a healthy profit in U.S. currency, the books are a natural extension of Whitecap's series on Canadian regions. Owl Books, like its fellow children's publishers Annick, Groundwood, Kids Can, and Tundra, has adopted American spellings so its titles won't appear foreign to teachers and librarians in the United States. Groundwood has gone a big step farther, developing Libros Tigrillo, a bilingual line of English-Spanish titles aimed at young Latino readers in the States and elsewhere.

At ECW Press, the partners, Jack David and Robert Lecker, have adopted an even more basic repositioning. Named for *Essays in Canadian*

Writing, the journal of literary criticism launched out of York University in the 1970s, ECW Press played a unique role for twenty-five years by publishing critical studies and bibliographies of Canadian authors, aimed at the scholarly and library markets. But in the mid-1990s, the press suddenly veered out of character, churning out fan biographies of American sports, music, and TV stars: David Duchovny of *X-Files* fame, *Buffy the Vampire Slayer*'s Sarah Michelle Gellar. In 1998 ECW unveiled Secret Guides, a series for hip travellers flagging out-of-the-way pleasures ("cruising," "occult," "raves," "God") in major North American cities. American sales grew to two-thirds of the press's volume and increased its revenues by 300 percent, to over $2 million, in just three years. David and Lecker have said the change of direction didn't skew their identity but grew out of an avid lifelong interest in American pop culture.

Looking to markets abroad is hardly a new trend. Canadians have been working the Frankfurt International Book Fair since 1962, the Bologna Children's Book Fair since the 1970s, and more recently they have been flocking to fairs in London, Paris, and Guadalajara. The federal government has encouraged an international outlook for the past three decades. Development of export markets was among Gérard Pelletier's original support measures in 1972, and the federally funded Association for the Export of Canadian Books underwrites export activities and operates the Canada stand at major fairs. Fuelling the whole process has been the mounting world acclaim accorded Canadian writers.

What's new is that, since the late 1990s, the American market has become an obsession. The United States is physically and culturally accessible, with an English-speaking population about twelve times larger than Canada's, and it's rich. Whereas Canadians once sold rights to American publishers, many now sell their own editions directly into the States. The University of Toronto Press was the first to establish a sales office in Buffalo, New York; Firefly followed suit, as did Stoddart Publishing. Stoddart also operated London Bridge, run by Nelson Doucet, which distributed British publishers in the United States. On the West Coast, Orca and International Self-Counsel Press both set up branch offices in Bellingham, Washington. As far as their customers in the United States are concerned, these are American publishers.

Why would a profession that flaunted its Canadianness in the 1970s and '80s distort its nationality this way? Publishers aren't necessarily above greed, given a choice. But their all-out pursuit of American readers has more to do with basic survival – and with a drastically altered market back home.

Chapters Inc. has transformed the Canadian retail book market so radically that it's startling to recall the corporation has existed only since 1994. But before its red and yellow logo and saturation advertising made its brand as ubiquitous as McDonald's, Chapters was just a bunch of venture capitalists looking for an industry to take over. They found it in the sedate, unsuspecting, underperforming world of Canadian book retailing.

Pathfinder Capital and Canadian General Capital Corporation were captained by a Canadian Forces paratrooper turned smooth-talking Harvard Business School grad named Lawrence N. Stevenson, Larry to his friends. He and his fellow acquisitors started by buying middlebrow SmithBooks, formerly W.H. Smith of Canada, in 1994. The chain had produced only modest financial returns after its purchase by Winnipeg's Federal Industries five years earlier. With lightning speed, Stevenson then bought up the other national bookstore chain, lowbrow Coles, from Southam. He merged the two and renamed the corporate entity Chapters, with himself as CEO and former Ontario premier David Peterson providing a patina of political respectability as chairman of the board.

SmithBooks had already absorbed the Melzack family's upmarket but overextended Classics chain in 1985. And so, where a decade earlier there had been three bookstore chains, each with a different style and product mix, now there was only one. The market power of Chapters was un-challenged, combining the Chapters, World's Biggest Bookstore, Coles, SmithBooks, Librairie Smith, Classic Books, and Book Company brands. Publishers no longer had a significant alternative customer in Canada; if the Chain didn't order a title, that book automatically lost access to half the domestic retail market. And hundreds of independent local bookstores faced a single-minded, predatory foe.

With a shrewd, smooth political campaign, Chapters passed lengthy scrutiny by the federal Competition Bureau. Despite warnings from the ACP and protests from the Canadian Booksellers Association, the bureau found in 1995 that the new retail giant wouldn't "unduly limit" competition in book retailing. With the formalities out of the way, Stevenson adopted a take-no-prisoners approach towards competitors and suppliers alike. He executed his strategy to open Canada's first book superstores, modelled on big-box outlets operated in the States by the Borders and Barnes & Noble chains; indeed, Barnes & Noble acquired a 20 percent interest in Chapters. The superstores, at least ten times bigger than an average bookstore, began opening in prime retail locations across the country. Within five years, Chapters had built seventy-one superstores throughout Canada; in the same period, it closed over 150 of the more than 420 Coles and SmithBooks outlets as part of its corporate rationalization.

With the objective of knocking long-established independents out of the game, the Chapters superstores offered bestsellers at discounts of 30 percent or more (offers duplicated by Coles and SmithBooks) and featured Starbucks coffee bars, comfortable armchairs for browsing, and cheery children's play centres. The strategy worked with stunning efficiency. Between 1997 and 2000, independent bookstores that had been cherished fixtures in their communities for decades fell before the Chapters blitzkrieg. Britnell's (established 1893), the Book Cellar, the Children's Bookstore, Writers & Co., and ten Lichtman's stores, all in Toronto; nine out of ten Duthie's stores in Vancouver; four Sandpiper stores in Calgary; Books Canada and Food for Thought in Ottawa; and dozens of booksellers in other cities all went out of business.

The Chain's drive for market share accelerated after it emerged from a three-year monitoring period imposed by the Competition Bureau. In 1998 it opened Chapters Online (listed, like Chapters Inc., on the Toronto Stock Exchange) to grab a slice of the expanding Internet book market pioneered by Amazon.com. Like many e-commerce ventures, Chapters.ca proved costly and unprofitable. It was soon followed by more dangerous developments.

In 1999 Chapters converted its huge warehouse and distribution centre in Brampton, Ontario, into a "wholesale" operation called Pegasus Inc. The actual core functions of Pegasus were filling orders for Chapters.ca customers and supplying books to the Chain's own stores. But by claiming Pegasus as a wholesaler, Chapters could demand the higher wholesaler discount from publishers. To make the pretense more credible, Pegasus pursued sales to libraries and schools and announced its intention of supplying the very independent bookstores that Chapters was driving out of existence.

Until then Canadian publishers had been ambivalently complicit in the gutting of the retail sector. They'd been happy with the sharp spike in sales resulting from the Chapters building boom, yet nervous about the unrealistic size of its orders and troubled by the loss of so many traditional bookstore customers. With the advent of Pegasus, publishers' worst suspicions were confirmed. Pegasus demanded from them a wholesaler discount of 50 percent-plus, in place of the 45 to 48 percent they'd been giving Chapters. Although the Chain claimed otherwise, publishers understood that if they wanted their books on sale at any Chapters, Coles, or SmithBooks outlets, they'd have to ship to Pegasus on its terms.

Since the extra discount points wiped out publishers' already paper-thin profit margins, they faced an invidious choice: either absorb the higher discount, raise book prices, and risk consumer resistance (as Stoddart did), or refuse to extend the discount and lose the Chain's business (as Firefly did). Some independent booksellers, such as Jim Munro of Victoria, mocked the publishers' dilemma, saying they'd helped create the monster in the first place and were now suffering the consequences. Most publishers felt they had no realistic choice but to play the Chain's game.

Firefly furnished an object lesson in what would happen if they didn't cooperate. Chapters responded by returning $1 million worth of books for credit, including titles from Annick, Owl, and the other presses distributed by Firefly.

Larry Stevenson became notorious in the trade for browbeating suppliers over the phone. Anna Porter complained to him that Key Porter's new book by Allan Fotheringham, who was then crossing the country on tour, had been shipped to Pegasus but still hadn't reached Chapters stores;

if the Chain didn't get its act together, Fotheringham was going to blast its inefficiency in *Maclean's*. In that case, Stevenson replied, he'd return every Key Porter book in his possession.

By the dawn of 2000, however, it was apparent that the belligerent business model wasn't working. For all its dominance, the behemoth had grown too quickly: no doubt expanding the market, as Stevenson often claimed, but also far outstripping the market's ability to grow. Publishers realized Stevenson hadn't been buying their books so much as borrowing them, fully returnable, to wallpaper his edifice complex. He'd extracted steep discounts and supermarket-type display fees, even charging publishers to attend his sales conventions; but his numbers didn't add up to a healthy business. Yet the Chapters stock price had stayed buoyant long enough, breaking $30 at its height, that Stevenson and other company executives made a killing selling their shares.

Mere days after the *Globe and Mail*'s *Report on Business* magazine put the grinning, denim-shirted Stevenson on its cover as "Man of the Year" for 1999, Pegasus began returning books to publishers in unprecedented quantities. Receiving a credit note for a big round sum, indicating their receivables from Pegasus were being reduced accordingly, publishers would wait, sometimes for weeks, for the books to come back. Often they arrived damaged, bearing the telltale traces of coffee-slurping browsers, even though industry standards require returns to be in resaleable condition. Equally disturbing, publishers found the value of the returns sometimes varied wildly from the credit being claimed. Physical distribution at Pegasus was as chaotic as its accounting practices. Thousands of books sat marooned in transport trucks lined up outside its warehouse. Rather than streamlining the supply chain, as advertised, Pegasus had created a bottleneck that delayed deliveries by weeks.

By that time, financial reporters had got wind that the book industry was in trouble again. Sniffing a story, they discovered that publishers' returns from the Chain were running at 50 to 60 percent of sales in early 2000, instead of the industry average 20 to 30 percent. And since Chapters/Pegasus was returning books in lieu of paying its bills, publishers' cash flow was drying up. Money that *was* trickling in paid for inventory that the retailer had purchased 120, 150, even 180 days earlier, instead of the standard ninety days. As the news became public, the Chain's share price sagged below $10. Larry Stevenson went on a counteroffensive, sniping at publishers over the phone and in the media. "Chapters Shoots Back at Publishers" ran a typical headline in the *Globe and Mail*.

By July 2000, Chapters was so delinquent in paying publishers that some had put the entire Chain on credit hold. Since Chapters by then represented 65 percent of Canada's English-language retail book trade, this was akin to publishers taking themselves off life support. It was reported that Chapters owed HarperCollins Canada over $10 million, much of it dating to before Christmas 1999. A few other firms also had Chapters on hold, but most were biting their tongues. Invited to go public before the House of Commons Standing Committee on Canadian Heritage, which was convening hearings into the book trade at the CBA's request, most publishers remained meekly silent, fearing Stevenson's retribution. Notable exceptions who gave evidence at the hearings, either in public or in private, were the ACP president, Michael Harrison of Broadview Press, the ACP vice-president, Susan Renouf of Key Porter, Karl Siegler of Talon Books on behalf of the Literary Press Group, Patsy Aldana of Groundwood, Sharon Fitzhenry of Fitzhenry & Whiteside, and Lionel Koffler of Firefly.

Publicly shamed at last, Chapters reached an agreement with HarperCollins and became somewhat more amenable to paying its other suppliers. Problems with payables and returns persisted, however, until late in 2000, when the drama took an unexpected twist. A battle for control of Chapters, and consequently for the Canadian retail book market, broke out between Stevenson and his only serious rival, Toronto-based Indigo Books and Music. The smaller but well-financed Indigo, with its chain of fifteen superstores, smelled blood.

Indigo had been founded in 1996 by the entrepreneur Heather Reisman, with whom Stevenson had conducted a bitter running feud. Reisman and her husband, the financier and takeover artist Gerry Schwartz, CEO of Onex Corporation, launched a takeover bid with an offer to Chapters shareholders in November 2000. The wealthy couple became media darlings as they shrewdly outmanoeuvred Stevenson and his management group at every turn. At the end of a four-month battle, marked by Stevenson's foiled attempt to snooker his rivals by merging with the Future Shop electronics chain, Indigo's gamble was crowned with success: first when Chapters shareholders accepted an enriched offer, and ultimately by rulings in Reisman's favour by federal regulators.

This time the Competition Bureau listened more diligently to publishers' concerns. With the aid of pressure from the bureau, the ACP and the CBPC entered into a form of collective bargaining with Reisman, hammering out a detailed code of conduct to govern terms of trade between the industry and the ever more dominant super-Chain. The five-year agreement placed limits, to be lowered in stages, on the new Chain's permissible returns levels and payment periods. The code of conduct reflected a truth that had never been understood by the previous Chapters management: if the book business is waged as a winner-take-all military campaign, it fails for everybody.

The prime casualty of Larry Stevenson's Seven Years' War had been Canadian publishers' domestic market. Chapters superstores had proved to be efficient vehicles for making bestsellers – celebrity bios, happiness guides, Oprah picks – sell even better. But selling literary fiction, history, children's books, or regional titles is a different matter. To market those genres effectively requires knowledge, taste, and an ability to marry customers with the right book. That skill, known as "hand selling" in the trade, had always been the strength of independent booksellers. But by 2000, Chapters had killed off so many of the independents, whose aggregate market share had shrunk from 60 percent a decade earlier to about 35 percent, that Canadian literary, children's, and regional publishers lost market share also.

Domestic publishers had another problem with Chapters. Consumers browsing the Chain's bestseller walls or new releases displayed face-up on its "power tables" naturally assume the books have merited that placement because of their quality or popularity. In reality, suppliers have paid hefty premiums to the Chain to place their books there. Since most Canadian-owned publishers can't pay that kind of money, their books have to make do with spine-out positions on the shelves, where a book can easily get lost in a 100,000-title inventory. In a parody of the free market, superstore bestsellers are decided in advance: they are the books whose publishers can afford to publish bestsellers.

It was scarcely any wonder that Canadian publishers had begun working the American market so feverishly. But even before the Chapters debacle, other forces of change had begun pushing them closer to the margins at home.

For years literary agents were even scarcer in Canada than wealthy writers. Until the late 1970s, a single Toronto agent, Matie Molinaro, represented many of the name authors, from Marshall McLuhan to Adrienne Clarkson. Gradually other professional agents, such as Bella Pomer and Beverley Slopen, began acquiring clients and cutting deals with publishers. But it was the Lucinda Vardey Agency and the Colbert Agency that completely undid publishers' comfortable assumptions about advances and author loyalty.

Young and vivacious, Vardey made an immediate impression upon arriving from London to handle publicity for William Collins of Canada. Her stunts to grab media attention in the mid-1970s sometimes rivalled Jack McClelland's. Vardey had a penurious start as an agent, playing piano in churches and bars to make ends meet; but before long, she was earning serious money selling rights to Canadian authors abroad and to British writers (Martin Amis, Julian Barnes, Ruth Rendell) in Canada. Her major coup came in 1985, when she orchestrated international advances totalling $1 million for *The Red Fox*, the first spy thriller by the Ottawa author Anthony Hyde. Vardey's confident, dazzling style, epitomized by her dramatic telephone auctions, helped banish forever what she termed "the oh-so-grateful-author syndrome."

Nancy and Stanley Colbert operated with a different style, more abrasive but equally effective. The American-born Colberts represented many of the country's most saleable authors, including their friend Timothy Findley, whom they moved from Clarke, Irwin to Collins. The couple's aggressive tactics won the gratitude of writers and the enmity of publishers. Joined in the business by their son David, the Colberts not only raised the bar for advances by a factor of ten or more but pioneered the sale of Canadian literary properties to television and the movies.

In 1989 the Colberts startled the trade by switching to publishing, contracting to manage the newly created subsidiary HarperCollins Canada for Rupert Murdoch. They sold the Colbert Agency to Linda McKnight and her Macmillan colleague Arnold Gosewich, who renamed it MGA. Eventually the venture capitalist Bruce Westwood bought both MGA and the Vardey Agency and merged them to create the country's biggest literary agency by far, Westwood Creative Artists.

Agents' commissions, usually based on 15 percent of their authors' royalties, swelled during the 1980s and '90s, thanks to two phenomena. One was the growing demand for Canadian fiction abroad, a demand that agents themselves helped to create. The other was the changing conduct of subsidiary publishers in Canada.

In the early to mid-1980s, the Canadian branches of Penguin, Collins, and Random House all sharply increased their interest in publishing Canadian trade books. The quickest way to build a list was to buy authors and projects off the shelf, and they resorted to it with abandon. Penguin made its half-million-dollar move on Peter C. Newman for his Hudson's Bay Company history in 1982. Random House spent a similarly whopping amount for one of its first Canadian titles, *The Canadian Living Cookbook*, a ready-made package. Doubleday Canada and Collins too joined the fray. In the late 1980s, subsidiaries coughed up unprecedented advances for new books, sometimes with no realistic prospect of earning the money back. It was a heady time for agents and their clients, and for international book packagers like Madison Press in Toronto, which sold publishers finished, turnkey projects such as the heavily illustrated *Titanic* books, bought by Doubleday Canada and publishers around the globe.

With the 1991 recession, advances deflated and cooler heads prevailed. The foreign-owned companies tended, at that point, to run hot and cold in their commitment to Canadian writing. Penguin, bullish on original Canadian fiction in the 1980s, bailed out into safer territory, returning in the late 1990s. Little, Brown Canada pursued a domestic trade program for several years under its publisher, Kim McArthur, until Time Warner

decreed that the $20-million subsidiary, although generating profit esti-
mated at $2 million, wasn't profitable enough; in 1998 head office shut the
Canadian branch down entirely.

That same year, Bertelsmann merged Doubleday with Random House
in the U.S. In reviewing the deal's impact, the Chrétien government made
little attempt to require benefit, net or otherwise, to Canada, and none
whatever to the Canadian-owned sector. The Department of Industry
blandly approved creation of a merged entity bigger than the five largest
Canadian-owned publishers combined: a colossus comprising the
Random House of Canada, Knopf Canada, Vintage Canada, Doubleday
Canada, Bantam, Dell, Seal, and Anchor imprints. The giant, called
Random House of Canada, would control 25 percent of Canada's English-
language trade market, according to an estimate by the editor of *Quill &
Quire*, Scott Anderson.

In approving the merger, the federal government could reasonably
have imposed conditions such as divestiture of one or more of the imprints
through a tendering process. That requirement would have extracted
meaningful net benefit for the Canadian industry, while mitigating the
conglomerate's ability to overwhelm its domestic competition. Precedents
existed; indeed, the Department of Canadian Heritage adopted that
approach the following year. After authority to regulate foreign investment
in the cultural industries was transferred to that department from
Industry, Heritage reviewed the merger of Addison-Wesley with Prentice-
Hall by the British conglomerate Pearson and granted approval only on
condition that Pearson divest some of its educational programs to
Canadian-owned publishers.

But the Random House–Doubleday deal sailed through without
collateral benefit. The only trade publishers now able to compete on an equal
basis with the Bertelsmann conglomerate were two other subsidiaries, both
of which, at the time of writing, are headed by former Random House of
Canada executives: HarperCollins, currently under president David Kent,
and Penguin, now part of Pearson Canada, under Ed Carson.

Literary agents were ready to sell the well-heeled trinity all the
manuscripts their money could buy. In addition to Westwood Creative
Artists, at least a dozen smaller agencies, headed by Denise Bukowski,

Dean Cooke, Anne McDermid, Don Sedgwick, Carolyn Swayze, and others, represented sizable stables of authors for whom they obtained advances reaching, with surprising frequency, into six figures. Lori Lansens, whose previous writing credits consisted of screenplays, received $500,000 for international rights to her novel *Rush Home Road* (Knopf in Canada). A second-time novelist, Nancy Richler, scored $400,000 for international rights to *Your Mouth Is Lovely* (HarperCollins in Canada). Doubleday Canada paid Nino Ricci a reported total of $350,000 in a two-book contract for *Testament* and a later novel. Occasionally a large indigenous firm, usually M&S, joined in the bidding, even though its publisher, Doug Gibson, tried to avoid the excesses of what he has termed "chequebook publishing."

By 2001, a new phenomenon had appeared. Agents were no longer waiting for promising young writers to emerge from incubation in the literary presses; they were snapping up their first efforts and selling them handily to the multinationals. In a kind of gold rush fever, writers in their twenties barely out of creative writing school were being signed for advances as high as $50,000. Graduates of the creative writing program at the University of British Columbia seemed especially favoured; it's estimated that thirty UBC graduates published or were about to publish books from 1999 through 2002. Their agents were discovering what Lucinda Vardey had proved fifteen years earlier with Anthony Hyde: first-time authors are attractive to publishers precisely *because* there is no track record – the writer is all potential.

Observers marvel why – when first novels typically sell 2,500 copies in Canada and earn the author less than $10,000 – multinational publishers are betting the farm to buy them.

But they aren't betting the farm. The subsidiaries' primary source of profit continues to lie, as it always has, in marketing the parent company's titles. The McGraw-Hill International executive Walter Wulff's pithy 1972 statement to *Publishers Weekly* still applies: "The prime objective of a foreign subsidiary is not its own publishing but the sale of the U.S. product." With the marketing and distribution infrastructure in place for that purpose, subsidiaries' costs on Canadian titles are amortized over much larger and more profitable sales volumes in imported books. Although they don't base their livelihood on Canadian publishing, the subsidiaries are wealthy enough to afford fishing expeditions for the next hot Canadian author. One rationale sometimes advanced – that multinationals take losses on Canadian publishing in order to be good corporate citizens, and thus keep government off their backs – doesn't hold water. Such an approach would catch up with them sooner or later, causing head office to apply the brakes.

Karl Siegler of Talon Books put forward another explanation. He conceived it after watching his former author Brian Fawcett leave for HarperCollins and a large advance for *Public Eye: An Investigation into the Disappearance of the World*, and after watching the novelist Michael Turner leave Arsenal Pulp Press for Doubleday and an advance reported as $60,000 for *The Pornographer's Poem*. Since neither book seemed likely to earn back the advance from sales, Siegler concluded (based on other supporting evidence) that the subsidiary publishers had simply decided to wipe their domestic competitors off the map, or at least push them to its far edges, by buying up author futures. He compared the tactic to the cola wars, in which Coca-Cola spared no expense to decimate its competition. And since the Canadian publishing equivalents of Coca-Cola were winning the war, Siegler prophesied, the great flowering of Canadian-owned publishing since the 1960s will eventually prove to have been a one-generation phenomenon.

A more nuanced explanation rests on the facts that the multinationals are competing essentially with one another, and Canadian fiction has become big business, replacing non-fiction as the most profitable category. In 1996, three extraordinarily successful Canadian novels changed the rules of the game. Anne Michaels's *Fugitive Pieces* (M&S), Ann-Marie MacDonald's *Fall on Your Knees*, and Gail Anderson-Dargatz's *The Cure for Death by Lightning* (both Knopf Canada) all sold huge quantities at home and abroad. And all were first novels. Suddenly fiction, particularly first fiction, appeared in a fresh light. If a company had even one such hit a year, the profits would be big enough to offset losses on numerous other books.

Subsidiary publishers began pursuing the Hollywood blockbuster strategy: out of every ten releases, most will lose money, two or three will break even, and one or two will be highly profitable. If companies spread their nets widely enough, their odds of landing a blockbuster improve. Among movie studios and record labels, this is known as risk reduction.

A risk reduction strategy works only if two factors are present. One is a commitment of major marketing money to each prospect. Hence the advertising budgets heralding Knopf Canada's "New Faces of Fiction" campaign, Random House of Canada's "Discover Your Next Favourite Author" campaign, and Penguin Canada's "Our Canadian Girl" campaign. And hence glossy advertorials such as Random's giveaway magazine *Read*, the production of free "reading guides" to promote new novels to book clubs, and full-colour HarperCollins catalogues tucked into copies of *Quill & Quire*. It's a numbers game few can afford, and it leads to what John Metcalf has acerbically termed "the manufacturing of celebrity by ignorant media and the manipulation of the audience by publicity budgets."

The other precondition for risk reduction is hiring outstanding editor-publishers to scout literary talent. This the subsidiaries have done brilliantly, giving executive positions to some of the best editors in the business. At Penguin, until her retirement in early 2003, it was Cynthia Good, a veteran trade publisher and architect of a nationalistic non-fiction program worthy of Jack McClelland in his prime, led by authors such as Linda McQuaig, John Ralston Saul, and James Laxer. At HarperCollins, it's Iris Tupholme and Phyllis Bruce, whose reputation rests in part on publishing award-winning fiction by Richard Wright, Bonnie Burnard, Sharon Butala, and Dennis Bock. At Random House of Canada, the editor-in-chief is Anne Collins, gifted author and former editor of *Toronto Life*; Knopf Canada has Louise Dennys and her colleague Diane Martin; the Doubleday Canada imprint comes under Maya Mavjee; and until spring 2003, John Pearce was executive editor-at-large for all Random and Doubleday imprints. Without the experience, discernment, and skill of such editors, the subsidiaries, for all their flash and cash, would still be churning out cookbooks and packaged titles.

The blockbuster syndrome is reinforced by the fact that Canadian fiction has its own version of the Man Booker Prize (as it's now known). Winning the Giller Prize and its $25,000 purse, first awarded in 1994, is only the beginning for a novelist; the Giller confers the Midas touch on sales too. The glitzy Giller gala is televised live every November from a Toronto hotel. The nominees are introduced to musical fanfares and video dramatizations before an invited audience that has just eaten a fine dinner; the suspense builds; the winner is announced to eruptions of publicity, kicking off the Christmas book buying season. With the Giller sending a winner's sales through the roof, large unearned advances for potential finalists become "a cost of doing business," according to HarperCollins's Phyllis Bruce. A Giller win can mean a sale of over 100,000 copies in Canada. Even being nominated can boost demand; publishers go back to press on the strength of the nomination alone. But since there can be only five nominees and one winner, the stakes are high, and the gambler needs strong nerves and plenty of cash.

Publishers may have other reasons for spending a lot of money for a book, Bruce explained, quite apart from its commercial potential – corporate reasons. The advance can be considered a long-term investment in an author who holds the promise of delivering future titles or, in some cases, a desirable backlist, to which rights may be available. Or the publisher may wish to make a billboard statement, displaying to writers and their agents the bankroll to become a major player, in the hope of attracting other authors. In the end, as Bruce acknowledged, it's all informed speculation anyway. Like portfolio managers in a mutual fund, only publishers whose hunches pan out more often than not will prosper.

Fortunately for those publishers, other factors besides the Giller come into play – what Penguin's Cynthia Good called "an inventory of possibilities" that can help a book take off. The title may be made into a movie or a television program. It may be bought by chains such as Price Club or Costco, which order relatively few titles but in very large quantities. It may become a book club selection; the most powerful book club by far is Oprah Winfrey's, which selected novels by the Canadians Ann-Marie MacDonald and Rohinton Mistry, stimulating previously unheard-of sales running into the hundreds of thousands. And on a smaller scale, a book may benefit enormously from that much-desired but elusive quality, word of mouth. Word spreads from reader to reader, sometimes through writers' festivals or private reading clubs. One of Good's authors at Penguin, Donna Morrissey of Newfoundland, overcame ho-hum reviews and media coverage for *Kit's Law*; the novel sold 35,000 copies because booksellers loved it and hand-sold it to their customers.

The biggest gambles publishers make are on new writers with no track record at all. Betting five or six figures on a first novel by someone hyped as the next Anne Michaels or the new Michael Ondaatje may be rational-ized as an investment in the author's future. But when sales are just fair to middling, and the advance remains unearned, a publisher's ardour cools. "I worry about the impact on younger writers' careers," one admired veteran editor mused. "When they get a whack of money and the book doesn't earn out, their ability to earn a decent advance on their second or third book is harmed."

The Giller Prize has had ancillary benefits. It has helped raise the profile of the older Governor General's Awards, whose juries have recently been more adventurous in their picks than most Giller juries. The Giller's popularity has also helped bring into existence a host of other national awards, from the Charles Taylor Prize for creative non-fiction and the Writers' Trust of Canada awards, two of them sponsored by the Rogers and Pearson corporations, to the Griffin Poetry Prize. At $40,000 each for both a Canadian poet and an international poet, the Griffin purse has made many in the media far more excited about poetry than they'd ever guessed they could be.

Certainly literary prizes heighten a sense of excitement around books – at least around those that are nominated – presumably driving people into the bookstores. One always hopes the glare of publicity will bathe other authors in reflected light. But the fixation with competition and success may only divide literature into a hierarchy of winners and losers, benefiting the chosen few. The *reductio ad absurdum* is the craze for "one-book" reading promotions, which exhort an entire population to read the same title. Even the Vancouver Public Library and CBC Radio have got into this act. In its Canada Reads competition, the public broadcaster features a panel of celebrity critics who review several Canadian novels and banish one after another from the island, leaving a single survivor (in 2002 it was Michael Ondaatje's *In the Skin of a Lion*; in 2003, Hubert Aquin's *Next Episode*) that all Canadians are urged to read.

Gigantism in the book trade, exemplified by superstore book retailing, big cash advances, and media-bedazzling prizes, has bred a form of literary cross-dressing. While cash-poor domestic publishers masquerade as Americans, foreign-owned conglomerates reach for the brass ring by showcasing Canadian writers. That new environment produced the first big publishing surprises of the millennium.

As the century turned, greying Canadian publishers were beginning to ask themselves if they had sufficient prospects, money, and energy to do business in the new environment. Avie Bennett was the first to answer that question.

In June 2000, stealing the headlines from the news that scientists had decoded the human genome, Bennett convened a media conference to announce the sale of McClelland & Stewart. Since he had no heir prepared to succeed him as a publisher, the trade had been speculating about such a sale for years. But no one was expecting Bennett to announce that he was donating 75 percent of M&S to the University of Toronto.

With a curious mixture of shyness and steely bravado, the seventy-two-year-old Bennett explained he'd structured the terms of his donation, with the federal government's blessing, so that the company could remain a separate, commercial publishing entity. M&S would shed its agency lines but keep its publishing staff, headed by Doug Gibson, and would be governed by a new board of directors chaired by Bennett. The university would hover in the background as majority owner, with control over five of the seven seats on the M&S board. But that wasn't all.

Bennett had sold the remaining 25 percent of Canada's most storied publishing company for an undisclosed sum, reliably assumed to be large, to a rival publisher. M&S's new minority partner wouldn't be Jack Stoddart, Ron Besse, or any of Bennett's other Canadian colleagues, as might have been expected from an outspoken nationalist. Instead it would be Random House of Canada, the local branch of the world's most ubiquitous and powerful multinational publisher. With two seats on the board for its one-quarter stake (the maximum a foreign investor could own if the company was to remain eligible for grants), Random would also take responsibility for many of M&S's most crucial operating functions: sales, distribution, accounting, and financial management. The Bertelsmann behemoth would have not a foot but a muscular shoulder inside the door of M&S.

Bennett's public comments suggested he'd made the move not only to recover some of the treasure he'd sunk into M&S over the years but to ally the company with the strongest player in the market. Anticipating the shock he'd create, Bennett had lined up the support of his most celebrated author, Margaret Atwood, whose bona fides as a cultural nationalist are impeccable. In a prepared statement, Atwood praised Bennett's "thoughtfulness, thoroughness and integrity" in making the donation to the university. She encouraged M&S authors to feel confidence in the new arrangement.

Others weren't so sanguine. Critics and competitors asked how long it would take before Random leveraged its 25 percent to acquire effective control. Some opined that it *already* exercised control. At the very least, Random held the purse strings and would be responsible for absorbing any operating losses, which could place it in a position to demand greater equity someday. Nor was it clear for how long the University of Toronto would continue to own M&S, or just how it would exercise its stewardship.

What about the federal objective of expanding Canadian ownership of the book industry? Was the government giving up on three decades of public investment, surrendering without a shot being fired? Although those questions were far from answered, books from "The Canadian Publishers" would be shipped out of Random's North American distribution centre in Westminster, Maryland. The symbolism was too potent to ignore.

Certainly Ron Besse noticed it.

By 2000, Besse had long since downgraded Macmillan's Canadian publishing program. But he'd also taken the process much farther. Two years earlier, he'd buried Macmillan inside a new company, CDG Books

Canada, 49 percent of which belonged to IDG Books, American publishers of the immensely successful Dummies guides.

Macmillan had been distributing the Dummies books in Canada. As sales of the series topped $10 million in this country, IDG had, predictably, wanted greater control. Other companies, such as Penguin Canada, were vying with Besse for the distribution rights; to preclude losing the lucrative agency, he offered IDG the biggest stake he legally could. The historic publisher of MacLennan, Creighton, Davies, and Munro was erased. As CDG Books began publishing titles for "Canadian Dummies," the dumbing-down of Macmillan was complete.

Or so it seemed. But Besse had another trick up his sleeve. Although his Canada Publishing Corporation, owner of Gage, legally retained 51 percent of CDG, there was little doubt who exercised effective control. By 1999 about 60 percent of CDG's $20-million annual volume was in IDG titles, the remainder in Macmillan books. Besse said in an interview that it was becoming less and less viable to run a trade agency in Canada; with a single chain dominating the retail market, all an American publisher had to do, in effect, was to sell to Chapters. "American publishers don't need a Canadian distributor now," Besse asserted, "so that stream of profitability is being shut off. You're going to have to make it on your Canadian publishing program. I'm not really sure whether our small Canadian publishers can make it work."

Bearing out his own prediction, Besse was party to shutting down CDG Books early in 2002. The American educational publisher John Wiley & Sons had bought IDG in the United States. Wiley's Canadian subsidiary assumed IDG's 49 percent stake in CDG, but it wanted to own 100 percent. Barred from doing so by federal regulation, Wiley refused to participate in the partnership structure that IDG and Besse had devised. Wiley pulled the plug on CDG.

Wiley's Canadian branch hired thirteen of CDG's thirty employees, not including the president, the highly respected Tom Best. It then assumed the Canadian distributorship of the Dummies guides, as it had a legal right to do. The Macmillan list was put up for auction in June 2002. Although there were reportedly other offers, John Wiley & Sons Canada, not surprisingly, was the successful bidder. Under federal investment guidelines, it's permissible for a foreign investor to purchase a Canadian-owned publisher's assets, as long as it doesn't purchase the company itself: a loophole of very considerable proportions. The practical effect was, in this case, the same. As Wiley's departing Canadian president, Diane Wood, confirmed, "This will provide a great foundation for us to expand our local publishing program."

No one in the industry, much less in the government, spoke out against the blatant end run. Clearly federal foreign investment rules, erratically enforced over the years, were made to be bent if not broken.

While Ron Besse was scuttling the good ship Macmillan, Jack Stoddart was in court, sinking in debt. Stoddart's empire, critically positioned at the heart of the industry's distribution network, was the most ruinous casualty of the wars of succession. For a demoralizing period in spring and summer 2002, the wreck of Stoddart Publishing threatened to take many other Canadian publishers down with it.

The company, which had made money for most of the years Stoddart owned it, had been especially vulnerable to Larry Stevenson's depredations. With a big Canadian trade list and a slew of agencies, Stoddart Publishing relied on the Chain for up to 70 percent of its sales of new releases. (More specialized niche or regional publishers, by contrast, might make only 30 percent of their sales to Chapters.) Stoddart's General Distribution Services also handled order fulfillment for some 200 other publishers, sixty-two of them Canadian, and processed $87 million in annual sales. When Chapters started playing dangerous games with credit notes and returns, GDS was directly in the line of fire. The only arms of Stoddart's business to escape were Irwin Publishing, because it operated in the educational market, and his American operations.

Stoddart held his breath and continued paying GDS client publishers, even though GDS itself still hadn't been paid by Chapters; moreover, massive returns still had to be sorted and passed on to their publishers. Two of the firms whose cash flow he was buffering in this way were Key Porter and Douglas & McIntyre, in which he'd invested. Another forty or so were small presses in the Literary Press Group. Stoddart was once heard to say that if he had to take 50 percent returns from his largest customer, he could scarcely stay in business; but if he had to take 50 percent returns and not get paid for the other 50 percent, staying in business was out of the question. Somebody should have been listening.

The company already had its share of problems, some self-inflicted. In 1998 GDS had moved to a new warehouse outside Toronto with 300,000 square feet of space, four times its previous capacity, much of it not yet needed. In addition to incurring increased leasing costs, GDS lost experienced staffers unwilling to make the trek out of town. A refit of its computer system in preparation for the turn of the millennium was reported to cost $2 million and caused serious disruptions to customer service; in the middle of the 1999 Christmas season, GDS was unable to ship for twelve days.

For the next two years, GDS continued bleeding cash, starving more profitable parts of the business. One of those was Irwin, whose president, Brian O'Donnell, had built it from a $3-million enterprise to $12 million, generating profits that benefited Stoddart's other operations. But all branches of the empire suffered when Stoddart was unable to arrange refinancing through a Canadian bank. Both the big five and smaller banks were leery of lending to a business with such a high proportion of its receivables from Chapters. In the end, ironically, Stoddart found an American lender, Finova, based in Arizona, which lent money on the basis of a company's assets instead of its balance sheet. Finova provided Stoddart with a line of credit of $20 million (Can.).

But in the midst of the cash flow problems generated by Chapters, Finova itself filed for bankruptcy in fall 2001. Stoddart had to scramble once again for financing. For ten weeks, the company went without a line of credit, still struggling against the perception that it was too dependent on a single customer. In November 2001, the Department of Canadian Heritage rode to the rescue. The department approved a loan guarantee of $4.5 million from its loan-loss reserve program, which went to the Bank of Nova Scotia, backstopping a new line of credit. As per his understanding with the government, Stoddart paid off much of the debt to client publishers, authors, and printers, all of whom had been suffering collateral damage from his woes.

Stoddart/GDS looked set to recover its footing. But in the first two months of 2002, returns from Chapters/Indigo were again heavy – Stoddart claimed to have received a whopping $5 million in debit notes – and GDS again had to delay payments. Key Porter and Douglas & McIntyre both made contingency plans to obtain distribution elsewhere, warning Stoddart they'd have to leave if things didn't improve. He urged them to stay, assuring them and other worried clients that everything would be fine by March. It wasn't. It seemed the bank didn't agree with Stoddart about how much of his credit line he could draw down: once the returns were factored in, according to the bank's lending formula, he'd used up his borrowing capacity. Suddenly his room to manoeuvre vanished.

On April 30, 2002, General Publishing – the company that held all of Jack Stoddart's publishing interests, 85 percent owned by him personally – filed for bankruptcy protection in the Ontario Superior Court of Justice. The company reported debts totalling $45.7 million. They included $16 million due to the first secured creditor, the Bank of Nova Scotia, $13 million to unsecured GDS clients and agency publishers (of which about $5 million was owed to Canadian firms), and $1.5 million to authors.

For many publishers, the court filing seemed to spell disaster. Their panic was equalled by a sense of outrage that they hadn't received adequate warning. The fortunate ones, relatively speaking, were clients who had notified Stoddart before the filing of their intention to leave GDS and move to other distributors, which meant they could at least take possession of their inventory. These included D&M (owed about $2 million), Key Porter (owed about $1 million), ECW Press (owed $340,000), and Goose Lane Editions (Susanne Alexander, its publisher, counted herself lucky that Stoddart had cut her loose the day she gave notice in mid-April). But small literary presses such as Coteau Books, Véhicule Press, and the Porcupine's Quill and mid-sized clients such as McGill-Queen's University Press (owed over $800,000) and Hushion House were less fortunate.

Already facing the prospect of losing their domestic sales revenue, GDS clients confronted the dilemma of whether to allow the distributor to continue filling orders for their books during the term of bankruptcy protection – thirty days at first, later extended to ninety – with no certainty they'd ever see a penny. Having lost all confidence in GDS, most instructed it to stop shipping. This had the effect of making the distributor decidedly less attractive to potential buyers. His clients' defection guaranteed, Stoddart would contend later, that the receiver would be unable to sell GDS itself and thus realize cash with which to pay the debts.

Only a few weeks earlier, some client presses had already suffered from bankruptcy protection accorded their American distributor, LPC Group. Able to recover their inventory from LPC but not their receivables, many were out sizeable amounts in U.S. dollars.

Amid the strange spectacle of Stoddart's lawyers battling lawyers representing the ACP, the LPG, and individual creditors, an Ontario judge brought down a ruling that crushed the client publishers. They'd argued that their accounts receivable were their property, held in trust by GDS; but the court's interpretation of their distribution agreements was that GDS owned the receivables. That meant, for all practical purposes, that when all Stoddart assets were liquidated, the bank would get whatever monies resulted.

The publishers' plight was graphically described by Véhicule's Simon Dardick and Nancy Marrelli in their "Open Letter to the President of the Bank of Nova Scotia" in May 2002. Calling the court ruling "the death knell for many publishers," Dardick and Marrelli appealed to the bank's tradition of helping small enterprises; they pleaded that publishers be allowed to go into the GDS warehouse to get their books back. "Without access to our inventory or the ability to sign with a new distributor," they wrote, "in two or three months we won't be here. Publishers cannot exist without sales revenues or without alternate means of distribution. The Bank of Nova Scotia is the only entity that has the power to allow the small-to-medium book publishers affected by the GDS debacle to continue in business."

Neither the bank nor the court was swayed. To add insult to injury, client publishers would soon find themselves forking over hefty court-mandated fees merely to recover their books from the GDS warehouse.

As arguments and recriminations flew, perhaps Jack Stoddart's only benefit was discovering who his friends were. Anna Porter was quoted as saying that the last time Stoddart had paid her, Jesus had been in short pants. Ron Besse, on the other hand – to whom Stoddart didn't owe money – commented that he felt sympathy for him: "Jack worked his butt off for this industry," Besse was quoted as saying, adding that some of Stoddart's harshest critics were those who'd benefited from his advocacy work. The *National Post* kicked Stoddart mercilessly while he was down, running a photograph that made him resemble a Mafia don as he left the courthouse in dark glasses. The paper's coverage was thick with ad hominem slurs on his conduct and character, coming from industry colleagues who sheltered behind anonymity.

Amid all the public and private blaming, one piece of analysis made sense. By taking on so many small-press clients at GDS, Stoddart had performed a service to the industry but a disservice to himself. Fulfilling small orders from numerous small accounts is an expensive business; yet Stoddart had charged the LPG presses exceptionally low fees, a feature that had naturally attracted them in the first place.

The bigger picture was that Stoddart, beset by upheavals in his professional and personal lives, had let management of his increasingly complex operation get away from him. Insiders concurred that he'd been too reluctant to cut costs and too slow to lay off employees when trouble struck, making few staff reductions even while the company was sinking. A serious case of denial had been at work: an eerie echo of the failure two decades earlier of Clarke, Irwin, another second-generation publisher that failed to adapt to harsh times.

There was some indication that Stoddart had realized he needed to integrate his disparate companies within a more coherent strategy. Late in 1999 he'd hired Paul Davidson, the former political aide and consultant who, in five years as the ACP's executive director, had proved a smart, articulate, and effective advocate for Canadian publishing. After a year as Stoddart's vice-president of administration, Davidson helped move the adult trade program into the black. But he felt there hadn't been a real opportunity for the management group, including Stoddart's minority partners, Nelson Doucet and Brian O'Donnell, to reposition the company. Although Davidson attributed its final downfall to cash hemorrhaging from GDS, he also speculated that trouble may have been inevitable, given the absence of internal management controls. Communication from the top, to colleagues both inside and outside the company, was inadequate: "You could count on the fingers of one hand the number of management meetings in the past two years. For whatever reason, Jack seemed unable to act on the advice of his senior managers, including those with decades of experience."

By the end of summer, Davidson joined 200 or so other Stoddart employees who had lost their livelihoods. But like industry colleagues such as Susanne Alexander and Bill Hushion, he refused to join the chorus who focused on Stoddart's errors in judgment while ignoring his accomplishments. "Right now," Davidson observed, "Jack could walk on water and people would say he couldn't swim."

The sentiment was echoed by the historian Christopher Moore, a former chair of the Writers' Union of Canada: "Jack Stoddart looks to me like a guy with big ambitions who had to bet his company to fulfill them. He'd be a hero if he'd won the bet."

As for Stoddart himself, he remained adamant (again like Bill Clarke) that his firm didn't have to go down. "The company was eminently savable," Stoddart insisted in late 2002. "Stoddart Publishing and Irwin were profitable – it was GDS that was losing money." He cited different scenarios in which the outcome could have been different: if he'd been paid by Chapters/Indigo in early 2002; if the GDS client publishers hadn't bailed out so quickly; if the bad news stories hadn't prevented him from closing a sale of Irwin to Gage; if the bank hadn't sent in their "hatchetmen."

Stoddart couldn't help feeling he'd been the fall guy for others: "We had millions of dollars of returns in the GDS warehouse. And everybody was saying, 'They're not mine.' Nobody had an answer to the returns problem except, 'Let it be Jack's problem.'"

From May to August 2002, Stoddart and his restructuring officer raised whatever cash they could by finding buyers for the various assets. Irwin Publishing went to Nelson Thomson Learning for a price reported at $7.5 million; Stoddart Kids went to Fitzhenry & Whiteside, which hired Nelson Doucet as a vice-president; Boston Mills Press was bought by Firefly, and Anansi by the millionaire Scott Griffin, of Griffin Poetry Prize fame. In the end, there was no buyer for Stoddart Publishing itself, or for GDS.

The question remaining was how badly the rest of Canadian publishing would be gored. But the industry's internal alliances and government relationships, to which Stoddart had once been crucial, helped salvage the situation. The LPG executive director, David Caron, the ACP executive director, Monique Smith, and their boards worked together to negotiate remedies with officials at Canadian Heritage, the Canada Council, and the Ontario government. To help the victims bridge the cash flow gap and ready their books for the fall season, Sheila Copps's department provided GDS's Canadian clients with substantial advances on their regular funding. The government wouldn't contribute monies beyond budgeted levels, but it allowed publishers to draw down advances against several years' worth of future contributions from the Book Publishing Industry Development Program. The Ontario government of the new Conservative premier, Ernie Eves, meanwhile, stepped up with $1.5 million in emergency assistance.

Significantly, the federal government, which had already rescued Stoddart Publishing once through the loan guarantee program, offered no help to keep the company afloat. Jack Stoddart's political capital in Ottawa was exhausted. He'd always maintained there was a need for greater consolidation in Canadian-owned publishing; now the process would have to go on without him. The wars of succession would continue. The stakes would be higher than ever.

Red Deer P R E S S

FIFTH
HOUSE

LONE
PINE

ANANSI

INSOMNIAC PRESS

ORCA BOOK PUBLISHERS

RED DEER PRESS | BROKEN JAW PRESS | RAINCOAST BOOKS

THOMAS ALLEN PUBLISHERS | SECOND STORY PRESS | FIFTH HOUSE PUBLISHING

GASPEREAU PRESS | LONE PINE PUBLISHING | HOUSE OF ANANSI PRESS

INSOMNIAC PRESS

16

NO PUBLISHER'S PARADISE

*All the evidence which we have examined leads, directly
or indirectly, to the conclusion that the Canadian book
publishing industry . . . is facing almost insuperable
economic pressures. These threaten either to force it under,
or so to attenuate it that it could only survive as an
enfeebled regional cultural activity.*

Canadian Publishers and Canadian Publishing,
Ontario Royal Commission on Book Publishing (1973)

Six decades after Morley Callaghan had termed Canada "no publisher's
paradise," the Stoddart/GDS failure put the future of indigenous publishing once again in doubt. Losing the industry's largest Canadian-owned
player was traumatic. The damage went far beyond GDS client publishers
and Stoddart employees: it struck authors whose royalties evaporated
and whose books vanished from the marketplace; freelance editors and
designers who didn't get paid; booksellers who lost access to thousands of
titles; and printers and other suppliers forced to write off large debts. Even
companies unconnected to GDS shivered in the chill emanating from
nervous bankers and investors. Simon Dardick described the experience as
"the worst time of our lives, when we could see everything we'd worked for
coming to an end."

And yet, as so often in the past, the industry proved remarkably
resilient. By August 2002, Dardick's Véhicule Press was among the Literary

Press Group members who had found new distributors and could start rebuilding their lives. Other GDS clients, including Douglas & McIntyre, Goose Lane Editions, Cormorant Books, and the Porcupine's Quill, ended up at University of Toronto Press Distribution. Key Porter went to H.B. Fenn & Co., the Toronto-area distributor whose $100 million in annual revenues, mainly from American agencies, now made it the industry's biggest Canadian-owned entity after Nelson Thomson and Harlequin Books. One of the worst-hit clients was the country's second-largest scholarly publisher; McGill-Queen's University Press banded together with the University of British Columbia Press and several other academic presses to obtain distribution from a relative newcomer, Georgetown Terminal Warehouses. Harbour Publishing found a safe port with Whitecap Books back home in British Columbia. Publishers had learned a hard but vital lesson: to insist, in their new distributor agreements, on ownership of their receivables, so that monies owed to them are held in trust and thus protected from their distributors' banks and other preferred creditors.

Most of the publishers had lost their spring season and seen fall 2002 seriously compromised. The problem was even worse for those affected by the insolvency of the American distributor LPC. One such was ECW Press; its rapid expansion in the United States had drawn admiring comment in *Publishers Weekly*, but as a combined result of the two receiverships, ECW lost half a million dollars in a single month. Jack David and Robert Lecker had reached the limits of their borrowing capacity and were forced to put the twenty-five-year-old press up for sale. While entertaining expressions of interest, however, they had some unexpected good fortune with *Ghost Rider*, a journal of family tragedy and healing by Neil Peart, drummer for the super-group Rush. Because it appeared after the GDS collapse, Peart's poignant and inspiring memoir got to market, became a bestseller, and gave ECW the best summer in its history. The press was able to stay alive and independent after all, thanks also to emergency aid from the federal and Ontario governments.

Even as it was providing welcome financial relief for publishers and writers, the federal government was sending mixed signals about the book industry. On the one hand, the Department of Canadian Heritage pressed ahead with its supply chain strategy, an initiative urged by the parliamentary heritage committee after the Chapters hearings. Enriched by a succession of annual surpluses, the government committed $8 million over three years to trying to save the industry from the excesses of its own trade practices. The initiative aimed to support the adoption of new technologies making physical distribution more efficient and helping publishers and booksellers to manage the inventory that constantly flows between them. These measures, it was hoped, would cut down on the waste and expense of returns, thus making the industry more profitable. On the other hand, the same government brought down foreign investment rulings that continued the dismal policy retreat begun by Investment Canada.

In 2002 the on-line retailer Amazon.com wanted to enlarge its market share by launching a Web site selling books to Canadians in Canadian dollars. It wasn't as if the American giant had been prevented from doing business in this country. The Internet already gave Canadian consumers full access to Amazon's huge title selection and discount offers, except that they had to pay currency exchange and customs duties on Amazon orders. Although the company had already taken a slice of the domestic market, Amazon wanted more – money-losing quasi-monopolies always do. All it had to do was "locate" in Canada by getting around the foreign ownership policy.

Amazon astutely hired a well-connected Liberal, former New Brunswick premier Frank McKenna, as its Ottawa lobbyist. As an inducement to obtain publishing industry support, the company committed itself to staying within the Copyright Act and to ordering its books from domestic sources. The losers, once again, would be Canadian booksellers – not just Chapters.Indigo.ca, the major Internet bookseller in the country, but every bricks-and-mortar store. Already decimated by the Chain, the ranks of independent booksellers could only expect to lose more business.

In June 2002, the government permitted Amazon's virtual entry into the Canadian market despite formal objections from Chapters/Indigo and the Canadian Booksellers Association. The Department of Canadian Heritage considered that Amazon.ca didn't contravene foreign investment guidelines because it wouldn't maintain a physical corporate presence in Canada, such as a warehouse and employees; instead it would contract out its operations to Canadian intermediaries – including the government's own Canada Post.

Technically, the decision made a certain kind of sense. But by ducking the political challenge of adapting the foreign investment guidelines to the new world of e-commerce, the government again backed away from its long-standing goal of a strongly Canadian-controlled book industry. Opposition to Amazon's arrival was muted, if only because so many publishers welcomed competition, any competition, for Chapters/Indigo.

The next federal decision didn't merely bend the foreign investment rules, it broke them outright. In November 2002, the government permitted Susan Stoddart, CEO of Distican, to sell her company to its major American agency, Simon & Schuster. S&S had reportedly stated it would refuse to work with any new Canadian owner of Distican, as the policy required; instead it would pull out of Canada, which represents about 7 percent of its $649-million (U.S.) operations, and go home. Executives at S&S's parent, Viacom, knew from experience how effective it can be to threaten the Canadian government.

The official explanation for the Distican ruling was that it represented "an exception" to the policy, necessary to save eighty Canadian jobs. In actuality, the government had been unprepared to call Viacom's bluff about walking away from a lucrative business arrangement worth nearly $70 million (Can.).

The federal foreign investment policy remained formally in place. But, coming in the wake of the Stoddart/GDS collapse, the two ownership decisions pointed to a demoralizing conclusion: as far as many government officials were concerned, the great game of creating a made-in-Canada book industry was all but over.

A similar outlook coloured a *Globe and Mail* feature article during the GDS grief in spring 2002. It airily dismissed Canadian publishers' troubles on the grounds that the multinationals were publishing most of the important fiction anyhow. The feature included puff pieces on the latest novels from the Canadian outposts of Random House, Knopf, HarperCollins, and Penguin that could have been produced by the companies' promotion departments. It was preposterous for Canada's national newspaper to banish two generations of seminal literary publishing in a sentence or two. For its part, *Quill & Quire* took the position editorially that Canadian ownership, whether in publishing or in bookselling, counted for little compared with the virtues of "competition."

The fact is that, in the long run, competition will decline and largely disappear if Canada's unique policy model is abandoned to raw economics. Diversity and competition in the Canadian book industry will be replaced by the dominance of a very few multinationals with no allegiance to this country. And precedents will have been established that allow any Canadian publisher, or for that matter Chapters/Indigo, to argue that the government has given itself no choice but to let them sell to foreign buyers.

In parallel with the government's apparent retreat from its policy objectives, certain challenges to the industry are worsening. In some respects, book publishing is regressing to conditions of the 1950s and '60s. One of those conditions, clearly, is the imbalance between the Canadian-controlled and foreign-controlled sectors. Others include the dilemma in retail bookselling, the state of school libraries, and inadequate media coverage.

The problem in bookselling isn't a lack of outlets, as it once was, so much as a shortage of community-based, independent retailers. In some communities, the Chain is practically all there is. Even in major cities such as Calgary, Ottawa, and Vancouver, independents are thin on the ground downtown and nearly non-existent in the suburbs.

That hegemony places a tremendous responsibility on Heather Reisman's $700-million operation. With 89 superstores and another 181 conventional outlets as of this writing, the Chapters/Indigo empire rules the book market with even less competition than Larry Stevenson's company. The onus remains on the retailer itself, on the publishing industry with which it negotiated terms of trade, and on the federal government, which approved the merger, to ensure that the Chain wields its market power in the public interest. Given the extent of that power, Chapters/Indigo cannot function as a completely unregulated semi-monopoly; and it cannot be permitted to fall under foreign control.

Canada's publishers still work in a climate conditioned by a decade of government deficit-fighting at both the federal and provincial levels, a process that resulted in drastic cutbacks to education and public libraries. The resulting decline in book purchases, especially by schools and school libraries, has hurt producers of educational and children's materials while severely undermining the quality of education.

That situation has now been recognized as critical. It prompted the founding in 2002 of the Canadian Coalition for School Libraries, an alliance of publishers, librarians, and parents committed to reversing the decline in book budgets and teacher-librarian staff positions across the country. Such initiatives are needed to boost the sales of quality Canadian materials by children's publishers, whose lists will otherwise become increasingly commercialized and oriented to the American market. As one of the coalition's founders, Patsy Aldana of Groundwood Books, has observed, "If we don't find ways to reach our own market, we'll see a real loss of Canadian content in the children's industry."

Another return to the past is represented by shrinking media coverage of books and authors. Many major dailies, with the chief exception of the *Globe and Mail*'s Saturday book supplement, have cut back on book reviews, especially of Canadian titles. A survey in the April 2003 *Quill & Quire* measured newspaper review coverage in 1997 and 2002. Although the number of book reviews had remained constant overall, most newspapers, with the exception of the *Globe and Mail* and the *Halifax Chronicle-Herald*, were reviewing fewer Canadian authors five years later. The drop was most precipitous at the former Southam papers now owned by CanWest Global, which featured overall reductions of 14 percent in total reviews, 25 percent in Canadian authors, 46 percent in books from small Canadian presses, and 49 percent in children's books. Cutbacks in coverage of books from Canadian-owned publishers was especially pronounced at the *Edmonton Journal* and the *Ottawa Citizen*; the latter was running far more syndicated material from American print and on-line sources.

Radio programs interviewing authors have also declined in number and opted for lighter programming, although at the traditionally book-friendly CBC Radio, book chat is on the rise again. Meanwhile television shows dedicated to books have increased. Long-running programs such as

TVOntario's *Imprint* and CBC's *Hot Type* were joined in 2001 by the digital channel Book Television, produced by Daniel Richler, and such programs as *Fine Print* on Rogers Cable. Small-screen coverage is naturally welcomed by publishers, but they continue to regard print as the natural and most effective medium for reaching book buyers; and print coverage is demonstrably slipping.

Beyond such challenges, the succession issue remains vital in the first decade of the twenty-first century. The existence of a diverse, creatively vibrant, genuinely national industry still depends considerably on public policy. But policies are only as good as the political will to implement them. Many publishing achievements of the past thirty years have resulted from an implied covenant between the private sector and the public sector; the industry has amply delivered the goods, but government needs to keep its end of the bargain.

In the absence of structural measures, indigenous publishers' ongoing need for working capital continues. Since English-language recipients of government funding receive on average only 6 percent of their revenues in grants and typically earn no more than 2 percent operating profit, governments must not only maintain existing funding but ensure that their programs keep pace with inflation. In addition to applying existing policies with conviction, governments can take other constructive measures to improve the environment for Canadian publishing and writing over the long term.

At the federal level, the Canada Council for the Arts (as the agency was renamed in 1997) should enact an ACP proposal to help Canadian-owned publishers offer more competitive royalty advances. By supplementing advances, such a program would enhance publishers' ability to retain their authors and would simultaneously benefit writers. The federal government should also facilitate the industry's transition to a new generation of owners by introducing the proposed equity investment tax credit. It would serve a double purpose: attracting human and financial capital to the industry and providing an exit strategy for owner-managers now nearing retirement. Improvements in tax treatment would permit Canadian publishers to realize the equity they've built in their firms, while protecting the public's investment in those firms and ensuring they can be taken to the next level.

Our newspapers, themselves kept in Canadian hands by favourable tax treatment, often advise the federal government to abandon its Canadian ownership policies for the book industry. Abandoning the current support for domestic control would be a grave error. It would not only break faith with a demonstrably fertile cultural industry but undermine Canadian literary production. A more positive step would be clarifying the objectives of ownership policy, spelling out a transparent, rules-based regime to achieve those objectives, and applying the rules consistently, for the benefit of both Canadian and foreign investors.

The provinces too have a critical role in strengthening Canadian publishing. In the educational and library fields, they must reverse declines in book purchases, which have compromised the quality of school and public library collections. And they must work towards restoring teacher-librarian positions in school systems across the country. In the tax field, other provinces would be well advised to emulate Ontario and now British Columbia, which provide publishers with a refundable tax credit on investments in new Canadian-authored books. Levelling the playing field with imported titles, that measure also gives Ontario- and B.C.-based publishers a competitive edge over colleagues in other provinces.

It's important to recognize that book publishing has grown prodigiously with support from a variety of measures implemented by both levels of government. And it's equally significant that these programs have been completely consistent with freedom of expression. No program has permitted or implied control over a book's contents by politicians or bureaucrats.

Whatever action governments may take, what are the prospects for Canadian publishing in the current environment? By 2003 the industry had reached a crossroads. It appeared possible that the Canadian-controlled sector could dwindle into, as the Ontario royal commission once put it, an enfeebled regional cultural activity.

Yet events don't need to slide in that direction. On close examination, the sector appears bloodied but still creatively robust and full of promise. If industry players build on that reality, and if government chooses to support them, the indigenous sector could return to being as vibrant as ever, as vital to articulating a distinct cultural and political existence for Canada.

Domestically owned companies continue to originate the vast majority of Canadian-authored titles. This is true not only for regional titles or uncommercial genres, such as poetry, but for every category of trade publishing. A study I conducted for the federal government in late 2000 found that, of 1,587 new Canadian trade titles listed that year in *Quill & Quire*'s spring and fall announcements, in some three dozen different categories, fully 87 percent, or 1,381, came from indigenous firms.

The fact that multinational subsidiaries published just 206 of those titles, or 13 percent, and yet manage to create the impression that they are responsible for publishing most of contemporary Canadian literature, is extraordinary – a tribute to their marketing power. Their ability to create name authors is particularly evident in the marketing of novelists, whose books and faces ("New Faces of Fiction," etc.) lend themselves to saturation advertising and eleven-city media tours. When the face is Barbara Gowdy's, say, or Andrew Pyper's, and the novel is titled *The Romantic* or *Lost Girls*, a big-budget marketing campaign has little difficulty persuading the media that *this* will be the season's big book.

Unquestionably, fiction has the biggest sex appeal for marketing purposes. The subsidiaries have invested heavily in novels, which number over a third of all the trade titles they publish. Yet even in that category, my study found that, during 2000, Canadian-owned firms published 171 novels out of 238, or 72 percent. In other culturally significant genres, the percentages from Canadian-owned publishers were far higher: in short fiction, sixty-six of seventy-four titles, or 89 percent; in art, photography, and architecture, 90 percent; in nature and environment, 92 percent; in children's picture books, 93 percent; in Canadian history, 95 percent; in drama, theatre, and dance, 98 percent; in poetry, 99 percent; in Native studies, 100 percent.

Despite the Stoddart/GDS setback, that record held up in autumn 2002. The *Quill & Quire* listings for that season reflected my findings of two years earlier, with minor variations. In novels, for instance, Canadian-owned houses published 115 of 154 titles, or 75 percent; in biography, memoirs, and letters, eighty of ninety-four titles, or 85 percent; and so on.

This isn't to detract from the excellence of the subsidiaries' Canadian programs but to document who is publishing what. For the multinationals, publishing Canadian books is an add-on to their prime directive of marketing the parent company's product. Their Canadian output, significant as it is, complements a substantially larger, more generically diverse output from indigenous colleagues, most of whom live or die on Canadian books alone.

Only a few Canadian publishers today could be described as financially secure. But after the vicissitudes of the past decade, the survivors are wily, entrepreneurial, and abundantly capable of reinventing themselves. Any overview of the industry's creative resources must start with the first rebirth after the dark days of the Stoddart failure.

The gloom over the trade began lifting with Scott Griffin's purchase of the House of Anansi. The news raised spirits when it was announced at the 2002 Canadian Booksellers Association trade show, now known, inevitably, as BookExpo Canada. One of the reasons for hope was Griffin's declared attitude towards Anansi. He'd probably paid more than he had to under the circumstances (reportedly $400,000), but it was what he acknowledged the press *should* be worth. He also announced he was retaining Anansi's publisher, Martha Sharpe, the business director, Adrienne Leahey, and the sales director, Matt Williams, and urging them on with the literary program they'd been creating under the Stoddart umbrella. Griffin made the youthful trio principals in the company and moved Anansi back onto Spadina Avenue, after its thirteen-year exile in Don Mills. Serendipitously, the thirty-five-year-old press's newest incarnation also received a 2002 Giller Prize nomination for *Open*, a story collection by the Newfoundland writer Lisa Moore.

Griffin wasn't the only Canadian investor taking a chance on publishing. The Giller winner for 2002, Austin Clarke's novel *The Polished Hoe*, carried what previously would have seemed an unlikely imprint, Thomas Allen Publishers. Although Thomas Allen & Son has been around since 1916, for decades it was content to distribute Houghton Mifflin and other agencies.

But Jim Allen, the fourth-generation CEO, was determined to reconstitute his great-grandfather's idea of a genuine publisher sustained by import revenues, and he approached the admired editor Patrick Crean with an offer Crean couldn't refuse.

Crean had made his reputation publishing fiction (Greg Hollingshead, Susan Swan, Barbara Gowdy) at Jane Somerville's now-defunct Somerville House. In 2000 he left Key Porter, where he'd had a personal imprint for a year, to build an ambitious trade program at Thomas Allen: fifteen to twenty titles annually, divided more or less evenly among literary fiction, high-end non-fiction, and commercial non-fiction. The authors Crean signed during his first twenty-four months were an interesting mix of younger talents like Larissa Lai and Melanie Little and established authors such as Leon Rooke, Sylvia Fraser, Brian Fawcett, and John Metcalf. With his program in only its second year, winning the Giller sent a signal that Thomas Allen would be a force in twenty-first-century Canadian literature.

Raincoast Books is another company building a trade program on profits from distribution. When it was started in 1979 by Mark Stanton and Allan MacDougall, Raincoast merely kept local stock for the sales agency the pair had bought from Jim Douglas and Scott McIntyre, later picking up distribution rights to individual titles. The company grew rapidly after becoming the distributor for several international publishers, particularly Chronicle Books and Conari Press from California, Bloomsbury from Britain, and Lonely Planet from Australia. "We took very seriously the old Mafia adage that distribution is key," McDougall explained. Earning a sterling reputation for customer service, Raincoast also made a successful wholesale operation out of its Book Express division and began dabbling in publishing. Although it found success with Nick Bantock's ingenious Griffin and Sabine picture books for adults, the typical Raincoast list ran heavily to books on gardening, crafts, cooking, and beautiful British Columbia.

On Stanton's retirement, the company made two critical moves: selling a 25 percent stake to a California-based distributor, Advanced Marketing Services, and securing Canadian rights to the astonishing Harry Potter books, published by Bloomsbury. Flush with cash (as of this writing, over

6 million copies of the first four Harry Potters are in print in Canada alone), Raincoast became more ambitious as a publisher. It recruited young editorial talent within the West Coast industry and acquired Polestar Book Publishers, a feisty three-woman operation headed by Michelle Benjamin. Under Benjamin's direction, Raincoast launched a program of literary and young adult titles alongside its non-fiction. But it also kept pushing the distribution side of the equation. Raincoast opened an eastern warehouse in Toronto and in 2002 acquired the Canadian branch of the American distributor Publishers Group West – moves that drove total revenues towards a heady $60 million. Although it's difficult to foresee how much importance Raincoast will accord original publishing, the company offers the same promise as Thomas Allen: the potential to evolve into a large, diversified Canadian-owned publisher with financial clout.

The question of balancing distribution and publishing arises for other companies. H.B. Fenn & Co. has started to publish original titles but appears risk-averse to date, perhaps wary about diverting too many resources away from profitably selling books for agencies such as Time Warner and Microsoft Press. McArthur & Company, started in Toronto by Kim McArthur after Little, Brown Canada was closed, is based on revenues from the large British publishers Orion and Hodder Headline; authors such as Maeve Binchy and Ian Rankin cross-subsidize McArthur's Canadian trade list, with its emphasis on crime fiction and gardening. Lionel Koffler's Firefly Books is a distributor that has jumped into publishing with both feet, specializing in children's books, sports, gardening, nature, and the outdoors. Given Koffler's drive and acumen, it seems certain to play an increasingly important role in the years ahead.

Distribution is no longer an issue for the ongoing experiment that is McClelland & Stewart. During fifteen years as owner, Avie Bennett worked thoughtfully at consolidating key pieces of the domestic industry to make M&S a more viable publishing entity. Buying Hurtig, Tundra, and Macfarlane Walter & Ross, he also entered a fifty-fifty distribution arrangement with Penguin Canada to create Canbook: a joint warehousing and order fulfillment venture, which was supposed to benefit from economies of scale but suffered chronic systems malfunctions. Bennett devised the University of Toronto–Random House of Canada ownership structure for

M&S. In the process, M&S shed all its agencies to a new company, Stewart House, owned by a former employee; but early in 2003, Stewart House sought bankruptcy protection.

What remains at M&S under its seasoned president and publisher, Doug Gibson, is the editorial, design, and production functions, plus rights and promotion, with everything else handled by Random House of Canada. Stripped down to its core creative roles, M&S has concentrated on building its trade program during the first three years of the new order. It has bulked up the already formidable fiction list under its vice-president and fiction publisher, Ellen Seligman. Particularly striking is the company's ability to inspire loyalty in many of the country's leading authors – Margaret Atwood, Alice Munro, Michael Ondaatje, Guy Vanderhaeghe, Rohinton Mistry, Anne Michaels, Jane Urquhart – while attracting its share of the next wave of literary writers, such as Thomas Wharton, Nancy Lee, and John Bemrose.

For now, M&S remains the flagship of Canadian publishing. It competes head-to-head, company executives insist, with the multinational imprints to which it is corporately allied. Some observers ask how independent M&S can be as long as it reports to Random House of Canada for sales, marketing, distribution, and financial management. By the venerable firm's 100th anniversary in 2006, both its co-owners may well have reassessed and clarified their singular arrangement – and outsiders' understanding of it. Whether control of M&S mutates yet again, and in what direction, is the industry's biggest imponderable.

The indigenous houses responsible for the bulk of Canada's publishing output occupy many niches. A major and well-established editorial resource is housed in the nation's university presses. The big three – University of Toronto Press under George Meadows and Bill Harnum, who oversaw the press's transition from university ward to corporate status during the 1990s; McGill-Queen's under Philip Cercone, who greatly expanded the press's publishing capacity and fields of interest; and University of British Columbia Press under Peter Milroy, the only Canadian after Marsh Jeanneret to preside over the Association of American

University Presses – maintain substantial scholarly programs of international stature. Their lists range across a variety of disciplines in addition to Canadian studies. Smaller university presses – Alberta, Calgary, Manitoba, Wilfrid Laurier – may publish less widely, but they are recognized in the scholarly community as publishers of distinction. The three western presses specialize in studies of their regions, and all the academic publishers regularly issue titles with trade as well as scholarly appeal. McGill-Queen's and Alberta have even ventured into contemporary literature.

Both the children's and literary press movements have been strengthened in recent years by newcomers with a keen nose for talent, and by older presses renewing their energies.

During the 1990s, a second wave of kids' publishers rolled principally out of the west. A former high school teacher, Bob Tyrrell, was remarkably successful in transforming Orca Book Publishers from an adult press of regional non-fiction into an internationally recognized children's publisher. Since being named CBA Publisher of the Year in 1993, Victoria-based Orca has reaped many of the national and regional awards now offered for Canadian children's literature and sells vigorously into the States. Dennis Johnson's Red Deer Press, first affiliated with Red Deer College, is now based in Calgary; and although it continues its vocation as a literary press issuing western writing in several genres, Red Deer has become best known for its award-winning children's program. Johnson gave the celebrated author Tim Wynne-Jones the chance to create a kids' list from scratch in 1989 – an unusual alliance, since Johnson is a staunch regionalist and Wynne-Jones lives near Perth, Ontario – but the pair fashioned an outstanding program now edited by another easterner, Peter Carver. Second Story Press similarly combines adult publishing with children's picture books and young adult fiction. Since its founding in Toronto by three principals locked out of Women's Press, Second Story has published imaginatively on themes such as child abuse and the Holocaust, and has sold rights to many of its children's titles abroad. The press is now owned by the veteran feminist publisher Margie Wolfe.

Literary presses have provided fresh troops for the guerrilla struggle. The new publishers are both tribal and global, seeking markets wherever they can find them, particularly in the United States. The standard-bearer is Mike O'Connor's Insomniac Press, which celebrated its tenth anniversary in 2002; it's an enterprising Toronto house with a signature *noir* style epitomized by Natalee Caple and Lynn Crosbie, and a recent bestseller in the popular singer Jann Arden's diaries. At Toronto's Gutter Press, Sam Hiyate showed a postmodernist wit by granting himself a personal imprint as he competed with Insomniac and the new Anansi to publish punk urban fiction. Also in Toronto, Beth Follet's Pedlar Press had a breakout novel in 2000, Camilla Gibb's *Mouthing the Words*, which won the City of Toronto Book Award and was sold to publishers in several countries; Gibb subsequently signed with Doubleday Canada.

In Fredericton, Joe Blades's Broken Jaw Press is a prolific source of new poetry. Anvil Press in Vancouver introduces many of the city's most exciting young literary talents and is responsible for the extraordinary photographic essay *Heroines*. Nightwood Editions in Roberts Creek, British Columbia, the much-mutated successor to blewointment press, publishes literary and children's titles. In Winnipeg, J. Gordon Shillingford divides his output of plays, poetry, and regional history among a variety of imprints. Perhaps the most unusual new venture is Gaspereau Press, because it's also the most traditional: operated in Kentville, Nova Scotia, by Gary Dunfield and Andrew Steeves, Gaspereau specializes in finely crafted books typeset and printed in-house, of which the most admired has been George Elliott Clarke's *Execution Poems*.

Paralleling Anansi's revival, certain presses have grown stronger editorially with age. Brick Books, a poetry press based in London, Ontario, that has been around in one form or another since 1975, has half a dozen volunteer editors scattered around the country, among them Stan Dragland and Don McKay. Brick has compiled a rich backlist including titles by P.K. Page, Anne Carson, and Jan Zwicky, and its authors are routinely among the poetry award winners and nominees.

Under Brian Lam, Arsenal Pulp Press has stayed hip and outrageous while blossoming into a cosmopolitan, continental marketer, publishing the novelist Michael Turner, literary anthologies like *Carnal Nation* and *Exhibitions: Tales of Sex in the City*, and equally edgy non-fiction. Arsenal Pulp's *Scrambled Brains*, considered too pungent for the book racks of BC Ferries, is the first Canadian cookbook to get itself banned. The press has also created one of North America's major gay and lesbian programs, helping fill the gaps left by Ragweed/gynergy and Press Gang, the Vancouver feminist press that had staked out new territory and won several prestigious Lambda Awards in the States.

Even Coach House Press, once defunct, has experienced an out-of-body rebirth. After being "rescued" in the early 1990s from its old unbusinesslike ways, the press came under new management by a group headed by a former Ontario Arts Council literature officer, Margaret McLintock. The group shunned the qualities considered by one member of the editorial collective, Frank Davey, to have been the press's natural virtues: being "subversive, mischievous, interrogative, or defiant toward various artistic, prosodic, theatrical, political, sexual, bureaucratic, or narrative conventions." Paid staff were hired, marketing undertaken, sales and distribution contracted out to M&S. Although sales grew 400 percent, the press also assumed much higher overheads, and when things started going wrong, it had less capacity to absorb the shock. First Coach House's American distributor went under; then, in 1996, the Mike Harris government terminated Ontario's loan guarantee program, triggering a move by the bank. McLintock and her fellow directors wound the press up, selling its inventory and contracts to Talon Books and other publishers.

The demise of such a prestigious imprint helped exert pressure on Ottawa to restore the BPIDP funding that had been cut a year earlier. The money came too late to save Coach House, but its founder, Stan Bevington, saw an opportunity. He reunited with Victor Coleman and Rick/Simon to realize a concept for a new kind of publishing house in cyberspace. In 1997 the three launched their idea under the name Coach House Books, and by year's end their Web site had published fourteen literary texts, all downloadable free. The publishers recommended readers "tip" the authors directly, in lieu of conventional royalty payments. The press also produced CD-ROM and print versions ("paper artifacts") of the texts, selling them on-line and through bookstores.

Darren Wershler-Henry, a poet and Coach House author, took over as editor, while Bevington and Rick/Simon continued to contribute design, and Coleman embarked on *onezerozero*, his on-line history of small-press poetry in Canada. During the Stoddart/GDS troubles, Wershler-Henry became an eloquent advocate for literary publishing. The fact that the ingenious Coach House title *Eunoia*, by Christian Bök, had just carried off the 2002 Griffin Poetry Prize while the book itself languished in the GDS warehouse lent Wershler-Henry's public statements a certain poignancy; he has since moved on to academic life.

Educational publishing has become dominated more than ever by the multinationals (one of which, Nelson Thomson, is Canadian-owned). Competition in the field narrowed severely during the 1990s because of mergers and acquisitions. One company alone, Pearson Education Canada, now combines the Canadian subsidiaries of five formerly separate educational publishers: Addison-Wesley, Collier-Macmillan, Ginn, GLC, and Prentice-Hall. But Canadian-controlled Gage Learning Corporation remains a serious competitor under the ownership of the Besse family, Chris Besse having succeeded his father, Ron, as CEO. Educational firms such as Broadview Press (publishing college texts in English and the social sciences), Crabtree Publishing (children's readers), Dundurn Press (history, social sciences, reference, and, more recently, trade fiction and non-fiction), and Fernwood Publishing have grown by specializing in niche areas. Broadview is particularly unusual, for a Canadian publisher, in listing its shares on the stock exchange to raise working capital. In Alberta the province's encouragement has fostered a vigorous community of educational publishers, including Arnold Publishing (now owned by Nelson Thomson), Weigl Educational Publishers, and Duval House, which exports English-as-a-second-language texts to China.

Indeed, regional publishing continues to thrive at many trade imprints in both the west (Altitude Publishing, Fifth House Publishers, and Lone Pine Publishing in Alberta) and the east (Formac Publishing, Nimbus Publishing, and Pottersfield Press in Nova Scotia). Lone Pine has been conspicuously successful by taking its innovative regional formula – low-priced yet high-quality illustrated paperbacks on Alberta's natural and human history, marketed on racks through non-traditional retail outlets – and applying it successfully to British Columbia, Ontario, and western regions of the United States.

To compete in a globalizing world, the Canadian publishing industry will need more than small niche players, however skilled. Just as John Gray of Macmillan once doubted that a national literature could be built from a succession of first and second books, an enduring national publishing industry can't subsist on authors who move on to the multinationals after a book or two. But the simple fact is, as Patrick Crean of Thomas Allen Publishers has observed, "publishing in Canada has become a capitalist's game, and you need an awful lot of cash to make it work." A subsidiary publisher intent on list-building such as Maya Mavjee, known for her show-stopping advances at Doubleday Canada, can blow competitors off the map by reaching into her company's treasure chest to win an author: Nino Ricci's two-book, $350,000 advance is a case in point. In the face of such largesse, most Canadian publishers can only look on with a mixture of dismay and disbelief.

Scott McIntyre, one of the industry's most knowledgeable players, most resourceful survivors, and sunniest optimists, has demonstrated his firm's ability to use passion, craft, and ideas, rather than dollars, to attract authors. And he feels intensely proud of the talent and professionalism in Canadian publishing. "What we've achieved in this country," he said recently, "is a cultural miracle, and that isn't going to change."

Nonetheless, McIntyre's dour conclusion was that the best days of the made-in-Canada publishing experiment are over. This may be especially true since a generation coming of age with globalization and the Internet feels less loyalty to the idea of cultural sovereignty. The dilemma for a company like Douglas & McIntyre, which has honed itself on Canada's publishing reality, is that its multinational competitors play by a whole different set of rules. "In the multinationals' feeding frenzy," McIntyre commented, "you see numbers that are insane. And that just gives the literary agents more stature than ever. All the writers go to them, and the agents go to the top dollar every time. So that hands the Canadian game to the people with the deepest pockets."

And yet by early 2003, McIntyre and his partners were far from conceding the game to anyone. D&M, with its related imprints, Groundwood and Greystone, has become arguably the leading wholly independent Canadian trade publisher. It navigated the GDS shambles and survived intact, in large part because of continuing stellar sales highlighted by burgeoning exports. With several titles on bestseller lists during 2002, D&M's potent program was equally capable of producing a beautiful, full-colour work of history like Derek Hayes's *Historical Atlas of Canada* and postmodern takes such as Douglas Coupland's *Souvenir of Canada* and Will and Ian Ferguson's *How to Be a Canadian*. Continuing to mix art books and Native studies with children's literature, fiction, history, humour, sports, food, and travel, the company seemed to have weathered all storms and to have attained that magic but elusive high ground somewhere between cultural relevance and commercial success. It has combined a frontlist of strong international appeal with the depth and breadth of a backlist containing over 700 titles. Its future looks if not golden, at least luminous.

A firm like D&M is testimony that Canadian publishers with enterprise, talent, guile, and staying power can make the Canadian game pay off for readers. That fact ought to reassure skeptics, inspire colleagues, and perhaps persuade those eternal doubters, bankers and investors. And it should remind government of the reasons why it adopted policies to support book publishing in the first place – and why it must remain committed to them for the long term. Although the dream of a predominantly Canadian-owned industry may have vanished, swallowed by globalization and free trade, government's role in ensuring the viability of the remaining indigenous publishers, and of those yet to come, is crucial.

The Canadian publishing experiment will always be risky. But no inexorable fate awaits to marginalize or destroy domestic publishing. When the Massey-Lévesque commission, like the Ontario Royal Commission on Book Publishing twenty years later, found a grim outlook for the industry, it urged action. In both cases, the decisive steps that followed made all the difference. Creating an environment in which indigenous publishing can flourish, allowing the nation to tell its story to itself, is essential to the existence of a healthy tribe of authors, readers, and citizens. It means that when the next young Canadian publishers come along, they will have fair prospects for discovering the next generation of Canadian writers, and for the incomparable adventure of publishing them to the world.

EPILOGUE

The day after this book was finished, its intended publisher, Macfarlane Walter & Ross, went on the auction block. McClelland & Stewart, which had owned MW&R for three years, announced in February 2003 that the prestigious non-fiction imprint was for sale. The reasons given were systemic: depressed book sales during the previous fall – an economically depressed time, with the world holding its breath in anticipation of the American invasion of Iraq – and especially depressed sales of quality non-fiction, the genre that MW&R specialized in.

After weeks of negotiation, M&S was unable to come to terms with interested buyers. The parent company then made good on its commitment to take responsibility for MW&R's contracts and other assets and to publish the titles as its own. The outcome for this particular book and this particular author, therefore, was favourable after all. But the portents for a certain kind of sophisticated, intellectually challenging Canadian publishing were not.

As MW&R's president, Jan Walter, affirmed when the closing was announced, the company had enjoyed "fifteen years of the most rewarding kind of publishing." The fact that those years could not continue underlined once more the unforgivingly narrow margins on which Canadian publishing operates, coupled with its vulnerability when adverse conditions strike. In this case, the adverse condition was a shrinking marketplace, with fewer retail outlets favourable to MW&R's intelligent, issue-oriented books on contemporary politics, society, and culture. The harrowing of the retail market described in chapter 15, "Wars of Succession," had claimed another victim. The lesson was not encouraging for readers seeking books that will give them a deeper understanding of their country, their times, and their place in the world.

There had always seemed a striking resemblance between what New Press tried to accomplish in the 1970s and what MW&R succeeded in accomplishing for a considerably longer period two decades later. Both publishers, it will be argued, paid insufficient attention to the market. But in MW&R's case, some stunning market successes were followed by lean times in which the retail marketplace itself had changed, becoming more than ever a mass-marketing machine – to the extent that the machinery practically dictates which kinds of books are likely to succeed. Working to make that marketplace more hospitable to good books of all kinds, and to good readers of all kinds, is the next major challenge facing the perilous trade. Canadians must hope it meets the challenge.

CHRONOLOGY

CANADIAN BOOK PUBLISHING, 1946 TO MAY 2003

1946
- John Gray appointed head of Macmillan of Canada.
- Jack McClelland joins McClelland & Stewart (M&S).
- First Statement Press starts up.

1947
- Doubleday establishes Canadian subsidiary.

1948
- William Toye joins Oxford University Press.

1949
- Clarke, Irwin ends alliance with Oxford University Press and resumes operating independently.
- Harlequin Books starts up.
- Royal Commission on National Development in the Arts, Letters and Sciences (Massey-Lévesque) appointed.

1950
- W.H. Smith chain opens its first Canadian bookstore, in Toronto.

1951
- Massey-Lévesque report recommends creation of the Canada Council and the National Library.

1952
- Contact Press starts up.
- Jack McClelland succeeds his father as operational head of M&S.

- Canadian Retail Booksellers Association (later Canadian Booksellers Association) created.

1953
- Marsh Jeanneret appointed director of University of Toronto Press.
- National Library of Canada established by Parliament.
- Federal government removes 10 percent sales tax on books.

1954
- CBC Radio begins *Anthology*, a weekly literary program.

1955
- Canadian Writers' Conference, Queen's University, Kingston.

1956
- Literary quarterly *The Tamarack Review* starts up.
- Mel Hurtig opens his first bookstore.

1957
- Canada Council (later Canada Council for the Arts) established by Parliament.
- Jack Stoddart Sr. buys General Publishing.
- Bill Duthie opens his first bookstore.

1958
- M&S launches New Canadian Library series.

1959
- Readers' Club of Canada starts all-Canadian book club.
- University of Toronto Press embarks on *Dictionary of Canadian Biography*.
- George Woodcock founds quarterly *Canadian Literature*.
- Canada Council made responsible for Governor General's Literary Awards; French-language awards added.

1960
- McGill University Press starts up.
- Lorne Pierce retires from the Ryerson Press.

1961
- Presses de l'université Laval joins *Dictionary of Canadian Biography* project.
- Canadian Book Publishers' Council created.

1962
- Gray's Publishing starts up.
- First Canadian stand at Frankfurt International Book Fair.

1963
- Copp Clark bought by British publisher Pitman.
- M&S drops twenty-three agencies to focus on Canadian books.

1965
- Coach House Press and Peter Martin Associates start up.

1966
- Oberon Press and Fitzhenry & Whiteside start up.

1967
- Contact Press winds down operations.
- House of Anansi Press, Hurtig Publishers, Talon Books, Tundra Books, and University of Manitoba Press start up.
- Canada Council offers grants for individual literary titles.
- More than 300 titles published to mark Canada's Centennial.
- New National Library building opens.

1968
- University of Toronto Press opens branch in U.S.

1969
- Hugh Kane leaves M&S to join Macmillan; Anna Porter joins M&S.

1970
- Ernst & Ernst report sets Canadian publishers' domestic market at $222 million, $5.5 million in exports.
- W.J. Gage publishing division sold to American-owned Scott Foresman; Ryerson Press sold to McGraw-Hill; Emergency Committee of Canadian Publishers protests takeovers.
- Ontario Royal Commission on Book Publishing appointed.

1971
- Independent Publishers' Association created.
- Jack McClelland announces M&S is up for sale.
- Ontario lends M&S $962,000; establishes loan guarantee program for Canadian-controlled publishers.

1972
- Macmillan of Canada bought by Maclean-Hunter.
- Ontario Arts Council begins block grants to book publishers.
- Federal government provides $1.7 million a year to book publishing through Canada Council and Department of Industry, Trade and Commerce.
- Longhouse (Toronto) and Books Canada (Ottawa), all-Canadian bookstores, open.

1973
- Ontario Royal Commission on Book Publishing issues final report.
- John Gray retires as president of Macmillan.
- Association for the Export of Canadian Books created.
- Writers' Union of Canada created.

1974
- Federal government regulates foreign investment in book industry through Foreign Investment Review Agency (FIRA).

1975
- Literary Press Group created.
- Canada Council supports book promotion and distribution.
- First Montreal International Book Fair (later Salon du Livre de Montréal).
- Harlequin bought by Torstar.

1976
- Canadian Children's Book Centre established.
- Canada Council Children's Literature Awards created.
- Pocket Books of Canada sold to General Publishing.
- Independent Publishers' Association becomes Association of Canadian Publishers.

1977
- M&S-Bantam created to publish mass-market paperbacks under Seal imprint.
- Gage Educational Publishing repatriated by Consolidated Graphics.
- Marsh Jeanneret succeeded as director of University of Toronto Press by Harald Bohne.

1978
- First Seal Book Award presented.
- Gage Educational Publishing bought by Ron Besse.
- Coles bookstores bought by Southam.

1979
- Canadian Book Publishing Development Program (later Book Publishing Industry Development Program) established by federal government to provide "industrial" support to Canadian-owned publishers.

1980
- Macmillan sold by Maclean-Hunter to Ron Besse; Canada Publishing Corp. created to hold Gage and Macmillan.
- Federal government appoints Federal Cultural Policy Review Committee (Applebaum-Hébert).

1981
- Peter Martin Associates bought by Book Society of Canada.
- Readers' Club of Canada closed.

1982
- Jack McClelland appoints Linda McKnight president of M&S.
- Applebaum-Hébert committee recommends public lending right and stronger federal support for book and magazine publishing.

1983
- Clarke, Irwin goes into receivership; assets bought by Book Society of Canada (later Irwin Publishing).

1984
- M&S obtains new financing from Ontario government and private investors.

1985
- M&S bought by Avie Bennett.
- Classics bookstore chain bought by W.H. Smith.
- Hurtig Publishers releases first edition of *The Canadian Encyclopedia*.
- Federal government announces Baie-Comeau policy on foreign investment in book trade.

- Government allows Gulf + Western to escape policy in acquiring Prentice-Hall of Canada, but requires it to divest Ginn Canada.

1986
- Book Publishing Development Program renewed, transfers $4.8 million to Canada Council block grant program.
- M&S hires Doug Gibson from Macmillan.
- Doubleday (U.S.) bought by Bertelsmann; Anna Porter installed as Canadian president.

1987
- Governor General's Literary Awards incorporate Canada Council Children's Literature Awards.
- Jack McClelland leaves M&S, sells Seal Books to Anna Porter.
- Avie Bennett appoints Adrienne Clarkson M&S publisher.

1988
- Lester & Orpen Dennys bought by Christopher Ondaatje, resold to Hees International Bank Corp.
- Irwin Publishing bought by Stoddart Publishing.
- New American Library bought by Penguin.
- Copyright Act amended to protect authors' and publishers' reprographic rights.
- Adrienne Clarkson leaves M&S, succeeded as publisher by Doug Gibson.

1989
- House of Anansi Press bought by Stoddart.
- HarperCollins created; Canadian branch placed under Stan and Nancy Colbert.
- W.H. Smith bought by Federal Industries; name changed to SmithBooks.

1990
- Federal government buys majority interest in Ginn Canada.

1991
- Federal goods and services tax introduced.
- Hurtig Publishers bought by M&S.
- Lester & Orpen Dennys closed; Knopf Canada starts up under Louise Dennys.

- Western Producer Prairie Books bought by Douglas & McIntyre.
- Anna Porter leaves Doubleday Canada.

1992

- Minister of Communications Perrin Beatty announces new federal publishing policy: Book Publishing Industry Development Program tripled; Baie-Comeau policy diluted; publishers' importation rights to be protected.
- HarperCollins receives federal approval under new policy.
- Anna Porter leaves Seal Books.
- Michael Ondaatje becomes first Canadian to win Booker Prize.

1993

- Carol Shields becomes first Canadian to win Pulitzer Prize for fiction.

1994

- SmithBooks and Coles bought by Pathfinder Capital and Canadian General Capital Corp.; merged into Chapters Inc.
- Federal Competition Bureau investigates Chapters merger.
- Federal government resells Ginn/GLC to Paramount (later Viacom).
- First Giller Prize awarded.

1995

- Chapters merger approved by Competition Bureau.
- First Chapters superstore opened.
- Department of Canadian Heritage cuts book industry funding by 55 percent.

1996

- Tundra Books bought by M&S.
- Federal government disallows entry of American bookstore chain Borders.
- Indigo Books and Music starts up, begins superstore rollout.

1997

- Copyright Act amended to protect publishers' importation rights.
- Minister of Canadian Heritage Sheila Copps restores funding cut to publishers and introduces loan guarantee program.

1998

- Kids Can Press bought by Nelvana animation studios.
- Little, Brown Canada closed by Time Warner.

- Macmillan of Canada becomes CDG Books, 49 percent U.S.-owned.
- Random House bought by Bertelsmann.
- Chapters, Indigo, and some independents start selling books over Internet.

1999
- Bertelsmann receives federal approval for Random House takeover and merger with Doubleday Canada.
- Pearson PLC buys Prentice-Hall; receives federal approval for takeover and merger with Addison-Wesley into Pearson Education Canada.
- Chapters establishes Pegasus as national wholesaler.

2000
- House of Commons Standing Committee on Canadian Heritage holds hearings into book industry.
- Avie Bennett donates 75 percent of M&S to University of Toronto, sells 25 percent to Random House of Canada.
- Margaret Atwood becomes second Canadian to win Booker Prize.
- Indigo makes takeover bid for Chapters.

2001
- Indigo succeeds in bid for Chapters, negotiates code of conduct with publishing industry.
- Department of Canadian Heritage dedicates funding to book industry's supply chain problems.

2002
- Stoddart Publishing and General Distribution Services enter bankruptcy.
- Irwin Publishing bought by Nelson Thomson; Stoddart Kids by Fitzhenry & Whiteside; House of Anansi by Scott Griffin; Boston Mills Press by Firefly Books.
- CDG Books wound up, assets purchased by John Wiley & Sons Canada.
- Amazon.com launches Canadian Web site.
- Simon & Schuster receives federal approval to take over Distican.
- Yann Martel becomes third Canadian to win Man Booker Prize.

2003
- M&S winds up Macfarlane Walter & Ross.

SOURCES

S ince this is the first general narrative of book publishing in English Canada, it draws on an eclectic variety of sources. No single volume served as a jumping-off point.

The most detailed record of developments in the publishing industry since 1935 has appeared in the monthly trade paper *Quill & Quire*. Without it, tracing the industry's chronological progress would be next to impossible. Fortunately the publishers of *Quill & Quire* have maintained a complete archive of back issues, to which I had frequent access. Another invaluable source of information is *The Oxford Companion to Canadian Literature*, second edition, Eugene Benson and William Toye, eds. (Toronto: Oxford University Press, 1997).

Introduction: A Canadian Experiment
The Ontario Royal Commission on Book Publishing made an authoritative and comprehensive set of observations three decades ago, when the industry looked very different in some ways from the present, very similar in others. The commission's two volumes were its *Background Papers* (Toronto: Queen's Printer and Publisher, 1972) and its final report, *Canadian Publishers and Canadian Publishing* (Toronto: Ministry of the Attorney General, 1973).

The cited 1950 listing of book publishers in English Canada appeared as "Key to Publishers" in a catalogue compiled by *Quill & Quire* for its January 1950 issue. I also cite the 1970 Ernst & Ernst report on the Canadian book publishing and manufacturing industry, commissioned by the federal Department of Industry, Trade and Commerce; based on 1969 data, the report was thoroughly summarized in the January 15, 1971, *Quill & Quire*. The most recent industry statistics are from *Survey of Book Publishers and Exclusive Agents, 1998–1999* (Ottawa: Statistics Canada, 2000).

Morley Callaghan's comment is from 1938, quoted by Bruce Whiteman in *Lasting Impressions: A Short History of English Publishing in Quebec* (Montreal: Véhicule Press, 1994).

1: The Publishing Life

My memories of starting out in publishing were refreshed by conversations with William H. Clarke Jr. and with Patrick Toner, Alden Nowlan's biographer in *If I Could Turn and Meet Myself: The Life of Alden Nowlan* (Fredericton: Goose Lane, 2000). Bill Clarke continues to teach in the astronomy department of the University of Toronto. Dennis Lee left publishing many years ago to pursue the arts of writing poetry and children's literature. Dave Godfrey still owns a publishing house, Beach Holme Publishing, now based in Vancouver.

2: At Mid-Century

Striking portrayals of Canadian publishing in another era appear in the *Report* of the Royal Commission on National Development in the Arts, Letters and Sciences (Ottawa: Queen's Printer, 1951) and *Writing in Canada: Proceedings of the Canadian Writers' Conference, Queen's University, 28–31 July 1955*, George Whalley, ed. (Toronto: Macmillan of Canada, 1956).

For information about late-nineteenth-century and early-twentieth-century Canadian publishing, I have drawn particularly on two background papers of the Ontario Royal Commission on Book Publishing: "The Development of Trade Book Publishing in Canada," by H. Pearson Gundy; and "Developments in Canadian Book Production and Design," by C.J. Eustace.

My predecessor at the Canada Council, Robin Farr, helped place the 1950s in perspective for me. The quotation from Farr's former colleague at the Ryerson Press, Campbell Hughes, comes from *Quill & Quire*, April 1985. Robert Fulford, whom I consider my mentor as a literary journalist, John Robert Colombo, and Robert Weaver shed further light on publishing conditions during the 1950s and '60s.

3: Gray's Luck

The primary source for John Gray's career at Macmillan of Canada up to 1946, and for Canadian publishing in general in the 1930s and '40s, is Gray's *Fun Tomorrow: Learning to Be a Publisher and Much Else* (Toronto: Macmillan of Canada, 1978). A.B. McKillop's *The Spinster and the Prophet: Florence Deeks, H.G. Wells, and the Mystery of the Purloined Past* (Toronto: Macfarlane Walter & Ross, 2000) describes Macmillan before Gray's arrival.

I was privileged to spend an afternoon in fall 1998 with Gladys Neale, the first of many remarkable women executives in Canadian publishing, speaking about Gray and her own career. Macmillan's launch of Morley Callaghan's *The Loved and the Lost* is recounted in Barry Callaghan's *Barrelhouse Kings* (Toronto: McArthur & Company, 1998). The Robertson Davies material relies on *Robertson Davies: Man of Myth*, by Judith Skelton Grant (Toronto: Viking, 1994). For details about Gray's relationship with Hugh MacLennan, I consulted *Hugh MacLennan: A Writer's Life*, by Elspeth Cameron (Toronto: University of Toronto Press, 1981). When writing an article about Malcolm Ross for the February 1987 *Saturday Night*, I received directly from Ross his version of proposing the New Canadian Library to Gray.

Interviews with James Bacque, Kildare Dobbs, Jim Douglas, Doug Gibson, John Gray the younger, and Donald Sutherland afforded many insights into life with Gray.

4: Toye and His Ilk

William Toye and Ivon Owen contributed interviews for this chapter. Robert Weaver and Dennis Reid gave first-hand accounts of undergoing the Toye treatment as an author.

The Sheila Egoff quotations are from the first edition of her study, *The Republic of Childhood: A Critical Guide to Canadian Children's Literature in English* (Toronto: Oxford University Press, 1967).

5: The Scholarly Entrepreneur

Marsh Jeanneret's *God and Mammon: Universities as Publishers* (Toronto: Macmillan of Canada, 1989), one of the very few memoirs of Canadian publishing, has been underestimated and generally forgotten. Handicapped by an archaic title and equally archaic jacket design, it is nonetheless full of well-told and often amusing tales, although it peters out into generalization towards the end.

The Ontario Royal Commission on Book Publishing's final report contains the ultimate elaboration of Jeanneret's ideas on publishing policy. He had previously shared those ideas in more basic form with the Canadian Book Publishers' Council and restated them in an article for the April 25, 1969, *Quill & Quire*.

Conversations with Jeanneret's colleagues Harald Bohne, Rik Davidson, Robin Farr, Francess Halpenny, Mary McDougall Maude, and Jean Wilson provided a richer sense of the man. Two of Halpenny's papers helped establish the historical context: "Making Canadian Studies Connections" (*Association of Canadian Studies Bulletin*, Vol. 18, No. 4, Winter 1996–1997) and "The Ambience of Scholarly

Publishing in Canada, 1955–1975," prepared for the founding conference of the History of the Book in Canada project held at the National Library of Canada, Ottawa, in May 1997.

Bill Harnum, senior vice-president for scholarly publishing at UTP, explained Jeanneret's impact on the press today. Harnum, Philip Cercone, director of McGill-Queen's University Press, and Peter Milroy, director of the University of British Columbia Press, enlightened me on the state of contemporary scholarly publishing.

6: Prince of Publishers; 7: Surviving Prince Jack

Jack McClelland was the first person interviewed for this book. After the first of our two interviews, McClelland gave me a draft outline, dated February 28, 1994, of his never-published autobiography, "My Rose Garden."

The best portrait of McClelland extant, if not the most detailed or up to date, is Elspeth Cameron's long, penetrating "Adventures in the Skin Trade" in the November 1983 *Saturday Night*, which won a National Magazine Award. Close behind are Judith Timson's "Jack McClelland Then and Now" (*Toronto Life*, July 1980) and Martin Knelman's "Business by the Book" (*Financial Post Magazine*, October 1, 1983). Anyone who writes about McClelland also owes a debt to the motherlode of information amassed in James King's biography *Jack, A Life with Writers: The Story of Jack McClelland* (Toronto: Knopf Canada, 1999). It should be read in tandem with the vastly entertaining *Imagining Canadian Literature: The Selected Letters of Jack McClelland*, Sam Solecki, ed. (Toronto: Key Porter Books, 1998). For the history of McClelland & Stewart's publishing program, I consulted *Bibliography of McClelland & Stewart Ltd. Imprints, 1909–1985*, by Carl Spadoni and Judy Donnelly (Toronto: ECW Press, 1994), which contains a useful introduction summarizing the firm's history.

Several biographies of Canadian authors discuss their subjects' relationships with McClelland. Those I consulted included *Irving Layton: A Portrait*, by Elspeth Cameron (Toronto: Stoddart, 1985); *Earle Birney: A Life*, by Elspeth Cameron (Toronto: Viking, 1994); *Various Positions: A Life of Leonard Cohen*, by Ira B. Nadel (Toronto: Random House of Canada, 1996); *The Life of Margaret Laurence*, by James King (Toronto: Knopf Canada, 1997); and *The Red Shoes: Margaret Atwood Starting Out*, by Rosemary Sullivan (Toronto: HarperCollins Canada, 2001).

Canadian publishers who learned their trade at M&S, at least in part, and with whom I spoke about McClelland, were Patrick Crean, Jim Douglas, Allan MacDougall, Scott McIntyre, John Neale, Anna Porter, and Jan Walter. Other former

M&S employees who were extremely helpful included Paul Audley, John Robert Colombo, Linda McKnight, Peter Taylor, Peter Waldock, and Catherine Wilson. For the writer's version of M&S, I interviewed Margaret Atwood, Pierre Berton, Sylvia Fraser, Graeme Gibson, John Metcalf, Farley Mowat, and Peter C. Newman.

8: Printed in Canada by Mindless Acid Freaks

The small-press movement in Canada began with First Statement Press and Contact Press. John Sutherland's 1951 quotation is from *The Letters of John Sutherland*, Bruce Whiteman, ed. (Toronto: ECW Press, 1997). For Contact's history, I spoke with the youngest surviving partner, Peter Miller, who provided a bibliography of Contact titles, from 1952 to 1967. I also consulted Miller's brief memoir, "Contact Press: The Later Years" (*Canadian Notes and Queries*, No. 51, 1997).

On the fabled second floor at Coach House Press, I conducted interviews on separate occasions with the founder, Stan Bevington, accompanied by the designer Rick/Simon, and with the sometime Coach House editor, author, and typesetter Victor Coleman. Dennis Reid spoke to me about the press's origins. The most detailed account of Coach House and its history, complete with avowed biases, appears in Frank Davey's journal *Open Letter*, 9th Series, No. 8 (Spring 1997). The National Library produced a catalogue to accompany its 1996 exhibition *New Wave Canada: Coach House Press and the Small Press Movement in English Canada in the 1960s*.

Matt Cohen was helpful in comparing two of the publishers with which he was associated, Coach House and House of Anansi Press. For this book and for my earlier pamphlet, *Making Literary History: House of Anansi Press, 1967–97*, I interviewed Arden Ford, Shirley Gibson, Dave and Ellen Godfrey, Dennis Lee, James Polk, and Ann Wall. I also consulted the Anansi papers at the National Archives of Canada. Douglas Fetherling's *Travels by Night: A Memoir of the Sixties* (Toronto: Lester Publishing, 1994) conveys a vivid sense of Anansi's beginnings. *Rochdale: The Runaway College*, by David Sharpe (Toronto: Anansi, 1987), contains colourful background on the Rochdale College era. Interviews with Margaret Atwood and Graeme Gibson supplied insight and indispensable humour.

The main sources for the New Press story are my own memory and records. I also spoke with my former partners, Jim Bacque and Dave Godfrey, and with Ellen Godfrey and two former New Press sales managers, John Bemrose and David Stimpson. I'm sure all of the above would tell the story differently if it were up to them.

9: On the Barricades

Canadian publishing's heroic period occurred in the heady days when the indigenous industry was fighting for its life. Some of the battles are documented in the records of the Independent Publishers' Association, held in the Simon Fraser University Archives, Vancouver, as part of the Association of Canadian Publishers papers (holdings that, at the time of writing, went up to only 1985). In addition to consulting those records, I interviewed the publisher James Lorimer and the former publisher Carol Martin, whose involvement with the industry extends from 1959, beginning with the Readers' Club of Canada, to her work with the Canada Council in the 1980s. Conversations with Paul Audley, Lionel Koffler, Dennis Lee, and Ivon Owen rounded out the picture.

10: Rise of the West

In researching publishing in British Columbia, I spoke with two veteran observers of the industry, Basil Stuart-Stubbs, former chief librarian at the University of British Columbia, and Alan Twigg, founder of *B.C. Bookworld*. I was fortunate to be able to interview Gray Campbell, a year before his death. Jim Douglas was a fount of knowledge about not only his own company, Douglas & McIntyre, but early days in the West Coast book trade. Scott McIntyre and Celia Duthie gave me valuable interviews. *Ocean/Paper/Stone*, by Robert Bringhurst (Vancouver: William Hoffer, 1984), is the highly informative catalogue of an exhibition on British Columbia publishing.

Mel Hurtig has documented his significant publishing achievements in *At Twilight in the Country: Memoirs of a Canadian Nationalist* (Toronto: Stoddart, 1996). I conducted lengthy interviews with Hurtig and the editor he hired to oversee *The Canadian Encyclopedia*, James Marsh. Other views of working with Hurtig came from Susan Kent, Jan Walter, and, from an author's perspective, John Robert Colombo.

11: A Clutch of Dreamers

Since Canada's literary presses are so many and various, I'm conscious of not having devoted equal space to all the deserving. Certain presses seem to me more emblematic than others of their time and place. This chapter draws on publishers' catalogues and Web sites (an invaluable resource for the researcher) and on conversations with the following publishers and editors: Susanne Alexander, David Arnason, Simon Dardick, Jack David, Manuela Dias, Sibyl Frei, Jan Geddes, Anne Hardy, Tim Inkster, Robert Kroetsch, Brian Lam, Michael and Nicholas Macklem,

Rolf Maurer, John Metcalf, Clyde Rose, Karl Siegler, and Howard White. The industry statistics on page 257 are drawn from my paper "Trade Publishing in English Canada," presented to the Book Publishing and Public Policy conference sponsored by the Writers' Union of Canada and the Association of Canadian Publishers, Ottawa, April 1981.

12: The Mavericks of KidLit

Sheila Egoff's background paper for the Ontario Royal Commission on Book Publishing is titled "The Writing and Publishing of Canadian Children's Books in English." Egoff's *The Republic of Childhood*, cited earlier, was updated with Judith Saltman and reissued as *The New Republic of Childhood: A Critical Guide to Canadian Children's Literature in English* (Toronto: Oxford University Press, 1990). Judith Saltman is also author of the valuable *Modern Canadian Children's Books: Perspectives on Canadian Culture* (Toronto: Oxford University Press, 1987). Saltman and colleagues at the School of Library, Archival and Information Studies, University of British Columbia, have launched a research project known as Canadian Children's Illustrated Books in English; the Web site is at www.slais.ubc.ca/saltman/ccib/home.html.

Children's publishers and editors interviewed included Patsy Aldana, May Cutler, Diane Davy, Valerie Hussey, Colleen MacMillan, Catherine Mitchell, Allan and Katherine Shute, Bob Tyrrell, Rick Wilks, Catherine Wilson, Margie Wolfe, and Tim Wynne-Jones.

13: A Very Difficult Business

Bill Clarke, Robin Farr, Gladys Neale, and John Pearce were sources for the Clarke, Irwin story. Malcolm Lester and Louise Dennys were interviewed separately about Lester & Orpen Dennys; their ill-fated partnership with Christopher Ondaatje was explored by the journalist Don Gillmor in the September 1991 *Saturday Night*. Avie Bennett and Ron Besse told me their own stories. Additional background on the McClelland & Stewart and Macmillan sagas came from interviews with Doug Gibson, Michael Harrison, Bill Hushion, Ellen Seligman, David Staines, Peter Waldock, and Jan Walter.

14: Net Benefit

The chapter draws on my work for the Association of Canadian Publishers between 1990 and 2000 and on a paper I wrote for the ACP, *Foreign Investment Policy and Canadian Books, 1974–1996*. That paper was in turn indebted to Paul Audley's *Book Industry Policy: A Review of Background Information and Policy Options*, a 1990 report prepared for the federal Department of Communications.

For an excellent account of the Mulroney government's treatment of Marcel Masse and his Baie-Comeau policy, see chapter 9 of Marci McDonald's *Yankee Doodle Dandy: Brian Mulroney and the American Agenda* (Toronto: Stoddart, 1995). The Masse quotation reflecting on his time in Ottawa appeared in the December 1994 *Canadian Forum*.

Material on Key Porter Books came from interviews with Anna Porter and Phyllis Bruce. Sources for Douglas & McIntyre were Jim Douglas, Scott McIntyre, Patsy Aldana, Rob Sanders, and Barbara Pulling. For material on General Publishing, Stoddart Publishing, and their affiliates House of Anansi Press and Macfarlane Walter & Ross, I interviewed Jack E. Stoddart, Nelson Doucet, Jim Polk, Ann Wall, and Jan Walter. General's twenty-fifth anniversary booklet, *It Can Be Done*, commissioned from Campbell Hughes (Toronto: General Publishing, 1982), provides background on Jack Stoddart Sr. and the firm's early development.

15: Wars of Succession; 16: No Publisher's Paradise

For events in these chapters, I drew on a variety of news sources including *Quill & Quire*, the *Globe and Mail*, and the *National Post*. Background on the workings of literary agents came from Dean Cooke, Linda McKnight, and Lucinda Vardey; and on recent strategies of multinational trade publishers in Canada, from Phyllis Bruce, Patrick Crean, Louise Dennys, Cynthia Good, David Kent, John Neale, and Karl Siegler.

For insight into the last days of Stoddart Publishing and General Distribution Services, I spoke with Jack E. Stoddart, Susanne Alexander, Philip Cercone, Simon Dardick, Jack David, Paul Davidson, Tim Inkster, and Scott McIntyre.

Below is an alphabetical list of ninety-nine individuals interviewed on tape for this book. Additional interviews were recorded in written notes; their subjects are mentioned above.

Patricia Aldana, Jan. 26, 2000
Susanne Alexander, Sept. 26, 1999
David Arnason (interviewed
   with Patricia Dowdall),
   May 28, 1998

Margaret Atwood (interviewed with
   Graeme Gibson), May 19, 1999
Peter Atwood, Sept. 27, 1999
Paul Audley, Aug. 28, 1998
Avie Bennett, July 16, 1999

Pierre Berton, Jan. 21, 1999

Ronald Besse, July 28, 1999

Stan Bevington (interviewed with
    Rick/Simon), Sept. 25, 1998

Harald Bohne, Oct. 22, 1998

Phyllis Bruce, July 14, 1999

Gray Campbell, Apr. 24, 1999

Philip Cercone (interviewed with
    Arden Ford), Apr. 20, 2001

William H. Clarke, Jan. 21, 1999

Victor Coleman, June 27, 2001

John Robert Colombo, Aug. 14, 1998

Simon Dardick, Apr. 20, 2001

Jack David, Aug. 26, 1999

Rik Davidson (interviewed with
    Susan Kent), June 26, 2001

Louise Dennys, Aug. 26, 1999

Kildare Dobbs, July 28, 1999

Frans Donker, Mar. 16, 1999

Nelson Doucet, Dec. 10, 1998

James Douglas, Feb 4, 1998, and
    Apr. 26, 1999

Patricia Dowdall (interviewed with
    David Arnason), May 28, 1998

Celia Duthie, Apr. 28, 1999

Robin Farr, Oct. 21, 1998

Arden Ford (interviewed with
    Philip Cercone), Apr. 20, 2001

Sylvia Fraser, June 3, 1999

Sibyl Frei, June 14, 2000

William French, Aug. 13, 1998

Robert Fulford, July 17, 1998

Douglas Gibson, Dec. 8, 1998

Graeme Gibson (interviewed with
    Margaret Atwood), May 19, 1999

Dave Godfrey (interviewed with
    Ellen Godfrey), Feb. 3, 1999

Ellen Godfrey (interviewed with
    Dave Godfrey), Feb. 3, 1999

Cynthia Good, July 27, 1999

John Gray, Jan. 25, 2000

Francess Halpenny, Oct. 23, 1998

Bill Harnum, Dec. 9, 1998

Anne Hardy (interviewed with
    Michael Macklem and Nicholas
    Macklem), Feb. 26, 2002

Mel Hurtig, Feb. 9, 2000

Bill Hushion, June 4, 1999

Jackie Hushion, July 15, 1999

Valerie Hussey, May 19, 1999

Shane Kennedy, Feb. 8, 2000

Susan Kent (interviewed with
    Rik Davidson), June 26, 2001

Lionel Koffler, Aug. 27, 1999

Brian Lam, Jan. 30, 2001

Dennis Lee, Sept. 17, 1999

Malcolm Lester, June 3, 1999

James Lorimer, June 16, 1999

Allan MacDougall, Feb. 11, 1999

Michael Macklem (interviewed with
    Anne Hardy and Nicholas
    Macklem), Feb. 26, 2002

Nicholas Macklem (interviewed with
    Anne Hardy and Michael
    Macklem), Feb. 26, 2002

James Marsh, Feb. 8, 2000

Carol Martin, Apr. 20, 2000

Rolf Maurer, Feb. 7, 1999

Jack McClelland, Oct. 7, 1997, and
    Dec. 9, 1998

Scott McIntyre, Feb. 8 and April 26, 1999

Linda McKnight, Jan. 20, 1999

Louis Melzack (interviewed with
    Rose Melzack), Mar. 16, 1999

Rose Melzack (interviewed with Louis
  Melzack), Mar. 16, 1999
John Metcalf, Nov. 2, 1999
Peter Milroy, Feb. 6, 1999
Catherine Mitchell, June 19, 2000
Dan Mozersky, Mar. 17, 1999
Gladys Neale, Sept. 23, 1998
John Neale, Jan. 27, 2000
Peter C. Newman, Feb. 2, 1999
Ivon Owen, Aug. 25, 1999
John Pearce, June 19, 2000
Anna Porter, Oct. 20 and Dec. 7, 1998
William Roberts, Apr. 12, 1999
Glenn Rollans, May 1, 1999
Clyde Rose, May 1, 1999
Rob Sanders, Feb. 10, 1999
Ellen Seligman, Jan. 20, 1999
Allan Shute (interviewed with
  Katherine Shute), Feb. 9, 2000
Katherine Shute (interviewed with
  Allan Shute), Feb. 9, 2000

Karl Siegler, Feb. 12, 1999
Rick/Simon (interviewed with
  Stan Bevington), Sept. 25, 1998
David Staines, Apr. 7, 1999
Jack E. Stoddart, Dec. 10, 1998
Basil Stuart-Stubbs, Feb. 2, 1999
Donald Sutherland, July 28, 1999
Peter Taylor, June 17, 1999
William Toye, Aug. 13, 1998
Alan Twigg, Feb. 10, 1999
Bob Tyrrell, Apr. 13, 1999
Lucinda Vardey, Jan. 25, 2000
Jan Walter, Dec. 8, 1998
Randall Ware, July 21, 1999
Robert Weaver, July 17, 1998
Howard White, Apr. 25, 1999
Rick Wilks, June 20, 2000
Kevin Williams, June 16, 1999
Catherine Wilson, July 16 and
  Aug. 12, 1998

ACKNOWLEDGMENTS

I could not have written this book without the contributions of a great many individuals and organizations.

The publishers, writers, and book people I interviewed are named in the sources. In most instances, I recorded the interview on tape; in other cases, I kept written notes only. Several people were interviewed more than once. To all who agreed to be interviewed (and no one declined), I extend my gratitude and thanks for investing effort in what turned out to be, in a sense, a collective memoir.

Encouragement from various quarters was helpful as I embarked on this five-year project. The journalist and author Robert Fulford and the critic David Staines, general editor of the New Canadian Library (and, at the time, a colleague on the editorial board of *The Canadian Forum*), affirmed that the book was needed. Paul Davidson, executive director of the Association of Canadian Publishers, and others among my former ACP colleagues were key to ensuring the practical means to get the job done. My wife, Suzette MacSkimming, appreciated how close to my heart this project was and cheered me on with unfailing and articulate support.

Scott Anderson, editor of *Quill & Quire*, and the magazine's publisher at the time, Sharon McAuley, kindly gave me the freedom of their archives. Colleagues who helped by sharing ideas and enthusiasm included Janice Bearg of the Writing and Publishing Program at Simon Fraser University, the writer John Bemrose, my literary agent, Dean Cooke, and Margaret Reynolds of the Association of Book Publishers of British Columbia.

Assistance with research and writing expenses came from several sources. The Department of Canadian Heritage, under Minister Sheila Copps, provided funding through the Canadian Studies Program and the Book Publishing

Industry Development Program. The Canada Council for the Arts awarded me a non-fiction writing grant. The Ontario Arts Council approved support through its Works in Progress and Writers' Recommendor programs. I thank all those institutions and their officials for recognizing the importance of documenting Canada's literary and cultural history. Their funding has produced, in addition to this book, a substantial oral history that in time will be available to researchers through an archival institution.

I was extremely fortunate in being able to work with the ideal publisher for this book, Jan Walter. Jan's publishing experience is far-reaching, her professional sagacity and dedication legendary. In my case, she also exercised infinite understanding and patience. Jan put the manuscript in the hands of two of the best freelance editors in the profession: Barbara Pulling, whose creative structural editing on this third collaboration between us made a huge difference; and Barbara Czarnecki, who exercised scrupulous care and thoroughness throughout the copy-editing and indexing. My gratitude goes also to the former managing editor at Macfarlane Walter & Ross, Adrienne Guthrie, to senior editor Alex Schultz at McClelland & Stewart, and to my three transcribers, who painstakingly moved dozens of interviews from tape to the printed page: Karen Bond, Rosemary Currie, and Patrick Delaney.

Grateful acknowledgment is made to the following for permission to quote or reproduce copyright material. Efforts have been made to contact copyright holders. The author and publisher would welcome any information regarding omissions or errors.

The Estate of John Gray, for material quoted from *Fun Tomorrow: Learning to Be a Publisher and Much Else* (Toronto: Macmillan of Canada, 1978).

Mrs. Marsh Jeanneret, for material quoted from *God and Mammon: Universities as Publishers*, by Marsh Jeanneret (Toronto: Macmillan of Canada, 1989).

Key Porter Books, for letters quoted from *Imagining Canadian Literature: Selected Letters of Jack McClelland*, Sam Solecki, ed. (Toronto: Key Porter Books, 1998, © Sam Solecki).

Wayne Tefs and Turnstone Press, for the quotation from *Due West: 30 Great Stories from Alberta, Saskatchewan and Manitoba* (Regina, Edmonton, and Winnipeg: Coteau Books, NeWest Press, and Turnstone Press, 1996).

For permission to reproduce photographs, the author gratefully acknowledges the following.

Photo Section 1: (1) Ashley & Crippen; (2) McKenzie/Darg; (3) courtesy *Quill & Quire*; (4) Jean Milner; (5) Robert Lansdale; (6) Barrie Davis/*Globe & Mail*; (7) Robert Lansdale; (8) McKenzie/Darg; (9) courtesy *Quill & Quire*; (10) D'Arcy Glionna; (11) courtesy *Quill & Quire*; (12) courtesy *Quill & Quire*; (13) courtesy *Quill & Quire*; (14) John Reeves; (15) courtesy *Quill & Quire*; (16) Greg Tjepkema; (17) courtesy *Quill & Quire*.

Photo Section 2: (1) *Maclean's*; (2) courtesy *Quill & Quire*; (3) courtesy Mel Hurtig; (4) courtesy *Quill & Quire*; (5) courtesy *Quill & Quire*; (6) courtesy *Quill & Quire*; (7) Greg Tjepkema; (8) courtesy *Quill & Quire*; (9) courtesy *Quill & Quire*; (10) courtesy *Quill & Quire*; (11) David Laurence; (12) courtesy Kids Can Press; (13) courtesy *Quill & Quire*; (14) Lee Davis Creal; (15) City of North York; (16) courtesy *Quill & Quire*; (17) courtesy *Quill & Quire*; (18) Sally Gibson: (19) courtesy *Quill & Quire*; (20) courtesy *Quill & Quire*; (21) courtesy *Quill & Quire*; (22) courtesy *Quill & Quire*; (23) courtesy *Quill & Quire*.

INDEX